"This book explores perennial question about knowing God. Considering vene their critics launches this endeavor. In conversation with the contribution of Walter Kasper at the crossroads of the heritage of natural theology and the confession of faith in the Triune God, this work navigates through postmodern frontiers and pioneers an aesthetic and performance approach to the encounter with the God of Jesus Christ that illuminates paths for Christian discipleship on pilgrimage in the world. An important achievement."

> —Bradford E. Hinze
> The Karl Rahner, SJ, Professor of Theology
> Fordham University

"Clear, very well informed, and admirably argued, this book shows how, after all the changes in Western thought, we are still justified in holding that God is simultaneously present (available and knowable) and absent (mysterious and uncontrollable). God's love answers the deepest human longings. This work is a splendid example of authentic natural theology."

> —Gerald O'Collins, SJ
> Jesuit Theological College
> Australia

"A theological gem. Godzieba engages the biblical and theological tradition, as well as contemporary theology, in a way that is easily understandable and illuminating. He also takes on the challenge of God's presence and absence in a way that is creative and original. It is a must-read for any Christian facing the mystery of God, and experiencing both the absence and presence of God in a time and in the world where God seems both near and far. The book will serve as a great introduction for courses on God."

> —Francis Schüssler Fiorenza
> Stillman Professor of Roman Catholic Theological Studies
> Harvard Divinity School

"A capstone achievement that harvests years of theological research and teaching, Anthony Godzieba masterfully illustrates what a phenomenological study of God should do. This brilliant new book gives attention to relevant biblical passages, significant philosophical positions, noteworthy works of art, and major contributions of contemporary theologians in a 'student-friendly' way."

> —Anne M. Clifford
> Msgr. James A. Supple Chair of Catholic Studies
> Iowa State University

"Anthony Godzieba's new book is a fascinating and informative passage through the main questions of Christian theology. It integrates a profound historical view on dogmatic theology, deep spirituality, and innovative theological concepts into contemporary research on God. Assessing the questions posed by the modern critique of religion, it offers convincing arguments on why we should neither cease to consider God as an essential topic of science nor as a possible dimension in our everyday lives."

> —Kurt Appel
> University of Vienna

"A theological masterpiece! In deeply learned and highly readable prose, with Walter Kasper leading the way, Godzieba follows the traditional ways of negation and eminence down modern and postmodern paths of construction and critique. While giving natural theology its due, he deftly works the dialectic between God's incomprehensible mystery and simultaneous presence into a genuinely theological theology. If these two approaches to God as present and absent don't exactly lie down together, they come to as much peace as we might expect in our times. This book bears many signs of Godzieba's long career in the classroom. If you have been waiting for a God book for your graduate course, *A Theology of the Presence and Absence of God* is it."

> —William L. Portier
> Mary Ann Spearin Chair of Catholic Theology
> University of Dayton

"We can rightly compare this God-book with an excellent bottle of wine from a renowned vineyard which has been gracefully aged in time-tested barrels, and now is presented to today's readers to drink. Like such a wine, it possesses a rich flavor and fresh aftertaste which lingers after we have finished drinking from it. Experience and tradition, faith and reason, reflection and imagination, ineffability and incarnation come here wonderfully together in one book which amounts to a presentation of the mystery of God's love, reflected upon, imagined and witnessed to for our days. It is to be highly recommended to connoisseurs of fine theological wines."

> —Lieven Boeve
> Catholic University of Leuven
> Belgium

Anthony J. Godzieba

A Theology of the Presence and Absence of God

LITURGICAL PRESS
ACADEMIC

Collegeville, Minnesota
www.litpress.org

Cover design by Monica Bokinskie. Cover image courtesy of Getty Images.

Chapter 4, "The Christian Response, II: Theological Theology," was previously published as chapter 3.2 in Francis Schüssler Fiorenza and John P. Galvin, eds., *Systematic Theology: Roman Catholic Perspectives*, 2nd ed. (Minneapolis: Fortress Press, 2011).

1   2   3   4   5   6   7   8   9

Library of Congress Cataloging-in-Publication Data

Names: Godzieba, Anthony J., 1951– author.
Title: A theology of the presence and absence of God / Anthony J. Godzieba.
Description: Collegeville, Minnesota : Liturgical Press, 2018. | "A Liturgical
    Press Academic book." | Includes bibliographical references.
Identifiers: LCCN 2018010934 (print) | LCCN 2017057023 (ebook) |
    ISBN 9780814663820 (ebook) | ISBN 9780814663585
Subjects: LCSH: God (Christianity)
Classification: LCC BT103 (print) | LCC BT103 .G6426 2018 (ebook) |
    DDC 231.7—dc23
LC record available at https://lccn.loc.gov/2018010934

Contents

Preface

This book starts with a simple question and ends with a simple answer. The question is this: in our secularized, consumer-driven, technologized world, can we still experience the mystery of God? The answer rests in the mystery of God's love which, as Walter Kasper phrases it, "is the answer to the mystery of the world and human beings, the answer to the deepest human longing for acceptance and love." Getting from one to the other is a process—an adventure, even—involving both faith and reason, especially wider notions of both than contemporary stereotypes allow. This book explores various facets of this process by delving into the rich and deep Christian tradition of thinking, speaking, and praying about God.

The attentive reader will detect the pervasive influence of Kasper's classic work *The God of Jesus Christ*, with its emphasis on a theology of the Trinity as the true "grammar" of Christian belief. While this book is in no way an in-depth analysis of or commentary on Kasper's argument, I have modeled my general approach after his: exploring how God became a "problem" in Western culture, reconstructing an authentic Catholic natural theology (as an alternative to an abstract modern theism), and then showing how this leads to a "theological theology" where faith and reason are mutually supportive in exploring the reality of God as Trinity. In filling out this outline, though, I have gone my own way with a different guiding theme, different emphases, a different diagnosis of the contemporary context, a different central pivot for the first part of my argument, and a much different conclusion, while still sharing Kasper's strong emphasis on the centrality of the Christian confession that "God is love" (1 John 4:16).

This book's origins go back to the late 1990s and grow out of a course of the same name that I have taught at Villanova University throughout my career there. It has gone through a number of permutations before becoming this particular work, and has racked up a number of debts of gratitude along the way. Many of the book's ideas were discussed with my good friend and *Doktorvater* Francis Schüssler Fiorenza who, in more ways than I can count, has been a continual source of wisdom, sharp insights, and encouragement; my gratitude to him is boundless. Lieven Boeve has also been a good friend and conversation partner, and I am grateful for his insights and for the many opportunities he has provided for fruitful interaction with his colleagues on the Faculty of Theology and Religious Studies at the Katholieke Universiteit Leuven. Other friends and colleagues have been generous in discussing the ideas presented here, reading portions of the manuscript with a critical eye, or providing encouragement when this project seemed stalled: Michael Marissen and Ray van Leeuwen (our "Bach and beer" group has often veered from music to theology), Anne Clifford, Terry Wright, Ed Sweeney, and the late John Jones. Special thanks go to Beth Johnson, who tipped me off to John Macquarrie's fine book many years ago. At a late stage Kurt Appel graciously invited me to his doctoral seminar at the University of Vienna for a helpful discussion of the concluding chapter. Thanks also to my Villanova students who discussed (with varying degrees of agreement and skepticism) the main ideas of this book with me in my classes, to my graduate assistant Marygrace Urmson who helped check proofs, and also to the enthusiastic participants in the graduate course I taught as a visiting professor at the University of Dayton. I am most grateful to Hans Christoffersen and the editorial and production staff at Liturgical Press for including this book as part of their strong commitment to vital contemporary theological reflection.

Chapter 4 originally appeared as "The Trinitarian Mystery of God: A 'Theological Theology'" in Francis Schüssler Fiorenza and John Galvin, eds., *Systematic Theology: Roman Catholic Perspectives*, 2nd ed. (Minneapolis: Fortress Press, 2011), 131–97. It appears here with minor revisions.

This book is dedicated to my late parents, Anthony and Regina.

As always, my overflowing gratitude to my wife, Dolores, who knows all the reasons why.

Memorial of Saints Basil the Great and Gregory Nazianzen
2 January 2018

CHAPTER ONE

God—Believers—Questions

Surely you dwell in light inaccessible
where is it? and how can I
have access to light which is inaccessible? . . .
I have never seen you, O Lord my God,
I have never seen your face. . .
Let me seek you by desiring you,
and desire you by seeking you;
let me find you by loving you,
and love you in finding you. . . .
Lord, I am not trying to make my way to your height,
for my understanding is in no way equal to that,
but I do desire to understand a little of your truth
which my heart already believes and loves.
I do not seek to understand so that I may believe,
but I believe so that I may understand;
and what is more,
I believe that unless I do believe I shall not understand.

—Saint Anselm of Canterbury, *Proslogion*, chapter 1[1]

Beloved, let us love one another, because love is from God;
everyone who loves is born of God and knows God. Whoever
does not love does not know God, for God is love. God's love
was revealed among us in this way: God sent his only Son into
the world so that we might live through him. . . . So we have
known and believe the love that God has for us. God is love,

---

1. *Proslogion*, in *The Prayers and Meditations of Saint Anselm*, trans. Benedicta Ward (Harmondsworth/New York: Penguin, 1973), 240, 243, 244; the versification of the prose original is the translator's.

and those who abide in love abide in God, and God abides in
them.

—1 John 4:7–9, 16

Can we still seek, experience, and talk about God?

When praying the Creed at Sunday liturgy, Christians profess faith
in the one God, Father, Son, and Holy Spirit. Every day we encounter
new possibilities of experiencing divine grace and salvation. Yet at
the same time, many of us are immersed in a technologized, consumer-
oriented culture that displays ambivalent feelings toward God, religion, and spirituality. Neither the New Testament's confession nor
Anselm's profession are any longer easily understood or accepted.
The question, then, is this: can we still confidently profess our faith
in God and our belief that "God is love"?

This book's answer is a resounding "yes." In the midst of our profoundly secularized, fragmented, and at times fear-saturated Western
culture, Christians can make the case for the loving, redeeming, liberating, transforming presence of God in human life and in the world.
The purpose of this book is to help make that case.

However, doing so is not simple. The traditional meanings of the
three important factors mentioned above—*God, human life,* and *the
world*—have been seriously challenged over at least the past century.
These challenges have led to a series of questions that go far beyond
the one raised by skeptics in the eighteenth and nineteenth centuries,
"is there a God at all?"—radical and shocking at the time, but raised
casually now in Western culture. Today's questions challenge a range
of issues whose certainties we had come to take for granted. How
should God be described or defined? Can God be described or defined
at all? Is there one authentic definition of "being human," and should
there be only one? What constitutes "our world" and whose experience counts when describing it? Are "reality" and "humanity" fictions, aesthetic constructs, the products of social, political, and
economic interests—or something else entirely? What is the nature
of the relationship between human beings and God? Is it real or an
illusion? Does it raise up our humanity or diminish it? Is faith in God
a liberating human response or an outdated and repressive relic with
no place in contemporary Western culture? Even the most steadfast

Christian must recognize that believers and non-believers alike ask these questions, and the answers influence their own image of God.

A traditional theological analysis of belief in God would begin with general definitions of theology and of the doctrine of God. It would explain that "theology" literally means saying a word or giving a reasonable explanation (the Greek *logos*) about God (*theos*). It would show that the doctrine of God is the most fundamental of all Christian teachings and plays a role in every theological discipline. One commentator has noted that "whether we are dealing with the world as created reality or with our own salvation, with the Church or with the sacraments, or whether we ask about the fulfillment of humankind and history, God always stands at the focal point as origin and as goal."[2] A traditional introduction might even quote a renowned theologian like Cardinal Walter Kasper, who illustrates the central role of the doctrine of God:

> The mystery which God is for the religious man or woman generally, is interpreted by the Christian faith as the mystery of an unfathomable and incomprehensible love, and hence as a personal mystery. *This mystery of God's love is the answer to the mystery of the world and human beings*, the answer to the deepest human longing for acceptance and love. . . .
>
> So according to Christian understanding, revelation and the mystery of God are the revelation and mystery of God's love; and everything else which Christian theology and the Christian creed have to say about God, his personal nature, and the threeness of his person, are no more than the unfolding—founded on revelation itself—of that single statement in the First Epistle of John: God is love.[3]

Kasper here focuses on one of the key scriptural texts that gives us insight into the nature of God: "So we have known and believe the

2. Wilhelm Breuning,"Gotteslehre," in *Glaubenszugänge: Lehrbuch der katholischen Dogmatik*, ed. Wolfgang Beinert (Paderborn: Ferdinand Schöningh, 1995), 1:201 (all translations are mine unless otherwise noted).

3. Walter Kasper, "Revelation and Mystery: The Christian Understanding of God," *Theology and Church*, trans. Margaret Kohl (New York: Crossroad, 1989), 30–31.

love that God has for us. God is love, and those who abide in love abide in God, and God abides in them" (1 John 4:16). Not only is this the key to the Christian understanding of God, but with refreshing candor Kasper claims that *every* question concerning humanity and the world is answered by it as well.

I endorse this understanding of God without reservation. It is the starting point of Christian *faith*. But as a fundamental *understanding* of the triune God, the statement that God is love is more properly the *conclusion* we desire to reach. It can no longer be considered theology's self-evident starting point because of all the uncertainties that have grown up around the word *God*.[4] We need to demonstrate this claim's plausibility as far as we are able, and thus it becomes the *goal* of our journey of reflection on the revelation of God in human experience. It is true that over the past several decades there has been a tremendous revival in the search for God and for spiritual roots, and a corresponding surge in the growth of Christianity in certain areas. The burgeoning numbers of Christians who identify themselves as "evangelical," the intense quest for deeper spiritual nourishment (as opposed to spirituality fads) on the part of many younger adults, and the intense interest among Roman Catholics in Catholic values and identity are all signs of the enduring attractiveness of a concrete relationship with God that can productively transform everyday life. The persistence of religion testifies to the fact that the late nineteenth- and early twentieth-century predictions of the demise of religious belief have not come to pass.

Nevertheless, the privatization or marginalization of the importance of God and of religious belief in mainstream society is a crucial aspect of Western culture and cannot be ignored. In the flow of everyday concerns, God is often treated as a stranger who plays little or no role in public life. Religious voices are often banished from the current public discussion of shared societal values, with the resulting impoverishment of that discussion. Many have emphasized the obvious ongoing secularization of Western culture, beginning with early

---

4. A claim supported by Thomas Aquinas' reflections on thinking and speaking about God. See *Summa theologiae*, Ia, q. 2, art 1–2, in *Summa theologiae*, vol. 2 [1a. 2–11]: *Existence and Nature of God*, trans. Timothy McDermott [1964; repr., Cambridge: Cambridge University Press, 2006], 5–11.

modern times, as one cause of this marginalization. As David Burrell has pointed out, this has led to the gradual dimming of our ability to recognize God's connection with our human experience. Society now endures "the absence of an enveloping tapestry in which we can locate ourselves," an absence that "leaves the imagination with a vast emptiness" that we attempt vainly to fill.[5]

This is only one element in the very complex story of why religious belief no longer functions as the social cement that binds our common experiences.[6] Edward Schillebeeckx, in discussing the difficulties faced by contemporary believers, spoke of the clash between God's essential inconceivability—the "hiddenness of God"—and the human need for concrete images of God. This need can become so strong that people may cling to an image of God that reflects their own social situation more than the authentic nature of God.[7] In addition, the success of the natural sciences in providing answers for our questions about reality as well as a consistent explanatory framework for our experience, the loss of a sense of "transcendence" and the shrinking of our worldview to mere present material particularities, the growing dismay and even anger of many at the institutions of Christianity, and the boredom of a late capitalist consumer society represent other key reasons for religion's marginalization in much of everyday life.

Today, belief in God and the very meaning of the word "God" remain very much contested. At times many people, even those of goodwill and strong Christian belief, keenly feel the eclipse of God in culture and in their own lives. It is as if "the dark night of the soul" that St. John of the Cross described as a prelude to an individual's mystical union with God has descended upon contemporary Western culture.

Little of this diagnosis of contemporary ambivalence about God is new. Already in the 1960s Martin Buber had noted the loss of meaning the word "God" had suffered as well as the contradictory and

5. David B. Burrell, *Knowing the Unknowable God: Ibn-Sina, Maimonides, Aquinas* (Notre Dame, IN: University of Notre Dame Press, 1986), 6–7.
6. See, e.g., Louis Dupré, *Passage to Modernity: an Essay in the Hermeneutics of Nature and Culture* (New Haven: Yale University Press, 1993); Charles Taylor, *A Secular Age* (Cambridge, MA: Belknap Press/Harvard University Press, 2007).
7. Edward Schillebeeckx, *Church: The Human Story of God*, trans. John Bowden (New York: Crossroad, 1990), 55–59.

even inhuman causes it had been made to support: "It is the most heavy-laden of all human words. None has become so soiled, so mutilated. . . . Generations of men have laid the burden of their anxious lives upon this word and weighed it to the ground; it lies in the dust and bears their whole burden. . . . They draw caricatures and write 'God' underneath; they murder one another to say 'in God's name'."[8] Walter Kasper has pointed out yet another persistent and uniquely chilling factor which has affected contemporary belief in God: the fundamental indifference to the whole issue of belief and unbelief in certain areas of Western culture.[9]

For all these reasons, the traditional introduction to the doctrine of God will fail. An introduction that does not take seriously the pervasive attitude of our times and the kinds of questions we raise will not succeed in leading anyone (*introducere*) to God but rather will lead them away.

What questions, then, do people ask?

1. Questions and Their Discontents

"Where is God?"

On its face, it is a simple and straightforward question, posed by all sorts of people, no matter what relationship they may have to Christian belief or to other religious traditions—a person at prayer, perhaps, or at study, or a person overcome with grief. It can be posed coolly by a skeptic or anxiously by a believer who, despite her or his best intentions, acutely experiences God's absence. It can be cried aloud in anguish by persons bound together in the struggle for hope and meaning in the midst of suffering and chaos.

"Where is God?" is not a request for information, but is a pointed question about the presence of the ultimate reality. Is God with us? Does God love us? Will God help us? Any serious answer relies on the answer to yet another straightforward question:

"Who is God?"

8. Martin Buber, *Meetings*, ed. Maurice Friedman (La Salle, IL: Open Court, 1973), 50–51.
9. Walter Kasper, *Transcending All Understanding: The Meaning of Christian Faith Today*, trans. Boniface Ramsey (San Francisco: Ignatius Press, 1989), 19–20.

This is the question many consider to be first and most fundamental. People who raise this question expect the answer to convey the essential, absolute nature of the transcendent reality we call "God." They expect straightforward answers from a religion's sacred writings, from those who have had intense personal experiences of God, and from theologians.

The Christian tradition has no shortage of what appear to be straightforward answers to the question "Who is God?" Take, for example, this reply from Scripture:

> But Moses said to God, "If I come to the Israelites and say to them, 'The God of your ancestors has sent me to you,' and they ask me, 'What is his name?' what shall I say to them?" God said to Moses, "I AM WHO I AM." He said further, "Thus you shall say to the Israelites: I AM has sent me to you." God also said to Moses, "Thus you shall say to the Israelites: The LORD, the God of your ancestors, the God of Abraham, the God of Isaac, and the God of Jacob, has sent me to you." (Exod 3:13–15)

Consider, too, this more contemporary theological reply:

> God is the supreme and supremely personal Source and Creator of the universe, revealed in creation and in the events of salvation history (covenant, prophecy, the Incarnation of Jesus Christ, and the ongoing presence of the Holy Spirit), and object of religious devotion and subject matter of theology.[10]

These replies offer similar affirmations: God, the God of Abraham, Isaac, and Jacob, *is;* God *is the ultimate ground of the universe.*

But the appearance of simplicity is deceptive. Even determining the most fundamental questions about God is not a simple matter. The theologian Christian Duquoc has pointed out the difficulties by demonstrating how the questions have changed over the centuries, depending on the circumstances in which they have been asked.[11]

---

10. Richard P. McBrien, ed., *The HarperCollins Encyclopedia of Catholicism* (San Francisco: HarperCollins, 1995), s.v. "God" (Catherine Mowry LaCugna).

11. Christian Duquoc, "'Who is God?' becomes 'Where is God?': The Shift in a Question," trans. John Bowden, in *Where is God? A Cry of Human Distress,*

The subjects and writers of the biblical books posed the question "who is God?" and found the answer in God's liberating actions: "nothing defines his identity or his presence except the action which he takes within a framework which he has fixed, the covenant, and a promise which opens up the present to the future in a positive way."[12] Early modern theologians and philosophers transformed the question into the more abstract "what is God?"; their answers were correspondingly abstract and emphasized the essence of divinity, illustrating it by qualities such as immutability, infinite goodness, and omnipotence. But for others in the modern and contemporary eras, especially those who have suffered at the hands of those who claim to believe in God, the question has become "where is God?" Bartolomé de las Casas, the sixteenth-century Dominican priest and missionary to the Americas, posed this question in his defense of the native population against the brutal treatment directed at them by the Spanish colonialists. How could the true God, whom the Conquistadors claimed was on their side, support such exploitation and death? De las Casas' protest, as Duquoc points out, still resonates today.

> The time of the conquest of America shattered the illusion that the actions of those who knew and rehearsed the identity of God were the concrete expression of his will in this world. Las Casas had denounced the perversity of this interpretation. . . . It is useless to ask who he is, but a matter of urgency to establish where he is. To know where he is amounts to discerning his action. For a long time people believed that those who laid claim to God's name were fulfilling his actions. Fractures were produced; from now on, no institution, not even any ecclesiastical institution, could be sure of housing God. God no longer had any official address. We too have become nomads again. Where is God?[13]

---

ed. Christian Duquoc and Casiano Floristán, Concilium 1992/4 (London: SCM Press, 1992), 1–10.
  12. Ibid., 3.
  13. Ibid., 6.

The question about the ultimate transcendent reality is frighteningly difficult to answer—after all, the ultimate reality never presents itself to our experience and understanding with the same clarity as do the tangible realities that we encounter every day. But an even more crucial problem with the "Who?" question, the one which most today would consider the most fundamental, is its very formulation. It is terribly inadequate, even impertinent. The seductive ease of the question is precisely what makes it problematic: it raises expectations that cannot possibly be fulfilled. The question anticipates in reply a precise definition, an objective account of the essential elements of God's identity (what traditional Christian theology calls the divine attributes), a description of the characteristics that make God "God" and set God off from finite being. But in turn these expectations presuppose a type of precise knowledge of the nature of God that is impossible for human beings to have.

When we ask that "simple" question, we expect an answer that enables us to conceptualize the divine nature, as if "God" were a normal object to be understood and explained. Such an answer would promise too much and deliver too little. Such an idea of God would only *appear* to apprehend God's divine nature; in reality, it would be shot through with all the limitations of our human perspective. A definition formulated in response to this question alone, then, would be woefully impoverished and miss the true character of God. The mystery of God transcends human concepts.

2. Asking Carefully

Does this mean that the "simple" question should be firmly disallowed, or that the basic human search for God is doomed to shipwreck on its own limitations? Anselm of Canterbury (c. 1033–1109) can guide us toward a solution. His *Proslogion*, written between 1077 and 1078, is famous in the history of Western thought particularly for the brilliant argument he presents on behalf of the existence of God, "that thing than which nothing greater can be thought."[14] This

14. *Proslogion*, ch. 2, in *The Prayers and Meditations of Saint Anselm*, 244 (see n.1). Further references to this edition are given in parentheses in the text (page number/line numbers).

argument is usually extracted from the prayerful, meditative setting into which Anselm placed it and discussed by philosophers and theologians as the "ontological argument."

The *Proslogion*, however, opens with a long prayer uttered by the believer who seeks a clear vision of God, a meditative preparation for the journey of understanding the believer is about to undertake. The prayer has three stations or stages: the seeker's withdrawal into contemplative solitude, the seeker's growing awareness of his limitations and estrangement from God, and his compunction of sorrow at this estrangement, which ultimately gives rise to his intense desire for God.[15] Thus, in response to the opening invitation to "put aside your weighty cares, let your burdensome distractions wait, free yourself awhile for God and rest awhile in him" (239/4–7), the seeker beseeches God for help in finding God.

But the journey of discovery appears utterly impossible: God dwells "in light inaccessible" (240/22) beyond the reach of the understanding of the "wretched" seeker burdened by sorrow, desire, ignorance, and sin: "I was my own impediment" (242/93). Parts of this prayer echo the famous characterization of God offered centuries earlier in the effusive prayer that opens *The Mystical Theology* by Pseudo-Dionysius, the mysterious late fifth- or early sixth-century C.E. Syrian theologian who assumed the identity of Dionysius the Areopagite, one of St. Paul's disciples. This brilliant thinker supplied Christian theology with what over the centuries has become the classic model of negative or apophatic theology—the peculiar, paradoxical, fully necessary way of knowing God which holds that whatever can be affirmed about God must also be denied, and that true knowledge of God consists not only of knowing who God is, but even more fundamentally of knowing what God is not and that God is beyond affirmations.

> Trinity!! Higher than any being,
>   any divinity, any goodness!
> Guide of Christians
>   in the wisdom of heaven!

15. Benedicta Ward, in the introduction to *The Prayers and Meditations of Saint Anselm*, 79.

Lead us up beyond unknowing and light,
>   up to the farthest, highest peak
>   of mystic scripture,
>   where the mysteries of God's Word
>   lie simple, absolute and unchangeable
>   in the brilliant darkness of a hidden silence.
>   Amid the deepest shadow
>   they pour overwhelming light
>   on what is most manifest.
>   Amid the wholly unsensed and unseen
>   they completely fill our sightless minds
>   with treasures beyond all beauty.[16]

Anselm's seeker expresses sentiments much like those of Pseudo-Dionysius: the distance between God and any human understanding of God seems infinite and unbridgeable. Imploring God for guidance, the seeker prays that the desire for God, which at first seemed to be a burden, an unfulfillable hunger, be transformed into something positive that directs him toward an understanding of God. The moment of the *transfiguration* of this desire occurs when the seeker realizes that the desire for God does not spring up from nowhere, but is sparked by a dim understanding of God that he already possesses: "I cannot seek you unless you show me how, and I will never find you unless you show yourself to me" (243/136–38). Feelings of emptiness and exile from God begin to dissipate in the knowledge that there is "a little of your truth which my heart already believes and loves" (244/153).

The human desire for God can itself be an indicator of the presence of God, who speaks directly to that desire. Merely by using the word "God" in a meaningful way, the seeker acknowledges having some understanding, faint though it may be, of what the word means and of the being to whom it refers. The seeker already has some relation

16. *The Mystical Theology*, ch. 1, in Pseudo-Dionysius, *The Complete Works*, trans. Colm Luibheid and Paul Rorem, The Classics of Western Spirituality (New York: Paulist, 1987), 135. See Paul Rorem, *Pseudo-Dionysius: A Commentary on the Texts and an Introduction to Their Influence* (New York: Oxford University Press, 1993); Andrew Louth, *Denys the Areopagite* (London: Geoffrey Chapman/Wilton, CT: Morehouse-Barlow, 1989).

to God, even before the search has begun. This, in fact, gets the search started in the first place.

No one begins the search for God from a position of absolute non-knowledge. Even the person who thinks that the best place to begin looking for God is an abstract philosophical proof "must already have some idea of what he wants to prove; any meaningful question supposes some pre-understanding of what the questioning is meant to ascertain; so too a proof of God presupposes a provisional concept of God."[17] This is a very real kind of faith or trust, a "transcendental faith" in the overarching mystery which grounds all existence. Anselm calls this mystery "God." But faith, in Anselm's words, is also *fides quaerens intellectum*, a "faith seeking understanding,"[18] a faith that is both an act of God's grace and at the same time a human act that "exists only in the medium of human hearing, understanding, assenting and also questioning."[19]

This detailed description of the believer's initial experience in seeking God is one of Anselm's major insights and derives from his great sensitivity to the seeker's situation. He makes it clear that our search for God implicitly involves much more than raising questions. "Who is God?" is also a *confession*, both about God and about ourselves. It reveals and proclaims God's utter transcendence, in contrast to our own finite, fragile, and fallible concepts, categories, and names. When we ask the question, we disclose not only our interest in God, but also the deficiencies in our knowledge. Why ask if we already had all the answers? We have so little knowledge because of God's "discretion"[20]—the fact that God does indeed "dwell in light inaccessible," that God evades our direct perceptual experience, that God is not an object of our knowledge in the way that other objects are, and is beyond the ordinary reach of human concepts and language.

17. Walter Kasper, *The God of Jesus Christ* [hereafter *GJC*], new ed., trans. [Matthew O'Connell and] Dinah Livingstone (London/New York: Continuun, 2012), 4.

18. *Proslogion*, preface, 239. According to Anselm, this was the original title for the *Proslogion*.

19. Kasper, *GJC*, 6–7.

20. Duquoc, "'Who is God?'," 3.

But at the same time God is near and available. The distance between ourselves and God is not unbridgeable. In our fragile and fallible situation we have been given a glimpse of the nature of God that we strive to flesh out and understand more clearly (Anselm attributes this preunderstanding to our being created in the image of God [*Proslogion* 243/144]). Our question arises from a limited but real encounter with the divine mystery. Faith (*fides*) and rational understanding (*intellectus*) are not strangers or antagonists, but mutually supportive human actions that have the potential to bring us closer to God.

When we approach God we will always find ourselves situated between absolute ignorance and absolute knowledge. Our answers to the questions "Who is God?" and "Where is God?" will never be definitive, but they will not be useless. They reveal some things about God, about ourselves, and about the relationship between God and ourselves, even if they will never provide a wholly adequate explanation of any of these realities. To persist in expecting definitive answers would not only be unrealistic or unproductive on our part, but downright idolatrous: they would give us a "God" created according to our own image and likeness, an object created by our own minds that fits our finite expectations, but not the God revealed by Jesus Christ who challenges our categories, shatters our expectations, and offers us the infinite and unfathomable love that is God's own nature, expressed in the trinity of persons. In the in-between state in which we live, we are like Anselm's seeker: "Lord, I am not trying to make my way to your height, for my understanding is in no way equal to that, but I do desire to understand a little of your truth" (*Proslogion* 244/150–52).

And so we begin again, with chastened expectations.

3. A More Humble Questioning

Anselm's emphasis upon the limited reach of our faith-guided understanding of God is especially pertinent today. Contemporary Christian theology is acutely aware of the historically-situated nature of all human knowledge and of faith as well. In other words, the person who responds to the revelation of God does not have some direct, unmediated grasp of the divine nature. The ultimate and absolute cannot be known absolutely. Rather, the believer's faith is mediated by the experience of the world and the culture in which it is situated. One's understanding develops within a particular historical perspective, a particular standpoint within a shared cultural tradition built up over time. The believer is a *someone* in a *somewhere* that is shared with *others.*

Christians thus stand within a tradition of interpreted experiences.[21] The tradition within which they practice and understand their faith is a living one—it is the ongoing reception of the message, practice, death, and resurrection of Jesus Christ through the continual attempts of believers to be disciples committed to Jesus' understanding of God. Christian faith today stands in the wake of previous Christian practices and understandings; it is rooted in and formed by the past, yet at the same time differs from these past understandings. This is because faith and our understanding of it always occur *historically*— that is, differently in different historical epochs, influenced by the presuppositions that determine the particular character of each epoch. Our faith experience, even when dealing with the transcendent reality that is God, is saturated with presuppositions and norms that are peculiar to our own time and place. These presuppositions are effects constituted over the course of human history down to our own epoch, where they are formatted according our own culture's fundamental modes of understanding.[22] Even when the revelation of God begins to outrun these presuppositions and shatter the usual norms of know-

---

21. See Edward Schillebeeckx, *Christ: The Experience of Jesus as Lord*, trans. John Bowden (New York: Crossroad, 1981), 30–79; Schillebeeckx, *Interim Report on the Books "Jesus" and "Christ,"* trans. John Bowden (New York: Crossroad, 1981), 10–19.

22. See Bernhard Welte, "Credo ut intelligam als theologisches Programm heute" [1962], in *Gesammelte Schriften*, vol. IV/3: *Zur vorgehensweise der Theologie und zu ihrer jüngeren Geschichte*, ed. Gerhard Ruff (Freiburg: Herder, 2007), 212–27; ET: "Credo ut intelligam—as a Theological Program for Our Times," trans. Fidelis J. Smith, *American Church Quarterly* 2 (1962): 143–52; Welte, *Heilsverständnis: Philosophische Untersuchung einiger Voraussetzungen zum Verständnis des Christentums* [1966], in *Gesammelte Schriften*, vol. IV/1: *Hermeneutik des Christlichen*, ed. Bernhard Casper (Freiburg: Herder, 2006), 19–193. See also Hans-Georg Gadamer, *Truth and Method*, 2d rev. ed., trans. rev. Joel Weinsheimer and Donald G. Marshall (New York: Crossroad, 1989).

ing—thus allowing the transcendence and otherness of God to appear—revelation is still understood in relation to those particular categories even when we recognize it as going "beyond" them. Any attempt on our part to forget the finite character of the perspectives that affect faith and its understanding and imagine that we might immediately grasp God is doomed to inadequacy, failure, and perhaps even idolatry.

Our "somewhere"—the particular historical and cultural perspective from which we think and speak—most assuredly affects our experience and understanding of God, along with the way we talk about God. The clue Anselm has given us says as much.

4. The Context of Our Questioning

The "somewhere" from which and for which I am writing is Western culture in the second decade of the third millennium, a culture that can be described in a bewildering number of ways. It comes in the wake of a century that witnessed breath-taking accomplishments but that also has been called the bloodiest and most violent century of human history. Alongside stunning progress in technology, ecological awareness, the advancement of human rights, and in breaking barriers between ethnic cultures there have occurred outbreaks of violent racism and nationalism, ecological destruction, and acts of genocide whose horrific consequences are simultaneously unimaginable and real. We have witnessed the end of the Cold War and the dismantling of the Berlin Wall, but also more war and more families ripped apart by war. The wholesale explosion of consumerism as a style and philosophy of life has migrated to almost every part of the globe, aggravating the gap between rich and poor into a seemingly unbridgeable chasm. And after 9/11 a world of comfortable familiarity and consistency has become a world seemingly threatened by terror without end.

A common way to characterize our current situation is to say that we are living in a postmodern context, a time of diversity and fragmentation which has (temporally) come after and (critically) gone after the certainties and systems of modernity. For example, many current commentators on culture echo the now-classic characterization of "the contemporary" proposed by Jean-François Lyotard. If by "modern" we mean a culture which justifies the truth of its view of reality and its moral value by appealing to certain overarching, objectively certain theoretical explanations ("metanarratives"), then, Lyotard argues, present-day culture is no longer "modern." Rather, it is "postmodern"—suspicious of all such overarching explanations and fragmented into various "language elements" that have no common thread and thus defy any overarching explanation.[23] Others, such as Jürgen Habermas, have called this kind of analysis one-sided. They argue instead that contemporary society, despite its flaws and traumas, is still progressive and "modern" because modern values such as democracy and human rights live on in society and need to be practiced more responsibly for their emancipative force to be felt.[24]

This shows that we need to be careful about such labels as "modern," "postmodern," or "contemporary" as we try to discern the context of our questioning. These terms are notoriously difficult to define; using them without further explanation invites only ambiguity. They represent not only disputed historical "periods" but also diverse ideological judgments regarding the fundamental presuppositions of these periods. Many discussions, for example, simply identify "modernity" with the rationalism of the eighteenth-century Enlightenment or the scientific method of the nineteenth and twentieth centuries. But a close study of the period of history beginning with the Renaissance shows that "modernity" cannot be reduced to the dominant values of one time-slice, but can be defined in various ways—there are many "modernities" and a variety of "modern"

23. Jean-François Lyotard, *The Postmodern Condition: A Report on Knowledge*, trans. Geoff Bennington and Brian Massumi, Theory and History of Literature, vol. 10 (Minneapolis: University of Minnesota, 1984), xxiii–xxiv. In fact, Lyotard judges any commitment to metanarrative to be laying the groundwork for totalitarian terror (see pp. 81–2).

24. See, e.g., Jürgen Habermas, "Modernity—An Incomplete Project," trans. Seyla Ben-Habib, in Hal Foster, ed., *The Anti-Aesthetic: Essays on Postmodern Culture* (1983; reprint, New York: The New Press, 1998), 3–15.

cultures.[25] Similarly, the terms "contemporary" and "postmodern" cannot be reduced to simple definitions, nor are they equivalent.

A closer look at two analyses of contemporary culture will provide a more detailed description of our situation. While the analyses diverge, both ask similar questions: "What is the character of contemporary culture?" and "If contemporary culture looks like this, then what is the role of religion in this culture?"

4.1. A sociological perspective

The first analysis comes from the social theorist Bryan S. Turner.[26] He views contemporary culture as an arena of contention between still-vital modern values and the flourishing postmodern critique of those values. Both "sides" have religious roots, but both have become secularized in their values and practices.[27]

Turner's definition of modernity is influenced by the sociological theories of Max Weber and Émile Durkheim. Weber argued that modernization was rooted in "the process of secularisation, whereby religious values lose their social force, and world-views become increasingly pluralistic and fragmented. . . . The ultimate consequence of this process is that, alongside the dominance of instrumental rationalism and experimental science, religious values become

25. See Anthony J. Godzieba, " 'Refuge of Sinners, Pray for Us': Augustine, Aquinas, and the Salvation of Modernity," in Lieven Boeve, Frederiek Depoortere, and Maarten Wisse, eds., *Augustine and Postmodern Thought: A New Alliance Against Modernity?*, BETL 219 (Leuven: Peeters, 2009), 147–65. See also Dupré, *Passage to Modernity* and Taylor, *A Secular Age*.

26. For Turner's views on contemporary culture, see, e.g., *Religion and Social Theory*, 2d ed., Theory, Culture and Society (London/Newbury Park, CA: Sage, 1991); introduction to Christine Buci-Glucksmann, *Baroque Reason: The Aesthetics of Modernity*, trans. Patrick Camiller (London/Thousand Oaks, CA: Sage, 1994) 1–36; "Recent Developments in the Theory of the Body," in *The Body: Social Process and Cultural Theory*, ed. Mike Featherstone, Mike Hepworth, and Bryan S. Turner, Theory, Culture and Society (London/Newbury Park, CA: Sage, 1991) 1–35; *The Body and Society*, 2d ed. (London/Thousand Oaks, CA: Sage, 1996); *Vulnerability and Human Rights* (University Park, PA: Pennsylvania State University Press, 2006).

27. *Religion and Social Theory*, ix–xxiv.

attenuated and symbols are emptied of their content." The origins of this process go back to the "Protestant ethic" derived from the theology of John Calvin and the Calvinist emphasis on asceticism and rationalism. For his part, Durkheim differentiated between pre-modern society (held together by a "collective consciousness" composed of shared beliefs, symbols, and ritual practices) and modern society (which grew out of the breakdown of this consciousness in the face of increased social complexity). In place of these greatly-weakened shared beliefs, modernity is held together by social actions regulated by a systematized division of labor. Weber and Durkheim generally agreed that the birth of modernity was linked in some way to the loss of the socially cohesive force of religious beliefs and practices, hand-in-hand with the ever-increasing control of social behavior by means of the imposition of rational systems.[28]

Turner synthesizes these two classic positions and goes further. In his analysis, modernity is a way of life grounded on certain fundamental values initially encouraged by the Protestant Reformation: individuality, rationalism, and asceticism. In other words, the still-robust modern world puts premium value on the free, autonomous individual who can make rational decisions about the course of his or her own life, on instrumental rationality (i.e., goal-oriented thinking) as the most authentic use of human reason, and on disciplining the human body and denying pleasure in service to a higher goal. Throughout modernity, these values became secularized and are considered universally valid explanations of the human condition. Note the paradox: modernity's values have sprung from religious experience, but once secularized, they have undercut the truth of religious experience for many.

Postmodernity, on the other hand, represents a movement against various tendencies of modernity, including "the idea of grand narratives, concepts of unity, a unified notion of rationality and the

---

28. Ibid., xvi–xvii; quotation from xvi. See Max Weber, *The Protestant Ethic and the Spirit of Capitalism* [orig. 1920–21], trans. Talcott Parsons (London/New York: Routledge, 1992); Émile Durkheim, *The Elementary Forms of the Religious Life* [orig. 1912], trans. Karen E. Fields (New York: Free Press, 1995); Durkheim, *The Division of Labor in Society* [orig. 1893], trans. W.D. Halls (New York: Free Press, 1984).

authoritative dominance of western forms of reasoning."[29] It can be viewed as an outgrowth of modernity, part of a longer series of oppositional social movements prefigured by the Catholic Counter-Reformation and the Baroque in the seventeenth and eighteenth centuries and the Romantic movement in the nineteenth. Already present within modernity, then, were elements of its own critique. For example, as alternatives to a one-dimensional emphasis on rationality and individualism, the Counter-Reformation promoted non-rational, affective, and mystical practices and values, artistic illusion, and the location of truth in the absolute.[30] Postmodernity can be viewed as a secularized continuation of these modern oppositional attitudes. Under this heading, Turner includes contemporary movements from both the left and the right of the political spectrum: feminism's critique of patriarchy, the "green" movement, the conservative critique of modernity, even diverse types of religious fundamentalism.

His basic argument, then, is that "the contemporary" is neither wholly modern nor postmodern. It is rather the arena where their respective values, now secularized, compete for dominance in society and thus continue a contentious relationship that stretches back at least three hundred years.[31]

What role does religion play in this era of contention? Due to the breadth of modern secularization, Turner argues, religion has lost its traditional functions. It no longer provides the "social cement" that it did in pre-modern times, when its beliefs and practices served as *the* foundation for a common social life. Secondly, it is no longer the sole provider of the intellectual account that explains the origins, order, and meaning of the world and of society. This type of religious

---

29. *Religion and Social Theory*, xviii–xix.

30. For more on postmodernism's affinities with the Counter-Reformation and the Baroque, see Turner, "Recent Developments in the Theory of the Body," 26–30. For a theological discussion which begins with Turner's premise and argues for the continuing relevance of certain Counter-Reformation and Baroque Catholic values within contemporary Catholicism, see Anthony J. Godzieba, "Prolegomena to a Catholic Theology of God between Heidegger and Postmodernity," *The Heythrop Journal* 40 (1999): 319–39.

31. *Religion and Social Theory*, xx.

explanation, a "theodicy," was traditionally defined as a rational justification of the goodness of God in the face of evil and suffering in the world. But Turner understands "theodicy" more broadly as a profound reflection on human existence and on "the contingency of human embodiment" which provides "a number of distinctive intellectual responses to the problem of human pain, the nature of sexuality and the moral problems of death."[32] Religion still offers such an account, but is no longer the sole provider. Today its rivals are philosophy, the natural sciences, psychology, and especially late consumer capitalism (with its own emphasis on the body).

Despite the loss of its traditional functions, Turner argues that religion still has an important role to play in contemporary society. Religious belief and practice can give rise to a desire for a future where oppression and injustice will be overcome. When believers, in the process of actualizing their religious commitments, protest against the status quo, they express not only their belief in transcendent realities whose powers are greater than those in everyday experience, but also their judgment on the inadequacies of the status quo and their belief in the ability of these transcendent realities to change present-day negative situations into life-enhancing situations in the future. Despite widespread secularization, then, religious language and symbols still retain their potential to "provide the sort of utopian motivation which is necessary for massive social change." For example, "the imagery of the Old and New Testaments continues to provide a vocabulary of protest against injustice which, in both radical Catholicism and radical Protestantism, creates a utopian mentality, which is the basis for a radical critique of existing societies." Turner sees an analogous oppositional and utopian mentality present in Islamic fundamentalism.[33] Implicit in his argument is the conclusion that such a potential for social critique of the status quo puts

---

32. Ibid., xiv–xv. Turner makes a cogent argument for the close connection between body and theodicy. Cf. also Turner's claims regarding "ontological frailty" in "The End(s) of Humanity: Vulnerability and the Metaphors of Membership," *The Hedgehog Review* 3, 2 (Summer 2001): 7–32. See also Anthony J. Godzieba, "Incarnation, Theory, and Catholic Bodies: What Should Post-Postmodern Catholic Theology Look Like?," *Louvain Studies* 28, 3 (2003): 217–31.

33. *Religion and Social Theory*, xxi.

religion squarely on the side of postmodern movements of opposition. Religion thus can play a vital role in today's society, even though our epoch has been characterized as being non-religious or even hostile to religion.

4.2. A philosophical perspective

The philosopher Leszek Kolakowski offers a much different view of "the contemporary" and of religion's role in it.[34]

He agrees that the contemporary epoch is marked by a process of secularization that began in modernity. But he takes issue with the usual definitions of "secularization," either as the measurable decline in organized religion or the gradual assumption of the functions of religion by secular institutions. These are based on unfounded modernist assumptions that somehow religion must be on the decline and be replaced by other forms of knowledge, or that religion is simply a coded mythological explanation of the world, destined to be replaced by more rational or empirical explanations. Such views of religion, he argues, are themselves the result of the imposition of other arbitrary presuppositions: either the evolutionary assumption that "primitive" religion must make way for more "sophisticated" forms of human life; or a philosophical assumption that the "latent meanings" of myths are always the "true" ones and the ostensible meanings are always the product of self-deception, mystification, or ignorance; or a contrary philosophical assumption that the most obvious social use of a phenomenon is its true meaning. Each of these positions misses the specifically *religious* claims of religious phenomena and fails to explain why human beings would even choose the "detour" through religious language to express their needs if religious language were only a code to be decoded.

---

34. See "The Revenge of the Sacred in Secular Culture," trans. Agnieszka Kolakowska and Leszek Kolakowski, in Leszek Kolakowski, *Modernity on Endless Trial* (Chicago: University of Chicago Press, 1990), 63–74; *Religion, If There is No God. . .: On God, the Devil, Sin and Other Worries of the So-Called Philosophy of Religion* (New York: Oxford University Press, 1982). See also *God Owes Us Nothing: A Brief Remark on Pascal's Religion and on the Spirit of Jansenism* (Chicago: University of Chicago Press, 1995).

> Religious values, if they are to be attributed to secular interests and aspirations, must previously have been recognized as such [i.e., as religious], independently of those interests and aspirations. If the words *God is on my side* are to serve as a defense of any cause, God's authority must already be recognized, not invented ad hoc for that particular defense. The sacred must exist before it may be exploited. It is therefore absurd to claim that the sacred is no more than the instrument of the various interests that have pressed it into service.[35]

In light of such deficiencies in the usual characterization of secular modern culture, Kolakowski suggests a third definition of "secularization": "It takes the form of a blurring of the differences between the sacred and the secular and a denial of their separation; it is the tendency to attribute to everything a sacred sense. But to universalize the sacred is to destroy it: to say that everything is sacred is tantamount to saying that nothing is, for the qualities, sacred and profane, can be understood only in contrast to one another; every description is a form of negation; the attributes of a totality are inapprehensible."[36] The universalization of the sacred leads to its obliteration; this is the characteristic mark of contemporary culture. This state of affairs is due not only to anti-religious factors in modernity but also, Kolakowski claims, to religion itself, particularly Christianity. He argues that, in order to embrace the world and be accepted by the dominant forms of modern culture, Christianity tried to become integrated into the world by sacralizing everything secular, without distinction. In this way, the sacred, the source of Christianity's identity, became submerged and Christianity's specific identity was lost.

Does religion still play a role in contemporary culture? For Kolakowski the answer depends on the correct interpretation of the dialectical relationship between the sacred and the profane. In this relationship the sacred plays two crucial roles. First, it is a "conservative" force: it provides a stable structure or "system of signs" that

---

35. "The Revenge of the Sacred," 63–67; quotation from 65–66. Cf. *Religion*, 14–16.

36. "The Revenge of the Sacred," 68.

gives transient things meaning by fixing their value within a significant order determined by the sacred, adding "a weight of the ineffable, as it were, to every given form of social life." Such boundary-setting involves the sacred in a constant tension with the changeability and developing possibilities of finite worldly realities, but this tension is necessary and inevitable. "This tension is proper to life; its dissolution would result in death, either by stagnation (if only conservative forces remained) or by explosion (if only the forces of transformation remained, in a structural void)."[37]

The sacred's other, more important role is related to the first. By admitting the existence of the sacred, one confesses that the secular or profane is precisely what it is: non-sacred, finite, contingent, never absolute, and never able to fulfill our desires. Without the presence of the sacred to expose the intrinsic, "incurable" imperfection of the profane, the danger exists that humankind will consider the profane—which would then be the only accessible plane of existence—complete and perfect in itself, or at least perfectible by human effort. As totalitarian political movements have shown again and again, such a misreading of the profane and such hubris is a recipe for catastrophe.

> Culture, when it loses its sacred sense, loses all sense. With the disappearance of the sacred, which imposed limits to the perfection that could be attained by the profane, arises one of the most dangerous illusions of our civilization—the illusion that there are no limits to the changes that human life can undergo, that society is "in principle" an endlessly flexible thing, and that to deny this flexibility and this perfectability is to deny man's total autonomy and thus to deny man himself.[38]

To reject the sacred is to reject our inherent limits and indulge in these dangerous illusions. It also means the rejection of the idea of evil, since the sacred is necessary in order for the reality of evil to be recognized and resisted. Our changeable impulses alone are not equal to the task of measuring evil and resisting it.

---

37. Ibid., 70.
38. Ibid., 72. For a more detailed treatment, see *Religion*, 19–58.

Religion's crucial role in contemporary society, then, is to render the sacred present, thereby revealing the intrinsic limitations of the profane, its inevitable lack of fulfillment, and the suffering such limitations impose on our experience. "A religious world perception is indeed able to teach us *how to be a failure*. And the latent assumption behind such teaching is that on earth everybody *is* a failure."[39] The religious worldview alone is the realistic view because it reminds us that the world and human experience have essential limits and achieve only degrees of perfection, never any totality or perfect fulfillment of our desires. "Religion is man's way of accepting life as an inevitable defeat. That it is not an inevitable defeat is a claim that cannot be defended in good faith. . . . One can accept life, and accept it, at the same time, as a defeat only if one accepts that there is a sense [i.e., a meaning] beyond that which is inherent in human history—if, in other words, one accepts the order of the sacred."[40]

4.3. A theological synthesis

The differences between Turner's and Kolakowski's analyses of the contemporary are so marked that at first glance one might wonder if they and the positions they represent help us at all in understanding the context of our questions about God.

Turner offers a complex portrayal of the contemporary as poised between a commitment to its still-vital modern heritage and the postmodern dissolution of this heritage. His analysis of postmodernity is complex as well. It is not simply a wholesale break with modernity. Rather, it develops from the critical, questioning eye which modernity has turned toward all its inherited ancient and medieval traditions, as well as from those critiques of the all-encompassing modern project that arose within modernity itself. It then turns the critical process back on modernity itself and on the values that modernity seeks to keep alive as essential to the human condition.

---

39. *Religion*, 40.
40. "The Revenge of the Sacred," 73.

Kolakowski, on the other hand, never mentions the word "postmodern." He makes it quite clear that he views the contemporary epoch as a continuation of the long march of modernity. But it is a contentious continuation, and his evaluation of it has a strongly negative cast. Since for the most part the contemporary world—with the help of Christianity—has gradually obliterated the distinction between the infinite sacred and the finite secular, the contemporary era courts meaninglessness and risks catastrophe. If humanity fails to recognize the sacred's infinite otherness and the limits that it sets on the exercise of human power, then humanity is in danger of becoming so intoxicated with its ability to alter its own circumstances that it might not see any limits to that power and unleash violent destruction instead. The result of modernity's ignorance of the sacred and of the limits of the profane is a contemporary epoch in which the most realistic evaluation of our human condition—that we cannot save ourselves, that human life is permeated with non-fulfillment, that life is a "failure"—escapes us, and we slide ever closer to chaos by chasing short-term pleasures or by taking comfort in idealistic speculation.

Turner's analysis is framed in "world-disclosing" language ("this is the way things are") which describes the varieties of attitudes within the current situation without recommending any specific one, whereas Kolakowski's language is "action-coordinating" ("this is what we need to do to make things better") that advocates a course of action necessary to transform our present condition.[41] But despite their differing estimations of the contemporary epoch, they reflect a deeper consensus that is helpful for our purposes: both expose the religious roots of modernity and criticize modernity's so-called "absolute" status, and both note the complexity of our current situation and the crucial role played by religious (and specifically Christian) values in its formation. Those values provoke a variety of responses but nonetheless contribute to contemporary society's fundamental character.

41. See an analysis of these two dimensions of language in Stephen K. White, *Political Theory and Postmodernism*, Modern European Philosophy (Cambridge/New York: Cambridge University Press, 1991), 23–28.

Turner and Kolakowski also agree on the continued importance of religion in contemporary society, whether one labels that society "modern," "postmodern," or both. In their view, religion continues to offer society an essential understanding of reality that provides an alternative to the truncated, reductionist one that has grown in dominance over the last five centuries. Against the modern individualist view of the human person and the attempt to define everything by means of a one-dimensional rationalist yardstick, and against the pretensions of human power that has styled itself as the only possible power, religious belief and practice has consistently offered an alternative worldview or construal of reality that challenges attitudes which have become accepted without question.

A religious worldview understands all things to be in the grip of, at the behest of, or in the care of "the sacred," which both transcends and exposes the limitations of every other humanly-constructed worldview. This does not necessarily mean that a religious worldview is purely "otherworldly" and therefore unrealistic. Quite the contrary: the religious worldview is *the most realistic of all* since it speaks directly to our desires for the transformation of an inadequate (and sometimes tragic or even brutalizing) present, for a productive future, and for human development and happiness. The alternative view which religion offers is emancipative: it can free us from the terrors of temporality and of the human worldview that can forget its limitations. The construal of reality articulated by a religious worldview is one that adherents believe has its origins in an unprompted divine disclosure—one that it is revealed, not rationalized. Revelation directly addresses the good desired by people, both for themselves and for the cosmos. Thus spirituality and politics, contemplation and action are always bound together in a religious worldview, whether believers acknowledge the connection or not.

Our questions about God thus arise within a context that has religion as one of its formative aspects. Turner and Kolakowski place the values of Christian religious belief at the origins of modernity; even the most secularized features of modern culture have Christian religious experience somewhere in their bloodline. Postmodern attempts to surpass modernity continue to have a connection with Christian religious belief as well: in one way, they continue the legacy of early modern Catholicism and its opposition to the modern autonomous self (which ceased to be recognized as the image of God) and to the dominance of instrumental reason (which tended to sweep religious experience aside). Religious belief and practice, then, touch all contemporary practices to some degree, no matter how non- or anti-religious they may appear to be.

The divine "otherness" made manifest in these religious beliefs and practices—whether portrayed in terms of the sacred's radical difference from the secular (Kolakowski) or in terms of religion's "oppositional" character (Turner)—emphatically points to the existence of a transcending vision of reality that has a greater scope than our own plans and undertakings, and surpasses the expectations we generate from our own experiences. This is a fundamentally sacramental way of understanding reality: what is finite and contingent can mediate the infinite and absolute. Religious belief and practice offer ways of addressing the multitudinous possibilities of existence. They also make it clear that the presence and the successful actualization of these possibilities are grounded in the divine mystery. The conditions for the fulfillment of human desire exceed the usual human expectations, planning, and power.

These possibilities are rooted in God's otherness, in what the theologian Johann Baptist Metz calls the "practical" and "irritating" character of God, to which revelation attests in various ways. "God simply cannot be thought without this idea irritating and disrupting the immediate interests of the one who is trying to think it. Thinking-God happens as a revision of those interests and needs that are directly organized around one's self."[42] The "irritation" comes from the fact that God's otherness exposes the non-absolute and non-necessary character of our own lives—our fallibility, our finitude, our mortality. Our desires for happiness, well-being, and fulfillment always outrun our ability to satisfy those desires; our understanding of new possibilities always collides with our inability to actualize those possibilities exactly as we choose. We cannot supply ourselves with the complete happiness and the freedom

---

42. Johann Baptist Metz, *Faith in History and Society: Toward a Practical Fundamental Theology*, trans. J. Matthew Ashley (New York: Crossroad, 2007), 62.

from evil and tragedy that we crave—indeed, many times we can't even seem to arrange our day-to-day affairs so that we might enjoy momentary happiness. Thus we confront the "practical" aspect of the reality of God when we "review" our "interests and needs" and discover the desire for salvation and fulfillment that we cannot satisfy on our own.

This way of thinking and speaking about the reality of God—a way of being authentically theological—is at once staunchly traditional and expressly postmodern. On the one hand, the theological commitment to God's otherness echoes the experience of God found in Scripture and is as old as theology itself. On the other hand, the postmodern aspect derives from the alternative understanding of reality that is ultimately grounded in the otherness of God. Our ability to respond to and to conceive this "difference," this fulfillment of desires that exceeds our "normal," rational expectations, is an example of what the philosopher Richard Kearney has termed the "poetic imagination," the way of thinking by which one can "begin to imagine that the world as it is could be *otherwise.*"[43] This is not "imagination" in the usual sense of "inventing fantasies," but rather a realistic response to our situation and a direct probing for new and better possibilities for existence that the situation presents. Christian religious practices and beliefs can be understood as the believing community's activation of poetic imagination in the light of divine revelation. The Christian community's religious imagination responds to the revealed "otherness" of God and of God's grace and probes our situations for new possibilities of existence in the light of God's relationship with humankind and with the cosmos. Christianity's "oppositional" nature, animated by the revelation of God in Jesus Christ, proclaims that life *can* be otherwise than a mixed bag of pleasures and tragedies, and that God *wills* that it be otherwise. For the Christian, Jesus' preaching of the Kingdom of God is his imaginative re-visioning of the world as God sees it, as the place where the action of grace promotes what is positive and humanizing. This refiguring

43. Richard Kearney, "Ethics and the Postmodern Imagination," *Thought* 62 (1987): 39–58, at 44. See also Anthony J. Godzieba, "Knowing Differently: Incarnation, Imagination, and the Body," *Louvain Studies* 32 (2007): 361–82.

of the world toward eschatological fulfillment begins with imagining *as possible* God's salvific power to transform seemingly hopeless situations. And this response to the mystery of the divine initiative is the first step toward participating in its ongoing actualization. In other words, conversion to God implies putting into practice the values of the Kingdom of God.

This, then is the context of our questioning. As we continue to seek answers, one other important principle will guide our subsequent theological reflections on God. Turner's and Kolakowski's arguments, though instructive, presuppose a disjunction between sacred and secular, believer and dominant society, church and world. This presupposition ignores the human need to know and understand *something* about God, even if God's true nature remains, as Pseudo-Dionysius says, "in the brilliant darkness of a hidden silence." What is also needed, then, is the exercise of the sacramental imagination. The sound theological principle that we will follow has been articulated by Bernhard Welte: "Salvation can only be salvation when it is *our* salvation; redemption is only redemption when it redeems *us*."[44] The presence of God's love and grace can be recognized by, be effective for, and be acted upon by human persons only when it appears in human categories of understanding, even while it surpasses these categories. We must experience and understand something about God in order for God to be *our* God.

The sacred cannot be completely identified with the profane if it is to retain its transformative power. But without a presence mediated by worldly categories—that is, without some way to perceive the presence of the divine mystery in human lives—God remains unglimpsed and unknown to human concerns and expectations. That is why Anselm, in his prayer to God, yearns "to understand a little of your truth which my heart already believes and loves," that he might be guided by that truth and experience its salvific effects *in and through* his life, not *in spite of* his life. In order for the sacred to be known, it must inhabit the same space as the profane and speak its

---

44. Bernhard Welte, "Die Wesenstruktur der Theologie als Wissenschaft" [1955], *Auf der Spur des Ewigen* (Freiburg: Herder, 1965), 351–65, at 354; also in *Gesammelte Schriften*, vol. IV/3, 167–83, at 171.

language, while remaining sacred. This is what the incarnational heart of Christian faith teaches us: God became human to redeem human beings. This faith principle guides what follows. We will articulate an incarnational and sacramental understanding of God, and attempt to maintain the delicate balance between God's transcendent otherness (which prevents us from reducing God to our terms) and God's presence (which touches our lives with the emancipative force of God's love). This is what we mean by "the presence and absence of God."

CHAPTER TWO

How God Became a Problem in Western Culture

How are we to think and speak about God today? To answer that, we first need to discover why our contemporary situation has the conflicted relationship to God that it has. In other words, we must explain how God became a problem in Western culture. The "history of the God-problem" recounted here has two purposes: to pinpoint the historical sources of our culture's checkered relationship with God, and to retrieve the positive, productive elements from that history, which in turn will help us discover new possibilities for thinking and speaking of that relationship.[1]

We begin with the biblically-based belief in God as both immanent and transcendent, the portrayal that we will call *the classical dialectical view* of God, the understanding that God is simultaneously "present" (knowable, available) and "absent" (mysterious, uncontrollable). This was the dominant Jewish and Christian view in biblical times and remained so in Christianity up through the end of the medieval period. Our narrative will then move on and consider the later view, which we will term *the extrinsic view*. This emphasizes—and at times has overemphasized—the transcendence, inconceivability, and even, as an extreme reaction, the non-existence of God. A crucial point in our narrative is the momentous shift away from the classical dialectical view, with its more fundamental understanding of God based on revelation, to the extrinsic view that owes more to

---

1. Other narratives are possible, of course. See, e.g., Karen Armstrong, *A History of God: The 4,000-Year Quest of Judaism, Christianity and Islam* (New York: Ballantine, 1993); Francis Schüssler Fiorenza and Gordon D. Kaufman, "God," in *Critical Terms for Religious Studies*, ed. Mark C. Taylor (Chicago: University of Chicago Press, 1998), 136–59.

modern philosophy and to changes in the shape of knowledge and society. This shift began in the late medieval period and has been a dominant factor in Western culture from the Renaissance up until our own day. Because the extrinsic view has perdured for so long, it appears to be so "normal" that most believers would consider it—and not the biblical, dialectical view—to be the authentic "classical Christian view" of God. However, not only is the extrinsic view an unhelpful distortion of the classical Christian view, but there is a real question whether it is Christian at all.[2] In a later chapter we will propose an alternative to the extrinsic view by retrieving the more biblical dialectical view and examining how this way of thinking and speaking is more fundamentally and authentically attuned to God's self-revelation as Trinity and more encouraging of a dynamic relationship between God and human beings.

But first we need to trace the genealogy of the present state of affairs.

1. The Dialectical View

1.1 Biblical Roots

The source of the classical dialectical view of God can be found in biblical revelation, particularly in the narratives of the ancient theophanies or "manifestations of God" that served as classic reference points not only for Judaism but also for Jesus, his Jewish followers, the early Jesus-movement, and its later development into Christianity. From among these theophanies, one is considered to be at the heart of the Hebrew Scriptures, namely the revelation of God to Moses on Mount Horeb (Exod 3:1–4:17).[3] This theophany discloses the funda-

---

2. Walter Kasper goes so far as to speak of "the heresy of Christian theism" when examining aspects of what we are calling the extrinsic view. See Kasper, *The God of Jesus Christ* [hereafter *GJC*], new ed., trans. [Matthew O'Connell and] Dinah Livingstone (London/New York: Continuum, 2012), 285, 294.

3. See Brevard S. Childs, *Exodus: A Commentary*, The Old Testament Library (London: SCM, 1974); Terence E. Fretheim, *Exodus*, Interpretation: A Bible Commentary for Teaching and Preaching (Louisville: John Knox Press, 1991); Dennis J. McCarthy, "Exod 3:14: History, Philology and Theology," *Catholic Biblical Quarterly* 40 (1978): 311-22; Tryggve N. D. Mettinger, *In Search of God: The Meaning and Message of the Everlasting Names*, trans. Frederick H. Cryer (Philadelphia: Fortress,

mental identity of God in a way that echoes down through the Scriptures and into Christian history. It generates a series of reflections whose conclusions will dominate the Christian understanding of God until the end of the medieval period.

The Exodus episode recounts Moses' experience of the revelation of God at the site of the burning bush and God's commissioning of Moses to lead Israel from Egyptian bondage to freedom. In the midst of their conversation, Moses asks God for a sign to confirm that God has indeed given him leadership of the Israelites. "Moses is given as that justification the very divine name; that is, in ancient thinking, the revelation of the divine personality and a share in the divine power."[4] This name not only amplifies God's earlier self-identification ("I am the God of your father, the God of Abraham, the God of Isaac, and the God of Jacob" [Exod 3:6]) but adds an unexpected and puzzling new dimension to God's identity.

> But Moses said to God, "Who am I that I should go to Pharaoh, and bring the Israelites out of Egypt?" He said, "I will be with you; and this shall be the sign for you that it is I who sent you: when you have brought the people out of Egypt, you shall worship God on this mountain. . . . But Moses said to God, "If I come to the Israelites and say to them, 'The God of your ancestors has sent me to you,' and they ask me, 'What is his name?' what shall I say to them?" God said to Moses, "I AM WHO I AM." He said further, "Thus you shall say to the Israelites: 'I AM has sent me to you.'" God also said to Moses, "Thus you shall say to the Israelites: 'The LORD, the God of your ancestors, the God of Abraham, the God of Isaac, and the God of Jacob, has sent me to you.'" (Exod 3:11-15)

The dramatic revelation of the divine name YHWH (Yahweh) in verse 15 (translated above as "the LORD") is the pivot upon which the entire episode turns. It is the justification of Moses' authority to lead and the promise of Israel's liberation from the grip of its oppressors. By this revelation Israel's present experience of God is linked with the experience of God had by Israel's ancestors. The meaning

1988), 14–49; John Courtney Murray, *The Problem of God, Yesterday and Today*, The St. Thomas More Lectures, 1 (New Haven: Yale University Press, 1964), 5–30.
   4. McCarthy, 317.

of the name is explained earlier in verse 14 as *'ehyeh 'ašer 'ehyeh* (translated as "I am who [I] am"), with its repetition of the Hebrew verb *hyh* (*hayah*, "to be"). The precise meanings of both the phrase and the divine name (the third person singular form of *hyh*) are difficult to determine and have long been controversial.

We can better understand the meaning and importance of this passage if we consider three issues: the role of names in the ancient world, the role of divine names in particular, and the character of this specific divine name. In the ancient Middle East, names were understood to reveal the reality of the thing or person named and to complete their existence, making them present and available. To know a person's name gave one access to the deepest aspects of their being and personality, because it made available the fundamental "essence" or "nature" of the one named.[5] In the biblical world "the connection between a name and its bearer is so intimate that it is hard to speak of a name as a quantity that can be clearly separated from the individual who bears it. A person's name tends to be her or his alter ego and reflects her or his nature, power, and reality."[6] The divinities of the ancient Middle East were not exempt from this connection. The names of gods and goddesses needed to be known in order for them to be recognized and to be available to their worshipers. Without knowing the name, how might one pray to the god or goddess and invoke that deity's power and protection?

To name and to know the essential nature, then, is to have power and control to some degree over the person or thing named. This accounts for the chanting of the names of goddesses or gods—the human attempt to compel the deities to be present and to bestow their benefits upon those who pray in this way. This is also why Adam names the animals in the second creation story in the book of Genesis (Gen 2:19–20); it symbolizes the Hebrew belief in God-given human mastery over the rest of creation.[7]

---

5. Mettinger, 6–11; John L. McKenzie, *A Theology of the Old Testament* (Garden City, NY: Doubleday/Image, 1976), 75.

6. Mettinger, 11; see also Murray, 6–7.

7. Cf. Richard J. Clifford and Roland E. Murphy, "Genesis," *The New Jerome Biblical Commentary*, ed. Raymond E. Brown, Joseph A Fitzmyer, and Roland E. Murphy (Englewood Cliffs, NJ: Prentice-Hall, 1990), 12.

The divine name revealed to Moses is like other names but also radically different. On the one hand, "YHWH" functions as do other names: it reveals God's presence and personality to the Israelites and signals God's availability as the supreme helper of their cause. But even though they know the name, Moses and the Israelites utterly lack power and control over YHWH because they cannot know precisely what the name means. This is due to the ambiguous verbal formulations evident both in the original Hebrew and in translation.

The phrase *'ehyeh 'ašer 'ehyeh* in verse 14 is puzzling and has been explained and translated in various ways.[8] One approach renders it as "I am who I am" and treats the passage as an instance of the biblical *idem per idem* style, that is, the repeated use of the same root in order to preserve the indefinite character of a statement. Another sees the emphasis on the verb *hyh* to be making a theological statement about God and translates the phrase as "I am the one who is" or "I am the existing one." Yet another takes *hyh* as a future tense and translates the phrase as "I will be who I will be" or "I shall really be with you to help." Finally, there is the argument that "YHWH" derives from the causative form of the verb *hyh* (thus "to cause to be") and that the original Hebrew should be emended to read *yahweh 'ašer yihweh*, "he causes to be what comes into existence." The current scholarly consensus for the most part has ruled out this latter approach and insists on taking *hyh* as the main stem of the verb "to be." But this still allows for various translations and interpretations, from "I am who am" to "he who is" to "[My name shall be] *Ehyeh* [I AM], because I am."[9]

This range of interpretation underscores our point. Even though we can narrow down the range of meanings to some form of the verb "to be," we seem not to have reached much understanding at all. Neither *'ehyeh 'ašer 'ehyeh*, nor *'ehyeh* alone (verse 14), nor *YHWH* can be rendered precisely because their meanings cannot be known exactly. The mystery inherent in the name defeats our attempts to find an exact definition and translation, just as it defeated Moses and the

8. Mettinger, 29–36; McCarthy, 315–19; Childs, 60–77; Murray, 8–11.

9. The second translation is McCarthy's preference (317), the last Mettinger's (36).

Israelites. This does not mean that the situation is hopeless and that we have no insight at all into God. While the divine name "Yahweh" conceals God, it also reveals. Though our knowledge is always inadequate and the true nature of God remains mysterious, we can know *something* of the character or the personality of God. God's personal name (a verb) discloses at the very least that God is best understood along the lines of person and personal relationship, even if such understanding is never fully adequate. "Naming entails distinctiveness; it sets one off from others who have names, including gods. Moreover, anyone whose name is known becomes a part of the community that has names; God thereby chooses to join the historical community. Even more, to give this name with reference to the God of the fathers ties this God to a certain history."[10] That history, and those who share in it, are tied to God in an intimate relationship that God has decided freely to enter. The name discloses God's dynamic role in that relationship: "Yahweh *is* above all others and this means active and helping, for being and acting effectively were not separated."[11]

In light of this analysis, then, an adequate translation of the divine name might be "I am here, ready to act [on your behalf]."[12] This respects the text's emphasis on *hyh* as "to be" but also does justice to God's effective activity and promise to be eternally faithful to this relationship: "This is my name forever, and this is my title for all generations" (Exod 3:15b). In this light even the future-tense translation of *'ehyeh 'ašer 'ehyeh* has merit, capturing some sense of the ongoing revelation of the mystery of God. "I will be who I will be" means, in effect, "You will see who I will be once I act [on your behalf]." God's true nature will progressively be revealed to the Israelites as they continue to experience different aspects of God's saving power throughout their history. As demonstrated in Exodus and throughout the Old Testament, that power is God's life-giving and liberating activity, especially on behalf of the powerless, shattering life-denying situations and transforming them into life-affirming ones.

10. Fretheim, 64–65.
11. McCarthy, 317.
12. Cf. Murray, 11: "I shall be there, actively, with you."

The very structure of the revelation of the divine name in the burning bush theophany illustrates the fundamental biblical understanding of God that we are calling "dialectical."[13] The name YHWH discloses the true reality of God, but since the name's precise meaning remains elusive, any statement about the nature of God is always tentative. In this paradox, the structural elements of the dialectical view of God become apparent. First, the revelation of the name YHWH announces that the way to understand "the one who is," above all others, is as a *person*, in terms of personality and personal interaction. God has a personal name and thus enters into a personal relationship with the human community and into its history. Next there are the dialectical patterns disclosed in the name itself:

  (a) *Knowability—Mysteriousness:* God is *known*, especially by the salvific deeds that God performs. But God remains *mysterious* because God's nature can never be fully apprehended;

  (b) *Availability—Uncontrollability:* God is *available*, since God enters into the historical human community and can be recognized, called upon, prayed to. Yet God is *not controllable*, since what it is to be God escapes definition and transcends human concepts;

  (c) *Immanence—Transcendence:* God is *immanent*; God's availability occurs within history, within the world, within human experience. Yet God is also *transcendent*, since "the one who is" could never be reduced to a circumscribed object within a "larger" world.

These dialectical elements can be summarized in this way:

  (d) In the biblical tradition, God is experienced as both *Present* and *Absent.*

"Absence" here does not mean God's non-existence. It refers instead to those aspects of the reality of God that exceed the categories

---

13. My use of the term "dialectical" owes much to John Macquarrie's incisive discussion in his sadly overlooked Gifford Lectures from the early 1980s. See John Macquarrie, *In Search of Deity: An Essay in Dialectical Theism*, The Gifford Lectures 1983–4 (London: SCM, 1984), 171–82. While I have worked out the notion of the dialectical view somewhat differently, I have found his arguments extremely helpful.

of human understanding and escape our vocabulary, leaving them seemingly empty. No one definition or image of God can ever claim to be definitive. "Absence" signals the *otherness* of God, God's *excess* that outruns our human ability to adequately "name" and conceptualize the characteristics of the personality of God.

Identifying the dialectical view as the fundamental biblical view of God is supported by other theophanies in the Hebrew Scriptures. For example, the encounter between God and Abraham in Genesis 22, the story of the testing of Abraham (the *Aqedah* or "the binding of Isaac"), is a horrifying yet riveting event. Abraham is told by God to take "your only son Isaac, whom you love" (Gen 22:2), and sacrifice him on Mount Moriah. In faithful obedience Abraham goes off, without a word, to obey the harsh and mysterious divine command. At the moment when Abraham is about to carry out the dreadful sacrifice, however, God stays his knife-wielding hand. Through an angelic messenger God acknowledges Abraham's total faithfulness and obedience, and allows him to spy a ram in the distance. Abraham catches the ram and "offered it up as a burnt offering instead of his son" (Gen 22:13).

Here the hallmarks of the dialectical view are clearly visible. First, the narrator has depicted God "as the Lord whose demands are absolute, whose will is inscrutable, and whole final word is grace."[14] But there is even more to understand. At the outset Abraham clearly understands the command of God in terms of one of the widely-held beliefs of the ancient Middle East, that child-sacrifice is necessary to appease the gods and stay in their favor. His faith, in other words, initially encounters God according to the cultural expectations of his own era. He believes in the essential correctness of that view and acts in accordance with it, proceeding on the assumption that this understanding of God is complete rather than partial—this is who God truly is and what God truly wants. However, his encounter with God results in a surprise that shatters these expectations. An aspect of God's character is revealed that could not have been generated from Abraham's cultural presuppositions: God does not want child-sacrifice. The God in whom Abraham has placed his faith and the

14. Clifford and Murphy, "Genesis," 25.

control of his life chooses to affirm life rather than violently deny it.[15] The theophany thus unveils an aspect of the mystery of the personality of God, an unexpected trait that is not a projection from previously-held assumptions. This encounter between Abraham and God is a revelatory event that displays the logic of the dialectical view in a way similar to the Exodus theophany: the reality of God exceeds our settled conceptions and images of the divine, and indeed may shatter them.

Another example is found among the cycle of stories connected with the prophet Elijah (1 Kgs 17–2 Kgs 2). A theophany decisively concludes the contest between Elijah and the prophets of Baal (1 Kgs 18:16–40), followed by the episode where Elijah, on the run from an angry Queen Jezebel and an ambivalent King Ahab, encounters God in prayer (1 Kgs 19:1-18).

The contest is proposed by Elijah to prove who is the true divinity, either Yahweh or Baal, the Canaanite god of storms and fertility. The proof will be an all-out display of power: the true God will be the one who acts. In this way, Elijah hopes to win back for Yahweh the wavering religious loyalties of the people. Baal's court-supported prophets ("four hundred and fifty") and Elijah ("I, even I only, am left a prophet of the LORD," 1 Kgs 18:22) each prepare a young bull as a sacrificial offering but are not to start the fire. Each side is to call on its deity to consume the offering, and "the god who answers by fire is indeed God" (1 Kgs 18:24). At their turn, Baal's prophets whip themselves into a frenzy and lacerate themselves (accompanied by Elijah's sarcastic comments), but nothing happens. Elijah then prays soberly to Yahweh, who responds with a spectacular show of power (1 Kgs 18:38). At the sight of this the people confess their loyal belief in Yahweh and assist Elijah in rounding up the pagan prophets, whom the prophet single-handedly slaughters.

---

15. Ancient Israel struggled with the implications of this particular revelation throughout its history. The Old Testament's polemic against those who practice child sacrifice (e.g., 2 Kings 16:3; Ezekiel 20:23–26; Micah 6:7) shows that it was still practiced in times of crisis. See Clifford and Murphy, 26 (on Gen. 22:13) and Mark S. Smith, *The Early History of God: Yahweh and the Other Deities in Ancient Israel*, 2d ed. (Grand Rapids: Eerdmans/Dearborn, MI: Dove, 2002), 171–81.

Elijah then meets Ahab and announces the arrival of torrential rains that end a terrible drought (1 Kgs 18:41–46). Both the drought and the rain symbolize Yahweh's power that overcomes the Baalism promoted by Jezebel and half-heartedly approved by Ahab. As a result, Jezebel rages against Elijah, who flees in fear into the desert to Mount Horeb (1 Kgs 19:1–18). While sheltered in a mountain cave, the prophet experiences another theophany. But this time God's self-manifestation does not occur as any display of power; in fact, the traditional forms of divine manifestation (wind, earthquake, fire) are expressly denied. Rather, Yahweh's presence becomes revealed in "a sound of sheer [*or* fine] silence" (1 Kgs 19:12)—the opposite of Elijah's expectations and also completely different from "the LORD's fire" that swept down powerfully from heaven during the contest.

How do these two incidents illustrate the dialectical view? The first, in fact, appears to contradict it. Elijah has identified Yahweh as the deity of absolute power, particularly power over nature, the realm claimed by the Baalists for their own god.[16] Here Elijah performs as prophet in the classical Hebrew sense of the term: he is *nabi*, the one who speaks and acts in Yahweh's name, who knows and communicates Yahweh's truth. Elijah's criterion for the contest is simple: the real God is the God who acts with power. Baal does nothing, and so is a false god. Yahweh's power is even mightier than expected; Yahweh is real. Since Elijah had identified "Yahweh" with "absolute power," the contest seemingly confirms that God is precisely as the prophet has imagined God to be. At the end of the first episode, Elijah acts according to his apparently confirmed understanding of the nature of God: on behalf of Yahweh, he exacts ruthless revenge on Baal's prophets and on the royal court that supports Baalism. The resulting slaughter shocks us. It is carried out in the name of a violent image of God that seems to be in blatant contradiction to the image of God revealed to Abraham, the God who does not desire death but rather bestows and supports life. On the basis of this first episode we might claim that Elijah has strayed from the fundamental dialectical view that is at the heart of the Abrahamic and Mosaic traditions. He

16. See Smith, *Early History of God*, 65–79.

has reduced the reality of God to a single trait, "absolute power"—
and then modeled his own brutal actions on this understanding.

Could Elijah be mistaken? From his point of view, the contest has
simply confirmed his expectation that the truth of God is wholly
identical with what can be learned about Yahweh's personality from
one particular incident and from one's immediate religious and cultural situation. When one mistakes a partial image for the whole
reality of God, one overemphasizes the "presence" side of the dialectic and thus violates the revelational logic that is at the heart of
God's self-revelation to Israel, the presence/absence structure. That
is why the second episode is vitally important. There the divine
self-manifestation corrects Elijah's understanding and exposes his
earlier portrait of God as partial, one that cannot and should not be
absolutized. The prophet's understanding of God develops under
the pressure of a revelation that shatters his expectations. In the midst
of his suffering and prayer, he learns that Yahweh can be present not
only in raging power but also in such an opposite and unpredictable
way (a "fine silence") that this presence might be missed. The stories
from the Elijah cycle, then, confirm the dialectical view in a negative
fashion: the initial image of God held by Yahweh's heroic spokesperson is eventually revealed to be deficient. It is shattered by an image
of God whose greater adequacy is not due to human ingenuity but
to God's own gracious initiative.

While the classical dialectical view of God has its source in biblical
theophanies, it is not found only there. The presence/absence structure of divine self-revelation permeates the Old and New Testaments;
biblical faith and theology is incomprehensible without it. The dialectical view is implied, for example, in the biblical faith in creation
and in the inspired authors' attempts to articulate the intimate relationship between God and the world.[17] The first creation story (Gen
1:1–2:4a) asserts that humankind is made in the image (*selem*) and
likeness (*demuth*) of God (Gen 1:26). Human beings are thus

17. Regarding biblical creation faith and creation theology, see Anne M.
Clifford, "Creation," in *Systematic Theology: Roman Catholic Perspectives*, ed. Francis Schüssler Fiorenza and John Galvin, 2nd ed. (Minneapolis: Fortress, 2011),
201–53, at 204–14.

representatives of God within the created universe, reflections of divine presence that are just shy (*demuth*) of being exact copies (*selem*) of their divine source.[18] Psalm 8 speaks in a similar fashion, using a bold image to capture the intimate-yet-not-identical relationship of humanity to its divine source:

> Yet you have made them a little lower than God
>   [*or* angels (in Hebrew, *elohim*)],
>   and crowned them with glory and honor.
> You have given them dominion over the works of your hands;
>   you have put all things under their feet. (Ps 8:5-6)

The image/likeness schema presupposes and closely parallels the presence/absence structure. As stewards of creation, human beings are a mirroring, a trace, a clue of God's available and active presence in the world. But they can never be thought to be identical to the mysterious reality of God, since their "image" is not an exact one. There is always a distance, however slight, between the original and the representation.

The non-human world too enjoys an intimate relationship with its Creator. Even though biblical creation faith insists on the world's autonomy and non-godly status and thus "effect[s] a denuminization of reality by distinguishing clearly and unambiguously between God the creator and the world as his creation," nevertheless it fundamentally understands creation to be theonomous (grounded in God) and thus

---

18. "The human is a statue of the deity, not by static being but by action" (R. Clifford, in Clifford and Murphy, 11). *Selem* and *demuth* are terms connected with royalty. *Selem* ("image, statue, exact copy") was used for the statues of the king placed in various parts of the kingdom as a symbol of royal power and authority, in order to remind the inhabitants of the true source of that power. In Genesis 1:26 the linking of *demuth* ("likeness, something like") with *selem* interprets and modifies the exactness of the representation, so that *selem* will not be taken to mean sheer identity. See Gerhard von Rad, *Old Testament Theology*, 2 vols. trans. D. M. G. Stalker (New York: Harper and Row, 1962), 1:144–46; Terence E. Fretheim, "Genesis," in *The New Interpreter's Bible*, vol. 1 (Nashville: Abingdon Press, 1994), 345. For a detailed treatment of Gen 1:26–27, see Claus Westermann, *Genesis 1–11: A Commentary*, trans. John J. Scullion, 2d ed. (Minneapolis: Augsburg, 1984), 144–58.

a clue or pointer to God's creative presence and authority.[19] The world's goodness and the sheer fact of its autonomous existence are signs of divine providence. "The heavens are telling the glory of God; and the firmament proclaims his handiwork" (Ps 19:1). Thus the world's relationship to God also follows a dialectical pattern: both autonomous and theonomous, creation offers us a glimpse—never to be mistaken for a complete portrait—of the transcendent divine power that grounds it. Psalms 8 and 19, along with Paul's assertion in the Letter to the Romans that God's "eternal power and divine nature, invisible though they are, have been understood and seen through the things he has made" (Rom 1:20), provide some of the biblical warrants for what the later Christian theological tradition will call "natural theology," the mode of knowledge of God available to finite human experience within the created world simply from the sheer fact of its createdness.[20]

A final example is Jesus' use of parables in preaching the Kingdom of God. Nowhere in the New Testament does Jesus give a definition of the infinite mystery of the Kingdom or a detailed description of the Father. Rather, his references are indirect, suggestive—never telling his audiences what the Kingdom of God *is*, only what it is *like*.[21] His comparisons rely on examples taken from everyday life (agriculture, the family, politics). For example, a narrative about ordinary human relationships can disclose the extraordinary character of the divine-human relationship, as in the parable of the prodigal son (Luke 15:11–32). Jesus' choice to speak in parables is itself an exercise in presence/absence; what is immanent and familiar serves as a sign of the transcendent and extraordinary. The rhetorical

19. Kasper, *GJC*, 17. Kasper points out that even after the medieval development of the understanding of creation as autonomous, "the autonomy of the world, based as it was on the idea of creation, remained part of a total context that was theonomous; in fact the autonomy itself was given a theonomous justification" (ibid.). See also Kasper, "Autonomy and Theonomy: The Place of Christianity in the Modern World," *Theology and Church*, trans. Margaret Kohl (New York: Crossroad, 1989), 32–53.

20. This differs in important ways from a purely *philosophical* understanding of natural theology, a difference to be spelled out in the next section.

21. See Paul Ricœur, "Listening to the Parables of Jesus," in *The Philosophy of Paul Ricœur: An Anthology of His Work*, ed. Charles E. Reagan and David Stewart (Boston: Beacon Press, 1978), 239–45, at 242.

"detour" taken by Jesus is a sign of his understanding that the deepest mystery of God and of God's salvific actions exceeds whatever can be captured in language or concept. God's extraordinary reality appears only through comparison and is hinted at in metaphors, which themselves manifest the immanence/transcendence dialectic, since they always mean more than they can say.

1.2 Greek Philosophy and the Ontotheological Supplement

The dialectical view of God remained the fundamental understanding of God from early Christianity up until the late Middle Ages. Early in the development of Christian theology, however, the dialectical view became linked with various Greek philosophical speculations about deity that many today call "ontotheology." Beginning with Plato, ancient Greek philosophy produced demonstrations of the existence of God or the gods or of the divine ground (in Greek, *archē*) of all reality using discursive reason. This discourse, framed in terms of "being," characterized deity as the "highest being" that grounds the existence of all other beings.[22] The recent use of "ontotheology" (*ontos* [being] + *theos* [god] + *logos* [word, reason]) as a shorthand reference for this kind of philosophy of religion is due to the philosopher Martin Heidegger. He polemically summarized the history of philosophy from Plato to Nietzsche as metaphysics (the search for the unifying ground of beings in a realm exterior to our immediate experience) and thus as an ontotheological pursuit.

> Because Being appears as ground, beings are what is grounded;
> the highest being, however, is what accounts in the sense of giving

22. See also Richard Schaeffler, *Religionsphilosophie*, 2d ed., Handbuch Philosophie (Freiburg/Munich: Karl Alber, 1997), 58–61; ET: *Reason and the Question of God: An Introduction to the Philosophy of Religion*, trans. Robert R. Barr and Marlies Parent (New York: Herder and Herder/Crossroad, 1999), 22–24. Schaeffler argues that philosophical theology was born from the insight that the idea of the "first cause of all movement and its numerical/temporal order"(i.e., "self-thinking being," the originary unmoved mover) and the idea of "the one, eternal, and transcendent principle of all diverse experiential reality" (i.e., absolute being) apply to the same reality, namely the "highest principle" who contains the "fullness of being" (58–59/22).

the first cause. When metaphysics thinks of beings with respect to the ground that is common to all beings as such, then it is logic as onto-logic. When metaphysics thinks of beings as such as a whole, that is, with respect to the highest being which accounts for everything, then it is logic as theo-logic. . . . Metaphysics is both ontology and theology in a unified way. . . . The insight into the onto-theological constitution of metaphysics shows a possible way to answer the question, "How does the deity enter into Philosophy?," in terms of the essence of metaphysics.[23]

A classic answer to Heidegger's question is found in one of Plato's last dialogues, *Laws*. Book X of *Laws* presents one of the earliest systematic *philosophical* articulations of "natural theology." The natural theology of Greek philosophy argues that "nature, and especially change or order, requires the divine as an ultimate causal explanation, and hence natural theology seeks to show the continuity between science and religion."[24] In *Laws*, the Athenian Stranger, the dialogue's main character, delivers an argument against what he calls "impiety," the atheism of the young skeptical materialists and naturalists who insist that the world is a product of purely natural causes governed by chance, and that religious doctrines and moral principles are human constructions, grounded in power relationships, having no foundation in any eternal principles.

The Stranger offers a counter-argument to prove that the gods do indeed exist. He claims that what the atheists see as merely unplanned mechanical movement is really movement that is subordinate to intelligent planned causation. The crux of the argument lies in Plato's association of movement with "soul." Soul, defined as "motion capable of moving itself," is the source of all other movements and has ontological priority over all matter.[25] Material bodies move, implying

23. Martin Heidegger, "The Onto-Theo-Logical Constitution of Metaphysics, in *Identity and Difference*, trans. Joan Stambaugh (New York: Harper and Row, 1969), 70–71.

24. Michael L. Morgan, "Plato and Greek Religion," in *The Cambridge Companion to Plato*, ed. Richard Kraut (Cambridge: Cambridge University Press, 1992), 240.

25. Plato, *The Laws*, trans. Trevor J. Saunders (Harmondsworth: Penguin, 1970), 426.

that each has an individual soul that causes that movement. The motions of the heavenly bodies imply the presence of soul as well. Since these more excellent heavenly movements reflect the operations of reason, they must be caused by souls that are "rational and supremely virtuous," that is, "the best kind of soul that cares for the entire universe and directs it along the best path."[26] Because these souls have every excellence and are the ultimate cause of every observable movement on earth and in the heavens, the Stranger concludes that souls are divine and that "everything is full of gods."[27]

Plato's argument is important not so much for its cogency (it is not especially rigorous) as for its method, and the fact that the attempt to prove the existence of the gods is even made. The proof attempts to determine the necessary condition for the existence of the state of affairs that we experience. In other words, Plato is looking for the ultimate "reason why," the necessary divine precondition that must exist behind or above or underneath our experience of observable movement. That precondition, he argues, is the existence of the gods, the divinities he calls "souls." In order to prove the necessity and reality of religious faith, Plato works out a "natural theology" in the usual sense: a rational demonstration of the existence of the divine as the ultimate causal explanation of the natural world. It is important to note the context of this type of philosophy of religion: the need to establish the existence of the gods by means of rational demonstration assumes a situation where the gods themselves have become questionable.

The influence of Greek philosophy (particularly Platonism) and its natural theology appeared within post-biblical Christian theology at an early stage. Linking faith with reason, however, provoked widely divergent responses. One type is represented by Clement of Alexandria (c. 150–c. 215), who argued for a close harmony between faith in Christ and Greek philosophical teaching, specifically the Middle

26. Ibid., 428.

27. Ibid., 431: "A soul or souls—and perfectly virtuous souls at that—have been shown to be the cause of all these phenomena, and whether it is by their living presence in matter that they direct all the heavens, or by some other means, we shall insist that these souls are gods. Can anybody admit all this and still put up with people who deny that 'everything is full of gods'?"

Platonism by which he was heavily influenced. In his *Stromateis* ("Miscellanies," c. 200 AD) he offered a positive evaluation of reason and praised the use of Greek philosophy as "conducive to piety" and "a kind of preparatory training" for faith in Christ.[28] He argued that philosophy also serves theology by helping to clarify the Scriptures' ambiguities. "And how necessary it is for him who desires to be partaker of the power of God, to treat of intellectual subjects by philosophizing! And how serviceable it is to distinguish expressions which are ambiguous, and which in the Testaments are used synonymously! . . . Is not speaking our business, and does not action proceed from the Word? For if we act not for the Word, we shall act against reason."[29]

The opposite response is represented by Tertullian (c. 160–c. 225). He acknowledged the affinities between biblical teaching and philosophical doctrine and used philosophy himself to make theological points.[30] But at the same time he argued strongly against the use of philosophy in defending the faith, claiming that there was no need for rational argument, that it led only to heretical doctrines.

> For [philosophy] is the material of the world's wisdom, the rash interpreter of the nature and the dispensation of God. Indeed heresies are themselves instigated by philosophy. . . . What indeed has Athens to do with Jerusalem? What concord is there between the Academy and the Church? What between heretics and Christians? Our instruction comes from the "porch of Solomon" [i.e., rather than the *stoa* (porch) from which Greek philosophers taught], who had himself taught that "the Lord should be sought in

28. Clement of Alexandria, *Stromateis* I, 5, in Alexander Roberts and James Donaldson, eds., *Ante-Nicene Christian Library*, vol. 4: *The Writings of Clement of Alexandria, Vol. I*, trans. William Wilson (Edinburgh: T. and T. Clark, 1867), 366: "Before the advent of the Lord, philosophy was necessary to the Greeks for righteousness. And now it becomes conducive to piety; being a kind of preparatory training to those who attain to faith through demonstration. . . . Philosophy, therefore, was a preparation, paving the way for him who is perfected in Christ."

29. *Stromateis* I, 9, in ibid., 380.

30. See Jaroslav Pelikan, *The Christian Tradition: A History of the Development of Doctrine, I: The Emergence of the Catholic Tradition (100–600)* (Chicago: University of Chicago Press, 1971), 49–50.

> simplicity of heart" [Wisdom 1:1]. Away with all attempts to pro-
> duce a mottled Christianity of Stoic, Platonic, and dialectic com-
> position! We want no curious disputation after possessing Christ
> Jesus, no inquisition after receiving the gospel! When we believe,
> we desire no further belief. For this is our [first article] of faith, that
> there is nothing which we ought to believe besides.[31]

Between these two extremes lay a mediating position, one that
recognized the irreducibility of truth of faith to rational proof as well
as the value of reason in theological reflection. This middle way,
acknowledging the perduring tension between faith and reason,
would eventually become the mainstream Christian position. One
example is the thought of Gregory of Nazianzus (329/30–389/90).
He too has an optimistic view of reason, which "proceeds from God
[and] leads us up to God through visible things."[32] But his appropriation of rational argumentation for theological purposes stands somewhere between Clement and Tertullian. He is less willing than
Clement to dissolve the tension between faith and reason, but also
less willing to divorce them as does Tertullian. Clearly he has been
influenced by Greek natural theology.

> Now our very eyes and the law of nature teach us that God exists
> and that he is the efficient and maintaining cause of all things: our
> eyes, because they fall on visible objects, and see them in beautiful
> stability and progress, immovably moving and revolving if I may
> so say; *natural law, because through these visible things and their order,
> it reasons back to their author.* For how could this universe have come
> into being or been put together, unless God had called it into exis-
> tence and held it together? (vi, 290 [my emphasis])

31. *De praescriptione haereticorum* (On Prescription against Heretics) 7, in
Alexander Roberts and James Donaldson, eds., *Ante-Nicene Christian Library*,
vol. 15: *The Writings of Tertullian, Vol. II*, trans. Peter Holmes (Edinburgh: T. and
T. Clark, 1880), 8–9.

32. Gregory of Nazianzus, *Second Theological Oration*, xvi, trans. Charles Gordon Browne and James Edward Swallow, in Philip Schaff and Henry Wace, eds.,
A Select Library of Nicene and Post-Nicene Fathers of the Christian Church, Second
Series, vol. 7 (New York: The Christian Literature Company, 1894), 294. Further
references are in parentheses in the text (book number, then page number of
the translation).

In fact, he cites with approval Plato's argument from the *Laws*.

> For I commend the man, though he was a heathen, who said,
> What gave movement to these [things in heaven and on earth],
> and driven their ceaseless and unhindered motion? Is it not the
> Artificer of them who implanted reason in them all, in accordance
> with which the universe is moved and controlled? Is it not he
> who made them and brought them into being? (xvi, 294)

Here Gregory understands God in the same way that Plato under-stands "soul," as the necessary condition of the universe, for which one can mount a rational demonstration.

But Gregory also displays an acute awareness of the tension between faith and reason and of the inadequacy of reason-based arguments for God's existence constructed by "natural philosophers with their knowledge of useless details" (xxvii, 298). He attempts to strike a balance, holding on to what we can know of God through rational argumentation while acknowledging the primacy of faith in God whose fundamentally incomprehensible reality exceeds reason's limitations: "even reason has nothing to lean upon, but only the will of God" (xxvi, 298). Occasionally, though, he seems caught in a dilemma between commending the worthiness of natural theology arguments and needing to acknowledge its inadequacies in the light of faith.

> And very wanting in sense is he who will not willingly go thus
> far in following natural proofs; but not even this which we have
> imagined or represented, or which reason has sketched for us,
> is God. But if any one has got even to some extent a comprehen-
> sion of this, how is God's being to be demonstrated? (vi, 290).

The inadequacy of arguments within the philosophy of religion is clearly due to the dialectical character of God, to which Gregory gives eloquent (and eschatological) expression.

> What God is in nature and essence, no man ever yet has discov-
> ered or can discover. Whether it will ever be discovered is a
> question which he who will may examine and decide. In my
> opinion it will be discovered when that within us which is

godlike and divine, I mean our mind and reason, shall have mingled with its like, and the image shall have ascended to the Archetype, of which it has now the desire. And this I think is the solution of that vexed problem as to "We shall know even as we are known" [1 Cor. 13:12]. But in our present life all that comes to us is but a little effluence, and as it were a small effulgence from a great light (xvii, 294).

Some other experience beyond the constructions of rational discourse is needed to fully grasp the realities of our experience of God.

Gregory's thought offers us a case study of the problems involved in trying to join the biblical revelation of God with the Greek natural theology tradition. In the end, his primary commitment is to the dialectical view of God and it is clear that his faith tempers his reliance on natural theology, which he nonetheless continues to find valuable. His attitude is a preview of the eventual direction that the mainstream Christian theological tradition will take, arguing that alongside the primary experience of faith as the response to revelation there is positive value in reason's ability to explicate the workings and meaning of faith. In other words, one's experience of God and of God's offer of salvation is indeed the experience of a human person who makes sense of this offer through the medium of human understanding. The act of faith is always an *intellectus fidei*, a "faith that understands." The believer's faith responds to God's revelatory initiative and appropriates the offer of salvation by concretely interpreting its possibilities, making these possibilities part of the believer's lived experience.[33]

But Gregory's thought is also an example of the difficulties involved in navigating a middle course between the extreme positions of making faith almost equivalent to rational religion (Clement of Alexan-

33. See Bernhard Welte, "Die Wesenstruktur der Theologie als Wissenschaft" [1955], *Auf der Spur des Ewigen* (Freiburg: Herder, 1965), 351–65; also in *Gesammelte Schriften*, vol. IV/3: *Zur vorgehensweise der Theologie und zu ihrer jüngeren Geschichte*, ed. Gerhard Ruff (Freiburg: Herder, 2007), 167–83; Welte, *Heilsverständnis: Philosophische Untersuchung einiger Voraussetzungen zum Verständnis des Christentums* [1966], in *Gesammelte Schriften*, vol. IV/1: *Hermeneutik des Christlichen*, ed. Bernhard Casper (Freiburg: Herder, 2006), 19–193, at 32–60, esp. 32–43; Anthony J. Godzieba, *Bernhard Welte's Fundamental Theological Approach to Christology*, American University Studies, series VII, vol. 160 (New York/Bern: Peter Lang, 1994), 87–120.

dria) and denying reason any role at all in the explication of our belief in God (Tertullian). Gregory's vacillations highlight the fundamental lack of fit between the biblical dialectical view of God and the particular exercise of rationality that is Greek ontotheological philosophy. This "lack of fit" results from a clash between two sets of basic presuppositions.[34] On the one hand, the biblical dialectical view is the expression of experiences that human beings have with the divine Other. It presupposes the sheer givenness of the loving presence of God within human experience and interpretation, a revealed presence that exceeds that experience and its interpretative categories. The Bible asks "who is God?" or "where is God?" and answers the question by means of a narrative. It offers no proofs of God's existence, only testimonies to experiences of God whose existence is taken for granted. These experiences are, in a real sense, self-authenticating. Greek natural theology, on the other hand, asks "is there a God/are there gods?" and argues for the existence of God or divine ground by using discursive reason (the *logos* in ontotheology). This approach is fundamental, despite occasions where there is an awareness of reason's limits in dealing with reality's ultimate principles, as in Plato's myths in *Timaeus* and *Phaedrus*. However, a rational demonstration implies the *need* for a rational demonstration. Greek ontotheology assumes a situation where various interpretations of reality are competing for primacy, where "the divine ground" is one choice among others, and especially where God or the gods are no longer assumed to be self-evidently present. Therefore the existence of divinity must be reestablished by rational criteria.

There are additional discordances. The biblical view understands God to be the ground and guarantor of the truth of religious experience, while Greek natural theology pursues a critique of religious experience and sees reason itself as the ground and guarantor of truth. The biblical understanding of God is fundamentally at home with the present/absent, immanent/transcendent dialectic, and therefore is

34. In formulating what follows, I am indebted to Schaeffler, *Religionsphilosophie*, 49–63; *Reason and the Question of God*, 18–25. See also Joseph Stephen O'Leary's comments on the "lack of fit" and on the task of a phenomenology of faith in *Religious Pluralism and Christian Truth* (Edinburgh: Edinburgh University Press, 1996), ix–x.

comfortable with mystery. Greek natural theology displays the need for rational clarity and certainty; the sheer givenness of "religious experience" is not certain enough. In its quest for certainty, ontotheology overemphasizes the "present" side of the dialectic and represents whatever has been discovered in terms of what is already known. The "shattering" that occurs in the light of the revelation of divine excess or "absence" is excluded. This particular clash between the biblical view and Greek philosophical theology accounts for the attempts of both Gregory and Tertullian to restrain reason. They sense that rational speculation can go either too far and distort religious experience, or—paradoxically—that it will never take one far enough in order to reach the mystery of the living God.

The classical dialectical view of God remained the dominant view from ancient Christianity until the later Middle Ages. The following chapter, on Christian natural theology, will give a more detailed examination of the medieval component of our story. It cannot be denied that throughout this period the classical view was articulated primarily in metaphysical categories and thus at times skirted close to ontotheology. But more careful thinkers did not permit metaphysics to overwhelm the basic biblical experience of God. They also maintained a healthy tension between rational categories and their faith experience and thus refused the extreme reactions of either denigrating rational reflection on faith or turning religion into philosophy. Such a middle-of-the-road strategy (a broad middle, to be sure) grew out of the conviction that the Bible's basic dialectical understanding of God was the original catalyst and the life-blood of the whole of the Christian tradition of theological reflection.

2. The Rise of the Extrinsic View

2.1 The Nominalist Impetus

The later medieval period marks a crucial turning point in the history of the God-problem. The development of nominalist philosophy and theology in the fourteenth century, influenced primarily by the work of William of Ockham (c. 1285–1347), signaled the beginnings of the breakdown of the dialectical view within Western culture and the rise of its eventual replacement as the "normal" Christian perspective, the extrinsic view. Late medieval nominalism styled itself as "modern" (*via moderna*) over against what it considered to be the excessive abstractions of the older style of theology (*via antiqua*) practiced by the followers of Thomas Aquinas and John Duns Scotus. The nominalists insisted upon God's omnipotence and transcendent freedom as the primary categories for interpreting God's nature, actions, and relationship to the world. This emphasis ultimately put God beyond the reach of metaphysical speculations that, from the nominalist standpoint, functioned only to cut God down to fit our limited intellects and thus offend God's omnipotent nature. The nominalists, as Walter Kasper puts it, "emancipated autonomy from its theonomous context and reference" but thereby provided "the presupposition for the rise of modern atheism. . . . Nominalism carried the idea of God's omnipotence and freedom to an extreme, turning him into an absolutist deity who acts in an arbitrary manner."[35]

The unraveling of the dialectical view did not begin with nominalism. Rather, nominalism captured a mood. It gave a philosophical and theological voice to a religious discomfort that had already surfaced within Christianity before the fourteenth century and had appeared in popular religious practices. It was rooted in the growing sense of distance between the ordinary believer and God. Such discomfort was indeed a reaction against the growing tendency, both in theology and in preaching, toward abstractness and an overemphasis on God's transcendence. This overwhelming sense that the presence of God was slipping farther away, out of reach of the pious believer, gave rise to spiritualities and devotional practices that attempted to bridge the gap or at least to narrow the distance in order to make it less severe.

The architectural design of the medieval cathedral can serve as a map of the religious and theological problem. The main sanctuary with its high altar where the clergy functioned (the area known as the choir) was separated from the remainder of the long body of the cathedral (the nave), from which the laity observed the liturgical actions. Mass was said in the sanctuary that was usually partitioned off from the nave by a screen. The cathedral's physical arrangement sent a clear message: since the sacred actions were performed on the

35. Kasper, *GJC*, 17.

choir side of the screen, the locus of holiness was in the sanctuary and was readily accessible to the clergy. The laity, on the other hand, watched from a distance in the nave, with no direct access to the sacred actions save the reception of the sacrament of the Eucharist— and this itself was a rarity.[36] And the laity were looked at in turn, the object of the "gaze" of Jesus on the distant cross high above the sanctuary and of the various saints whose visages peered out from mosaics, altarpieces, and sculptures. The cathedral's design reinforced the experience of a wide gap, both physical and psychological, between the "mundane" world of the laity, full of the sufferings, the fears, and the desire for the miraculous that suffused the later middle ages, and the "holy" world of the clergy, who had direct access to the sacred actions.

How did popular religiosity respond to this situation? Devotional handbooks and religious art of the fourteenth and fifteenth centuries clearly illustrate that more and more emphasis was placed on the humanity of Christ, particularly his sufferings and death, and on devotions to the Blessed Virgin and the saints. Religious art in general became more realistic and indeed more somber, emphasizing sadness, tragedy, suffering, and death.[37] The purpose of this heightened realism was to fill the devout with emotion, evoking the compassion of the believer so that she or he could truly feel the presence of the love of God as mediated through the human life of Christ or through the intercession of Mary and the saints. Popular spirituality employed diverse forms of affective experience in order to bridge the growing

36. The decline in the reception of the Eucharist was accompanied by the growth of the veneration of the Host both within and outside of the liturgy. See Richard Kieckhefer, "Major Currents in Late Medieval Devotion," in *Christian Spirituality: High Middle Ages and Reformation*, ed. Jill Raitt, Bernard McGinn, and John Meyendorff, World Spirituality, vol. 17 (New York: Crossroad, 1988), 75–108, at 96–100. In these cases, *gazing in adoration*, whether at the consecration of the Mass or during extraliturgical Eucharistic exposition, bridged the distance between the laity and the altar and acted as compensation for the lack of actual reception. *Seeing* became the way for the laity to experience (and hold on to) the distant presence of God.

37. Emile Mâle, *Religious Art in France: The Late Middle Ages: A Study of Medieval Iconography and its Sources*, ed. Harry Bober, trans. Marthiel Mathews (Princeton: Princeton University Press, 1986), 81–82.

gulf between suffering humanity and God whose transcendent "otherness" was the focus of theological attention. Piety attempted to compensate for the overemphasis on the "absence" side of the dialectic and thereby slow the unraveling of the classical biblical view.[38]

We see this quite clearly in the late medieval growth in devotion to the humanity of Jesus. It became the focal point of the medieval ideal of imitating Christ. One aspect was the widespread devotion to the infancy and childhood of Jesus that developed during the thirteenth and fourteenth centuries.[39] An even more poignant development was the growth in devotion to Christ's passion and death. The thirteenth century saw the displacement of the usual Romanesque crucifix depicting a living Christ triumphant over death by the *Christus patiens* type that depicted Christ as already dead, hanging lifeless with eyes closed. The intent was to stress Christ's horrible suffering and thus evoke the empathy and compassionate response of the viewer.[40] After 1300 the crucifixion and its aftermath were even more tragically and pathetically portrayed, both in public images and in smaller works created for private devotion.[41] The realism of these images mirrored "the desire of Christians to take seriously, and if possible to imitate in their own lives and bodies, every aspect of Christ's life on earth."[42] The aim of such depictions and devotions was to point to the overwhelming presence of God's love that was revealed through Jesus' humanity, especially in his sufferings and death, and to persuade the believer to participate in the most personal way in this great event of incarnate love through the feelings of compassion evoked by such images and devotions. "The physicality of

38. For evidence of this, see Hans Belting, *Likeness and Presence: A History of the Image before the Era of Art*, trans. Edmund Jephcott (Chicago: University of Chicago Press, 1994); Giles Constable, "The Ideal of the Imitation of Christ," *Three Studies in Medieval Religious and Social Thought* (Cambridge: Cambridge University Press, 1995), 143-248; Kieckhefer, "Major Currents in Late Medieval Devotion," 75–108; Mâle, *Religious Art in France: The Late Middle Ages*, chapter 3; Ellen Ross, *The Grief of God: Images of the Suffering Jesus in Late Medieval England* (New York/Oxford: Oxford University Press, 1997).

39. Constable, 232–35.

40. Belting, 358.

41. See Constable, 231–32 (and the literature cited there); Mâle, 86–94.

42. Constable, 232.

the wounded Jesus, presented with shocking palpability in medieval art and narratives, manifested the reality of divine presence in Jesus Christ and made tangible the doctrinal claim that the Divine became human."[43] Affective spiritual experience thus became a major way of combatting the overly-abstract way in which God was conceived and presented by late medieval theology. Through the imitation of Christ and the deep feelings of compassion that devotional life evoked, God's presence remained actual, the life of the believer was transformed, and the distance between God and the believer was overcome.[44]

If we put the nominalists back into this context, their effect on our narrative is an ironic one. At first glance, nominalist theology appears to have shared in the same discomfort at the distancing of God that drove affective medieval spirituality. After all, both movements displayed an aversion to the metaphysical abstractness with which mainstream theology spoke of God. But the nominalists objected to the dominant characterizations of God and the metaphysical arguments for God's existence for different reasons. They objected first on logical grounds, holding that these arguments were worthless because of their logical inconsistencies. Second, they objected on the grounds that God has been revealed as supremely omnipotent and free, thereby putting the nature and existence of God beyond the reach of rational argumentation. These objections had an effect exactly opposite that of affective medieval spirituality. This nominalist understanding of God rendered God more transcendent than ever, with God's nature considered to lay so far beyond the boundaries of human experience

43. Ross, *The Grief of God*, 6. Although her argument is based on an examination of late medieval English sources, her remarks can apply to continental European images and devotions as well.

44. See Ross' comments (ibid., 131–38), especially regarding the incarnational emphasis and the complexity of the medieval spiritual experience of the humanity of Jesus: "In a theologically and emotionally sophisticated manner, medieval art, drama, sermons, and devotional literature project a common spiritual cosmos in which the person is transformed from being a sinner to being an intimate of the Divine in the encounter with the suffering Jesus. . . . Jesus' suffering is a somatization of divine love insofar as the intensified enfleshment of the suffering body becomes the very source of the manifestation of divine presence to humanity" (131).

that reason was incapable of forming any sort of real idea of God beyond what had been given to human experience by faith.

The best example of this can be seen in the thought of William of Ockham, whose theology presupposes his widely-influential theory of knowledge and his critique of traditional metaphysics.[45] For Ockham, our experience of the world consists of the immediate experience of individual contingent beings. Only these individuals exist. Universals such as "human nature" are not substances that exist independently outside the mind, as the medieval Platonists and Aristoteleans held. Ockham rejected all varieties of such realist claims as logically absurd: "no thing outside the soul is universal, either through itself or through anything real or rational added on, no matter how it is considered or understood."[46] Rather, universals exist only in the mind; they are terms (*nomina*) for classes of individual things, conventional signs that arise from our direct experience with particular beings and the abstractive concepts based on those direct, concrete intuitions. Thus our use of the concept of "human nature" arises from the abstractive comparison we make between our acts of awareness of two individuals, not because we recognize some separable essence of "humanity" that exists apart from those individuals. Something very similar occurs in our experience of causality. Ockham claimed that we may indeed have an experience of A causing B, but that nothing in that empirical fact itself could ever be proven by reason to be necessary and applicable to all such instances. We might project that particular causal relation to apply to other causal relations, but that is an abstractive act of the mind and not a direct "reading" of reality, since for Ockham there were no necessary relations

---

45. See Claude Panaccio, "William of Ockham," in *The Routledge Encyclopedia of Philosophy*, ed. Edward Craig (London/New York: Routledge, 1998), 9:732–48; Paul Vincent Spade, ed., *The Cambridge Companion to Ockham* (Cambridge: Cambridge University Press, 1999); Thomas Pfau, *Minding the Modern: Human Agency, Intellectual Traditions, and Responsible Knowledge* (Notre Dame, IN: University of Notre Dame Press, 2013), 160–82. An older but still worthy resource is F. C. Copleston, *A History of Medieval Philosophy* (New York: Harper and Row, 1972), 230–56.

46. *In libros Sententiarum* I.2.7, as cited in Paul Vincent Spade, "Ockham's Nominalist Metaphysics," in *The Cambridge Companion to Ockham*, 100–17, at 117n.74.

between individual beings. He found it logically absurd to assume, as did traditional metaphysics, that such abstractions and likenesses refer to extra-mental, non-empirical substances.

These epistemological claims had important consequences for Ockham's theology of God. He was dismissive of philosophical natural theology, since proofs for God's existence, in order to succeed, would need to rely on a concept of God that would disclose qualities that are proper to God alone. But for Ockham no such concept is available to human reason, since we have no direct intuitive knowledge of God. We can form some concepts about God (such as "absolutely supreme and perfect being," "creator," "immortal"), but all of these are generated from our finite experiences within this world (e.g., "creator" connotes knowledge of creatures, "immortal" negates our prior knowledge of death).[47] Ockham did consider possible a proof that argued for a first conserving cause of the world (i.e., the cause that maintains things in being), and that this could be God. But reason could not prove "that there should be only one such cause at any moment and that this cause should be identified with God: a celestial sphere or an angel could do equally well."[48] In any event, the resulting picture of God would fall far short of Christian view of the revealed God, whose essential qualities are articles of faith. God's omnipotence and absolutely free will—God's *potentia absoluta* (absolute power) as opposed to *potentia ordinata* (God's power as related to what has actually been created)—put God beyond the grasp of human reason. Whatever we know about God must come through divine revelation, which might even contradict reason. In fact, "God is no longer understood to owe anything to his creation, including human life, but, instead, is thought as forever free to renounce or remake the created world *and* the laws defining it."[49]

Ockham's goal was to purify Christian theology of Greek philosophical speculation, which he felt endangered Christian doctrine. Natural theology was an affront to God's omnipotence and freedom,

47. Panaccio, 742–43.
48. Ibid., 743.
49. Pfau, *Minding the Modern*, 165.

since it effectively trapped God in a rational system formed under the constraints of our own logical expectations. In Ockham's view, the God of revelation possesses a transcendent freedom that breaks free of all these rational constraints, even to the point of being able to impose a law that is contrary to human reason (provided that law is not also self-contradictory).

It would seem, then, that we should laud Ockham and his fellow nominalists for preventing the "presence" side of the dialectical view of God from becoming too "available" or rationally predictable, and for protecting the dissolution of God's "absence" by emphasizing divine transcendence. But whatever the nominalists' intent had been, the subsequent result was precisely the reverse of any defense of the dialectical view. Nominalism, in fact, marks the beginning of its collapse. While the nominalists intended to protect God's revealed freedom and power from ontotheological betrayal, the resulting overemphasis on the "absence" side of the dialectic rendered God foreign to human experience. After all, Ockham claimed that "what we know immediately are concepts which are not really God but which we use in propositions to stand for God."[50] Such a claim assumed a fundamental rupture between human experience and the presence of God. This whole way of thinking constituted a sharp turn away from the biblical natural theology that was based on a theology of creation. By overemphasizing the qualities of transcendence and freedom in order to emancipate God from human control, nominalism portrayed a God who was fundamentally untouchable by any sort of human experience. Thus God slips out of our reach—we are left with the abstract portrait of God that medieval affective spirituality attempted to counteract and that nominalism criticized at the outset. The *via moderna* of nominalism signals the beginning of the accelerated development of the problem of God that carries over into modernity, where God becomes "an absolutist deity who acts in an arbitrary manner" and "who does not liberate human freedom but oppresses it."[51]

50. *Ordinatio*, dist. 3, q. 2 as cited in Copleston, *A History of Medieval Philosophy*, 251.

51. Kasper, *GJC*, 17.

2.2 Modernity, Autonomy, and the Intensification of Extrinsicism

Over the course of the modern period (extending from the sixteenth century to the early twentieth century) the extrinsic view of God became established as the "normal" Christian view. The dialectical view did not disappear altogether; it continued to live on in various forms of Christian spirituality, but away from the higher-profile theological and philosophical debates over God's nature and existence. These debates, for the most part, tacitly assumed the extrinsic view as the only view. How did this "normalization" occur? In this section, as we track this religious and intellectual event, we should keep in mind the ambiguities involved in defining "modernity." We should ask, too, whether the modern analyses of the Christian belief in God had the Christian belief in God in view at all, or whether instead they were wrestling with a post-nominalist fiction that had less to do with biblical revelation and more with philosophical projection and convenience.

The modern discussion about God involves an overwhelming amount of material. To make our analysis somewhat easier, we will divide the material into two subject areas. First, we will examine the type of modern thinking that was driven by concern with the autonomy of nature and culture. Next we will look at that type concerned with the autonomy of human subjectivity.[52]

A. The autonomy of nature and culture. The sixteenth and seventeenth centuries witnessed the growing dominance of humanist claims that argued for the emancipation of the arts, politics, economics, and the sciences from their previously-assumed theonomous grounding. The awareness of God's presence did not disappear, as the humanist emphasis on the person as "image of God" and as Renaissance and Baroque religious art make very clear.[53] But the insistence on the autonomy of

---

52. I follow Kasper's outline here; see *GJC*, 20–46.

53. For examples of early modern religious art and spirituality that rely heavily on a sacramental (and dialectical) view of the world's relationship to God, see my "Prolegomena to a Catholic Theology of God Between Heidegger and Postmodernity," *The Heythrop Journal* 40 (1999): 319–39 and "Caravaggio, Theologian: Baroque Piety and *Poiesis* in a Forgotten Chapter of the History of Catholic Theology," in David M. Hammond, ed., *Theology and Lived Christianity,* The Annual Publication of the College Theology Society, vol. 45 (Mystic, CT: Twenty-Third Publications, 2000), 206–30. See also Charles Trinkaus, *In Our*

the products of both culture and scientific experimentation set the stage for the later modern situation where "the world becomes godless, God worldless and—in the strict sense of the word—objectless."[54]

The development of the natural sciences during the Renaissance, for example, contributed to the eventual eclipse of what might be called the late medieval "sacred canopy" understanding of God's relationship with the natural world.[55] Such thinking assumed the existence of a direct causal link between the finite natural world and the supernatural activities in the heaven beyond it; in other words, natural events have direct supernatural causes. In the mid-fourteenth century, then, perhaps what would have been considered the most coherent explanation of the plague that devastated Europe would have been one that asserted a direct supernatural cause, such as God's punishment for widespread sin. But Renaissance science hastened the decline of the sacred canopy model by arguing that natural events have natural causes. From this viewpoint the most intelligible explanation of the plague appears to be an organic one, namely, the vermin that entered Europe through Marseilles and other ports. Those working in the natural sciences saw the world as a set of symbols to be decoded, and viewed their own work as a search for the patterns, causes, and natural laws that lay behind the observable events of life and death, the wonders of nature, and the movements of the heavens. On closely examining the world, the natural sciences did not find instances of direct divine action but rather discovered natural processes of cause and effect. Explanatory appeals to God's direct activity were becoming superfluous.

Image and Likeness: Humanity and Divinity in Italian Humanist Thought (Chicago: University of Chicago Press, 1970); Brendan Bradshaw, "Transalpine Humanism," in *The Cambridge History of Political Thought 1450–1700*, ed. J. H. Burns and Mark Goldie (1991; repr., Cambridge: Cambridge University Press, 2004), 95-131; Anthony J. Godzieba, " 'Refuge of Sinners, Pray for Us': Augustine, Aquinas, and the Salvation of Modernity," in Lieven Boeve, Frederiek Depoortere, and Maarten Wisse, eds., *Augustine and Postmodern Thought: A New Alliance Against Modernity?*, BETL, vol. 219 (Leuven: Peeters, 2009), 147–65.

54. Kasper, *GJC*, 19.

55. "Sacred canopy" is Peter Berger's term; see his *The Sacred Canopy: Elements of a Sociological Theory of Religion* (Garden City, NY: Doubleday, 1967).

Clearly, the "ripping off" of the sacred canopy did not banish God from Western experience. Many in fact tried to balance a newfound confidence in science with their belief in God and in God's providence, and conflicts were argued out under the assumption that God did indeed still have a real relationship with the world. This situation, however—where natural science and Christianity offered competing explanations of this relationship—was complex and fraught with tensions, as the "Galileo affair" clearly illustrates.[56] Galileo Galilei (1546–1642), of course, rejected the age-old geocentric view of the world and, on the basis of his astronomical experiments, argued in favor of a heliocentric view that the Catholic Church eventually condemned in 1633.[57] Both Galileo and his major opponent, the eminent Jesuit theologian and cardinal Robert Bellarmine (1542–1621), realized that the status of biblical interpretation was one of the central issues in their debate. Both agreed that the traditional principles of Catholic exegesis (based on the medieval "four senses of Scripture") allowed for authentic interpretations of the Bible beyond the literal. And on the basis of their shared Christian belief in creation and the Incarnation, both agreed with the principle of the unity of truth, thus rejecting any solution that viewed scientific truth and religious truth as mutually exclusive.[58] But they disagreed decisively over what to do when scientific truth and religious truth indeed came into conflict. In these cases, Galileo argued, it was obvious that biblical assertions about the physical world had been written "for the sole purpose of accommodating popular understanding." To solve "disputes about

56. For details, see Richard J. Blackwell, *Galileo, Bellarmine, and the Bible* (Notre Dame: University of Notre Dame Press, 1991).

57. The "normal" view of the cosmos before Galileo's epoch—that the sun did indeed travel around the earth in accord with normal appearances—was considered to reflect the state of the cosmos after its creation by God. Geocentrism was thus considered to be a "divine" truth that had been confirmed not only by centuries of tradition but more importantly by Scripture and its interpreters. But this view was actually a convergence of Platonic assumptions, arguments by Ptolemy and Aristotle, and Biblical passages (such as Joshua 10:12–14) that seemed to assume the central position of the earth in the cosmos.

58. For these two points, as well as the argument that after the condemnation of Copernicanism in 1616 the grounds of discussion had changed from principles of biblical exegesis to issues of authority, see Blackwell, 165–79.

natural phenomena," Galileo argued, "one must begin not with the authority of scriptural passage but with sensory experience and necessary demonstrations. For the Holy Scripture and nature derive equally from the Godhead, the former as the dictation of the Holy Spirit and the latter as the most obedient executrix of God's orders."[59] Bellarmine rejected this solution. He held that the claims of the natural sciences, while offering plausible assumptions, had not been demonstrated to be absolutely true and certain, and thus should not take precedence over centuries of biblical exegesis and natural philosophy.[60]

Today's popular opinion considers Bellarmine's response and Galileo's subsequent condemnation to be examples of the "recalcitrant" Church's ill-considered resistance (in defense of dubious dogmatic claims) to the "correct" and "modern" scientific view of the world represented by Galileo. But in reality the debate over the truth of Galileo's assertions was a sophisticated one on all sides, and was carried out by all parties under the influence of their belief in the fundamental truth of the dialectical view.

However, the dominance of the dialectical view was fast waning. The subsequent reception of Galileo's arguments (in spite of his own conciliatory intentions) served to hasten its decline. The impetus given to extrinsicism by nominalist philosophy and theology was increased not only by the successes of the natural sciences but also by the influence wielded by theories of society and political

59. From Galileo's "Letter to the Grand Duchess Christina" (1615), in *The Galileo Affair: A Documentary History*, ed. and trans. Maurice A. Finocchiaro (Berkeley: University of California Press, 1989), chapter 2 [translator's numbering], 92–93.

60. See Bellarmine's 1615 letter to Paolo Antonio Foscarini, translated in Blackwell, 265–67. Foscarini, a Carmelite priest and theologian, had published a treatise in defense of Copernicus' theories earlier that same year. In his letter, Bellarmine offered a joint response to Foscarini and Galileo, whose arguments he considered to be similar. See especially Bellarmine's third point: "To demonstrate that the assumption that the sun is located in the center and the earth in the heavens saves the appearances is not the same thing as to demonstrate that in truth the sun is located in the center and the earth in the heavens. The first demonstration, I believe, can be given; but I have the greatest doubts about the second. And in case of doubt one would not abandon the Sacred Scriptures as interpreted by the Holy Fathers" (Blackwell, 266).

governance such as those of Nicolò Machiavelli (1469–1527) and Hugo Grotius (1583–1645). Each had sketched out views that removed political action and law from their theonomous moorings. Grotius, for example, claimed that such a view "would have a degree of validity even if we should concede that which cannot be conceded without the utmost wickedness, that there is no God, or that the affairs of men are of no concern to him."[61] During this period, then, God became viewed as more extrinsic than ever, residing on the periphery of the world or outside the world altogether, needed only to explain those things that human reason could not explain—the "God of the gaps," whose function was to fill in the deficiencies of the human knowledge of the cosmos.

Against this progressive exiling of God from the world, theologians and philosophers crafted arguments and developed new formulations of the God-world relationship. But in making these arguments they presupposed the same extrinsicist model as did their opponents. Deists, for example, presented various systems of natural religion that reconciled human rationality with belief in God. The most familiar version of deism attempted to demonstrate how scientific rationality and the Christian belief in creation could be joined together. It portrayed God in terms of a clockmaker who created the world and then absented himself, leaving the world to function on its own according to the intelligible natural laws engrafted into it at creation. On those occasions when natural laws ceased to function, God intervened in the world by means of miracles that put the world aright. More sophisticated types of deism argued for a rational religion that transcended particular religious confessions (which many viewed as sources of social inequities and sectarian violence) and their claims to mediate special divine revelation.[62] They argued that revelation was unnecessary and even contradictory, since all human beings had access to the divine truths evidenced in nature by the unaided use of the power of human reason. God was seen as the wholly transcen-

61. Hugo Grotius, *Prolegomena to the Law of War and Peace* [*De Jure Belli ac Pacis*, 1625], trans. Francis W. Kelsey (Indianapolis: Bobbs-Merrill, 1957), 10.

62. See Michael J. Buckley, *At the Origins of Modern Atheism* (New Haven: Yale University Press, 1987), 37–41.

dent divine being who never intervened; such action would indeed contradict God's omnipotence and unchangeable eternal nature. In these cases the extrinsicist presupposition is clear. An ironic result of such arguments, especially in their Christian guise, is that they succeeded only in undercutting the dialectical view. These attempts to make God more present and knowable resulted in an overemphasis on God's transcendence and unavailability. Another irony is that the extrinsicism embraced by Christianity in the wake of scientific claims for the autonomy of the world and human culture prepared the ground for vociferous arguments on behalf of atheism that would appear in the late eighteenth and nineteenth centuries. Finally, the severing of culture from its theonomous roots increasingly deprived religion of its public "voice" among other human pursuits, with the result that "religion," in order to continue to be meaningful, became increasingly privatized, identified with a subjective and individual relationship to God. In any case, the concept of God that governed all these discussions had been irrevocably altered.

B. The autonomy of human subjectivity. Modern philosophers concerned with articulating the rational basis for human life gave these claims for autonomy an even sharper edge. In fact, the concept of the autonomy of the world (whether the "natural world" of the sciences or the "social world" of humanist culture) owes a great deal to the exploration of the autonomy of human freedom, at first tentatively probed by the nominalists and Renaissance humanist thinkers, then more deliberately examined by the European rationalist philosophers of the sixteenth through early nineteenth centuries.

The understanding of subjectivity introduced by René Descartes (1596–1650) was an overwhelmingly decisive factor. His search for the objective and absolutely certain foundations for all true knowledge led him to find those foundations in the "thinking self." His search, laid out in *Discourse on Method* (1637) and in *Meditations on First Philosophy* (1641), was occasioned by nagging doubts about the certainty of his knowledge about the self, the world, and God, as well as his frustration over the lack of any clear philosophical method for eliminating these doubts. This "Cartesian anxiety," as the philosopher Richard Bernstein has called it, appears in the *Meditations* in terms of "a grand and seductive Either/Or. *Either* there is some support for our being, a fixed foundation for our knowledge, *or* we cannot escape the forces of darkness that envelop us with madness, with intellectual and moral chaos."[63] By turning his debilitating doubts into a productive method—thus deferring judgment on the truth of the body, the world, and God until he had more "clear and distinct" evidence—Descartes found his solution in what remained, namely the thinking self.

> But immediately I noticed that while I was endeavoring in this way to think that everything was false, it was necessary that I, who was thinking this, was something. And observing that this truth *"I am thinking, therefore I exist"* [*cogito ergo sum*] was so firm and sure that all the most extravagant suppositions of the sceptics were incapable of shaking it, I decided that I could accept it without scruple as the first principle of the philosophy I was seeking.[64]

Since doubting is an act of thinking, in the midst of the most radical doubting there must be a doubter/thinker in existence to perform that operation. This is a peculiar "self," to be sure—a thinker thinking thoughts even before it has been ascertained whether these thoughts refer to anything outside the intellect. This absolutely certain existence of the thinking subject (the *cogito*, also called the *res cogitans*, a "thinking thing"[65]) becomes for Descartes the firm foundation, the starting point for determining the truth of reality and our ideas about it. If any idea is "presented . . . to my mind so clearly and distinctly that I had no occasion to call it into doubt,"[66] then it is judged to be a "clear and distinct idea," a true idea.[67] Here, then, is the revolu-

63. Richard Bernstein, *Beyond Objectivism and Relativism: Science, Hermeneutics, and Praxis* (Philadelphia: University of Pennsylvania Press, 1983), 18. For his discussion of "Cartesian anxiety," see pp. 16–20.

64. Descartes, *Discourse on Method*, part four, in *Descartes: Selected Philosophical Writings*, trans. John Cottingham, Robert Stoothoff, and Dugald Murdoch (Cambridge: Cambridge University Press, 1988), 36.

65. *Meditations on First Philosophy*, Second Meditation, in *Selected Philosophical Writings*, 82.

66. *Discourse*, part two, in *Selected Philosophical Writings*, 29.

67. "So I decided that I could take it as a general rule that the things we conceive very clearly and very distinctly are all true" (*Discourse*, part two [*Selected Philosophical Writings*, 36]); "But whatever method of proof I use, I am always

tionary cure for "Cartesian anxiety": the *subject* who is the judge and guarantor of truth.

This remains true even in the face of both Descartes' insistence that God is the source of truth and the guarantor of the truth of our ideas, and his confession that his existence and the truth of his knowledge depend completely on God.[68] But we should be suspicious of these philosophical claims (and not Descartes' personal religious claim) because of the structure of his argument. He arrives at the "clear and distinct ideas" in a particularly meaningful order. First there is the self as *res cogitans*, followed by the world as *res extensa* ("extended substance"), then God, and finally the relationship of soul and body. If God were indeed the guarantor of truth and if the idea of God could not be more "self-evident," as Descartes claims,[69] then why is the "God-idea" the *third* clear and distinct idea rather than the *first?* The answer must be that it is the *cogito* that determines the truth or falsity (the degree of clarity and distinctness) of our ideas, including the "God-idea." God has been replaced by the *cogito* as the ground of reality. The human person might indeed experience God, but that experience occurs and is judged to be true in the preestablished arena of human subjectivity. With this step we are far from the ancient and medieval claim that the essential identity of human beings (as the "image of God") is grounded in God. The Christian claim might still be visible in Descartes' "turn to the subject," but the philosophical anthropology that once supported it has gone off in another direction. Human subjectivity is now self-justifying; it claims its dignity autonomously. Descartes' arguments for the existence of God result in a situation similar to the one we saw earlier: the irony of the affirmation of extrinsicism despite his attempts to speak of the connection

---

brought back to the fact that it is only what I clearly and distinctly perceive that completely convinces me" (*Meditations*, Fifth Meditation [ibid., 109]). Descartes' use of the visual metaphor to describe knowledge (knowing is analogous to seeing; the "true" is what is "clear" and "distinct") as well as his "foundation" metaphor (truth is grounded upon an unchanging, unshakable foundation located beyond time-bound ordinary experience) are key contributions to the modern history of objectivism. Cf. Bernstein, *Beyond Objectivism and Relativism*, 8–20.

68. Meditations Three, Four, and Five, *Selected Philosophical Writings*, 86–110.
69. Meditation Five, ibid., 109.

between God and the world. The attempt to articulate God's *presence* through rational proofs justified by and to subjectivity emphasize instead God's *absence:* subjectivity has displaced God as ground, made God questionable—and arguments are needed to "bring God back."

French and German Enlightenment thinkers after Descartes took this insight even further by emphasizing the power inherent in autonomous reason, though without Descartes' religious compunction or adherence to scholastic categories.[70] For the various *philosophes* and *Aufklärer*, nothing seemed able to stand in the way of the inevitable progress of the human intellect, especially after the successes it was able to claim in science, politics, and the arts. Belief in the universality of human nature led quite logically to the optimistic conclusion that since human reason is universal, all human beings eventually could agree, without coercion, on the moral, scientific, political, and even religious truths that are necessary for human happiness, and that the epochs of conflict that had ravaged Europe were about to come to an end. This optimism, the hallmark of Enlightenment humanism, extended to the attempts to understand the structure of reason itself, usually explained in naturalistic or mechanistic terms suggested by the natural sciences. The chief task was to free human reason, and thereby human beings, from the so-called tyrannies of authority, tradition, superstition, and from what were perceived to be the irrationalities of institutional religion, particularly Christianity. Some thinkers, influenced by Benedict Spinoza, took their investment in reason in even more radical directions, seeking "to demolish the foundations of Revelation, authority, and tradition, while at the same time consciously undermining the legitimacy of monarchy and aristocracy," in order to emancipate all persons from "the bogus bonds of authority" and thereby "reinstate human liberty" in all its forms.[71]

---

70. See Peter Gay, *The Enlightenment: An Interpretation*, 2 vols. (New York: Knopf, 1966-69); Roy Porter, *The Enlightenment,* Studies in European History (Atlantic Highlands, NJ: Humanities Press International, 1990); Buckley, *At the Origins of Modern Atheism*, 37–67.

71. Jonathan I. Israel, *Radical Enlightenment: Philosophy and the Making of Modernity 1650–1750* (Oxford: Oxford University Press, 2001), 703.

Apart from these more radical thinkers, Enlightenment attitudes toward the general *concept* of religion were mostly favorable. While rigorous, systematic atheism did indeed develop during the latter half of the eighteenth century (*philosophes* such as Denis Diderot and Baron d'Holbach are prime examples), most intellectuals of the time rejected atheism and saw the need for religion, and even for public religious ceremonies that contributed to the social order.[72] What they rejected was confessionalism, specifically Christianity, which an increasingly secularized European culture branded as devious "priestcraft" and blamed for centuries of social divisiveness and physical horrors. They argued that a more enlightened and humane search for God was one carried out independently of the established religious traditions.

Here again the "natural religion" represented by deism plays an important role. For example, Diderot (1713–84) defended a rationalist deism before eventually becoming an atheist. He complained of the "ugliness" of the historical religions and argued instead that natural religion, which offered its truths directly to human experience, is the foundation of all religious experience, including confessional religion.[73] Such a claim represented the thinking of many of the epoch's intellectuals. They rejected supernatural revelation and advocated instead the abilities of human reason to discover the existence of God and religious truth in the evidence of nature, which was available to all. "Most believed that science and philosophy, though casting doubt upon the existence of the specifically Christian, humanoid 'God of miracles', nevertheless pointed to some sort of presiding Deity, a supernatural Creator, Designer and Mind."[74] While evidence of the existence of the "supernatural Designer" was discoverable within human experience, clearly the Deity's essential "character trait" was transcendence. God's relationship to the world and to human beings was discussed abstractly, being reduced to arguments from design and explanations of God's providence as exercised from afar. Little mention was made of Christ as the incarnate presence of

72. Porter, 32–41; Buckley, 38–40.
73. Buckley, 39.
74. Porter, 35.

God within human history, even by theologians.[75] Rather, he was most often presented as the supreme moral teacher. The image of the Deity as "supernatural Designer," needless to say, was the late eighteenth-century version of the extrinsic view.

The critical philosophy of Immanuel Kant (1724–1804) encouraged the further entrenchment of this extrinsicism, despite his efforts to establish a connection between God and the human experience of moral obligation. His claim in the *Critique of Pure Reason* (1781/1787) that he "found it necessary do deny *knowledge*, in order to make room for *faith*" (B xxx; 29)[76] is a sign that the dichotomies between religious belief and key areas of human experience, which had to be argued for earlier in modernity, were now taken for granted. Kant denied that speculative reason could reach the idea of God and considered natural theology's metaphysical arguments for God's existence (the ontological, the cosmological, and the "physicotheological" proofs) to be useless.[77] This claim is based on his analysis of what he argued was the limited scope of human reason. Our cognitive faculties shape our knowledge of the world of our experience. Real knowledge is possible only on the basis of sense perception (sensuous intuition) and the formal principles of reason. But since God is beyond our

75. Buckley, 41–67. Even an eighteenth-century cultural icon such as George Frideric Handel's *Messiah* (1741) reflects this attitude. Contrary to one's expectations, it lacks specific references to Christ's historical life. Musicologist Clifford Bartlett (in his notes to the CD recording EMI CDS 7 49801 2 [soloists, Taverner Choir and Players, conducted by Andrew Parrott]) points out that the text provided to Handel by Charles Jennens was constructed precisely to avoid these specifics, since "a life of Christ drawn from the gospels would have offended" a mid-eighteenth-century English audience that was more comfortable with "the Messiah [presented] more as a theological concept than a personality" (13).

76. *Critique of Pure Reason*, trans. Norman Kemp Smith (New York: St. Martin's Press, 1965). In the text, "A" and "B" followed by a page number refer respectively to the first (1781) and second (1787) editions of the work. The page number of the translation appears after the semicolon.

77. For overviews see Allen W. Wood, "Rational Theology, Moral Faith, and Religion," in *The Cambridge Companion to Kant*, ed. Paul Guyer (Cambridge: Cambridge University Press, 1992), 394–416; James C. Livingston, *Modern Christian Thought, Volume I: The Enlightenment and the Nineteenth Century*, 2d ed. (1997; reprint, Minneapolis: Fortress, 2006), 58–69.

empirical experience, and the ontological components (or "predicates") of the idea of God as highest and supremely perfect being (*ens realissimum*) are not given in sensuous intuition, the necessary existence of God cannot be proven, either by the ontological argument (since " 'Being' is obviously not a real predicate" and is "merely the positing of a thing . . . the copula of a judgment" [A 598/B 626; 504], it thus adds nothing to our idea of God) or by the cosmological of physicotheological arguments (since both presuppose theories of causality that are derived from our empirical experience and are thus inapplicable to the "highest Being" [A 603–30/B 631–58; 507–24]).[78]

However, the inability of pure speculative reason to know God with certainty did not close off all approaches to God. In the *Critique of Practical Reason* (1788) Kant argued that a rational faith in God could be grounded in pure practical reason, the source of our knowledge of morality. Our moral disposition (our desire for happiness and our recognition that virtue is the way to fulfill that desire) demands two elements: first, the *summum bonum* ("highest good") toward which we strive (composed of both the "moral good" or virtue and the "natural good" or happiness in proportion to virtue); second, the condition that ensures the possibility of the coincidence of perfect happiness with perfect virtue. Even though virtue does not always result in the amount of happiness we expect, we continue to be virtuous because our moral reason tells us that such a perfect coincidence (*perfect* happiness as the result of *perfect* virtue) ought to be possible. Our own limitations confirm that this possibility is not grounded in ourselves. In fact, the *summum bonum* demands a cause adequate to its effect of "perfect proportion." Thus Kant postulates the existence of God, the "higher, moral, most holy, omnipotent being who alone can unite the two elements of this good"[79] and who would ground the supreme goal of our moral actions. "Now, it was a duty

78. For the same reasons, of course, the existence of God cannot be *disproved* with certainty.

79. *Religion within the Boundaries of Mere Reason*, preface to the first edition, in *Religion within the Boundaries of Mere Reason and Other Writings*, trans. Allen Wood and George di Giovanni, Cambridge Texts in the History of Philosophy (Cambridge: Cambridge University Press, 1998), 34 (= 6:5 of the German Academy of Sciences edition of Kant's collected works).

for us to promote the highest good; hence there is in us not merely the warrant but also the necessity, as a need connected with duty, to presuppose the possibility of this highest good, which, since it is possible only under the condition of the existence of God, connects the presupposition of the existence of God inseparably with duty; that is, it is morally necessary to assume the existence of God."[80] In other words, God must be assumed to exist for human morality to be meaningful for us. Theism is a moral postulate of pure practical reason, "a special point of reference for the unification of all ends."[81] It is not the necessary knowledge of suprasensible divine reality, but a rational supposition that answers a subjective need founded upon duty. "Morality in no way needs religion (whether objectively, as regards willing, or subjectively, as regards capability) but is rather self-sufficient by virtue of pure practical reason." Morality is thus the foundation for religion and not vice versa.[82]

In the wake of these arguments, then, it is clear that we should be as critical of Kant's employment of God as we were of Descartes'. His claim regarding God's "moral necessity" did bring God back into the Enlightenment conversation, but at the same time Kant was at pains to emphasize the fundamental autonomy of the self and the consequent "non-necessity" of our knowledge of God. This is a further intensification of Descartes' move of giving human subjectivity primacy over all other reality.[83] The "necessity" of the divine postulate is a secondary move that derives from our understanding of our duty to the moral law, an understanding reached independently of any religious element. The idea of God that Kant holds out as the only possible understanding of God thus testifies to the continued dominance and supposed self-evidence of the extrinsic view, again under

80. *Critique of Practical Reason*, trans. Mary Gregor, Cambridge Texts in the History of Philosophy (Cambridge: Cambridge University Press, 1997), 105 (5:125).

81. *Religion within the Boundaries of Mere Reason*, 35 (6:5).

82. Ibid., 33–34 (6:3–5); citation at 33 (6:3).

83. Cf. Robert Solomon's comment that Kant "complete[s] the move that Descartes began, recognizing not only the importance of the first-person point of view, but also its all-encompassing nature" (*Continental Philosophy since 1750: The Rise and Fall of the Self*, A History of Western Philosophy 7 [Oxford/New York: Oxford University Press, 1988], 29).

the guise of a set of arguments designed to articulate God's presence and knowability. The epistemological presuppositions of Kant's *Critique*, which led to a repudiation of metaphysics and natural theology, confirm how transcendent to human experience and thus how extrinsic God had become.

Might the speculative idealism of Georg Wilhelm Friedrich Hegel (1770–1831), who succeeded Kant in philosophical importance, be interpreted as an antidote to the overwhelming dominance of the extrinsic view? After all, Hegel's system integrates God into the history of the world by portraying God as the Absolute Spirit that comes to know itself through history. God is "the One who exists *necessarily* because he is not merely *a* concept but *the* concept, the concept of the all-real, the most-real, the perfect."[84] Absolute Spirit comes to complete self-knowledge by expressing itself in history and realizing itself throughout history in nature and in human self-consciousness.

Crucial to Hegel's whole system is the dialectical understanding of the development of history. Every thesis gives rise to its antithesis; reason eventually unites the contradictory positions into a higher synthesis. In this synthesis, the negative elements in both positions are themselves negated and the once-differentiated positive elements are brought together into a higher unity that Hegel termed *Aufhebung* or "sublation" (where thesis and antithesis are at the same time "cancelled" and "preserved at a higher level" [*aufgehoben*]). This dialectical struggle that is also part of the structure of all rational consciousness, whereby one comes to know oneself by setting oneself off from what is non-self, affects Absolute Spirit as well. Thus history is necessary for God—"history" truly understood as Absolute Spirit's self-externalization and journey of reconciliation to itself, culminating in perfect self-knowledge. Absolute Spirit's consciousness articulates itself in the finite materiality of creation (i.e. what is non-God, including the finite spirit of human consciousness), struggles with the self-alienation inherent in this external self-manifestation, and finally overcomes all alienation at the end of history with the achievement

---

84. Peter Hodgson, "Georg Wilhelm Friedrich Hegel," in *Nineteenth Century Religious Thought in the West*, 3 vols., ed. Ninian Smart et al. (Cambridge: Cambridge University Press, 1985), 1:90.

of pure freedom in pure self-knowledge.[85] In coming to realize itself through the dialectical process, the Absolute needs the finite consciousness of human subjectivity as the arena for this realization. "God is God only so far as he knows himself: his self-knowledge is, further, a self-consciousness in man and man's knowledge *of* God, which proceeds to man's self-knowledge *in* God."[86] At the end of history Absolute Spirit will have been purified of any finite mediation and will be fully realized as pure consciousness, pure idea, pure self-thinking thought.

Hegel's systematic integration of God into history—or better, his re-definition of all history as the process of God's self-realization—would seem to have eliminated extrinsicism and restored the presence/absence structure that we have argued is central to Christianity. The universal, infinite, ideal nature of Absolute Spirit, while present both in and as history, is perfectly realized only at the *end* of history. The truth, Hegel insisted, is found in the whole process, not in the isolated parts. This led him to argue, however, that Christianity—the "absolute" religion where the self-revelation of Absolute Spirit had been realized—also needed to become *aufgehoben*. In its present earthly state Christianity had not yet reached its goal of being "absolute knowledge" because of its dependence on representations of God (e.g. as Father and as Son). While representation is a necessary stage in the realization of the Absolute, Hegel claimed that every representation of God, even as transcendent person, remains on the level of the finite and the historically contingent. Spirit is only fulfilled when it transcends the particular and achieves universal conceptuality. Thus historical Christianity is incomplete as it presently exists and must be transcended. It must become philosophy.

All this looks quite different from the God-arguments offered by Descartes and Kant. But, in an ironic twist, Hegel's conception of God also fails to overcome the power of the modern extrinsic view. By overemphasizing the role of rationality in bringing God to presence,

---

85. Van A. Harvey, "Ludwig Feuerbach and Karl Marx," in ibid., 1:293.

86. Hegel, *Encyclopedia of the Philosophical Sciences* (1830), §564 (citing C. F. Göschel [1829]), in *Hegel's Philosophy of Mind*, trans. William Wallace and A. V. Miller (Oxford: Clarendon Press, 1971), 298.

Hegel renders God extrinsic by insisting that the completely abstract conceptual nature of Absolute Spirit in its fullness is the ultimate truth of God. This critique might at first seem outrageous. Surely Hegel's philosophical articulation of God's intimate involvement with the history of the created world is as close as modernity had gotten to the fundamental biblical understanding of this relationship and to the Christian version of "natural theology." But the truth of our critique is supported by Peter Hodgson's insight that Hegel is "forgetful" of transcendence: "Although transcendence clearly is present in Hegel's thought . . . the great stress on the *revealedness* of the Absolute, its rational comprehensibility, its implicit identity with the human subject, means that Hegel inevitably downplays the mysterious, violating, numinous, revealing/concealing power of Being vis-à-vis human consciousness. Hegel certainly does not forget the Absolute, but he tends to forget the transcendence of the Absolute, confident that the Absolute can be known *absolutely.*"[87]

This extrinsicism appears on two levels. At the explicit level, Hegel argues that the fullness of God at the end of the historical process is pure idea, without remainder. Christian notions of "person" or "relationship" in reference to God are contingent representations, dependent on feeling and imagination, which must be surpassed and sublated. In his defense of Christianity, Hegel felt that he had to define the true nature of God as the *necessarily extrinsic* Absolute Idea in order to save God. But, as some of Hegel's contemporary critics pointed out, the resulting abstraction empties God of all content.[88] This move in turn is grounded on the more covert aspect of the problem. Within what we have called the fundamental classical biblical dialectical view, the absolute knowability that Hegel demands as part of God's

---

87. Hodgson, "Hegel," 1:111–12 (his emphases).

88. This accusation was made both by Hegel's orthodox ecclesiastical critics and, after his death, by his "left-wing" followers (e.g., Ludwig Feuerbach, Karl Marx, and Bruno Bauer in his work *The Trumpet of the Last Judgment upon Hegel the Atheist and Antichrist* [1841]). The latter group claimed that Hegel's system was indeed atheistic (having replaced God with human self-consciousness) and had set in motion (positively, in their view) the overcoming and dissolution of Christianity. See Livingston, *Modern Christian Thought, Volume I*, 126–27; Kasper, *GJC*, 27–28.

perfection would be equivalent to absolute presence, absolute control, and—in a strange reversal—absolute immanence. Hegel confirms this in the passage quoted above: God's self-knowledge is "a self-consciousness in man and man's knowledge *of* God." This is of higher value than the presence/absence structure of revelation that is fundamental to Christianity. But this move puts too much of a burden on rational concepts and ignores the fundamental metaphorical (concealing/revealing) structure of religious symbols.[89] The true nature of God, according to the fundamental Christian claim, is revealed according to the grammar of the presence/absence structure: both *knowability* as well as *the mystery of divine "discretion"* (which is also divine "excess") belong to the very essence of God. When Hegel equates God with an idea of God that fulfills modern subjectivity's standard of rational clarity, this clearly violates the grammar of revelation and results in a distortion, a "God" who is not God but rather an image generated by reason. The reality of Absolute Spirit mirrors the structure of subjectivity, while the "excess" of the revealed God, which disrupts all names and concepts and can never be sublated or deduced, remains unthought, excluded from the rational schema that claims to be complete. The living God continues to remain "worldless" in modernity, despite Hegel's obvious intent—an ironic result.

2.3 Taking Stock: A Preliminary Conclusion

Earlier we emphasized how the medieval nominalists' over-emphasis on divine transcendence had encouraged the "unraveling" of the classical dialectical view. But this only set the stage for the crucial shift in Western culture's predominant image of God. Only in modernity did the view of God as a distant "Deity" or as a "problem to be solved" develop into the dominant view. The result was the eclipse of the classical dialectical view by the doctrine of the transcendent and extrinsic God. By the eighteenth and nineteenth centuries, the portrait of the "Christian God" bore little resemblance to the

---

89. Cf. Hodgson, "Hegel," 1:113: "Concepts can fall into 'transcendental illusion' by forgetting their limited character and function: while constituting the 'horizon' or 'logical space' for the clarification of meanings, they cannot provide *objective* knowledge of the Absolute."

trinitarian God of Christian belief. By and large the "Christian God" who was worshiped, proven, and critiqued was the extrinsic God, a modern construct owing much more to the theistic arguments of modern philosophy than to biblical experience. Walter Kasper, as we noted before, argues that this construct is "heretical" and "repeatedly turns into the atheism which it is intended to prevent."[90] While it is true that Hegel's systematic integration of God into history stands out as a special case, his ultimate failure to overcome the extrinsic view illustrates how entrenched it had become by the nineteenth century.

Those who considered themselves believers still saw God as being in touch with humanity and the world. But the "objective" vocabulary that one might have used to explain this relationship had already been co-opted by the natural sciences and the modern philosophy of subjectivity. Christian faith in God was now judged to be more of a private matter, best practiced in moments of interior prayer and best explained non-rationally through the language of affect. And so in 1799, when Friedrich Schleiermacher first mounted his virtuoso defense of religion against its "cultured despisers," he described religion in terms of "intuition and feeling" and defined it as "the sensibility and taste for the infinite."[91] In fact, he was codifying Christianity's already-established privatization and confirming the failure of both philosophy and theology to deal with the progressive marginalization of the living God.

3. The Nineteenth-Century Critique of Religion

The strongly influential rejection of religious belief in God carried out by the nineteenth century atheist critics Ludwig Feuerbach, Karl Marx, and Friedrich Nietzsche marks the final stage of our history of the God-problem. A major catalyst for their atheism (which they shared with a host of lesser figures) was the success of modern arguments for human autonomy. Another was the continued presence of

---

90. *GJC*, 285 ("the heresy of Christian theism"), 314–15 ("theistic" faith already undermined by the Enlightenment and leading to atheism).

91. *On Religion: Speeches to its Cultured Despisers* [1799 ed.], trans. and ed. Richard Crouter, Cambridge Texts in the History of Philosophy (Cambridge/ New York: Cambridge University Press, 1996), 22, 23 (Second Speech).

the anti-Christian sentiment of the Enlightenment, strengthened by the French Revolution. But more importantly, nineteenth-century atheism can be read as a direct reaction to the extrinsic view of God. It was a reaction both to modernity's identification of the extrinsic view as the "normal Christian view" and to the failure of the early modern and Enlightenment theistic project to legitimate it.

In the cases of Feuerbach and Marx, an even more specific cause can be found. The contradictory tendencies within Hegel's system led to the split of his followers into right- and left-wing camps after his death. "Left" or "Young" Hegelians such as Feuerbach and Marx saw him not as the philosophical savior of historical Christianity but rather as the one who had laid the groundwork for its dissolution and its displacement by a more radical humanism.[92] Due to the close alliance between religion and the state in early nineteenth-century Germany, their radical religious critique led inexorably to a radical political critique that deemed the contemporary social and political conditions to be "irrational," oppressive, and in need of radical "rational" reform. Although they end up with different interpretations of the essence of religion, both Feuerbach and Marx began their critiques of religion from the same place.

Nietzsche, while not identified with the Young Hegelians, can be seen as taking this radical critique of religion to its extreme limits. His own critique is carried out in direct dialogue with the extrinsic view. The haunting power of his pronouncement that "God is dead . . . and we have killed him"[93] stems directly from his insights into modernity's failure and the ambivalent legacy of autonomy.

Even at the distance of more than a century and a half, their critiques continue to exert a force that is impossible to ignore. Any contemporary theological reflection on God needs to wrestle with

92. See Robert Nola, "The Young Hegelians, Feuerbach, and Marx," in *The Routledge History of Philosophy, Volume VI: The Age of German Idealism*, ed. Robert C. Solomon and Kathleen M. Higgins (London/New York: Routledge, 1993), 290–329; Livingston, *Modern Christian Thought, Volume I*, 214–36; Harvey, "Ludwig Feuerbach and Karl Marx," in *Nineteenth Century Religious Thought in the West*, 1:291–328. See also the literature mentioned above in n. 88.

93. *The Gay Science*, no. 125, in *The Portable Nietzsche*, ed. and trans. Walter Kaufmann (1954; reprint, Harmondsworth: Penguin, 1983), 95.

them. It is no overstatement to say that at these critics' hands, the extrinsic view virtually collapses.

3.1 Feuerbach: Religion as Projection

Ludwig Feuerbach (1804–72) began his career as a student of theology and a disciple of Hegel, but soon became an anti-theologian and materialist. The humanist atheism of his major work *The Essence of Christianity* (1841) had a tremendous influence on Marx and others because it demonstrated how to reconfigure Hegel's philosophy into a critique of Christianity and a manifesto for change.

Feuerbach's critique of religion rests upon certain presuppositions. His fundamental view of human nature was completely materialist: what is most real, he argued, is not some "spiritual" human nature but rather the universal essence of humanity that results from natural processes. Central to this essence are our sense of community with others (that does not in any way dissolve our individuality) and most importantly our "infinite" consciousness which distinguishes us from other animals—that is, human subjectivity's consciousness of its own infinite nature and its ability to transcend its limited environment by means of the intentional desire for the infinite. While Hegel argued that the intentional striving of human consciousness participates in the realization of infinite Absolute Spirit, Feuerbach interpreted this philosophical doctrine as the substitution of self-consciousness for God or the identification of God with infinite human nature. Feuerbach thus reversed Hegel's polarity by interpreting the infinite intentionality of human consciousness in a completely material way—it points toward human fulfillment rather than to the Absolute Spirit at the end of history.

Religion is the result of this human desire for the infinite. "Religion . . . is consciousness of the infinite; thus it is and can be nothing else than the consciousness that man has of his own—not finite and limited, but infinite nature."[94] In order to explain the development of historical religion, Feuerbach traced the stages of what he considered to be the causal origins of religion back to human experience. In the

94. *The Essence of Christianity*, trans. George Eliot (New York: Harper and Row, 1957 [orig. 1854]), 2.

first stage, humanity desires absoluteness and oneness with its infinite nature, but this desire cannot be fulfilled by humanity itself. And so humanity objectifies and projects its infinite capabilities, highest aspirations, and most positive qualities outside itself onto a "God." For Feuerbach, precisely this is the source of all religion: God is created by humanity according to humanity's image and likeness.

> Consciousness of God is self-consciousness; knowledge of God is self-knowledge. By his God thou knowest the man, and by the man his God; the two are identical. . . . God is the manifested inward nature, the expressed self of a man—religion the solemn unveiling of a man's hidden treasures, the revelation of his intimate thoughts, the open confession of his love-secrets.[95]

In the second stage, humanity forgets that this projection has occurred. God has become the "divine object," independent of us. In the wake of this forgetfulness, humanity becomes alienated from itself. Having given over to God all of its positive qualities, it retains only negative ones. Humanity sees itself in God but can no longer recognize these qualities as its own. This is the first alienation which humanity suffers on account of religion. In the third stage, God has ceased to be the "divine object" and becomes the Divine Subject who looks down on humanity, now the object of the divine gaze. Here occurs humanity's final alienation, its objectification at the hands of the God that it has created.[96]

For Feuerbach, then, religion is not a response to divine transcendence but rather a human creation that leads to humanity's own alienation and negation. Only by undoing the projection can humanity return to its essence and retrieve its true identity. Feuerbach's version of a true humanism thus can only be atheism, which negates the nega-

95. Ibid., 12–13. See also p. 14: "The divine being is nothing else than the human being, or, rather, the human nature purified, freed from the limits of the individual man, made objective—*i.e.*, contemplated and revered as another, a distinct being."

96. Ibid., 31: "God is the highest subjectivity of man abstracted from himself; hence man can do nothing of himself, all goodness comes from God. The more subjective God is, the more completely does man divest himself of his subjectivity, because God is, *per se*, his relinquished self. . . ."

tion of humanity and unmasks religion by showing its origins in human consciousness. The atheist critique of religion is proposed as the exercise of human freedom, reversing the alienating illusion that religion has perpetrated. It argues that "the beginning, middle and end of religion is MAN,"[97] that theology is and has always been anthropology, that faith in God has always been faith in humanity but unconsciously so. Atheism is thus said to bring humanity to authentic consciousness and frees it to see its infinite capabilities and to live them in community with others. Religion and prayer, once they have been dismantled by atheist philosophy, will be replaced by politics.

3.2 Marx: Religion as Illusion

Karl Marx (1818–83) read Feuerbach, especially *The Essence of Christianity*, and was profoundly influenced by him. His early writings took up Feuerbach's atheist critiques of Hegel and of religion and combined these with his own atheist, humanist, and materialist standpoint.[98] As his "Theses on Feuerbach" (1845) show, however, Marx also criticized Feuerbach for not going far enough in his critique. In Marx's estimation, Feuerbach saw alienation only as a psychic or mental matter, and identified the cure for alienation as a reorientation in our thinking, the intellectual discovery of the true nature of religious illusion. For Marx, this missed the main questions: what concrete social and political conditions made the illusion of religion necessary in the first place, and what social and political changes needed to be carried out in order to make this illusion unnecessary? "The chief defect of all hitherto existing materialism—that of Feuerbach included—is that the thing, reality, sensuousness, is conceived only in the form of the object or of *contemplation*, but not as *human sensuous activity*, *practice*, not subjectively."[99] In other words, Feuerbach

97. Ibid., 184.
98. For an example of Marx's indebtedness to Feuerbach, see the opening sections of his essay "Critique of the Hegelian Dialectic and Philosophy as a Whole," one of the "Economic and Philosophic Manuscripts of 1844," in *The Marx-Engels Reader*, ed. Robert C. Tucker, 2d ed. (New York: W. W. Norton, 1978), 106–08.
99. "Theses on Feuerbach," Thesis I, *Marx-Engels Reader*, 143 (all emphases here and in other citations from Marx are original).

claimed to be a materialist, but was not materialist *enough*. By rooting the problem of alienation in the realm of thought rather than in the material world, Feuerbach revealed that he was still caught up in Hegel's abstract metaphysics.

What Marx argued instead was that the problem of human alienation has its deeper roots in the social, political, and economic framework that conditions humanity, not simply in "bad thinking." Religion is only a symptom, albeit the most important one. Self-alienation can be resolved only when the social, political, and economic obstacles to self-realization are removed through "praxis" or concrete action.

> [Thesis IV] Feuerbach starts out from the fact of religious self-alienation, of the duplication of the world into a religious, imaginary world and a real one. His work consists in resolving the religious world into its secular basis. He overlooks the fact that after completing this work, the chief thing still remains to be done. . . . After the earthly family is discovered to be the secret of the holy family, the former must then itself be criticized in theory and revolutionized in practice.

> [Thesis VIII] Social life is essentially *practical*. All mysteries which mislead theory into mysticism find their rational solution in human practice and in the comprehension of this practice.

> [Thesis XI] The philosophers have only *interpreted* the world, in various ways; the point, however, is to *change* it.[100]

Marx's atheist critique of religion has three basic elements.[101] First, religion is best understood as projection—not in Feuerbach's sense of flawed or "inverted" self-consciousness, but as "inverted world consciousness" in response to debilitating political and social relations.[102] Belief in God and the need for such a belief thus have a material, not spiritual, source. Second, religion is simultaneously an illusion and a

---

100. Ibid., 144–45.
101. Cf. Kasper, *GJC*, 34–35.
102. "Contribution to the Critique of Hegel's *Philosophy of Right*: Introduction," *Marx-Engels Reader*, 53–54, at 53 (further references appear in parentheses in the text).

consolation that people give themselves, in order to compensate for the alienating material conditions in which they live. "Religion is the sigh of the oppressed creature, the sentiment of a heartless world, and the soul of soulless conditions. It is the *opium* of the people" (54). Religion will disappear only when the social and economic oppressions that create the need for religion are overcome. Lastly, religion's "illusory happiness" (the promise of eternal life beyond this world) is both a legitimation of domination and a protest against that domination. With its promise of eternal life *beyond* this world and thus the elimination of any desire for change *within* this world, religion keeps people enslaved, especially when used to thwart social change and keep the entrenched oppressors in power. But religion also articulates a hope for a better world and thereby represents a critique of the negativities of the present. "*Religious* suffering is at the same time an *expression* of real suffering and a *protest* against real suffering" (54).

In Marx's view, then, belief in God is not simply negative but can act as a positive catalyst: the "sigh of the oppressed creature" is both a symptom of the deeper material estrangements and a strong reaction against them. Religion's diagnostic value for exposing alienating relationships is the reason why Marx insists that "the criticism of religion is the premise of all criticism" (53). The goal of atheism's critique of religion is not to leave humanity without consolation, but to call humanity to its full realization.

> Criticism has plucked the imaginary flowers from the chain, not in order that man shall bear the chain without caprice or consolation but so that he shall cast off the chain and pluck the living flower. The criticism of religion disillusions man so that he will think, act and fashion his reality as a man who has lost his illusions and regained his reason; so that he will revolve about himself as his own true sun (54).

3.3 Nietzsche: The End of Metaphysics and the Death of God

The critique of religion made by Friedrich Nietzsche (1844–1900) is difficult to summarize because it touches not only belief in God but every aspect of culture. "He confronts us . . . with the question of being or not being; his focus is on the foundations of our entire

Western culture, both Greek and Christian. He unveils its nihilistic tendency and sees nihilism coming as a result."[103] His critique comes wrapped in his polemic against Christianity (his exemplar for all religions) which he interprets as resentment, a revolt against life. For our purposes, we must limit ourselves to Nietzsche's caustic comments on the God of Christianity and metaphysics.

Nietzsche vigorously argued for a "perspectivism" that regards "absolute and eternal" truths as rhetorically-intensified fictions that satisfy our need to deny our mortality.[104] All truths, ideas, ideals, values and systems are illusions; they claim universal and atemporal status, but this masks the real situation in which we find ourselves, a situation of individuals and irreducible differences known only from our limited perspective, not from some "eternal" viewpoint. The human desire for stable truths, in its lust for "sameness," eradicates these unique differences. "The same" is non-existent, but the human intellect posits it nonetheless in an "absolute" and "eternal" form in order to meet our psychological needs. "Absolute truth," then, is a falsehood, a distortion of real life.

> What then is truth? A movable host of metaphors, metonymies, and anthropomorphisms: in short, a sum of human relations which have been poetically and rhetorically intensified, transferred, and embellished, and which, after long usage, seem to a people to be fixed, canonical, and binding. Truths are illusions which we have forgotten are illusions. . . .[105]

For Nietzsche, any metaphysical claims are thus impossible,[106] and the time-honored philosophical distinction between the "true" (meta-

---

103. Kasper, *GJC*, 43.

104. For Nietzsche's succinct argument concerning the material-experiential origins of "truths" and the human need to universalize and thereby falsify these "sensuous" experiences, see *On Truth and Lies in a Nonmoral Sense*, in *Philosophy and Truth: Selections from Nietzsche's Notebooks of the Early 1870's*, trans. and ed. Daniel Breazeale (1979; reprint, Atlantic Highlands: Humanities Press International, 1990), 79–91.

105. Ibid., 84.

106. E.g., see his case against the "thing-in-itself" in §§557–60 of *The Will to Power*, trans. Walter Kaufmann and R. J. Hollingdale (New York: Vintage, 1967), 302-03.

physical) world and the "apparent" (material-empirical) world appears as a persistent Platonically-inspired error, raised to sacred status by a pernicious Christianity ("Christianity is Platonism for 'the people' "[107]) but finally recognized and overcome, we are assured, by Nietzsche himself.[108]

Ultimately, Nietzsche's suspicious analysis attempts to unmask all metaphysical truth-claims and label them as illusions. And in the Western intellectual tradition, it is the God of Christianity who has been identified as the highest instance of metaphysics ("Supreme Being," *ens realissimum*, etc.) and the ground of all being and truth. But the moment Nietzsche discovers a traceable genealogy for "absolute truth" or for "belief in God" is for him the moment when the insight dawns that they are illusions, and God is the ultimate illusion ("our most enduring lie"[109]). Since metaphysical essences and the very idea of God are said to have their origins in human experience as answers to specific human needs, then their claims to absoluteness, eternity, and universality are meaningless, since they have a *beginning* and a specific *history.* There is nothing "necessary" about them that demands that they be viewed as "eternal." After having been exposed as a metaphysical illusion, God is truly dead and can be disposed of—indeed, over the course of modernity God had already been rendered a fiction. This is the main thrust of the madman's announcement in *The Gay Science*—proclaiming the death of God, but also the

107. *Beyond Good and Evil: Prelude to a Philosophy of the Future*, trans. Walter Kaufmann (New York: Vintage, 1966), 3.

108. See the section of *Twilight of the Idols* entitled "How the 'True World' Finally Became a Fable: the History of An Error," in *The Portable Nietzsche*, ed. and trans. Walter Kaufmann (1954; reprint, Harmondsworth: Penguin, 1983), 485–86. Note especially no. 6: "The true world—we have abolished. What world has remained? The apparent one perhaps? But no! *With the true world we have also abolished the apparent one.*" For these aspects of Nietzsche's thought, see Alexander Nehamas, *Nietzsche: Life as Literature* (Cambridge, MA: Harvard University Press, 1985), esp. 42–105, and Maudemarie Clark, *Nietzsche on Truth and Philosophy*, Modern European Philosophy (Cambridge: Cambridge University Press, 1990), esp. 95-125.

109. *The Gay Science*, §344, trans. Walter Kaufmann (New York: Vintage, 1974), 283.

destruction of the metaphysical foundation (the Greatest Being) that anchored all values and judgments.

> "Whither is God?" he cried; "I will tell you. *We have killed him—* you and I. All of us are his murderers. But how did we do this? . . . What were we doing when we unchained this earth from its sun? Whither is it moving now? Whither are we moving now? Away from all suns? Are we not plunging continually? Backward, sideward, forward, in all directions? Is there still any up or down? Are we not straying as through an infinite nothing? Do we not feel the breath of empty space? Has it not become colder? Is not night continually closing in on us? . . . Do we smell nothing as yet of the divine decomposition? Gods, too, decompose. God is dead. God remains dead. And we have killed him. How shall we comfort ourselves, the murderers of all murderers?"[110]

Nietzsche argues that the result of the end of metaphysics and the death of God is a feeling of new freedom but also the realization of the true consequences of this event: nihilism ("are we not straying as through an infinite nothing?") and the end of all values. The true legacy of Christianity and its God, he claims, is this nihilism, since both are a "no" to life.

> The Christian conception of God . . . is one of the most corrupt conceptions of the divine ever attained on earth. . . . God degenerated into the *contradiction* of life . . . . God as the declaration of war against life, against nature, against the will to live![111]

110. Ibid., §125, 181. Nietzsche claims that this insight is too recent to have made an impact on his nineteenth-century contemporaries ("I have come too early," the madman says, "this tremendous event is still on its way" [ibid., 182]). Martin Heidegger comments on this passage: "The terms 'God' and 'Christian God' in Nietzsche's thinking are used to designate the suprasensory world in general. God is the name for the realm of Ideas and ideals. . . . The pronouncement 'God is dead' means: The suprasensory world is without effective power. It bestows no life. Metaphysics, i.e., for Nietzsche Western philosophy understood as Platonism, is at an end" ("The Word of Nietzsche: 'God is Dead'," in *The Question Concerning Technology and Other Essays*, trans. William Lovitt [New York: Harper and Row, 1977], 61).

111. *The Antichrist*, §18, in *The Portable Nietzsche*, 585. See also §58 (ibid., 647–50).

The state of nihilism is not the carefree situation that one might expect but rather a chilling one. Humanity is now faced squarely with the responsibility for its own freedom. Nietzsche proposes to give new meaning to life in the "revaluation of all values," the reconstitution of a life of value that overcomes metaphysically-based Christian moral principles and is thus "beyond good and evil."[112] His exemplar is the "Overman" (*Übermensch*), who with the will to life overcomes all alienations, is "faithful to the earth," and refuses to believe in "otherworldly hopes."[113]

This critique takes us far beyond Feuerbach and Marx, who were still fundamentally modern thinkers. They jettisoned God in favor of their commitment to the modern autonomous subject (even if, as in Marx, it appears in its social guise). And though their subject is layered with false consciousness and is hardly as "transparent" as the Cartesian *cogito*, they have retained the modern belief in the power of reason to get to the bottom of all illusions, especially those of religious faith, and find the bedrock truth on which to found a new, more authentic humanism. Nietzsche's thought, however, presents a much more complex case. His subject is still the modern autonomous subject, but now with the look of the isolated Romantic hero standing over the abyss, defying moral conventions and traditional ideas of transcendence, reminiscent of nineteenth-century artistic, musical, and literary depictions of the heroic individual in splendid, passionate, even agonized solitude.[114] He jettisons both humanism and reason, indeed all foundations of the self. The autonomy of this "groundless" subject has been pushed to extremes: its rational intellect, rather than offering the solace of Cartesian clarity, serves up nothing but deceptions.[115] Against this background, Kasper's evaluation of Nietzsche as an "uncannily contemporary thinker" is persuasive: "In Nietzsche faith in reason and thus in

---

112. See *The Antichrist*, ibid., 565–656; *Beyond Good and Evil: Prelude to a Philosophy of the Future*, trans. Walter Kaufmann (New York: Vintage, 1966).

113. *Thus Spake Zarathustra*, §3, in *The Portable Nietzsche*, 125.

114. Tellingly evoked, for example, by Casper David Friedrich's painting *Wanderer Above the Sea of Fog* (c. 1818).

115. See, for example, *On Truth and Lies*, 80: "the intellect unfolds its principle powers in dissimulation."

modernity is shattered. He reveals the lack of meaning and direction, the boredom of modern civilization. He knows the consequences of de-divinization, including the emptying out of the world which Platonism and Christianity together had built and which achieved its full practical results in modern science and technology. The statement that God is dead is as it were an abbreviated expression of this far-ranging process."[116]

3.4 The Shattering of Extrinsicism, an Authentic Chance for God

Did the nineteenth-century critique of religion lead to the end of religious belief in Western culture? Obviously not, as the continued presence of religion in contemporary culture demonstrates. But a closer look shows that our culture's ongoing conflicted relationship with God owes much of its persistence to the shattering of the traditional Christian notion of God that Feuerbach, Marx, and Nietzsche effected. Their attack on God as a dehumanizing construction that needed a rigorous philosophical critique has been successful in many ways. Present-day criticisms of images of God as mere projections, tools of ideological manipulation, or as burnt-out metaphors without the ability to inspire are so common within the secularized society of the West that they need no special demonstration.

Besides their cultural influence, however, the nineteenth-century critiques raise more complex issues that can contribute to our evaluation of the extrinsic view of God. The philosopher Paul Ricœur has brought some of these issues to our attention, and theologians owe him a great debt for his analysis and insightful interpretation of those whom he calls the "masters of suspicion."[117] His interpretation focuses on three elements: the identification of the kind of critique that

---

116. Kasper, *GJC*, 43–44.

117. See Paul Ricœur, "The Critique of Religion" and "The Language of Faith," trans. R. Bradley DeFord, in *The Philosophy of Paul Ricœur*, ed. Charles E. Reagan and David Stewart (Boston: Beacon Press, 1978), 213–22; 223–38; *Freud and Philosophy: An Essay on Interpretation*, trans. Denis Savage (New Haven: Yale University Press, 1970), esp. 32–36. See also Richard Kearney, "Religion and Ideology: Paul Ricœur's Hermeneutic Conflict," *Irish Theological Quarterly* 52 (1986), 109–26.

nineteenth-century atheism practices, an analysis of the specific operations of this critique, and the unexpected suggestion as to how Christian believers might use this "external critique" in order to help strengthen their faith in God.[118]

First, the nineteenth-century critique can be characterized as a "hermeneutics of suspicion." In other words, these critics have introduced a new theory of interpretation that presupposes that the meanings of all discourse—religion included—are "double meanings," that there is a break or rupture between a discourse's obvious meanings (which must be questioned) and its real "hidden" meanings which the obvious has actively suppressed. These true meanings must be excavated from underneath the discourse that masks them. The reason for this particular interpretational tack, Ricœur points out, is that the nineteenth-century critics claim to have discovered the fundamental problem of modernity, namely "false consciousness" (to use Marx's term), the fact that consciousness is not as "clear" as early modern and Enlightenment thinkers had assumed. It has layers, depths, motivations, and strategies that are hidden even from the most rational subject. Consciousness can signify one thing yet mean another; it both reveals and conceals. This is not simply a "problem" that one can solve by means of some Cartesian meditative methodic doubt. Rather, "illusion is a cultural structure," a factor embedded in modern Western culture that cannot be excised but only unveiled.[119] All expressions of human consciousness, then, have a "double meaning" to which we must apply a "double hearing," an interpretational strategy that acknowledges both the obvious (illusory) sense and the

118. Ricœur names Freud as one of his "masters of suspicion" and omits Feuerbach. Since Feuerbach's projection theory plays a more decisive role in our narrative than does Freud's theory of religion, I have substituted Feuerbach for Freud in what follows. Freud's materialist critique of God as illusory is based on philosophical presuppositions that are largely derivative of the more fundamental nineteenth-century philosophical critiques that we have already discussed. For an appraisal of Freud on religion, see Hans Küng, *Freud and the Problem of God*, trans. Edward Quinn (New Haven: Yale University Press, 1979). For support in considering Feuerbach one of the "masters of suspicion," see Van A. Harvey, *Feuerbach and the Interpretation of Religion*, Cambridge Studies in Religion and Critical Thought 1 (Cambridge: Cambridge University Press, 1995).

119. Ricœur, "The Critique of Religion," 214.

masked/hidden/suppressed meaning. It is this suspicious herme-neutic that the nineteenth-century critics applied to the discourse of religion in order to decode what they considered to be its more authentic underlying message of oppression.

Second, Ricœur depicts the specific operations of this hermeneutic as a deciphering that leads to a critique of culture. The nineteenth-century critics performed a "demystification" and "demythologiza-tion" of religious language not in order to criticize its specific content, but in order to return to what they considered to be the true historical source of the entire human turn to religion. Thus Marx interpreted religious discourse about "heaven" not as signifying the perfect realm beyond earth where God, angels, and saints dwell, but rather as a coded message of domination and submission. Have the poor pray to God for salvation in heaven, Marx held, and they will not question the social and economic conditions that hold them enslaved, nor will they challenge their enslavers. Thus religious discourse is interpreted as a mythology driven by ideology that serves the interests of the rich and powerful. "Substitute paradise for the submissive, ideo-logical justification for the powerful, and you have a perfectly valid and legitimate reading of religion and a kind of denunciation of what religion falsely proclaims in ignorance of its economic *motivation*."[120]

Nietzsche enacts a similar decoding. His "genealogy of morals" is what Ricœur calls an "archeology" that attempts to discern the true original directing cause (*archē*) of Christian values.[121] These values, as well as the Western cultural system that they support, are projec-tions or objectifications of the working of the will. The task of gene-alogy is to get behind these manifestations to see the will itself (the "willing will") and precisely how it articulates its values (the "willed will").[122] Since Nietzsche interpreted Christianity as a "no" to life, he felt that he had exposed its value system as the manifestation of a weak and deformed will, which refused to deal with the differential forces of life. For him, this "weak will" is the true *archē* of religion.

120. Ibid., 216.
121. See Friedrich Nietzsche, *The Birth of Tragedy and The Genealogy of Morals*, trans. Francis Golffing (New York: Anchor/Doubleday, 1956).
122. Ricœur, "The Critique of Religion," 216; *Freud and Philosophy*, 35.

What is needed in its place is a strong will, the will to power, and the value of self-responsibility ("beyond good and evil") that it expresses.

Both Marx and Nietzsche—and Feuerbach as well, with his assertion of human infinite consciousness—thus considered the suspicious hermeneutic of religion and God-talk to be necessary in order to overcome the false consciousness embedded in culture and to show human beings the way to be fully human, without the presence of the God they considered to be a dehumanizing idol and without the "hidden meanings" of ideology. But Ricœur insists that what he terms their "external critique" of religion is necessary *for believers* as well, since "to smash the idols is also to let symbols speak."[123] In other words, a hermeneutics of suspicion, by correctly divesting religion of its ideologically-driven masks, clears the way for the disclosure of the *real* meaning of religion and religious discourse. The *external* critique of the hermeneutics of suspicion can be extended by the *internal* critique of a hermeneutics of affirmation performed by believers themselves.

These two forms of hermeneutics differ in the direction of their focus.[124] A *suspicious* hermeneutic proceeds *archeologically*. It looks backwards to the past, to the *archē* or originating inner-worldly cause, and considers it to be completely determinative of the phenomenon being examined. In the case of religion, the nineteenth-century critics found an inner-worldly origin in either the unsatisfied desire for absoluteness (Feuerbach), economic injustice (Marx), or a weak will (Nietzsche)—the "hidden meaning" within the double meaning of religious discourse. An *affirmative* hermeneutic of religion, on the other hand, proceeds *eschatologically*. It looks forward to the *eschaton*, the future arrival point of religious hope that is disclosed in religious language and symbol. A hermeneutics of affirmation can illustrate that religious symbols have more than a past, and indeed more than one *archē* in their past. They have future meanings and intentions. They anticipate a freedom or a truth or an act of justice which is a

---

123. "The Critique of Religion," 219.

124. See Ricœur, "Existence and Hermeneutics," trans. Kathleen McLaughlin, in *The Conflict of Interpretations: Essays in Hermeneutics*, ed. Don Ihde (Evanston: Northwestern University Press, 1974), 22–24; Kearney, "Religion and Ideology," 116–18.

genuine human hope but which is beyond anything that we have experienced or that we might accomplish on our own. They speak, in other words, of transcendence. Only a hermeneutics of affirmation can disclose the eschatological dimension *in front of* a religious symbol, a new possibility for human existence which has a footing in our experienced reality but whose fulfillment lies in the future, and thus can *only* be symbolized. "With symbolic language, we are in turn faced with a language that says more than what it says, which says something other than what it says and which, consequently, grasps me because it has in its meaning created a new meaning."[125]

An illustration is the Christian claim that "only God can save us." This religious language suffers from what Ricœur calls "cultural estrangement," because the dependence on God described by this discourse clashes so fiercely with our values of autonomy and self-reliance. But at the same time this discourse offers an "available believable" because it speaks of the fulfillment of authentic human existence that is revealed by God and available to all.[126] A hermeneutics of affirmation, in its own way, acknowledges a more positive "double meaning" of religious language that both conceals and reveals, and thus demands a "double hearing" as well.

Ricœur's framework gives us a way to redeem the claim we made earlier, that the nineteenth-century critics shatter the extrinsic view of God. Clearly these external critiques have been effective at "smashing the idols." This stems largely from two factors. First, Feuerbach, Marx, and Nietzsche are heirs to the legacy of the modern arguments for the autonomy of subjectivity. Granted, their "subject" is a more complex, layered reality than the Cartesian *cogito*, but it is still possible to draw a relatively straight line from Descartes to the nineteenth century and to find that those at the end of the line have just as strong an investment in the power of subjectivity as early modern thinkers before the awareness of "false consciousness." Secondly, the nineteenth-century critics linked this effectiveness to another factor that they especially targeted, namely the inarguable presence of human expectations within every portrait of God. This link between "self"

125. Ricœur, "The Language of Faith," 233.
126. "The Critique of Religion," 219–20.

and "God" had been made before, but not quite in this way. The masters of suspicion employed the inexorable logic and power of autonomy to claim either that the link was an oppressive equivalence (Feuerbach and Marx) or that subjectivity had obliterated whatever notion of God had remained in modernity and had now claimed life as its sole possessor (Nietzsche). This insight into the tendency of human expectations to overrun the image of God captures that moment when one's image of God has become an idol. And the critics' objective was to rid culture of that dehumanizing idolatrous presence.

But who is this idol that has been smashed? Who is the God who is called a projection and an alienation? Who is the God who is dead? On our reading of the history of the God-problem, it is clear that it is the God bequeathed to the nineteenth century, *the extrinsic God*, who has been identified as the oppressive "Christian" God. Feuerbach, Marx, and Nietzsche are reacting to and confirming a movement of thought that began with William of Ockham. Their attack on Christianity applies to the only image of God with which they were familiar, the extrinsic God that had been at the forefront of Christian consciousness for so long that it had been mistaken for the authentic view of God and identified with Christianity. Their criticism is at once negative and positive, a bracing critique that clears the decks, so to speak, of those images of God that have become wasted and ineffective. The masters of suspicion give us the means to read the history of the God problem backwards, allowing us to discover when the "Christian" God became an idol and how the standard image of God ceased to be a response to transcendence and became instead the extrinsic and determined fulfillment of human need.

In light of the power of the nineteenth-century critique, it is legitimate to ask whether authentic Christian belief in God is still possible. Our answer is "yes"—once the idols of modern theism have been smashed, it is possible to "let the symbols speak," to allow the dialectical understanding of God to appear again in its revealed fullness and be recognized as the authentic vivifying force of Christianity. In the following chapters we will craft a theology of the presence and absence of God that acknowledges the insights of a hermeneutics of suspicion but proceeds by means of a constructive hermeneutics of affirmation. Our goal is to retrieve the traces of the living God of revelation within the Christian tradition (our affirmative hermeneutical glance backward toward the *archē*) and to use the contemporary religious imagination to discern the present-day manifestations of the truly "excessive" presence of God who is our future (our forward glance toward the *eschaton*). In the following chapter, we will begin by constructing a natural theology that responds to transcendence and yet knows its limitations.

CHAPTER THREE

The Christian Response, I: Natural Theology

How should Christian theology respond to the "eclipse of God"? How might we increase the chances for an authentic thinking and speaking about God after the shattering of extrinsicism?

Our first step is to craft a *Christian natural theology*, as the prelude to a Christian "theological theology" of God. Natural theology highlights those aspects of human experience which act as pointers to the presence of God and as presuppositions for faith. It sketches out that "clearing" within our experience where God's self-communication occurs and can be recognized by us in faith for the salvific reality that it is. We will refine this rough definition, but for the moment it is an acceptable starting point.

There are good reasons for being cautious in pursuing this approach. We already observed how the meaning of "natural theology" has shifted over the centuries and remains ambiguous. There have been biblical claims for a natural knowledge of God, natural theologies associated with the Greek philosophers, and modern rationalist natural theologies, all having different assumptions about the roles played by reason, faith, experience, history, and cultural expectations in determining how human experience has access to the reality of God.[1] In

1. Because of these ambiguities, the term "philosophical theology" has been suggested as a more precise substitute, since it emphasizes both the *rational* as well as the strongly *theological* character of this kind of reflection (e.g., Max Seckler, "Theologie als Glaubenswissenschaft," in *Handbuch der Fundamentaltheologie 4: Traktat Theologische Erkenntnislehre*, ed. Walter Kern, Hermann J. Pottmeyer, and Max Seckler [Freiburg/Br.: Herder, 1988], 185). I prefer "natural theology" since it is more often used in English-language contexts. However, I understand the term as interchangeable with "philosophical theology" precisely for the reasons that Seckler notes.

contemporary theology the topic is controversial, especially in light of Karl Barth's radical critique of it in the name of a theology of the Word of God (claiming that the "analogy of faith" trumps the "analogy of being"), and in the light of recent Barth-inspired critiques of theological method, such as those raised by postliberal theologians and by those associated with "radical orthodoxy."[2] We need, then, to carefully delineate natural theology's character and show its proper place within the Christian reflection on God. And we will need to identify and avoid certain pitfalls that could very well turn our reflections into the philosophical "theism" that we have already labeled a dead end.

1. The Meaning and Necessity of Natural Theology

The fundamental claim of any Christian natural theology is that there is some connection—always needing further specification—between our everyday experience and our experience of the reality of God. Our experience of God has some footing in our everyday life-world. Experiences that may appear merely ordinary and natural can, upon careful analysis, be seen as pointers toward the extraordinary, the supernatural.

But why insist on what seems to be a mere truism? The widespread contemporary "culture of disbelief," the "eclipse of God" acutely experienced by many individuals, the uncertainties which permeate even the God-talk of believers—all these are indications that the connection between the experience of God and human experience can be tenuous, and perhaps literally inconceivable, for many. Mainstream contemporary culture, often equating image with reality and claiming the immediate and the immanent to be the highest values, at times even puts

2. For Barth, see e.g. *Anselm: Fides Quaerens Intellectum*, trans. Ian Robertson (Richmond: John Knox Press, 1960 [German orig., 1931]); idem, *Church Dogmatics, volume I, part 1: The Doctrine of the Word of God*, trans. G. W. Bromiley et al. (Edinburgh: T. & T. Clark, 1957), x: "I regard the *analogia entis* [analogy of being] as the invention of Antichrist. . . ." For postliberal theology, see George A. Lindbeck, *The Nature of Doctrine: Religion and Theology in a Postliberal Age* (Philadelphia: Westminster, 1984). For radical orthodoxy, see John Milbank, Catherine Pickstock, and Graham Ward, "Introduction: Suspending the Material: The Turn of Radical Orthodoxy," in *Radical Orthodoxy: A New Theology*, ed. John Milbank, Catherine Pickstock, and Graham Ward (London/New York: Routledge, 1999), 1–20.

the very possibility of transcendence into question.[3] Contemporary thinking about God, then, is caught in a dilemma. When society loses "the basic presuppositions needed for understanding [the Christian message about God]," as Walter Kasper puts it, it can lose "the very ability to believe" as well as lose contact with "the dimension of mystery."[4] Whenever theology finds itself lacking "the language and the adequately developed categories that would enable us to speak unambiguously about God,"[5] a developed natural theology is absolutely vital. We need to articulate it in such a way so that it can express the intersection of the mystery of God with human experience as well as provide adequate categories for reflecting on this intersection.

Where might we find a usable definition or description? Unfortunately, the most prevalent understanding of natural theology, such as that found in standard theological reference works, offers little help. It shows clear signs of a bias that distorts the relationship between human experience and the reality of God.

> [Natural theology is] the body of knowledge about God which may be obtained by human reason alone without the aid of Revelation and hence to be contrasted with "Revealed Theology."[6]

> Natural theology [is] the study of God solely through the use of human reason. Typically, theology relies upon God's revelation for knowledge about God. . . . Natural theology, however, works independently of the content of revelation. Processes observable by any human person, along with human reason, provide the sources for the knowledge of God gained by natural theology.[7]

---

3. Cf. Richard Kearney, "Ethics and the Postmodern Imagination," *Thought* 62 (1987): 39–58; idem, *The Wake of Imagination: Toward a Postmodern Culture* (Minneapolis: University of Minnesota Press, 1988), 1–33.

4. Walter Kasper, *The God of Jesus Christ* [hereafter *GJC*], new ed., trans. [Matthew J. O'Connell and] Dinah Livingstone (London/New York: Continuum, 2012), 65.

5. Ibid., 64.

6. *The Oxford Dictionary of the Christian Church*, 3rd ed., ed. F. L. Cross and E. A. Livingstone (Oxford/New York: Oxford University Press, 1997), 1132 (s.v., "Natural Theology").

7. *The HarperCollins Encyclopedia of Catholicism*, ed. Richard P. McBrien (San Francisco: HarperCollins, 1995), 908 (s.v., "natural theology").

These definitions, with their emphasis on "human reason alone" and "reason independent of revelation," are merely restatements of the modern rationalist definitions of natural theology which presupposed a strict distinction or even opposition between nature and human reason on the one hand and supernatural revelation and faith on the other. They immediately betray their indebtedness to Enlightenment (and particularly Deist) discussions of rational religion. As we noted previously, these seventeenth- and eighteenth-century arguments held that although God was a wholly transcendent being, the powers of unaided human reason could discover divine truths which were disclosed in nature. These truths, along with the rational means to grasp them, were presumed to be available to all human beings and transcended the particularity of Christianity and all other religious traditions. Special divine revelation and the faith needed to recognize and appropriate it were considered unnecessary and even contradictory to human nature.

The "standard" definitions of natural theology presuppose this position and obscure its historical context and contingent, polemical character. They thereby replicate not only the absolute oppositions assumed by modern rationalist religion (reason vs. faith, natural vs. supernatural) but also its more fundamental presuppositions: an extrinsicist understanding of God, a definition of "nature" which assumes it to be a closed system, and a theory of human nature which overestimates the powers of human reason and renders faith either privatized or else irrelevant because it is considered irrational. To define "natural theology" in this way, then, reinstates the very problem of God that we are trying to overcome, and leaves us with an anthropology whose truncated rationalist assumptions are hardly an adequate fit with contemporary human experience.

What we need is a more adequate conception of natural theology, one consonant with our efforts to articulate both a dialectical view of God and a more open and integrated understanding of human experience, one which views faith and natural knowledge not as opposites but rather as different mutually supportive aspects of human experience.

Both the Bible and later Christian tradition already suggest this sort of in-depth description of human experience. The biblical traditions reflect the consensus that creation conveys a "natural" knowledge of the divine power and glory which grounds both the person and the cosmos. These traditions also hold human beings accountable for such knowledge. Psalm 8 praises the majesty of God which can be glimpsed "[w]hen I look at your heavens, the work of your fingers, / the moon and the stars that you have established" (Ps 8:3). The author of the book of Wisdom criticizes as foolish those who do not perceive the obvious link between creation and the Creator: "For from the greatness and beauty of created things / comes a corresponding perception of their Creator. . . . [F]or if they had the power to know so much / that they could investigate the world, / how did they fail to find sooner the Lord of these things?" (Wis 13:1, 5, 9). In the New Testament, Jesus' parables draw on a wide range of ordinary human experiences and show how they can be clues to the presence of the Kingdom of God and intimations of eschatological salvation. And the traditions which reflect Pauline teaching assert explicitly that a knowledge of the reality of God can be derived from creation (Acts 14:15–17; Rom 1:19–20).

As Christianity developed, these insights became more fully developed, first through the ancient Church's insistence upon the close relationship between creation and salvation (against the world-denying doctrines of the Gnostics)[8] and later through the medieval scholastic reflections upon the mutual supporting links between nature and grace and the preambles to faith available within the natural knowledge of God.[9] More recently, nineteenth- and twentieth-century Roman

---

8. E.g., Irenaeus of Lyons' arguments in *Adversus Haereses*. See *Against the Heresies, Book I*, trans. Dominic J. Unger, rev. John J. Dillon, Ancient Christian Writers, no. 55 (New York/Mahwah: Paulist Press, 1992).

9. E.g., Thomas Aquinas, *Summa theologiae* Ia, q. 2, a. 2, ad 1: "For faith presupposes natural knowledge, just as grace does nature and all perfections that which they perfect" (*Summa theologiae*, vol. 2 [1a. 2–11]: *Existence and Nature of God*, trans. Timothy McDermott [1964; repr., Cambridge: Cambridge University Press, 2006], 11.)

All further references to the *Summa theologiae* are taken from the Blackfriars edition, trans. Thomas Gilby et al., 61 vols. (1964–76; repr., Cambridge: Cambridge University Press, 2006). The short form of reference in parentheses in the text follows this format: *ST* and the part, question, article, ad [= response] (vol. no. of the Blackfriars edition: page[s]).

Catholic theology, reacting against modernity's overestimation of the role of reason in human experience and effacement of the material world's theonomous grounding, developed arguments regarding reason's openness to divine truth and the positive value of natural knowledge for faith. These positions are reflected in the official statements of the First and Second Vatican Councils. Vatican I in 1870 took a stand between the repudiated extremes of rationalism and fideism by proposing "a twofold order of knowledge" of God, one attainable by natural reason, the other attainable only by faith.[10] It taught that God "can be known with certainty from the consideration of created things, by the natural power of human reason."[11] However, because "God [has] directed human beings to a supernatural end"[12] and "there are proposed for our belief mysteries hidden in God which, unless they are divinely revealed, are incapable of being known" by natural reason,[13] faith in supernatural revelation is also necessary in order for human beings to overcome reason's natural deficiencies and reach a knowledge of the fullness of God. Vatican II (1962–65) reaffirmed these teachings explicitly[14] as well as in a more personalist way: "the Church holds that the acknowledgment of God is in no way at odds with human dignity, since this has God for its basis and fulfillment."[15]

10. *Dogmatic Constitution on the Catholic Faith*, *"Dei Filius,"* ch. 4, in Norman P. Tanner, ed., *Decrees of the Ecumenical Councils*, 2 vols. (London: Sheed and Ward / Washington: Georgetown University Press, 1990; hereafter *DEC*), 2:808 (Latin orig. and Eng. trans. on facing pages); *Enchiridion symbolorum definitionum ed declarationum de rebus fidei et morum/Compendium of Creeds, Definitions, and Declarations on Matters of Faith and Morals*, ed . Heinrich Denzinger, Peter Hünermann, et al., 45th ed. (San Francisco: Ignatius Press, 2012; hereafter DH), DH 3015 [DH normally provides slightly different English translations].

11. *Dei Filius*, ch. 2, (*DEC* 2:806; DH 3004). Note that the Council defines the *possibility* of knowing God *(certo cognosci posse)* and not the absolutely fulfilled actual success of that process (e.g., by means of a rational proof of God's existence). Cf. Kasper, *GJC*, 69.

12. *Dei Filius*, ch. 2 (*DEC* 2:806; DH 3005).

13. Ibid., ch. 4 (*DEC* 2:808; DH 3015).

14. *Dogmatic Constitution on Divine Revelation*, *"Dei verbum,"* §6, (*DEC* 2:973; DH 4206), citing *Dei Filius*, ch. 2.

15. *Pastoral Constitution on the Church in the Modern World*, *"Gaudium et spes,"* §21 (*DEC* 2:1080; DH 4321).

However, reflecting the changed circumstances of the later twentieth century, Vatican II acknowledged the presence of atheism and the fact that contemporary culture can render the appropriation of the natural knowledge of God more difficult. The council emphasized, along with Vatican I, the ultimate insufficiency of natural knowledge and taught that the only complete and certain answers to the question of God and the quest for human meaning come from the revelation of God in Jesus Christ.[16]

Both the biblical testimonies and the teachings of the Christian tradition offer a view of human experience which challenges the radical dichotomies assumed by rational religion. Understanding always already exists as a *possibility* for human existence, as the possible fulfillment of the intentional desire for meaning.[17] Reason and faith are mutually implicating intentional acts of human conscious awareness. In other words, the concrete experience of understanding reveals reason to be an *active intentionality*—an openness to and consciousness of what is other than the self, the active capability of grasping what is "non-I." Reason itself thus presupposes what we might call a kind of "faith," although in a secular mode: a faith in the principles which govern the intentional actions of reason but whose truth cannot be demonstrated by reason; a commitment to the non-objectifiable, transcending horizon of the whole of being which is the presupposition for the fulfillment of meaning.[18] The process of natural knowledge must rely on what is beyond the immanent and the empirical in order to make sense of both the evidence of experience and its own operations in dealing with that evidence. Here, at the limits of what is rationally demonstrable, reason manifests its fundamental openness to what is beyond those limits. Without such

16. Ibid., §§19–22 (*DEC* 2:1079–82; DH 4319–22).

17. Cf. Karl Rahner, *Foundations of Christian Faith: An Introduction to the Idea of Christianity*, trans. William V. Dych (1978; reprint, New York: Crossroad, 1989), 14–39.

18. Cf. Walter Kasper, *Transcending All Understanding: The Meaning of Christian Faith Today*, trans. Boniface Ramsey (San Francisco: Ignatius Press, 1989), 44–46; Wolfhart Pannenberg, "Anthropology and the Question of God," in *The Idea of God and Human Freedom*, trans. R. A. Wilson (Philadelphia: Westminster, 1973), 80–98, at 91.

a faith in the indemonstrable yet necessary conditions for thinking itself, reason would be paralyzed. This "secular faith" and the openness beyond immanence that it symbolizes can contribute to a developing religious faith in God, the Holy Mystery who grounds the conditions of reality and supports the fullness of the meaning of our existence in the face of the non-availability of this fullness on our own terms and by our own abilities.[19]

On the other hand, if one's faith in God is to be considered a truly human act it must involve the whole person, including human rationality. Since Christian faith claims to speak the truth of salvation to all human beings, it cannot focus solely on private religious experiences but must also "refer to what all human beings have in common and what links them as human beings amid all their cultural differences: their reason or understanding."[20] Within the act of faith, one way in which the believer experiences the truth of salvation offered by God is by understanding it as a possible mode of human existence. In other words, faith grasps the revelation of the presence of God as *meaningful* for the believer—the act of faith interpretively lays out the possibilities-for-living which have been offered in revelation and grasped as salvation by the one who believes. This interpretive dimension of faith is carried out through the categories of human understanding. The theologian Bernhard Welte puts it this way:

> That the Word of God has an addressee belongs to the essence of the proclaimed Word of God itself. The Word is spoken, and then it is heard, appropriated, and finally believed. But in [the believer's] appropriating hearing an *understanding* is always at work, an understanding from the side of the hearer. The hearer would not at all hear correctly if he did not enter into the message with *his* thought, and if it were not clear to his thinking what the Word said to him.[21]

---

19. Walter Kasper, *An Introduction to Christian Faith*, trans. V. Green (New York: Paulist Press, 1980), 32–33.

20. Kasper, *GJC*, 71.

21. Bernhard Welte, "Was hat die Philosophie in der Theologie zu tun?" [1974], *Gesammelte Schriften IV/3: Zur Vorgehensweise der Theologie und zu ihrer jüngeren Geschichte*, ed. Gerhard Ruff (Freiburg: Herder, 2007), 153–62, at 153–54 (my translation; his emphases).

This in no way denies the basic Christian claim that religious faith is a gift from God. But if faith is to be at the same time an authentic human response to revelation—if "faith comes through what is heard" (Rom. 10:17)—then it is inherently "a hearing which understands," an active response which necessarily brings into play the believer's rational categories and the culturally-influenced presuppositions which inform them.[22] Faith is never simply a passive "blind faith" or an unmediated grasp of raw information. If it were, one could not claim that revelation as such had indeed occurred, because the address of salvation to the person would have been short-circuited and the appropriation of the object of the faith-act by the *whole* person would not have been accomplished. We might say, then, that Anselm's classic formulation takes on a wider meaning. Faith is always *fides quaerens intellectum*, "faith seeking understanding."[23] But it is also an *intellectus fidei*, a "faith developed in understanding." Revelation occurs within a relationship; it is addressed to a "someone" who hears and makes sense of this salvific offer through the various forms of human understanding. Rational reflection is thus linked inextricably to faith and plays a critical role in the constitution and appropriation of the revelatory event.[24]

Faith, then, is neither something irrational nor a mere epiphenomenon but rather a constitutive element of the full meaning of human experience. Reason, for its part, while it experiences limitations, is not a closed system oriented solely toward the empirical world. Rather, it is an exercise of open-ended intentionality whose transcending axiomatic conditions are necessarily "taken on faith." Faith is not

---

22. See Bernhard Welte, *Heilsverständnis: Philosophische Untersuchung einiger Voraussetzungen zum Verständnis des Christentums* [1966], in *Gesammelte Schriften*, vol. IV/1: *Hermeneutik des Christlichen*, ed. Bernhard Casper (Freiburg: Herder, 2006), 19–193, at 34–35.

23. Anselm of Canterbury, *Proslogion*, in *The Prayers and Meditations of Saint Anselm*, trans. Benedicta Ward (Harmondsworth/New York: Penguin, 1973), preface, 239.

24. See Bernhard Welte, "Credo ut intelligam als theologisches Programm heute" [1962], in *Gesammelte Schriften*, vol. IV/3, 212–27, at 214; ET: "*Credo ut intelligam*—as a Theological Program for Our Times," trans. Fidelis J. Smith, *American Church Quarterly* 2 (1962): 143–52, at 145.

knowledge, nor are rational reflection and faith identical. But neither are they opposing aspects of human experience. Faith and reason have a mutually implicating relationship, and this overlapping character demands a description of natural theology broader than the standard definitions, a description which does justice to faith's "reasonableness" and reason's openness to what is beyond the empirical and discursive.

We move in a more productive direction, then, if we define natural theology as that type of thinking which seeks "the natural 'access-point' of faith"[25] and describe its task as one of demonstrating "the internal reasonableness of a faith which has its substantiation in and from itself."[26] In other words, natural theology pursues the knowledge of God's presence without an overt appeal to supernatural revelation, but nevertheless remains sensitive to the fact that its conclusions can be fully articulated only by an *intellectus fidei* developed in the light of the self-disclosure of the horizon of ultimacy towards which faith is oriented. Natural theology's fundamental task is to demonstrate that human experience by its very nature is open to infinite transcendence and participates in a dynamic movement toward God that can be more fully articulated through a faith commitment to God's further self-revelation. This revelation, providing a fuller knowledge of God's character than that achieved by reason alone, nevertheless is not opposed to reason, since it fulfills reason's intentional drive. Natural theology can articulate the general character of the divine mystery that we seek, the fundamental characteristics of the world through which we have access to that mystery, and the characteristics of the human seeker of the mystery.

This more expansive vision of natural theology is important for a number of reasons. First, it demonstrates how belief in God is rationally plausible and how the natural knowledge of God can serve as a "clearing" wherein human experience is already in touch with the mystery of God and already open to the possibility of a more intimate relationship with God which revelation brings about. Second, it shows that we can avoid the radical dichotomies of rationalist reli-

25. Kasper, *An Introduction to Christian Faith*, 20.
26. Kasper, *GJC*, 71.

gion and maintain that reality and salvation are not contradictory. Lastly, it provides insights whereby we can articulate even more clearly the claim made by the *intellectus fidei*, "faith developed in understanding," that our rational discernment of God's presence within human experience and within the cosmos can provide us with the basis for the most comprehensive understanding of reality and help us identify the most meaningful possibilities for human liberation.[27]

Today natural theology is usually considered synonymous with proofs for the existence of God. Over the past several centuries these proofs have been the primary means for expressing the claims for the natural knowledge of God, and they remain so for many today. A glance at history of natural theology, though, shows that this was not always the case. The biblical sources testify to a natural knowledge of God but offer neither philosophical proofs nor any systematic theological argument. The earliest Greek natural theology was interested in the question of the nature of the divine origin of things. It was not until Plato and Aristotle that "the question of the nature of the divine origin merged into an argument for its existence"[28] and that the proofs became the major vehicle for natural theology. From this point on, arguments for the existence of God (as in Plato's *Laws*, book X) assumed the double duty of demonstrating the reality of the divine and exploring the attributes of the divine nature (such as unity, eternity, and immortality) in addition to its status as the origin of reality. Early Christian theology appropriated this form of philosophical theology (not without some uneasiness, as shown in the previous chapter) in order to demonstrate that "its claim could be taken seriously that the God who redeems us in Jesus Christ is the Creator of heaven and earth and thus the one true God of all peoples."[29]

The almost myopic emphasis on the proofs as objectively certain demonstrations occurred only after the extrinsic view of God became

27. Cf. ibid., 78–79.

28. Wolfhart Pannenberg, *Systematic Theology*, 3 vols., trans. Geoffrey W. Bromiley (Grand Rapids, Eerdmans, 1991–98), 1:78. See also in the same volume (1:63–118) Pannenberg's valuable overview of the history of natural theology and assessment of its contemporary task.

29. Ibid., 1:79.

dominant in early modernity. This shift in focus was encouraged by the growing dominance of the natural sciences with their conception of nature as a closed system (which led to the demotion of the "sacred canopy" view of the world) and by the developing forms of rational religion discussed earlier. But it was also encouraged among Catholic theologians, ironically enough, by the disputes over the relationship between nature and grace which occurred during the sixteenth century. In order to refute heretical claims such as that of Michel Baius (1513–89) that grace is not a supernatural gift but rather is owed to nature and necessarily belongs to it, Catholic theologians of the Baroque period created the construct of "pure nature" as an aid in formulating a theological argument which would safeguard the total gratuitousness of grace. Eventually what began as a hypothesis gradually hardened into a description of two dichotomous realms, the natural and the supernatural. This served as the backdrop for the modern type of Catholic theological argumentation which dominated the period from sixteenth- and seventeenth-century Baroque Scholasticism all the way up to the Neo-Scholasticism of the late nineteenth and early twentieth centuries with its emphasis on objective deductive demonstrations and rigorous distinctions.[30]

This checkered heritage does not delegitimate the proofs for God's existence, as some contemporary critics have claimed. Rather, it changes the way we view them and the goals for which we employ them. Today it is certainly true that when these arguments are presented as objective demonstrations with inarguable conclusions, they most often fail to convince the disaffected Christians, the skeptics, and the non-believers at whom they are aimed. Few are moved by

30. Cf. Kasper, *GJC*, 73–74; Pannenberg, *Systematic Theology*, 1:81–82; Henri de Lubac, *Augustinianism and Modern Theology*, trans. Lancelot Sheppard (New York: Crossroad, 2000); de Lubac, *The Mystery of the Supernatural*, trans. Rosemary Sheed (New York: Crossroad, 1998). For the broader fundamental theological background to these developments, see Francis Schüssler Fiorenza, "Systematic Theology: Task and Methods," in *Systematic Theology: Roman Catholic Perspectives*, ed. Francis Schüssler Fiorenza and John Galvin, 2 vols. (Minneapolis: Fortress, 1991), 1:3–87, at 27–34; Anthony J. Godzieba, *Bernhard Welte's Fundamental Theological Approach to Christology*, American University Studies, series VII, vol. 160 (New York/Bern: Peter Lang, 1994), 18–30.

the "indubitable" claims of such arguments, except perhaps to dispute their logic. This is because the arguments are usually seen from the point of view of the rationalist natural theology that we have sought to overcome here. Although much contemporary Western culture has inherited that tradition and used its dualistic assumptions to define the roles of faith and religion, its God-arguments do not seem to carry much persuasive force. Its assumptions of a link between "logic" and "God" and of the complete separation of faith and reason are not shared by the disaffected or the non-believer in a way that might open up a path to belief. In fact, to insist that the conclusions of these arguments must be "indubitable" and "inarguable" removes the act of free assent which is a necessary element of the human act of faith.

But if we view God-arguments with the expanded understanding of natural theology that we have proposed, the proofs then retain their value. As explorations of our ability to know the existence and attributes of God, they continue to have the important function of "commend[ing] a form of knowledge of God that is compatible with us and our human nature."[31] Substantiating this particular claim in the context of contemporary culture is vitally important, especially after the hermeneutics of suspicion of Feuerbach, Marx, and Nietzsche. As rational arguments, the proofs should clarify the warrants for this knowledge and show how the sources of this knowledge have a footing in human experience. They are not self-contained quasi-geometric demonstrations. Rather, they are reasonable pointers to God's reality and character, as well as testimonies to the inherent capacity of human experience to acknowledge the presence of God even before the explicit recognition of religious faith. They mark the point of intersection between finite human experience and the infinite reality of God which begins to be grasped by reason but which ultimately exceeds reason's limits.[32] These limits are not the defeat of

31. Pannenberg, *Systematic Theology*, 1:81.

32. Cf. Kasper, *GJC*, 100: "It is not surprising, therefore, that a proof of God's existence must be of a different kind from a proof in mathematics or the natural sciences. The 'proofs of God's existence' reach beyond the dimension of the physical and of the purely rational into the metaphysical world and the realm of the infinite, which by its very nature can no longer be conceived and com-

reason but a positive disclosure of "the natural access-point of faith." At the point where its capacities are exhausted and its categories break down, natural theology provides a clearing where faith's desire for God becomes clearly visible and where its encounter with God's self-revelation is rendered plausible. But the God-arguments of natural theology can go no further than this and must concede any further knowledge of the nature of God to revelation and faith. We must be mindful that we can evaluate faith as inherently reasonable and yet recognize that the ultimate substantiation of faith must come from faith itself and from self-revelation of God which is the object of its intentional striving.

2. Some Classical and Contemporary God-Arguments

Arguments for the existence of God can be classified into two general types. Those which look to the natural world as a source of evidence for our natural knowledge of God are *cosmological arguments.* Their point is to trace the contingency of the world to the necessary divine cause of its existence. *Anthropological arguments* take their evidence from the human experience of self and the structure of human subjectivity. They attempt to argue for a similar necessary connection between the contingent self and its divine ground.[33] This typology has lent itself to a general chronological division suggested by some commentators: ancient and medieval arguments are fundamentally cosmological while modern and contemporary ones are necessarily anthropological. Wolfhart Pannenberg offers some reasons for this typical division:

---

prehended in finite definitions. If we were to attempt to prove God as though he were just like any other being . . . then, far from knowing him, we would profoundly fail to know him."

33. Earlier, Kant had classified what he considered "the only three possible ways of proving the existence of God by means of speculative reason" as the physico-theological (arguing to the reality of God as supremely perfect being from the contingent structure of the sensible world), the cosmological (arguing from the existence of the sensible world), and the ontological (arguing from concept of being itself). See *Critique of Pure Reason*, trans. Norman Kemp Smith (New York: St. Martin's Press, 1965), 499–500 (A 590–91/B 618–19).

Plato stands at the beginning, and Kant at the significant turning point for modern man, of a process which can be described as one of the continuous anthropologizing of the idea of God. Of course for Plato, the human soul was already distinguished by being particularly close to divinity. . . . But for Plato the soul was still embedded in the world of nature, and rooted, together with this world, in a divine origin. The philosophical theology of the modern age, on the other hand, has been guided by the apprehension that there is no assured way leading from nature to God, and that therefore the whole burden of proof of the truth of faith in God falls upon the understanding of man, upon anthropology.[34]

The turning point to which Pannenberg refers is the development of the principle in early modern science that bodies in rest or in motion persist in that rest or motion without any particular cause, thus eliminating any need for an explanatory "first cause" or "first impulse"—a development prepared by William of Ockham. "If continuance in being and in movement had become something that could be taken for granted, then there was no longer any place for God in an account of nature."[35] Modern science seemed to make nature's relationship to God ambiguous at best, and the Platonic links among nature, soul, and God became impossible to maintain. If a way to the knowledge of God is to be found anywhere today, Pannenberg argues, it can be only within human experience itself. And even this search is made more difficult by the effects of the rise of atheism during the nineteenth century. In a way similar to the challenges posed by modern science, atheism challenges theology's assertion of the necessary connection of the human person to God. "If it cannot be shown that the issues with which religion is concerned, the elevation of man above the finite content of human experience to the idea of an infinite reality which sustains everything finite, including man himself, are an essential [element] of man's being . . . then every other viewpoint with which one may concern oneself in this field is an empty intellectual game, and what is said about God loses every claim to

34. Pannenberg, "Anthropology and the Question of God," 82.
35. Ibid., 83. See also *Systematic Theology*, 1:86–88.

intellectual veracity."[36] Even though "no anthropological argument can prove God's existence in the strict sense," theology is obliged to demonstrate, as far as it is able, "that we are referred to an unfathomable reality that transcends us and the world, so that the God of religious tradition is given a secure place in the reality of human self-experience."[37] This is precisely the task of natural theology: not rational demonstration apart from faith, but the clarification of the presuppositions of faith in God, the portrayal of the human encounter with divine revelation as a real possibility for human experience to act as a clearing for the appearance of revelation and thus provide an opportunity for the free assent of faith.

The cosmological-anthropological grid is a useful tool for evaluating the presuppositions of the admittedly selective group of God-arguments that we will discuss here. What is less useful is the division of the types into periods of dominance before and after modernity or Kant; the contemporary evidence refutes it. Overtly cosmological arguments are still in use (as we will see) and still prove useful for explicating how a person, within the contingencies of the world and of everyday life, remains open to the presence of God precisely by means of one's ordinary experience rather than in spite of it.[38]

Here we will discuss five God-arguments. The first two are classics within the Christian tradition: Anselm's so-called "ontological argument" and Thomas Aquinas' cosmological arguments (the "five ways"). They are the touchstones for Christian natural theology, and no subsequent argument escapes their influence, either positive or negative. The latter three are contemporary: Hans Küng's influential argument based on "fundamental trust"; a post-metaphysical argument (with variations by Jean-Luc Marion and John Dominic Crossan) that tries to come to terms with the critique of ontotheology; and

36. "Anthropology and the Question of God," 88–89.
37. *Systematic Theology*, 1:93.
38. Even Pannenberg has moved away from a strict periodization. In his later *Systematic Theology* (1:93–94) he says that even though cosmological arguments have an anthropological basis, "there can be no strict [anthropological] proof because the existence of God would have to be proved in relation not only to us but above all to the reality of the world. This is why cosmological proofs remain important and are still of interest today."

Walter Kasper's argument based on the human desire for freedom and for universal meaning. Each of these three has been chosen specifically because it explicitly confronts head-on the continued influence of the nineteenth-century hermeneutics of suspicion in our immediate historical context, and each seeks to provide a way to speak plausibly of God after Nietzsche.

In fact, this "applicative" move is our major concern throughout. Our goal is not merely to analyze five inherently interesting attempts to do natural theology but also to answer the question of whether natural theology is possible at all after the hermeneutics of suspicion. The classic arguments of Anselm and Aquinas are steeped in metaphysics—can they be retrieved for our contemporary situation after Nietzsche has proclaimed the end of metaphysical truth-claims and the death of God? Do our three contemporary examples truly confront the implications of the hermeneutics of suspicion and nevertheless successfully assert "that the concept of God is an essential part of a proper human self-understanding"?[39] We will evaluate all five arguments, determine whether they offer any retrievable elements which survive the suspicious critique of religion and metaphysics, and attempt to support the claim made at the outset of this chapter that Christian natural theology can serve as a prelude to the Christian revelational theology of God.

2.1. Anselm of Canterbury and the Ontological Argument

We are already familiar with Anselm's *Proslogion* (written c. 1078–79) from our opening chapter. There we adopted his method of "faith seeking understanding" in order to orient our own questions about God and situate them as faith-guided questions within the journey of the believer who is suspended between absolute ignorance and absolute knowledge of God.[40] The *Proslogion* was a sequel to the

---

39. Pannenberg, *Systematic Theology* 1:93.

40. *Proslogion*, in *The Prayers and Meditations of Saint Anselm*, trans. Benedicta Ward (Harmondsworth/New York: Penguin, 1973), 238–67; references in the text are taken from this edition (Anselm's chapter numbers followed by page number of the translation). Another translation (by M. J. Charlesworth) is in *Anselm of Canterbury: The Major Works*, ed. Brian Davies and G. R. Evans, Oxford World's

Monologion (c. 1076), a meditation on the "the essence of the divine" which Anselm had composed at the behest of his fellow monks at the Abbey of Bec in central Normandy.[41] The earlier work, he tells us in the *Proslogion's* preface (*proemium*), was written for those who had wanted "an example of meditation on the meaning of faith . . . by silent reasoning in [one's] own mind." But eventually he grew dissatisfied with it because it seemed to be merely "a connected chain of many arguments." What he desired instead was a more elegant solution, "one single argument, needing no other proof than itself, to prove that God really exists." The search for this caused him much anxiety and frustration, until at one point "it began to force itself upon me with increasing urgency, however much I refused and resisted it" and he welcomed its discovery with great joy (*Proslogion* proem., 238).[42]

Anselm has structured his "one single argument" as a four-step dialogue between the believer and the "fool" or unbeliever.[43] In response to the *unbeliever* [1] who, like the *fool* of Psalm 14, "says in his heart, 'There is no God' " (Ps 14:1), the *believer* [2] offers a defini-

---

Classics (Oxford/New York: Oxford University Press, 1998), 82–122. See also G. R. Evans, *Anselm and Talking About God* (Oxford: Oxford University Press, 1978); Evans, *Anselm*, Outstanding Christian Thinkers Series (London: Chapman; Wilton, CT: Morehouse-Barlow, 1989); Klaus Kienzler, *Glauben und Denken bei Anselm von Canterbury* (Freiburg/Br.: Herder, 1981); R. W. Southern, *Saint Anselm: A Portrait in a Landscape* (Cambridge: Cambridge University Press, 1990). The ontological argument has provoked controversy and numerous commentaries; for a partial listing, see Kienzler, *Glauben und Denken*, 220 n.2.

41. *Monologion*, Prologue, trans. Simon Harrison, in *The Major Works*, 5. The monks desired a form of meditation wherein "nothing whatsoever [was] to be argued on the basis of the authority of Scripture, but the constraints of reason concisely to prove, and the clarity of truth clearly to show, in the plain style, with everyday arguments, and down-to-earth dialectic, the conclusions of distinct investigations" (ibid.)

42. Anselm's biographer Eadmer reports that in 1078, "one night during Matins, the grace of God shone in his heart and the matter became clear to his understanding, filling his whole heart with immense joy and jubilation" (*Vita Anselmi* I, quoted by Southern, 128).

43. The term "the ontological argument" was first used by Kant (see n. 33). Anselm presents the argument complete in chapter 2. Chapters 3 and 4 are further explications of the last two steps.

tion of God as "that being (*aliquid*) than which nothing greater can be thought" (*Proslogion* 2, 244), thus bringing the image of God before human thought.[44] Having heard the definition, the *fool* [3] understands it—that is, he has formed a concept of "the greatest being" and thus has given it intra-mental existence. He still, however, denies that any such being exists outside the mind. In an aside Anselm reminds us there are two levels of existence, the ideal (intra-mental) and the real (extra-mental): "it is one thing to have something in the understanding, but quite another to understand that it actually exists" (*Proslogion* 2, 244).

This is the precise point which the *believer* uses in the final step [4] to clinch the argument and show that the fool's persisting unbelief is a logically impossible position. The "being than which nothing greater can be thought" must have extra-mental as well as intra-mental existence, since to be "the greatest being" means that no perfection is lacking. "For if it exists only in the understanding, it is possible to think of it existing also in reality, and that is greater" (*Proslogion* 2, 245). It would be contradictory for the fool to claim that "the being than which nothing greater can be thought" exists only in the mind and not in extra-mental reality. In making this particular assertion the fool would *claim* to have in mind the "greatest being," but a closer inspection would reveal it to be not the "greatest" at all—one could continue on and conceive a being still greater than this, one which is actually exists extra-mentally. "For it is possible to think of something existing which it is not possible to think of as not existing, and that is greater than something that can be thought not to exist" (*Proslogion* 3, 245). But once one has truly conceived God as the "being than which nothing greater can be thought"—that is, once one has performed the third step and truly understood the definition—the inevitable conclusion is that "there can be no doubt at all that something than which a greater cannot be thought exists both in the understanding and in reality" (*Proslogion* 2, 245) and that "he [God] is of such a kind of existence that he cannot be thought not to exist" (*Proslogion* 4, 246).

44. "Aliquid quo maius nihil cogitari possit." *Aliquid* is translated as "that thing" by Ward, "something" by Charlesworth (*The Major Works*, 87). I have modified the translation slightly.

Any analysis of Anselm's brilliant argument must acknowledge that its definition of God has an antecedent in Augustine's work (some of which was available at Bec), although it appears there without the logical precision that Anselm adds.[45] In *De doctrina christiana* Augustine says that "when the one God of gods is thought of . . . he is thought of in such a way that the thought seeks to attain something than which there is nothing better or more sublime."[46] And in a more important way the heritage of Augustine's theology and its Platonic presuppositions act as the broader background for Anselm's reflections. One important presupposition is that "reality" is "primarily a property or attribute of that which is most highly abstract and spiritual and only secondarily attaching to the concrete and particular exemplifications of it which we should now be inclined to call 'real'."[47] Another posits the necessary relationship of thinking with being: thought is inconceivable except as a participation in being and as an interpretation of being. Between idea and reality an ontological connection is always assumed, even if not completely articulated. In the *Proslogion* Anselm intensifies this principle: the ontological connection between the *idea* of the "being than which nothing greater can be thought" and the *reality of God* to which it refers is a truth which is disclosed to us by the presence of God within the human person who is created in the image of God: "I confess, Lord . . . that you have made me in your image, so that I can remember you, think of you, and love you" (*Proslogion* 1, 243). By its sheer created status human reason has already been informed by revelation; its autonomy is theonomous. The fulfillment of our desire to know God will not be the result of our own efforts, but of our efforts illuminated by the presence of God "who gives understanding to faith" (*Proslogion* 2, 244). Our awareness of the conceptual horizon within which Anselm worked helps us to avoid misunderstanding his argument, either by

45. See Southern, *Saint Anselm*, 128–29. Southern notes that Seneca's *Quaestiones naturales* (a copy of which was also available in the library at Bec) contains a formulation which is closer to Anselm's wording than is Augustine's, although it is not known whether Anselm consulted it.

46. *On Christian Doctrine*, book I, 7, trans. D. W. Robertson, Jr., The Library of Liberal Arts (Indianapolis: Bobbs-Merrill, 1958), 11.

47. Evans, *Anselm*, 52.

seeing it as a philosophical trick or by dismissing it as an empty speculative attempt to bestow objective reality upon the "mere idea" of an absolutely necessary and supreme being.[48]

By "saying in his heart" that there is no God, the fool denies that the word "God" has any real referent. The believer's reply is carefully crafted. The definition of God as "the being than which nothing greater can be thought" is designed to be as general as possible so as to conceptually grasp the broadest common denominator of all experience of divinity, without demanding immediate assent. The fool, by understanding the idea of "the being than which nothing greater can be thought," admits that the existence of God is at least possible. In step four Anselm discloses the idea's full implications. To understand the meaning of "the being than which nothing greater can be thought" is to have in mind the idea of "the greatest being," the all-perfect being. Since "all-perfect" means that no perfection is missing, the greatest being necessarily implies real (i.e., extra-mental) existence. In other words, if we were to present the résumé or list of the perfections of the greatest being, the space for "real existence" would have to be filled. If that space were empty, then this in fact would not be the résumé of the greatest being, but rather of the being one step removed, the "greatest-being-minus-one." This is the contradiction in which the fool is involved: if one claims to have in mind the idea of "the being than which nothing greater can be thought" and yet at the same time denies that this idea has an extra-mental referent, then the believer in turn can rightly insist that the fool does not have in mind the greatest being at all, but rather the greatest-being-minus-one. The fool has not truly extended his mind to its ultimate limit, as he claimed, but rather has stopped one step short. "For if it exists only in the understanding, it is possible to think of it existing also in reality, and that is greater" (*Proslogion* 2, 245). In other words, the being who is greater is indeed the one who has all the perfections of the greatest-being-minus-one, as well as extra-mental existence—this is the absolutely unique "being than which nothing greater can be thought." All of the perfections are accounted for, including that of real, extra-mental existence.

48. The latter is Kant's criticism. See *Critique of Pure Reason*, 500–07 (A 592–602/B 620–30).

This point is the basis for Anselm's answer to his contemporary critic Gaunilo of Marmoutiers, whose book "on behalf of the fool" (*Liber pro insipiente*) claimed that Anselm's argument was invalid because it had made an illogical move from the ideal to the real.[49] Gaunilo proposed as a counter-example the idea of a "Lost Island" which is "more excellent than all other lands" but whose extra-mental existence is far from certain.[50] Anselm replied that the idea of "the most excellent island" is unlike the idea of the greatest being. The latter is absolutely unique because the necessity of its extra-mental reality is inherent in the idea itself; "the being than which nothing greater can be thought" must include all the perfections. An idea of "the most excellent island" is not one which includes all the perfections nor does it contain an inherent necessity. It is rather the idea of a determinate reality (an island) composed of a limited set of "perfections" extrapolated from everyday experience, none of which *has to* have extra-mental existence. It is not contradictory to speak of a "merely possible most excellent island." However, if God is possible—that is, if the idea of an all-perfect and necessary being contains no contradictions—then God *must exist*, since it would be absurd to speak of a "merely possible necessary being."

At a deeper structural level, Anselm presents us with a limit-concept, a unique concept which lies at the limits of rational consciousness yet points to a reality beyond those limits.[51] He indicates this when he confesses, "Lord, you are then not only that than which nothing greater can be thought; you are something greater than it is possible to think about" (*Proslogion* 15, 257). The idea of God brings the reality of God before human consciousness in a way which expresses the dynamic openness of finite human subjectivity to the infinite, with no attempt to define or constrain that infinite to fit a

---

49. *Pro Insipiente (On Behalf of the Fool)*, trans. M. J. Charlesworth, in *The Major Works*, 105–10. Anselm considered this defense of the fool so eloquent and important that he directed that Gaunilo's work, along with his response *Liber apologeticus adversus responentem pro insipiente* (*Reply to Gaunilo*, trans. M. J. Charlesworth, ibid., 111–22) be published along with the *Proslogion* (cf. Davies and Evans in the introduction to *The Major Works*, xiv).

50. *On Behalf of the Fool*, ch. 6, 109.

51. See Kasper, *GJC*, 110–15.

certain determination. Here reason opens out to faith in God. At the very limits of reason ("nothing greater can be thought") the mind encounters the incomprehensibility of God and tries to articulate within these limits the "pre-apprehension of irreducible mystery"[52] already given to human experience. In other words, "we do, at least, understand . . . that we cannot understand this."[53] This limit-concept "points" in two directions and is disclosive in two senses (thus akin to Paul Ricœur's "symbol"). It reveals both the finitude of human rationality (seen in the "nothing greater") and the divine ineffability which lies beyond the grasp of the concept. The *limitation of the concept itself*, the idea of God as it is grasped by the human mind, is *enabling* rather than disabling; it discloses what is beyond limits of the mind, namely the incomprehensible greatest being who lies beyond the finite categories of reason. And yet the certainty of the reality of the divine mystery is available to human thought; the unique reality of God unveils itself at the very point where reason's abilities are exhausted. As Kasper puts it, "in the end thinking necessarily transcends itself, inasmuch as it thinks something which it is essentially incapable of thinking out any further, because the infinite cannot be captured in any finite concept. God, therefore, can be known only through God; he can be known only when he himself allows himself to be known."[54] The ontological argument attempts to articulate this paradox.

Anselm's argument presents in a more formal way the development of his insight into "faith seeking understanding" which we characterized in chapter one as "the desire for God which is awakened by God." The journey into the knowledge of God does not start from a blank slate or a zero-point of absolute ignorance, but with a radical openness to the ultimacy and mystery that we come to learn is God and with a *Vorgriff* (a pre-understanding or pre-apprehension), vague and unarticulated though it may be, which the believer already has of the meaning of the word "God" and the being to whom the word refers. Despite the believer's initial despair over the seemingly

52. Ibid. 114.
53. *Monologion*, ch. 64 (*The Major Works*, 70).
54. *GJC*, 112–13.

unbridgeable distance between God and the believer (because of God's apparent inaccessibility and the believer's own sinfulness), nevertheless the enabling cause of the journey into greater knowledge of God is this *Vorgriff* which undergirds the structure of human experience created in the image of God. "I cannot seek you unless you show me how, and I will never find you unless you show yourself to me. . . . I do desire to understand a little of your truth which my heart already believes and loves" (*Proslogion* 1, 243–44). The ontological argument is the logical articulation of this *Vorgriff*. It is an *anthropological* argument because it examines the structure of human experience in order to discover precisely where within our finitude lies the access-point of faith in God. And of all the aspects of human experience that might be analyzed, Anselm focuses on rationality and its clearly experienced limits. It is, however, a rationality informed by the faith or trust in ultimacy which the *Vorgriff* represents. In the course of pushing rationality to its limits he articulates where our pre-understanding of God is most intensely experienced and where God's own self begins to be more clearly manifest to us—but *only begins* to do so, since a rationality informed by faith is still a human activity with limits, an activity which reaches only to the incomprehensible mystery of God but can go no further. The particular characteristics of that mystery can only be revealed by God's own self and accepted in faith—a rationally-informed faith, a faith seeking understanding. The surprising aspect of this analysis should not be underplayed: Anselm considers the structure of rational human experience to be the best pointer we have of the existence of God.

2.2. Thomas Aquinas and the Cosmological Argument

Nothing reveals the contrast between the positions of Anselm and Thomas Aquinas (c. 1225–1274) better than Thomas' abrupt dismissal of the ontological argument.[55] He disputes Anselm's claim that the

---

55. Our analysis of Thomas Aquinas' approach follows his own outline of the issues as presented in the first part of the *Summa theologiae*, question 2: why Thomas' approach differs from Anselm's; what method should be followed in this different approach; what arguments flow from this method. See *Summa theologiae* Ia, q. 2 (2:4–17 [see n. 9]).

proposition "God exists" is self-evidently true and needs no demon-stration.[56] He rejects, in other words, any argument claiming that the existence of God proves itself once the meaning of the word "God" (as "the being than which nothing greater can be thought") is under-stood. In fact, Thomas' criticism of Anselm's argument is similar to that raised by Gaunilo.

> [First,] it is not known by all, even including those who admit that God exists, that God is that than which a greater cannot be thought. After all, many ancients said that this world itself was God. . . . What is more, granted that everyone should under-stand by the name *God* something than which a greater cannot be thought, it will still not be necessary that there exist in reality something than which a greater cannot be thought. . . . Now, from the fact that that which is indicated by the name *God* is conceived by the mind, it does not follow that God exists save only in the intellect. Hence, that than which a greater cannot be thought will likewise not have to exist save only in the intellect. (*SCG* I, 11 [81–82])

The meaning of "God" is more ambiguous than Anselm is willing to allow (*ST* Ia, q. 2, a. 1, resp. [2:6–7]), due to the limitations of the human intellect. It is "because we are not able to conceive in our minds that which God is, that God exists remains unknown in relation to us" (*SCG* I, 11 [81]) and must be demonstrated rationally.[57] This criticism also stems from Thomas' commitment to a fundamentally Aristotelian theory of knowing: intellectual knowledge is initially dependent upon our sense knowledge of the world, and this latter

56. See *Summa contra Gentiles* book I, chs. 10–11, in *Summa Contra Gentiles: Book One: God*, trans. Anton C. Pegis (Notre Dame: University of Notre Dame Press, 1975), 79–83; further references are given in parentheses in the text (*SCG* I, book, chapter [page(s) in the translation]). The critique appears in shortened form in *ST* Ia, q. 2, art. 1 (2:4–9).

57. See also book 14, where Thomas recommends the method of remotion or negation *(via negationis)* as the most appropriate way of investigating the char-acteristics of God's being. "For, by its immensity, the divine substance surpasses every form that our intellect reaches. Thus we are unable to apprehend it by knowing *what it is*. Yet we are able to have some knowledge of it by knowing *what it is not*" (*SCG* I, 14 [96]).

is eventually made intelligible through the process of abstraction.[58] The presence of the idea of God in the intellect would first have to come through the senses, yet "God transcends all sensible things and the sense itself" (*SCG* I, 12 [85]). This principle renders Anselm's purely intellectual starting point invalid and his anthropological argument suspect.

Is the access to God through human experience thereby cut off? By repudiating the fundamentally Augustinian-Anselmian mode which heretofore had dominated the discussion, Thomas leaves us in a precarious position. But he proposes what he considers to be a more adequate alternative. While God does indeed transcend the senses, "his effects, on which the demonstration proving his existence is based, are nevertheless sensible things" (*SCG* I, 12 [85]). And so our access to God can begin with our experience of the extra-mental world in all of its order and fragility. Starting from these "effects" we can inquire about the ultimate cause of the cosmos, which we can name "God."

This approach depends on the success of isolating the quality or qualities shared between sensible effects and God which might lead us from these finite effects to the infinite divine cause. Thomas describes this shared quality in metaphysical terms: the inner connection between sensible effects and God lies at the most fundamental level of reality, existence itself. He works out the implications of this position in a brilliant synthesis of Neoplatonic "henology" and participation theory with Aristotelianism.[59]

---

58. See the discussion in *ST* Ia, 84, especially arts. 6 and 7 (12: 4–47, esp. 32–43. See also *Quaestiones disputatae de veritate* q. 2, a. 3, 19, "whatever is in our intellect must have previously been in the senses" (*The Disputed Questions on Truth*, trans. Robert W. Mulligan et al., 3 vols. [Chicago: Regnery, 1952–54], 1:68).

59. "Henology," the argument that the "One" (*hen*) is the fundamental organizing principle of reality, is usually associated with the Neoplatonism. See Reiner Schürmann, "Neoplatonic Henology as an Overcoming of Metaphysics," *Research in Phenomenology* 13 (1983): 25–41; Dierdre Carabine, *The Unknown God: Negative Theology in the Platonic Tradition: Plato to Eriugena*, Louvain Theological and Pastoral Monographs, 19 (Louvain: Peeters/Grand Rapids: Eerdmans, 1995), 138–47. For the centrality of the theory of participation in Thomas' thought, see W. Norris Clarke's classic presentation, "The Meaning of Participation in St. Thomas," *Proceedings of the American Catholic Philosophical Association* 26 (1952):

Thomas expresses the relationship between the infinite cause and finite effects in the language of being and participation: the act of existence itself (*esse*) is the "thread" tying them together, the perfection shared by the divine Ground and the effects as contingently grounded.[60] Finite beings do not exist independently; rather, they are contingent upon and thus participate in the act of being itself which Thomas identifies with "the divine essence."

> [B]eing itself (*ipsum esse*) is present in all things: whence others participate in it but it does not participate in anything else. But that-which-is, a being (*id quod est, sive ens*), although this is a most common expression, is nevertheless referring to something concrete and so it participates in *ipsum esse* not as the more common is participated in by the less common, but it participates in *ipsum esse* as the concrete participates in the abstract.[61]

> The divine nature or essence . . . is itself its act of being (*eius esse*), whereas the nature or essence of any created thing is not its act of being but participates in being from another. In God,

147–60. Clarke defines participation as "a theory for rendering intelligible . . . the common possession in many subjects of a given attribute, whether in the logical or the ontological order, by reference to a higher source from which all receive or participate in some way the perfection they possess in common" (150). He emphasizes both the Neoplatonic roots of Thomas' doctrine and his realistic tempering of the Neoplatonic insight by means of its "transposition" into the framework of Aristotle's potency-and-act analysis (154–55). See also L.-B. Geiger, *La participation dans la philosophie de S. Thomas d'Aquin*, Bibliothèque thomiste XXIII, 2d ed. (Paris: J. Vrin, 1953). Regarding the influence on the Neoplatonism on the *Summa theologiae*, especially its overall structural plan of *exitus* (the procession of creatures from God) and *reditus* (the movement of creatures back to God), see Marie-Dominique Chenu, *Toward Understanding Saint Thomas*, trans. A.-M. Landry and D. Hughes (Chicago: Regnery, 1964 [French orig., 1950]) and Paul Rorem, *Pseudo-Dionysius: A Commentary on the Texts and an Introduction to Their Influence* (New York: Oxford University Press, 1993), 169–74.

60. Clarke, "The Meaning of Participation," 152.

61. *In Boethii de hebdomadibus* 1, 2 (*An Aquinas Reader*, trans. and ed. Mary T. Clark, 2d ed. [Bronx: Fordham University Press, 1988], 52, translation modified). For the Latin text, see *S. Thomae Aquinatis Opera omnia ut sunt in Indice Thomistico*, ed. Roberto Busa, S.J. (Stuttgart-Bad Cannstatt: Frommann-Holzboog, 1980), 4:540, col. 1.

> accordingly, the act of being is pure, because God is his own
> subsistent act of being (*ipse Deus est suum esse subsistens*); but in
> the creature the act of being is received or participated.[62]

This metaphysics rests on Thomas' fine-tuning of Neoplatonic participation theory by means of his insight into Aristotelian "potency"
as the *limiter* of actuality. Neoplatonism, especially as represented by
Plotinus (c. 205–270), had argued that the unity of reality was due to
all things' likeness to and participation in the One or the Good, the
divine first principle, from which all things receive their being and to
which all things return.[63] For Thomas these insights into participation
and the unifying aspect of the first principle were crucial, but as a
Christian he could not accept the inevitable pantheism that resulted
from this view. As a "brake" on the pantheistic implications, he turned
to Aristotle. Aristotle had argued that all living beings, at their metaphysical level, are composed of potency (possibility) and act (actuality, real individual existence); this explains their change and
development, when potentiality is made actual. This combination
reappears in Thomas with the language of essence and existence, but
he takes the metaphysical principle much further than Aristotle. *All
things* are composed of essence (potency, which limits the act of existing to being *this particular individual being*) and existence (actuality, the
act of "to-be" [*esse*] whereby the possibilities inherent in essence
become *real*); the two are joined in a mutually-implicating relationship.
Thus finite beings have *esse*/existence, but have it in a limited, dependent, *participative* way, according to the possibilities granted them by
their essence. This Platonism-cum-Aristotelianism allows Thomas to
hold on to the insight that *esse* is the true meta-category, the most
adequate philosophical way to articulate the nature of reality without
falling into the pantheism which is obviously ruled out by his Christian "realism" (which asserts the connection between creatures and
Creator as well as the obvious finitude of creatures).

By means of this schema Thomas is able to articulate and clarify the
simultaneously-present dual nature of the reality of creatures: they

---

62. *De veritate*, q. 21, a. 5 (*Disputed Questions on Truth*, 3:26). For the Latin text,
see *Opera omnia*, 3:125, col. 3.

63. On Plotinus' doctrine of God, see Carabine, *The Unknown God*, 103–53.

participate in the divine life, but do so in a dependent, finite way.[64] God and creatures share *esse*, not in the univocal sense of the Neoplatonists, but analogically: God *is* being, creatures *have* being; God is subsistent being itself, the being of creatures is derived from God and is limited by their essence. Creatures thus display both autonomy and theonomy—the very message of the Genesis creation stories, here transposed into metaphysical categories.[65] Creatures are the fore-grounded participative effects of the divine cause and thus can lead us back to the unifying Ground (the "pure act of being") without being identical with that Ground. This analogically "adjusted" theory of participation is at the heart of Thomas' arguments for God's existence. By rendering this divine Ground rationally plausible, such arguments thus can serve as preambles to faith (*ST* Ia, q. 2, a. 2, ad 1 [2:10–11]).

This metaphysical theory of reality leads to an important methodological point. Thomas argues for the proper use of reason to demonstrate God's existence in reply to objections that the existence of "the unseen God" lies beyond rational demonstration and definition, and that since "God and his effects are incommensurable . . . effects incommensurate with their cause cannot make [that cause] evident" (*ST* Ia, q. 2, a. 2[2:8–9]). The key here is "proper use." Demonstrating the cause-and-effect connection in the mode which proceeds from the evident cause to the effect (*per causam et dicitur propter quid*) will certainly not work when it comes to God, precisely because what-it-is-to-be-God (that is, God's nature *in se*) is not self-evident; indeed, God-as-cause is the very point to be proven. But there is another mode of demonstration that is useful in the present case, one which argues from evident effect to non-evident cause (*per effectum et dicitur demonstratio quia*).

> Now any effect of a cause demonstrates that the cause exists, in cases where the effect is better known to us, since effects are

---

64. Cf. *ST* Ia, q. 4, a. 3, ad 3 (2:58–59): "Creatures are said to resemble God, not by sharing a form of the same specific or generic type, but only analogically *(secundum analogiam tantum)*, inasmuch as God exists by nature, and other things partake [of] existence *(Deus est ens per essentiam et alia per participationem)*.

65. For the notions of autonomy and theonomy in the biblical creation stories and in Aquinas, see Walter Kasper, *Theology and Church*, trans. Margaret Kohl (New York: Crossroad, 1989), 34–38.

dependent upon causes, and can only occur if the causes already
exist. From effects evident to us, therefore, we can demonstrate
what in itself is not evident to us, namely, that God exists (*ST* Ia,
q. 2, a. 2, resp. [2:10–11]).

There are, then, some truths about God that we can know from our
limited perspective (*quoad nos*) by the proper use of human reasoning
(here Thomas echoes Paul's Letter to the Romans, 1:19–20). These truths
are not faith nor do they replace faith, but rather are authentic preambles to faith, reasonable pointers to God. "For faith presupposes natural
knowledge, just as grace does nature and all perfections that which
they perfect" (*ST* Ia, q. 2, a. 2, ad 1 [ibid.]). We must remember, though,
that effects give us only the limited knowledge *that* God exists, and
cannot give us comprehensive knowledge as to *who* God is (*ST* Ia, q.
2, a. 2, ad 3 [ibid.]). Thus Thomas acknowledges the finitude of reason
and the limitations of the "clues" available to human experience, while
at the same time arguing that knowledge of God is an authentic possibility within human experience if reason is employed correctly.

The famous "five ways in which one can prove that there is a God"
(*ST* Ia, q. 2, a. 3, resp. [2:12–17]) are illustrations of this method. While
each of the ways has a different focus (motion, causation, contingency,
degrees of perfection/being, purposeful action), they all have in
common a four-step procedure:[66]

(1) beginning with an observation of ordinary experience,
we note things that are changing, dependent, temporally
limited and contingent, evaluated according to a standard, or goal-directed . . .

(2) . . . which leads to the question of what else is implied
which makes sense out of our experience—the necessary
precondition, as it were, for our experience to be this way
. . .

(3) . . . which turns out to be itself unchanging, independent,
eternal and necessary, unlimited and absolute, and not
directed by another . . .

(4) . . . and this we call "God."

66. Thomas Gilby, "Appendix 5: The Five Ways," in *Summa theologiae*, 2:189.

The first way exemplifies this process (*ST* Ia, q. 2, a. 3, resp. [2:14–15]). (1) We observe change (*motus*) in the Aristotelian sense of movement from potency to act: the transition from one condition to another and thus the actualization of inherent possibilities. "To cause change is to bring into being what was previously only able to be and this can be done only by that which already is," that is, some other agent which already possesses that actuality. "Of necessity therefore anything in process of change is being changed by something else"; it cannot give itself what it does not already have in actuality, but needs something else, an outside agent to start the movement from potency to act.[67] (2) Theoretically, the sequence of "outside agents," each moved from potency to act by a previous agent and so on, could be traced backwards into infinity.[68] But Thomas thinks such an infinite sequence is irrational: "Now we must stop somewhere, otherwise there will be no first cause of the change, and, as a result, no subsequent causes." Without an initial cause, there would now be nothing; our experience tells us otherwise. Thus, something else is implied which allows our experience of the chain of ontologically dependent changes to be what it is. (3) What is implied is an "outside agent" to start off the process of movement from potency to act, but which itself is unchanged/unmoved, that is, not dependent on any other "outside agent." Thus this "unmoved mover" or first cause of change stands outside the process of change while influencing what occurs within the process. (4) "And this is what everybody understands by God."

The first way is echoed by the second and third ways as well; indeed, they are all variations on a single type of argument. Where the first focuses on change, the second substitutes causation and the third substitutes contingency. Thomas considered the first way to be "the most obvious" (*ST* Ia, q. 2, a. 3, resp. [2:12–13]). The third way,

67. Thomas' example is fire, actually hot, which sets wood, actually cold but potentially hot, on fire. For his use of examples, see *Summa theologiae*, 2:12, n.b, and "Appendix 3: Existence and Causality," 2:181–85.

68. Thomas is not describing an infinite temporal or historical sequence, but rather "an infinite series in the ontological order of dependence" (Frederick Copleston, *A History of Philosophy, Book One: Volume II, Augustine to Scotus* [Garden City: Image/Doubleday, 1985 (orig. 1950)], 342.), which he will consider to be impossible.

however, is the most fundamental since it argues a claim that cuts across the first three (and arguably all five) ways, namely that all temporal and contingent beings must have a sufficient reason for their existence.[69] In the case of the third way, this is the necessarily existing being "which owes [its being] to no other thing than itself; indeed it itself is the cause that other things must be" (*ST* Ia, q. 2, a. 3, resp. [2:14–15]).

The fourth way (*ST* Ia, q. 2, a. 3, resp. [2:14–17]) is a surprising retrieval of Anselm's "greatest being" within Thomas' cosmological framework—it might even be seen as an ironic *tour de force*. The theory of participation, appearing here in its strongest form, is "rehabilitated" by Thomas in accord with his epistemological commitments and his metaphysics of the analogy of being. Its opening move departs somewhat from the pattern of the first three ways. (1) In our everyday experience we make comparative judgments about things. These evaluations seek to determine how things are more or less approximate to an absolute standard which embodies to the fullest degree the quality which is being compared (e.g., goodness, beauty, truth). The being we judge to be "more" or "less" in comparison to a "best" already participates in the quality represented by that "best." (2) But this implies that there indeed exists that standard of perfection which is covertly known by us. This "best," this standard of perfection of one kind (goodness, beauty, or truth) itself must participate in (3) the ultimate cause of all perfection, which itself must be perfect—in short, the *supreme* being which is the fullness of perfection and which does not get its perfection from another but is self-existing, the Highest Being or Good (4) whom we call "God."

The fifth and final way (*ST* Ia, q. 2, a. 3, resp. [2:16–17]) presents the most unique variation on the four-stage pattern. (1) The starting point is our experience of "the orderedness of actions to an end," a plan or pattern within reality which guides all things, even things without intelligence, to their proper *telos* or fulfillment. (2) Such a teleological arrangement cannot proceed purely by chance, but connotes a rational intentionality (3) which in turn presupposes an over-

---

69. Cf. Copleston, *A History of Philosophy, Book One: Volume II*, 346.

all intelligent being which gives order and purpose to everything, (4) "and this we call 'God'."

If we take an overall view of the five ways, it is clear how they perform the function of natural theology as we described it earlier in this chapter, namely the rational search for the natural access-point of faith. They can be legitimately divided into two categories: the first three proceed by way of *negation* (God does not have the limitations that we experience either in ourselves or in the world), the last two by way of *analogy* (God has perfections with which creatures are acquainted, but has them without limitations, to the highest degree). As variations on a single basic cosmological orientation, they are responses to what Thomas considers to be the realistic assessment of our historically-situated standpoint, the finite condition of human reason and faith. In sum, our experience is not explainable on its own terms but opens out to the ultimate transcendental ground called "God" who is the necessary condition for the very possibility of experience. The transcendence which we come to know through a close analysis of the "stuff" of our experience is certain and has intelligible characteristics. But we can never on our own, through the sheer force of human rationality, penetrate to God's essence in order to know *what or who* God is in God's own self (*in se*). Our knowledge is always only an indirect knowledge of God "from our perspective" (*quoad nos*), a knowledge *that* God exists and *how* God is toward us. Thomas believes that this respect for the limits of human rationality is preferable to Anselm's rational introspection, precisely because it is more true to our experience.

And yet for all the distance which Thomas seeks to put between himself and Anselm, his cosmological arguments share a structural similarity with the ontological argument in that they, too, deal with a limit-concept, here introduced by the idea of contingency.[70] The third way puts it most bluntly: why is there something rather than nothing? Finite beings do not have to be; their time in being is spent "suspended over the abyss of non-being . . . inclined toward nothingness and

---

70. Kasper, *GJC*, 102–03. See also Bernhard Welte, *Religionsphilosophie*, 5th ed., ed. Bernhard Casper and Klaus Kienzler (Frankfurt am Main: Knecht, 1997), 142–51.

controlled through and through by nothingness."[71] But despite their precarious status, beings exhibit a wondrous resiliency: they persist and resist the tendency toward nothingness. Thomas attributes their persistence to their participation in God who is unconditioned subsistent being itself (*ipse esse subsistens*) and the groundless Ground. There is something of "the unconditioned in the conditioned" which becomes apparent when we meditate on the limited status of all reality, conditioned as it is by nothingness, and wonder at its power to resist nothingness. What is revealed through our experience of such absolute limitation is the answer to the question: it is by virtue of the ultimate, groundless Ground that there is anything at all. The idea of the groundless Ground is a limit-concept which points in two directions: back to an awareness of our limitations, yet forward to a reality beyond our conceptual categories. This limit-concept brings about a conversion of thought where we "put aside our explanatory thinking and trust ourselves to the absolutely Groundless. . . . Even in its incomprehensibility, the knowledge of God is authenticated by the fact that it makes the world and its order intelligible and thus proves its authenticity by means of the phenomena of reality."[72] This conceptual limit, which in reality is no closure at all but rather a precise point of human openness to transcendence, describes the clearing where a dialogue between gratuitous divine revelation and the human response in faith may take place.

2.3. Hans Küng and the Argument from Fundamental Trust

Among contemporary approaches we have chosen, Hans Küng's is the one most reminiscent of the classical Christian natural theology tradition.[73] But this does not render his constructive argument any less contemporary. He replies directly to the critique of religion made by the "masters of suspicion" and seeks to counteract the broader post-Enlightenment attempt to argue religion away as superfluous.

71. Kasper, *GJC*, 102.
72. Ibid., 103.
73. Hans Küng, *Does God Exist? An Answer for Today*, trans. Edward Quinn (Garden City: Doubleday, 1980 [German orig. 1978]), 552–83. Subsequent page references in the text (in parentheses) are to this edition.

It is clear that here we no longer comfortably inhabit the thought-world of the medievals.

Küng, in his diagnosis of the contemporary context for the discussion about God, notes that while the nineteenth-century critique of religion had promised the eventual withering away or even destruction of religion, clearly this has not happened. Rather, complex affirmations of the value of religion have developed, new signs of openness to religion and religious experience which by no means unambiguously support traditional religious institutions but which nevertheless indicate a growing appreciation of the function of religion in human life. For example, there has developed a more positive relationship between science and religion, despite the mistrust that has often existed between them. From the side of the natural and social sciences there has been an increased openness to religion, particularly among physicists and those who have argued for the necessity of a framework of ethical responsibility to guide scientific and technical activity.[74] There also has been the growth of what Küng terms "secular quasi-religiousness," the tendency for secular groups or movements to resemble and take on the functions of religious groups, a sign of "the recognition of the permanence of man's religious needs, needs of course that might be satisfied in a 'secular' way" (555).

Most importantly, there is the widespread recovery of a sense of transcendence within contemporary culture. Sociologists have shown that faith in the general order of existence plays a crucial constitutive role in the development of all aspects of human consciousness. Küng calls attention to Peter Berger's notion that various "signals of transcendence" are disclosed within everyday life, signs of a reality which transcends the immanent empirical world and to which human beings are open by nature. One crucial signal is a "faith in order," a "fundamental trust" in reality that is apparent in as ordinary a scene as a mother comforting her frightened child and assuring the child that everything is all right. "Man's propensity for order is grounded

---

74. Küng's optimistic (and almost prophetic) assessment has been affirmed by a flood of work over the past few decades seeking to develop a positive relationship between science and religion.

in a faith or trust that, ultimately, reality is 'in order,' 'all right,' 'as it should be.' Needless to say, there is no empirical method by which this faith can be tested. To assert it is itself an act of faith."[75]

From these and similar instances of the desire for religious experience or something close to it, Küng discerns a common recognition, by believers and non-believers alike, that our world is "not in order." This widespread discomfort keeps alive a common yearning for some value system or set of norms by which all is put back into order, for the ultimate ground of meaning which makes sense out of the whole of reality—a common yearning for something which approximates or is identical to religion. "Genuine religion . . . is found only where this ground of meaning, this absolutely final concern, that with which I am unconditionally involved, is not something merely of this world (secular) but something that is in the broadest sense 'divine' ('absolute', 'holy')" (561). Behind this diagnosis, however, lurks a crucial and unavoidable question: does this common yearning for the ultimate reality point us toward an *actually existing* ultimate, absolute reality? Theology cannot avoid the fact that "signals of transcendence" can be ambiguous and arise from some other impulse. Thus the question "does God exist?" is a genuine question, demanding "an absolutely unequivocal answer" (561).

Küng's answer has two parts. First he considers how the anxieties of existence and the desires for meaning might be fulfilled if God were assumed to exist—a hypothesis proposed as a response to Fyodor Dostoevsky's chilling statement "if there is no God, everything is permitted" and a positive counterproposal which is "more difficult" to develop (562).

He develops this hypothesis first by considering reality as a whole. In the face of "the *thoroughgoing uncertainty of reality* in the ontic, noetic, and ethical senses" (565), human beings exhibit a fundamental trust in the cohesion of reality and in its ultimate meaningfulness. Reality is precarious precisely because of its contingency; it appears groundless, evolving without any aim, "its unity repeatedly threat-

---

75. Peter L. Berger, *A Rumor of Angels: Modern Society and the Rediscovery of the Supernatural* (Garden City, NY: Doubleday, 1969), 71–72, cited by Küng, *Does God Exist?*, 557.

ened by disunion, its meaningfulness by meaninglessness, its value by worthlessness" (567). Despite this state of affairs, human beings expect reality to be coherent, and search for the universal meaning which will "make sense" out of everything. In our experience of reality, there is something which engenders our trust, but our expectations alone do not alter the precarious character of reality. "Trust in uncertain reality does not eliminate its radical uncertainty. Reality, which can justify a fundamental trust, appears itself to be mysteriously *unjustified*. . . . Reality is there as a fact, but enigmatically, utterly lacking in any manifest ground, support, or purpose" (565). If reality is truly this precarious, what is our trust ultimately based upon? "What, then, is the *condition of the possibility of this uncertain reality*" (565) and of our trust in its cohesion and persistence?

If God exists, then we would have a reason why reality, despite its radical uncertainty, holds together, why it supports out trust: because God would be the ground, support, and primal goal of reality. "If God exists, then reality suspended between being and nonbeing is not ultimately under suspicion of being a void. Why? Because God is then the being itself of all reality" (566). If this hypothesis is true, then our fundamental trust in reality would be supported not by reality itself but rather by reality's ultimate ground, God. We would also have a reason why reality itself *is* radically uncertain: "Because uncertain reality is itself *not God*. Because the self, society, the world, cannot be identified with their primal ground, primal support and primal goal . . . with being itself" (567).

If we were to formulate the hypothesis from the point of view of individual human existence, the formulations would be similar. Why is it that, despite "the riddle of my persistently uncertain human existence"—despite the menacing factors of emptiness, meaninglessness, sin, and death—we have a fundamental trust in the coherence and meaningfulness of our own existence? Again, if God exists, we would have an answer: because God would be "the primal source . . . ultimate meaning . . . all-embracing hope of my life" (567). We would, too, have a reason why human existence itself appears so precarious: "because man is *not God*. Because my human self can *not* be identified with its primal source, primal meaning, primal value, with being itself" (568).

Does the hypothesis about God, from the point of view of either reality as a whole or individual human existence, indeed point to the reality of God? In the second part of his argument, Küng considers the alternatives.

The complete denial of God is possible. Indeed, "atheism cannot be eliminated rationally. It is irrefutable" (568). The assertion of God's unreality presupposes an emphasis on reality's radical uncertainty. It relies on what the atheist would interpret as empirical or "realistic" evidence which definitively points away from any primal ground or support or goal. The atheist alternative is a choice, a *personal decision* based on a reasonable evaluation of the evidence of experience, an evaluation of reality as a whole which accounts for the evidence in a certain way. That evaluation in turn is guided by a presupposition, a judgment whose truth has been assumed in advance, namely, that reality's radical uncertainty is the fully adequate framework for understanding the conflicting evidence that reality provides. The ultimate decision, then, is that reality gives no indication whatsoever of any covert divine support; there is no God. "Neither a strict proof or an indication of God can prevail against such an assertion. For this negative statement rests on a *decision*, a decision that is connected with the fundamental decision for reality as a whole" (569).

On the other hand, the affirmation of God is just as possible and cannot be rationally refuted. The theist's assertion of God's reality is based on the experience of reality as well, but one which emphasizes fundamental trust and thus a confidence in reality's fundamental coherence. The theist alternative, too, is a *personal decision* based on a reasonable evaluation of the evidence of experience, an evaluation of reality as a whole which accounts for the evidence in a certain way. And that evaluation in turn is guided by a presupposition, a judgment whose truth has been assumed in advance, namely, the consistency and meaningfulness of reality which are also evident. The assertion of God's existence is grounded in a confidence in reality as a whole and points to the condition which renders this confidence and meaningfulness possible, namely the primal ground, support, or goal of reality. "Atheism . . . cannot prevail against such confidence imposed on us in the light of reality itself. The affirmation of God also rests, in the last resort, on a *decision*, which, again, is connected with the fundamental decision for reality as a whole. This, too, is rationally irrefutable" (596).

Which alternative is true? Is this a stalemate? After all, each appears to explain reality with equal cogency. Each represents as well a personal decision to interpret ambiguous reality in a particular direction, a decision grounded upon an assumption which is not strictly provable.

> Since reality and its primal ground, primal support and primal goal are not imposed on us with conclusive evidence, there remains scope for man's freedom. Man must decide without intellectual constraint but also without rational proof. Both atheism and belief in God are therefore ventures, they are also risks. The critique of the proofs of God itself shows that belief in God has the character of a decision, and—conversely—a decision for God has the character of belief. (570)

What helps break any apparent stalemate is the correct understanding of the roles played by faith and reason in these decisions. Küng emphasizes that a reasonable trust or belief, rather than absolute rational certainty, is involved in both steps of each argument. The evaluation of the status of reality (first step) provides a basis for the decision for either belief or unbelief in God (second step). Belief in God is rooted in "a trusting commitment to an ultimate ground, support, and meaning of reality" (570), a trust which is reasonable without being exclusively rational. Unbelief, on the other hand, is the refusal of trust in an ultimate ground and is instead a belief that uncertainty and contingency together form the sole overarching truth. Each position interprets the evidence of reality as a whole (and of one's individual life as well) from a critical rational perspective. But this rational interpretation itself depends on a prior act of trust in an overarching presupposition which itself escapes the certainty of rational proof.

This resolution of the question of reality's fundamental character, however, is only the first step. The judgment regarding the ultimate meaning and telos of the evidence of reality is the final step and results from the a person's free decision to trust in the guiding presupposition and to make sense of reality with the hypothesis which is the most adequate to the evidence. In other words, this final step goes beyond the decision "for or against reality as such" to the deeper and unavoidable decision concerning the reality of God (570). And a decision regarding God is ultimately a risk based on the interpreted evidence of reality, taken, in the end, without absolute certainty or the Cartesian clarity that would have marked an older natural theology.

But this does not mean that atheism and theism offer equally valid construals of reality. Although one cannot rationally refute a "personal decision" to construe the evidence of reality as either leading toward or away from God, one can judge each decision's relative adequacy to the evidence and evaluate its existential consequences—the choice does matter. Thus, atheism's denial of God can be judged irrational. "Denial of God implies an *ultimately unjustified* fundamental trust in reality. Atheism cannot suggest any condition for the possibility of uncertain reality. If someone denies God, he does not know why he ultimately trusts in reality" (571). The atheist, along with everyone else, acknowledges the day-to-day "workings" of reality with a fundamental trust and experiences reality's order and positivity amidst its uncertainty. But the atheist either will not or cannot account for these factors, leading to an unjustified assent to reality and "a freewheeling, nowhere-anchored and therefore paradoxical fundamental trust. . . . For this reason [atheism] lacks not perhaps all rationality but certain a radical rationality . . ." (571). It can thus give no satisfactory answers to the perennial questions regarding the truth of our knowledge, the efficacy of our actions, and the object of our hope.[76] The ultimate price of the denial of God is to leave oneself open to the experience of the "hollowness of reality" (571) and the danger of existential meaninglessness and despair.

Theism, on the other hand, can be judged as rationally justified. "Affirmation of God implies an *ultimately justified* fundamental trust in reality. A radical fundamental trust, belief in God can suggest the

---

76. Echoing throughout Küng's chapter are Kant's famous three questions from the *Critique of Pure Reason:* "All the interests of my reason, speculative as well as practical, combine in the three following questions: 1. What can I know? 2. What ought I to do? 3. What may I hope?" (635 [A 804–05/B 832–33]). For Küng's citation, see pp. 563–64.

condition of the possibility of uncertain reality. If someone affirms reality, he knows why he can trust reality" (572). By means of the affirmation of God as primal ground, support, or goal, the theist can indicate where one's trust in reality is ultimately anchored. One's fundamental trust, while directed to reality, is not grounded in uncertain reality itself but rather in the condition which makes reality possible. And the theist can show why this decision in favor of God's existence is rationally justified, having been led in that direction by the evidence provided by reality which supports one's fundamental trust. While taking seriously reality's multiple and even contradictory aspects (negative and positive, ordered yet precarious, "hollow" yet meaningful [567]), the theist's affirmation of God as the primal ground is a construal of reality which is at once more reasonable, more encompassing, even more "realistic" than the atheist's denial of God.

Küng's strong advocacy of theism in the face of the hermeneutics of suspicion falls within our definition of natural theology (the search for the natural access-point of faith), despite the fact that he explicitly denies that he is doing natural theology, since for him the term refers to any reflection on God which presupposes a radical discontinuity between the natural and the supernatural (as in Neo-Scholastic natural theology) or which assumes "an autonomous reason capable of demonstrating a foundation of faith but having nothing to do with faith itself" (577). But what Küng in fact rejects is what we rejected as well at the outset of this chapter: the truncated, modern rationalist version of natural theology.[77] He argues instead for a belief in God that is both rationally justified and yet also dependent upon God's revelatory initiative. This is a strongly Catholic position which mirrors the teachings of both Vatican I and Vatican II regarding the validity and the limitations of the natural knowledge of God as well as the human need for divinely-given faith. For Küng, both reality as a whole and the course of an individual human life mediate the presence of God as primal ground, support, or goal. Rationality is active throughout the process of interpreting uncertain reality, particularly as human

77. See sec. 1 of the present chapter. For Küng's detailed analysis of natural theology, see *Does God Exist?*, 509–28, 577–78.

beings probe for reality's authentic depths. Reason cannot prove the existence of God with absolute certainty, since reason is too limited and reality is too enigmatic for that.[78] But the act of rational probing opens the mind to the possibilities of truth beyond the empirical, thereby preparing the way for an act of trust in God as the ground of reality. Within this openness, belief is accomplished at the convergence of two movements, the human decision to trust and God's revelation of God's own presence through reality. "For what cannot be proved *in advance* I experience *in the accomplishment, in the very act of acknowledging what I perceive*" (573). This act of faith in God, supported by reality, confirms both the reasonable nature of our fundamental trust and the validity of our reason itself, while also pointing up the gratuitous character of God's act of mediated self-disclosure. "Belief in God is a *gift*. Reality exists before me. If I do not cut myself off, but open myself entirely to reality as it opens out to me, then I can accept in faith its primary ground, its deepest support, its ultimate goal: God, who *reveals* himself as primal source, primal meaning and primal value" (576).

I opened this section by claiming that Küng offers us an argument that is strongly reminiscent of the classical arguments. This is due to the resolutely metaphysical categories which he uses to characterize the reality of God and the relationship between God and reality. By defining religion as "a particular social realization of a relationship to an absolute ground of meaning" (560–61) and by describing God as the absolute ground, support, and goal of reality and of human existence, Küng places his argument squarely in the ontotheological tradition which we described in the preceding chapter—that is, the tradition which speaks of God as the *archē* of reality or the "highest/deepest" being who grounds all other beings. There are strong echoes of Thomas Aquinas' "five ways" as well, heard in Küng's claim that our knowledge of God is mediated by our experience of the world, in the "foundational" language with which he characterizes God,

---

78. "But also like fundamental trust, trust in God cannot simply be decided on, willed, extorted or produced. I cannot simply create or produce ultimate certainty, security, stability, for myself. God . . . is not an object of immediate experience. . . . It is just because of this that belief in God is seen as a *gift*" (575).

and especially in the way that both the structure and the basic goal of his argument recall the underlying four-stage pattern of Thomas Aquinas' "five ways."[79]

This does not mean, though, that Küng simply replays the classical arguments in a more contemporary idiom. Two major differences that make this obvious. First, in Küng's reading of the contemporary situation, reality is not as easily interpretable in the direction of God's presence as it was for the scholastics. According to Thomas, for example, once one had an insight into being and how participation-in-being formed the backbone of the metaphysical structure of reality, one could trace the "effects" of creation back to their necessary cause without much difficulty. For Küng, however, reality is polyvalent and hence ambiguous, "utterly lacking in any manifest ground, support, or purpose. That is why the question of reality, of being or not-being, of fundamental trust or nihilism, can emerge again at any time" (565). On its surface, our experience can support either belief or unbelief. Only when one reflects more closely on both reality and our situated experience of it do their fundamental structures and presuppositions appear.

The other difference involves the estimation of the power of reason. Although both Anselm and Thomas were clearly aware of the limits of rationality, they were optimistic about reason's ability to demonstrate God's existence with certainty and thereby give support to one's faith. Küng is less optimistic; for him, rationality plays a more ambivalent role. On the one hand, reason at first plays an evaluative role in dealing with the evidence of reality. But it does not and cannot fully determine a person's stance toward God since, as Küng repeatedly emphasizes, this is the result of a personal decision to construe the evidence along the lines of a presupposition whose validity is plausible yet rationally unprovable. Reason therefore contributes to one's decision but is not the sole determinant of the content of that decision. Rational certainty has been scaled back; neither atheist nor theist arguments *per se* can be rationally refuted. On the other hand, rationality returns at the conclusion of the argument as a criterion, and the final arbiter of the overall *results* (rather than the *content*) of

79. For the four-stage pattern, see above, sec. 2.2.

one's personal decision and judges its relative value vis-à-vis all other construals of reality based on the amount of evidence for which it can account. In this light, atheism is the irrational choice, theism the rational and hence better choice.

Finally, when we ask how Küng's argument fits into the anthropological/cosmological typology for classifying natural theology arguments, we find that it is not a perfect fit since it is both types at once. The cosmological argument, employing our experience of reality with its positive and negative elements, is the apparent starting point. But *only* apparently, for Küng clearly shows that an anthropological argument is simultaneously at work which describes how the structure of human subjectivity—seen here as the act of fundamental trust which supports all other human acts—functions as a clue pointing toward God's existence while mediating the cosmological element's own value as a clue. Küng's natural theology demonstrates that the cosmological argument is not simply a remnant of a pre-modern worldview but can still be effective after the hermeneutics of suspicion and after the collapse of the hegemony of modern rationality. But it demonstrates as well Wolfhart Pannenberg's point that, after the modern turn to the subject, the way to the knowledge of God in the contemporary situation must take the structure of human experience as a primary piece of evidence. The rehabilitation of the cosmological argument does not take place without a strong link to an anthropological argument. By combining the two, Küng's argument respects the insights of the older Christian tradition while also responding to the problems and possibilities of a new situation.

2.4. Natural Theology after Metaphysics?

The critique of metaphysics intensified during the last half of the twentieth century, particularly under the influence of the philosophy of Martin Heidegger (1889–1976). It continues to have a profound effect, and the scope of its influence and subsequent reception have only recently begun to be made clear.[80] It is not too dramatic to say

80. See, for example, Stephen K. White, *Political Theory and Postmodernism* (Cambridge/New York: Cambridge University Press, 1991) and Graham Ward's

that the radical nature of Heidegger's critique of both metaphysics and ontotheology marks a rupture in recent Western intellectual history. That "mark" affects the history of the Christian theology of God as well, dividing it so clearly into periods of "before" and "after" that Christian reflection on God after Heidegger's "overcoming of metaphysics" looks fundamentally different from what came before. The widespread reception of this critique destabilized the traditional identification of God with Being and forced a reevaluation of the role of metaphysics within Catholic theology, especially the Catholic theology of God and Christology.[81]

Heidegger claims that philosophy's intrinsic identity as metaphysics is revealed in its obsessive quest for the unifying ground of beings. In searching for the Being of beings in a realm exterior to our experience, "metaphysical thinking departs from what is present in its presence, and thus represents it in terms of its ground as something grounded."[82] The consistent objectifying representation of Being as a being, the tendency to ignore the fundamental phenomenality of beings (that is, their sheer givenness as modes of presencing), and the persistent misunderstanding of reality in terms of dualistic oppositions (e.g. Being as "ground" over against beings as "grounded") all add up to the fatal flaw of metaphysical thinking: despite its totalizing claims, metaphysics misses what Heidegger calls the "ontological difference," the very condition which makes the differentiation between Being and beings possible. Rather than the two elements which metaphysics wrongly identifies as fundamental, there are rather *three* which become apparent to thought: Being (the process of presencing), beings (which are present and take their stand within our field of attention), and the differentiating process which

editorial introduction to *The Postmodern God: A Theological Reader*, Blackwell Readings in Modern Theology (Malden, MA/Oxford: Blackwell, 1997), xv–xlvii.

81. See Anthony J. Godzieba, "Ontotheology to Excess: Imagining God Without Being," *Theological Studies* 56 (1995): 3–20; Godzieba, *Bernhard Welte's Fundamental Theological Approach to Christology* (see n. 30).

82. Martin Heidegger, "The End of Philosophy and the Task of Thinking," *On Time and Being*, trans. Joan Stambaugh (New York: Harper and Row, 1972), 56.

simultaneously connects and holds them apart—*dif-fers/de-fers* them, hence the "difference."[83]

Metaphysics compounds its errors by representing the ultimate unifying principle as the "highest being," the divine ground. Here, Heidegger argues, is where metaphysics becomes ontotheology. "When metaphysics thinks of beings with respect to the ground that is common to all beings as such, then it is logic as onto-logic. When metaphysics thinks of beings as such as a whole, that is, with respect to the highest being which accounts for everything, then it is logic as theologic."[84] God enters philosophy when identified with *Being*, the unifying Ground of the perduring of beings.

However, this God is thereby inscribed within a metaphysical schema which is "bigger" than God, so to speak. This all-encompassing schema employs God as part of the dualistic formatting of experience. God thus rests in the grip of the differentiating process which is always already present ahead of the Divine Highest Being who is distinct from beings. In other words, both the character of God as Being and the relationship of God to beings is determined by an always already-present third "factor," the ontological difference. This God, in Heidegger's famous description, is "the god of philosophy. Man can neither pray nor sacrifice to this god . . . can neither fall to his knees in awe nor can he play music and dance before this god."[85]

What are the consequences of Heidegger's critique of ontotheology in the light of the ontological difference? Is every image of God identified with the God of ontotheology? Is all talk of God automatically illegitimate? Some recent commentators would read Heidegger's critique in such an extremely unilateral way, as rendering *all* theistic discourse impossible, *all* images of God identical with "the God of philosophy" and thus illegitimate, *all* faith in God suspect because of its alleged totalizing tendencies. But it is clear, even in the passage from *Identity and Difference* cited above, that such extreme readings are mistaken if they claim to explain Heidegger's intent. He recog-

---

83. See "The Onto-Theo-Logical Constitution of Metaphysics," the second essay of Heidegger's *Identity and Difference*, trans. Joan Stambaugh (New York: Harper and Row, 1969), 42–74.

84. Ibid., 70–71.

85. Ibid., 72.

nizes the legitimacy of belief and of theistic discourse; indeed he
wants to speak of an experience of God which reaches back beyond
the image of God constructed by ontotheology and philosophical
theology to the God before whom one can indeed "play music and
dance." The critique of ontotheology in the light of the ontological
difference is Heidegger's way of clearing the decks, saying in effect
that human reason's attempts to use the idea of God to gain the
highest metaphysical vantage point and thus make the whole of being
intelligible are instead betrayals of the divine God who is beyond
"the God of philosophy."

This interpretation finds support in an analysis by Merold Westphal, who argues that the extreme readings of Heidegger's position
are mistaken and unsupported by Heidegger's own texts, whether
early or late.

> The explicit critique of onto-theology in the forties and fifties,
> and important anticipations of it from the twenties are directed
> toward the *how* rather than the *what* of our God-talk. . . . That
> is to say, they do not provide or seek to provide a philosophical
> case against belief in a personal Creator (as is all too often im-
> plied); they rather seek to keep open the space for religiously
> meaningful God-talk. . . . What is necessary to overcome
> onto-theology is not the abandonment of theistic belief but the
> avoidance of this temptation to have God at our disposal, con-
> ceptually speaking.[86]

What Westphal depicts as a Pascalian project of protecting the
experiential content of faith (the "what") from any sort of theoretical
distortion (the "how") has its sources in Heidegger's early lectures
on the philosophy of religion. There Heidegger presented a phenomenology of faith derived from his reading of Paul (Galatians, 1
and 2 Thessalonians) and Augustine (*Confessions*, especially book
10), a reading very much influenced by Luther and Kierkegaard.
His later critique of the metaphysical objectification and dissolution
of "the divine God" was a development of an explicitly Lutheran

86. Merold Westphal, "Overcoming Onto-Theology," in *God, The Gift, and
Postmodernism*, ed. John D. Caputo and Michael J. Scanlon (Bloomington: Indiana
University Press, 1999), 146–69, at 160.

view of faith's relation to theology which he had already laid out in the 1920s.[87] Taking this longer-range context in account, Westphal concludes that the critique of ontotheology "is not directed toward the God of the Bible or the Koran, before whom people do fall on their knees in awe, pray, sacrifice, sing, and dance." Rather, this critique is directed at "the 'metaphysical' tendency, whether found among philosophers or theologians, to imprison theological discourse within a primacy of theoretical reason under the rule of the principle of sufficient reason."[88] In this way Heidegger intends to open the way toward other possibilities of meaningful discourse about God.

The periodizing and destabilizing nature of Heidegger's critique of ontotheology marks a clear dividing line. On the one hand no Catholic natural theology of God which comes after Heidegger can afford to be un-reflectively metaphysical without a rigorous argument which demonstrates how its fundamental understanding of being escapes the Heideggerian definition of metaphysics as objectifying, controlling, stultifying representationalism. But on the other hand Heidegger's thought offers little help in constructing a "post-ontotheological" natural theology. No Catholic theology of God which is committed to incarnation and sacramentality can simply follow Heidegger's subsequent path and take up the rather diluted apophatic notion of *das Heilige* ("the Holy") which he articulated in his later works.[89] What sorts of possibilities, then, does Heidegger's proposal of "the end of metaphysics" open up?

87. See Martin Heidegger, *Phänomenologie des religiösen Lebens*, Gesamtausgabe, II. Abteilung: Vorlesungen 1919–1944, Band 60 (Frankfurt a. M.: Klostermann, 1995); *The Phenomenology of Religious Life*, trans. Matthias Fritsch and Jennifer Anna Gosetti-Ferencei, Studies in Continental Thought (Bloomington, IN: Indiana University Press, 2004). See especially the lectures on the phenomenology of religion (1920–21, which include the Pauline interpretations) and on Augustine and neo-Platonism (1921). See also Heidegger's 1927 lecture *Phenomenology and Theology* in *The Piety of Thinking*, trans. James G. Hart and John C. Maraldo (Bloomington: Indiana University Press, 1976), 10–11.

88. Westphal, "Overcoming Onto-Theology," 148, 160.

89. See, for example, "What Are Poets For?," in *Poetry, Language, Thought*, trans. Albert Hofstadter (New York: Harper and Row, 1971), 91–142 (orig. "Wozu Dichter," 1946); "Letter on Humanism," trans. Frank A. Capuzzi and J. Glenn

The philosopher Jean-Luc Marion takes Heidegger's rejection of the metaphysical/ontotheological tradition seriously and does not attempt to construct any sort of natural theology argument or proof. Rather, he suggests a way to think and speak about God at the limits of rationality. He attempts to redeem the Christian experience of God by liberating God from Being and dares to propose what Heidegger has ruled out: a re-situating of God as transcendental horizon or as *archē*. He puts the fundamental issue in this way: "does Being relate, more than anything, to God? Does God have anything to gain by being? Can Being . . . even accommodate any(thing of) God?"[90] Heidegger cannot provide the answers, he says, since his hoped-for "divine god" to be announced by the poets is still conditioned by ontotheology. In other words, the conditions wherein it is possible to encounter God still involve the thought of Being and the constraints of human subjectivity.[91]

Marion attempts to escape the bind of Being by providing another reading of the history of the God-problem, different from the one which we proposed in chapter two. In Marion's view, this history is constituted from the interplay of the "idolatrous" and "iconic" ways of signaling God's presence. An *idol* is the result of human projection, the exhaustion of the aspirations and expectations of human subjectivity and the freezing of them into an image which does no more than reflect these expectations back to the viewer. "The idol thus acts as a mirror, not as a portrait: a mirror that reflects the gaze's image, or more exactly, the image of its aim and of the scope of that aim" (12). With its starting point within human subjectivity, this concept is destined to exhaust the capacities of its limited raw material and to repeat its limitations. The idol, by providing a visible stop to the "gaze" of subjectivity, acts as a barrier which "admits no beyond."

Gray, in *Basic Writings*, rev. ed., ed. David Farrell Krell (San Francisco: Harper-Collins, 1993), 217–65 (orig. *Brief über den Humanismus*, 1947).

90. Jean-Luc Marion, *God Without Being: Hors-Texte*, trans. Thomas A. Carlson (Chicago: University of Chicago Press, 1991), 2 (parentheses in the original). Subsequent page references (in parentheses) are to this text; all emphases are original.

91. Marion quotes a number of passages which indicate how much Heidegger's anticipated "new thinking" about God is indeed conditioned by ontotheological thinking; see ibid., 38–43, 66–73, 207–08 n. 23.

Subjectivity, considered as a kind of sight, marks off as "thinkable" only that which can be encompassed and repeated within the visual metaphor (13). In Marion's reading, modernity's arguments both for and against God proceed in this idolatrous manner and thus silence God. Theistic metaphysics controls God by generating the conditioning idol-concept, and atheism simply substitutes another idol-concept during its critique.

But the idol is not the only way to think or the only way to think about God. With a phenomenology of the *icon* Marion argues that there is an experience "which does not result from a vision but provokes one" (17). There is thinking which is not simply the mirror of human experience but which shatters the controlling and generating mechanisms of subjectivity and presents a new possibility to be thought. The icon gives access to the divine by rendering the invisible visible, and finds its perfect counterpart in the face which presents to us the visage of infinite and unconstrainable depth, "which gazes at our gazes in order to summon them to its depth" (19).[92] Marion articulates a logic at work in reality which differs from the logic discerned by being-oriented subjectivity. Iconic thought is a response to an address from an origin beyond subjectivity, "an origin without original" which outstrips subjectivity's limited grasp (20). It recognizes that reality is based on "donation, abandon, pardon," on an excess which grants and clears space and allows beings to be, independent of Being. Thus iconic thought outwits ontotheology and the ontological difference by thinking the very condition or horizon which gives rise to the ontological difference: gift, giftedness, graciousness. The difference between Being and beings is not simply *there*, not simply a neutral presentation, but is a gift, the graceful unfolding of distance and difference. "*The gift delivers Being/being.* . . . [It] delivers . . . in that it liberates being from Being or, put another way, Being/being from ontological difference, in rendering being free from Being, in distorting being out of its subjection to Being" (100–01). And since the gift can be understood only as accomplished by the

---

92. Here Marion echoes the phenomenology of the face from Emmanuel Levinas' *Totality and Infinity: An Essay on Exteriority*, trans. Alphonso Lingis (Pittsburgh: Duquesne University, 1969), 187–219.

giver who is on the other side of the distance, "doubtless we will name it G⌀d, but in crossing G⌀d with the cross that reveals him only in the disappearance of his death and resurrection" (105).[93]

The graphic crossing-out of "God" is Marion's response to a dilemma: how to do justice to "the intimate gap between the giver and the gift," the distance that does not permit the giver to be identified with the gift but which nonetheless allows "the giver [to be] read on the gift" (104)? In other words, how can one name the divine presence which is beyond all names without freezing that reference into an idolatrous representation? Hence we see the appropriateness of the metaphor of personal relation and above all of the face as personal invitation to a depth beyond the reach of subjectivity. No wonder the eastern Church has revered the icon as a window into heaven, since it preserves the personal invitation to eternal life with God along with the divine revelation's dialectical play of presence/absence. Iconic thought, in its openness to the giver in the gift, overcomes (i.e., comes over, reaches over and beyond) metaphysics to rejoin the biblical experience which sees all revelatory events as a revealing concealing of the divine giver, whether they occur on Sinai or on Golgotha.

While the idol is characterized by the constraining control of subjectivity—making "being" the condition of the thinkable and measuring (and reducing) the divine to the range of being—the icon is characterized by excess, the unmeasured access to the infinite which provokes thought and to which thought's image responds. Thus not only is modernity's thinking about God idolatrous, but so is Heidegger's: his attempt to think God "beyond" the ontological difference and "beyond" metaphysics still permits the ontological difference to determine the character of what can be thought.

For examples of such iconic thought of God which "outwits" Being by getting beyond the conditions of being-language and which is open to "the difference that is indifferent to the ontological difference"

---

93. The "x" through "God" is Marion's typographic convention, modeled after Heidegger's strategy in *The Question of Being* (trans. William Kluback and Jean T. Wilde [New Haven: College and University, 1958]). There, Heidegger crosses out *Sein* (Being) as a graphic means of discussing being after the critique of metaphysics.

(84–85), Marion turns to Scripture. For instance, Paul writes to the Corinthians of God's choice of the foolish to be wise, the weak to be strong—in short, of God's call to "non-beings" (when viewed in an ancient economic and political context) to annul the difference and become full beings (1 Cor. 1:26–29). Iconic thought is also seen in the First Letter of John (e.g., 1 John 4:8: "Whoever is without love does not know God, for God is love") and in the parable of the prodigal son (Lk. 15:11–32), where the quality of this divine love is demonstrated in a comparison to a contentious family relationship brought to a successful outcome by an unexpected and unrequitable overflow of love and care. The point of these examples is to emphasize the graciousness, the *grace*, the gift-character of God's presence which is revealed to us on God's own initiative and which can neither be uncovered by the operations of reason nor trapped within the horizon and the possibilities of the metaphysics of being. "God gives Himself to be known insofar as He gives Himself—according to the horizon of the gift itself. The gift constitutes at once the mode and the body of his revelation. In the end the gift gives only itself, but in this way it gives absolutely everything" (xxiv).

Natural theology in the modern rationalistic sense is idolatrous and thus rigorously excluded. Reason, though, still plays a crucial role in providing some kind of access to faith (Marion's interpretation of this role is almost Anselmian). For when reason reaches the limits of its abilities in its encounter with the phenomenality of the world (i.e., when reason experiences a "saturated" phenomenon which exceeds and thus exhausts the conceptualizations of rational intentionality) what is revealed to us is the logic of sheer givenness and love which is truly immanent to that phenomenality, a truth that reality "imposes" on us that cannot be deduced by us but to which we respond—in fact, our knowledge is constituted by that response.[94] At rationality's limits, human subjectivity can experience something of the immanent presence which transcends and overwhelms rationality. Reason, though, can go no further; to understand this logic as the presence of God requires faith. Marion's position thus parallels

---

94. Jean-Luc Marion, "The Saturated Phenomenon," trans. Thomas A. Carlson, *Philosophy Today* 40 (1996): 103–24.

somewhat that of Vatican I: there exists the *possibility* of knowing God in a certain way (*certo cognosci posse*) but the full supernatural reality of God always exceeds reason's inherently insufficient "gaze."[95]

A somewhat different reaction to the end of metaphysics occurs in the work of the biblical scholar John Dominic Crossan. Although he is much better known for his many contributions to the study of the historical Jesus,[96] his early programmatic work *The Dark Interval* opens with "a theology of limit" that is really a natural theology that provides the framework for his emphasis on story and parable as primary modes of encounter with God.[97] The crux of this theology is a post-metaphysical argument for God which, though barely mentioning Heidegger, is obviously indebted to his critique of ontotheology. It offers one of the clearest explanations of the results of uncoupling of God from metaphysics as well as being one of the clearest examples of the "linguistic turn" in theology.

The argument is built upon the twin concerns of limits and language, and how they are linked. The "inevitability of limitation" presents itself to us not only in our mortality but also more profoundly still in the meaningful, historically-situated "stories" we tell about ourselves and the world of our experience.

> Indeed, death may be only a sign and a reminder of this more fundamental limit. This is the limit of language, that is, *the limit which is language itself.* Our intentions, our theories, our visions are always confined within both language and story. A theology of limit seeks above all to explore this limitation which is posed by the inevitability of life within story, of existence in this story or that but always in some story. (2)

95. Stijn Van den Bossche, "Kataphasis Beyond Apophasis—The Challenge of Jean-Luc Marion's *Étant donné* for Philosophy of Religion and Theology," typescript, 7–8.

96. E.g., *In Parables: The Challenge of the Historical Jesus* (New York: Harper and Row, 1973), *Four Other Gospels: Shadows on the Contour of the Canon* (Minneapolis: Winston/Seabury, 1985), and *The Historical Jesus: The Life of a Mediterranean Jewish Peasant* (San Francisco: HarperCollins, 1991).

97. *The Dark Interval: Towards a Theology of Story*, rev. ed. (Sonoma, CA: Polebridge Press, 1988 [orig. ed. 1975]). Subsequent pages reference to the revised edition appear in parentheses in the text.

This, Crossan suggests, is why we enjoy playing games: we are fascinated and challenged by their limits, which mimic the limits inherent in our own existence. By testing ourselves over against the limitations imposed by a game's rules, we explore our abilities to cope when confronted with our own finitude. We want to discover how much freedom and success we may have by playing against the limits without ever beating them. In doing so, we participate in both "a very serious practice session for life and death" (the ultimate limit) and a very necessary "experiment in disciplined failure" (5).

The haunting inevitability of limit brings Crossan to suspect all those "stories" that claim to circumvent the limits of experience and purport to "objectively" describe the "timeless facts" of reality "beyond" our experience. (We might label these stories "metaphysical," representing the same sort of thinking which Heidegger claimed to overcome.) Crossan identifies three of these "master claims" or "master paradigms" and confesses that he no longer believes any of them.

> The first great master claim is one which makes a distinction between *art* (or faith, or imagination) and *science* (or fact, or reason) and then postulates for each a different language and a different destiny. Having established this complete disjunction, the claim then situates one term in hierarchical supremacy over the other. . . .
>
> The second master claim is that of evolutionary progress . . . not taken merely as a story, a possible and most interesting way of seeing it, but as objective and realistic fact, open and obvious to the unprejudiced viewer.
>
> The third master claim is the postulate that there is an external reality *out there*, extrinsic to our vision, our imagination, and our intellect and that we are gaining objective knowledge and disciplined control over this extra mental reality. (6)

Their fundamental flaw is that they "deny their own being as story and maintain that they are telling us how it really is and not how I-you-we-they have agreed to imagine it." They are thus no longer "interesting"—that is, none of them offers an explanation of reality "that best opens up the possibility of transcendental experience for here and now" (7). And so Crossan proceeds to debunk them.

The error of the first claim is that no matter which type of language is considered to be more true to reality and thus privileged, the very choice of science over art or art over science implies that the "privileged" way of thinking has a comprehensive, direct, unmediated grasp of the truth of reality and that its language can express this truth. Crossan questions the very validity of the distinction. "The real distinction would not be between the direct language of science and the indirect language of poetry but between language, whether in science or in poetry or in anything else, which is aware of its limits and language when it is fossilized and totally oblivious to the yawning chasm beneath its complacency" (12–13). Different types of thinking and speaking are simply *approximations* to the truth, never direct expressions of it, and hence cannot be hierarchically arranged.

The second master claim has made the word "evolution" equivalent to "improvement" and "change" synonymous with "progress." Crossan attempts to refute this by adducing evidence for change without progress, evolution without improvement. Does it make any sense to say that contemporary art is "better than" Paleolithic cave paintings? Or would a more authentic estimation be that they are simply *different* and that no hierarchical comparison is even possible? Art, he claims, falls outside any schema of evolutionary progress; its different forms demonstrate change without progress. [98] Another example is the history of science as seen through Thomas Kuhn's theory of paradigm shifts.[99] Kuhn argued that this history as told by "normal science"—a story of smooth, steadily accumulative, linear progress—is fundamentally at odds with the real practice of science

---

98. He cites with approval T. S. Eliot's judgment that "art never improves, but . . . the material of art is never quite the same. . . . This change is a development which abandons nothing *en route*, which does not superannuate either Shakespeare, or Homer, or the rock drawing of the Magdelenian draughtsmen" (T. S. Eliot, "Tradition and the Individual Talent" [orig. 1932], in *Perspectives on Poetry*, ed. J. L. Calderwood and H. E. Toliver [New York: Oxford University Press, 1968], 259–66, at 261, as cited in *The Dark Interval*, 14).

99. Thomas S. Kuhn, *The Structure of Scientific Revolutions*, 2d ed. (Chicago: University of Chicago Press, 1970). See also the analysis of Kuhn's theory provided in Richard J. Bernstein, *Beyond Objectivism and Relativism: Science, Hermeneutics, and Praxis* (Philadelphia: University of Pennsylvania Press, 1983), esp. 51–108.

that is marked not only by consensus but also by crises and intuitive leaps. A time of consensus in a scientific discipline is a period governed by a dominant working model or paradigm which becomes more precise as it is explains new evidence and solves new problems.[100] However, when a paradigm fails, despite continual adjustment, to exhibit comprehensive explanatory value in the face of mounting anomalies—in other words, when a paradigm fails to "stretch" far enough to account for the discrepancies brought on by the latest evidence—that paradigm suffers a breakdown and a crisis ensues. This is the period of "extraordinary science" when rival paradigms are proposed and no one paradigm has the upper hand. A scientific discipline regains its stability once one of the rivals can be shown to explain everything the old paradigm explained, along with the latest evidence. Kuhn likens this "shift" in paradigms to a revolution. Of course, the new dominant paradigm will be subject in the future to the same fine-tunings and eventual crisis as the previous dominant paradigm. What is apparent in this more authentic history of science is that "there are no criteria of logical proof or any straightforward appeals to evidence that are *sufficient* to resolve the dispute" between the former dominant paradigm and its rivals and among the rivals themselves.[101] Indeed, the new dominant paradigm cannot be logically derived from the old, nor can any complete point-by-point comparison be made between the two. Despite this *incommensurability* of rival paradigms, however, judging their relative adequacy clearly involves rational evaluation. But it is an expanded type of rationality, "a judgmental activity requiring imagination, interpretation, the weighing of alternatives, and application of criteria that are essentially open."[102] Crossan employs both these examples to illustrate his claim that "evolutionary *progress* is simply a piece of major Western arrogance" (18) and that we have no superior, ahistorical standpoint from which to judge whether one period of art is "better" than another or whether one scientific paradigm is "the best" of all.

100. Kuhn defines paradigms as "universally recognized scientific achievements that for a time provide model problems and solutions to a community of practitioners" (*Structure of Scientific Revolutions*, viii).
101. Bernstein, *Beyond Objectivism and Relativism*, 22.
102. Ibid., 56.

There is change, there is difference, but our limited historical stand-point prevents us from "concoct[ing] claims of progress with our-selves at its present peak" (18).

The third and final master claim is fundamentally epistemological, and Crossan's refutation of it is perhaps the culmination of his pre-vious criticisms. Over against the naïve realist assertion that "there is an external reality *out there*" that we can know objectively, inde-pendent of our limited standpoint, he argues that *standpoint* is pre-cisely the issue: how might one conceivably "get outside" or "get around" one's historically-conditioned, linguistically-sedimented standpoint? That quest is impossible. The mind is not a camera, nor are ideas pictures of the world-as-it-is. Since we understand by means of our stories, interpretations, and theories, there is never any neutral and atemporal "seeing" or thinking. But rather than halting at this point and arguing something akin to Kant's noumenon/phenomenon distinction (while we cannot know absolutes absolutely but only in limited ways, we do not question the existence of those absolutes), Crossan pushes the perspectival argument to its logical limit:

> At this point it does look like something beyond idealism or realism is at work, something which might be termed relativism, if that word were not already reprobate. If it will not abuse the language too much we might call this new theory "relationism." Reality is neither *in here* in the mind nor *out there* in the world; it is the interplay of both mind and world in language. Reality is relational and relationship. Even more simply, reality is language. What is there before us and is without language is as unknowable as the answer to the question of how we would feel had we never been born. (22)

Crossan's radical epistemological perspectivism is clearly the ulti-mate source of his other critiques. If "being human means living in language and calling that process reality" (23) and if "'reality' is the world we create in and by our language and our story" (25), then both the claim of a privileged neutral language and the claim of a privileged position from which to evaluate progress are specious, because for Crossan there are no language-free, neutral, uninterpreted standpoints. Therefore none of the three construals can claim absolute value. Their explanations are simply stories that at one time were more likely than other stories but which are now dispensable. Over time "they have become boring, uninteresting, and in direct conflict with some more challenging and exciting new stories" (24).

How does this apply to our experience and knowledge of God? One could argue that it amounts to an extension of Heidegger's critique of ontotheology, with Nietzsche's repudiation of metaphysics not far in the background. Crossan notes that his linguistic perspectivism presents him with a troubling dilemma: either God is an idolatrous projection or else God is unknowable and religion is impossible.

> If there is only story, then God, or the referent of transcendental experience, is either inside my story and, in that case, at least in the Judeo-Christian tradition I know best, God is merely an idol I have created; or, God is outside my story, and I have just argued that what is "out there" is completely unknowable. So it would seem that any transcendental experience has been ruled out, if we can only live in story. (25)

What is definitely ruled out is the ontotheological understanding of God as transcendent Highest Being. Crossan restates this "classical vision" as the story of "the Lighthouse Keeper."

> Once upon time there were people who lived on rafts upon the sea. The rafts were constructed of materials from the land whence they had come. On this land was a lighthouse in which there was a lighthouse keeper. No matter where the rafts were, and even if the people themselves had no idea where they actually were, the keeper always knew their whereabouts. There was even communication between people and keeper so that in an absolute emergency they could always be guided safely home to land. (25–26)

The rumor of the death of God, announced by Nietzsche's madman, was a major factor in the destruction of this vision.[103] But an even more chilling version, Crossan believes, is provided by Emily Dickinson:

---

103. *The Gay Science*, §125, trans. Walter Kaufmann (New York: Vintage, 1974), 181. See also above, chapter two, section 3.3.

Finding is the first Act
The second, loss,
Third, Expedition for
The "Golden Fleece."

Fourth, no Discovery—
Fifth, no Crew—
Finally, no Golden Fleece—
Jason—sham—too.[104]

This, for Crossan, amounts to nothing less than the end of the onto-theological view.

> In that "sham" one hears the chilling slam as the door closes on
> the classical vision of a fixed center out there somewhere. What
> had died was the fixed center outside language, and for many
> who attended the funeral that could only mean the burial of God
> since they equated the two. When one believed in a fixed reality
> out there, apart from us and independent of us, one could easily
> imagine God as the one who really knew all about it. . . . Yet
> who would need such a God if reality was not outside us but
> inside our language? So, with the loss of credibility in a fixed
> reality independent of us, there soon followed the loss of faith
> in a God whose chief role was to guarantee that reality's validity.
> (27–28)

If God is no longer to be identified with "the fixed center out there,"
if there is nothing but story, can belief in God survive? Or is God
merely an "idol," a character whom we control in a story that we
generate out of our own experience? Crossan's way out of the
dilemma is to tell another story:

> There is no lighthouse keeper. There is no lighthouse. There is
> no dry land. There are only people living on rafts made from
> their own imaginations. And there is the sea. (28)

104. "Finding is the First Act," in *The Poems of Emily Dickinson*, ed. T H.
Johnson, 3 vols. (Cambridge: Belknap Press of Harvard University Press, 1955),
2:647–48, #870, as cited in *The Dark Interval*, 27.

Consider the rafts to be analogous to language and story—limited yet coherent "realities" upon which or within which we live our lives. Can we encounter God there? If God is "on the raft" and inside our story, then God is an idol of our making, a character we construct out of our own experience who thereby loses the "otherness" which is part of God's nature. If God is the ontotheological lighthouse keeper who is "off the raft" and outside language, completely independent of our narrative constructions, then God is unknowable. Either way, God ceases to be God for us and we will have no authentic experience of God.

> There is only one possibility left, and that is what we can experience in the movement of the raft, in the breaks in the raft's structure, and above all, what can be experienced at the *edges* of the raft itself. For we cannot really talk of the sea, we can only talk of the edges of the raft and what happens there. Our prayer will have to be, not "Thank God for edges," but "Thank edges for God." (29)

This is Crossan's contemporary version of the "transcendental move" which we have seen in every natural theology argument that we have examined thus far. This move states that only from the standpoint of the finite can we gain a sense of the infinite and that the finite opens out beyond itself to infinite transcendence. In Crossan's linguistic argument, the very limits of language disclose in a general way what is beyond those limits; they are the conditions for the possibility of our discovery of what is "beyond" and "other than" those limits and the world which those limits circumscribe. The possibility of an experience of transcendence and thus of an experience of God occurs only when we have reached the edges of language, when we have exhausted our narrative abilities and have reached the limits of our own conceptual abilities to constitute a world. Of course, if we had been astute enough about limits and edges we might already have gleaned such an interpretation of transcendental experience from a story told by Crossan much earlier in the chapter.

> There was once a man who owned some property on a high cliff which overlooked the sea. He spent many years of careful

construction on a road from his house to the very edge of the cliff. When the road was finished, he spent hours each day standing on the extreme edge where he could feel the thrill of the sea. The people who lived round about were practical and sensible folk, and they said that he was a very good roadbuilder and that he certainly liked to walk a lot. (8)

Only at the edges can we experience the transcendence of the "infinite" sea—not in the middle of land or the raft (because there we are surrounded by a constituted finite reality) nor off over the edge (because we would then be out of our world and drowned in the abyss). Only while standing at the edge can we feel the thrill of a "beyond" (the sea) which we do not grasp but rather which grasps us, which encompasses our story and, in a sense, holds it afloat. "There are no mysteries on the raft but, as Galileo might have said, still it moves" (29).

Despite their differences, I have paired Crossan and Marion because their arguments give a very clear indication of one major direction taken by natural theology in the wake of Heidegger's critique of ontotheology. The fact that Crossan's linguistic argument looks quite informal when placed next to Marion's rigorous application of phenomenology should not obscure Crossan's sophistication nor the striking similarities of both authors in dealing with reason and with the transcending openness of human experience. Both argue for the contemporary possibility of experiencing God after the hermeneutics of suspicion and after the notion of "God" has been uncoupled from metaphysics. And both insist on recognizing stringent limitations to all human interpretations of the presence of God and label as idolatrous any interpretation that claims to be adequate.

Finally, there are striking similarities in their attempts to offer a contemporary version of apophatic or negative theology. Because this postmodern version has a complex relationship to human experience—suspicious of it yet at the same time requiring it—it is somewhat different from the classic type we discussed previously.[105] Here, the points noted in the previous paragraph are intensified.

---

105. See the discussion of Pseudo-Dionysius in connection with Anselm in chapter one, section 2.

Marion and Crossan both assume a radical discontinuity between human experience and the experience of God rather than a continuity between human yearnings for salvation and the God who fulfills them. They stake their positions on an almost zero-sum interpretation of the relationship of faith and reason: the activities of reason and subjectivity in trying to know God are ultimately acts of hubris which must be diminished in order for any authentic experience of God to take place. Only with the collapse of reason, the shattering of the products of rational reflection, or the total surpassing of the abilities of human subjectivity are faith and revelation held to be possible. At the same time, Marion and Crossan still consider human subjectivity to be the necessary clearing where the experience of God occurs, but only on the condition of its absolute insufficiency; it adds nothing to the process of knowing the presence of God. This suspicion of human experience illustrates the tendency of post-metaphysical philosophical theology to emphasize the radical otherness of God and either to be much less optimistic than classical natural theology about what reason can achieve in the knowledge of God, or, in extreme cases, to impute to human subjectivity all sorts of inherently despicable motives (constraining God, betraying God, "freezing" God into a conceptual projection, etc.).[106]

The result is that the post-metaphysical natural theology argued by both thinkers strongly affirms the experience of transcendence while being reluctant to speak directly in any way about God's presence and attributes. Recall that Crossan's argument leaves us with only the barest notion of God, a general experience of transcendence "in the movement of the raft, in the breaks in the raft's structure, and . . . what can be experienced at the *edges* of the raft itself."[107] Only transcendence itself can reveal any of its characteristics to us. For Crossan this revelation occurs in the parables of Jesus, which are

106. For a critique that sees a latent anti-humanism within Marion's later work, see Anthony J. Godzieba, "As Much Contingency, As Much Incarnation," in *Religious Experience and Contemporary Theological Epistemology*, ed. Lieven Boeve, Yves De Maeseneer, and Stijn Van den Bossche, Bibliotheca Ephemeridum Theologicarum Lovaniensium, vol. 188 (Leuven: Leuven University Press/ Uitgeverij Peeters, 2005), 83–90.

107. *The Dark Interval*, 29.

"stories which shatter the deep structure of our accepted world . . . remove our defenses and make us vulnerable to God. It is only in such experiences that God can touch us. . . ."[108] Marion's idol/icon distinction conveys a similar message, although he maintains that at least a glimmer of the personality of the Giver (the quality of transcendence-as-love) reaches through to impoverished reason:

> Because God alone could accomplish [the crossing of Being], and because at best, we can glimpse God only in the intermittent half-times of our idolatries, in the meantimes of our mirror games, . . . we perceive this crossing only from time to time. For that which crosses Being, eventually, has the name *agapē*. *Agapē* surpasses all knowledge, with a hyperbole that defines it and, indissolubly, prohibits access to it. . . . We fall—in the capacity of beings—under the government of Being. We do not accede—in the capacity of "sinners"—to *agapē*.[109]

In the context of the "history of the God problem" that we laid out in the previous chapter, this postmodern delegitimation of rational subjectivity is to a large degree understandable: it is a rejection of the pretensions of reason which in modernity had rendered God more and more extrinsic and, in radical cases, led to atheism. It is also a rejection of Enlightenment natural religion with its hostility to revelation. But this is a vastly different understanding of natural theology than either Anselm, Thomas, or even Hans Küng proposed. Their emphasis on incarnation and their optimistic view of creation led them to see reason and faith as partners in the common project of bringing human beings to salvation understood as union with God. Reason by itself was considered insufficient, of course, but its essential virtue was that it sought the infinite God as its true end, thereby opening itself to be fulfilled by faith and revelation. Reason was thus considered redeemable. Not so in the post-metaphysical versions of natural theology we have seen thus far: reason can only be related to faith in the most negligible of ways, exhausting itself in its search for the all-encompassing view of reality and then getting out of the way so

---

108. Ibid., 100.
109. Marion, *God Without Being*, 108.

that a "true" religious experience may occur. And so our definition of natural theology as that type of thinking which seeks the natural access-point of faith is acknowledged here, but in a minimalist fashion. For a more optimistic view of the relationship of reason to faith and to the experience of God after metaphysics, we need to look elsewhere.

2.5. Kasper's Natural Theology: Freedom and Person

It is appropriate that our concluding example of natural theology be Walter Kasper's, for he summarizes and responds to many of the issues we have encountered thus far. He demonstrates the reasonableness of faith and articulates the point where human experience and God's presence intersect, as far as that is possible, and thereby attempts to rehabilitate natural theology after the crisis of ontotheology. This argument forms part of his larger project to show that the Christian belief in God as Trinity is the answer to atheism and to the contemporary eclipse of God.

Kasper's reaction to metaphysics is at once less polemical and less straightforward than Marion's. In describing faith's contemporary context, he acknowledges its post-metaphysical character and recognizes the modern turn to subjectivity and historicity as major contributing factors. He notes how the relationship between being and God presupposed by classical metaphysics has been rendered questionable by modern and contemporary philosophy. He also underscores the crucial roles that both Nietzsche and Heidegger have played in those critiques.[110] In this new context, faith and theology have been forced to rethink their basic presuppositions and raise the most fundamental question concerning the relation between God and being, "that is, whether we must ask the question of God within the horizon of the question of being, or the question of being within the horizon of the question of God" (*GJC*, 64).

But rather than agree completely with the contemporary critique of metaphysics, he offers instead a more general defense. He insists that

---

110. *GJC*, 46. Throughout this section, subsequent references appear in the text (*GJC*, page number). The latest German edition (*Gesammelte Schriften*, ed. George Augustin and Klaus Krämer, vol. 4: *Der Gott Jesu Christi* [Freiburg/Br.: Herder, 2008]) has also been consulted.

"the regaining of the metaphysical dimension [is] one of the most important tasks of contemporary theology."[111] Our talk about God, "the reality that includes and determines everything," demands a metaphysics "which enquires not about individual beings or realms of being but about being as such and as a whole" (*GJC*, 15). Metaphysics seeks "the final, all-determining and cohering foundations, wisdom about the oneness and wholeness of reality," and without such thinking and its attendant language, Kasper believes that discourse about God becomes an impossible task and theology itself is thereby plunged into crisis.[112]

However, Kasper is careful to delineate the type of metaphysics he believes is necessary. It must exhibit a thinking that "keeps open the question about the meaning of the whole" (*GJC*, 15), that is open to the overarching horizon of mystery that grounds the transcending character of human experience (*GJC*, 84–85), and that rigorously avoids absolutizing the finite (*GJC*, 114). He thereby distances himself from God-arguments based on an essentialist or "substance" metaphysics and rejects any thinking which objectifies the transcendent, all-determining horizon of experience in order to represent it in terms more appropriate to finite beings (*GJC*, 100).[113] This indicates that he has taken seriously Heidegger's criticism of the objectifying, calculative tendencies of metaphysics. And this sensitivity provides a basis for Kasper's negative evaluation of modern philosophy's various attempts to prove God's existence: the traditional ontotheological arguments simply lead to the atheism represented by Nietzsche. "In the final analysis it is impossible to prove God's existence from some authority external to him; he must show himself" (*GJC*, 109).

111. Walter Kasper, "Postmodern Dogmatics: Toward a Renewed Discussion of Foundations in North America," trans. D. T. Asselin and Michael Waldstein, *International Catholic Review: Communio* 17 (1990): 181–91, at 189. See also Kasper, "How to Do Theology Today," in *Speaking Truth in Love: The Theology of Cardinal Walter Kasper*, ed. Kristin M. Colberg and Robert A. Krieg (Collegeville, MN: Liturgical Press, 2014), 248–57.

112. "Introduction" to *Theology and Church* [see n. 63], 1–16, at 10; for his comments concerning "the true and deepest crisis of present theology" without metaphysics, see ibid., 3.

113. See also his stronger statement in "Postmodern Dogmatics": "Without a transcendent ground and point of reference, statements of faith are finally only subjective projections or social and ecclesial ideologies" (189).

This is why Anselm can be considered one of Kasper's major influences, in a sense, for he points out precisely *where* God's own self can be revealed to human experience. In the ontological argument, the one "to which all the other arguments boil down" (*GJC*, 109), Anselm has demonstrated the dynamic openness of finite human subjectivity to the infinite without attempting to define or constrain the infinite to fit a certain determination.[114] Anselm's fundamental achievement, according to Kasper, is that he has shown how "in the end thinking necessarily transcends itself, inasmuch as it thinks something which it is essentially incapable of thinking out any further, because the infinite cannot be captured in any finite concept. God, therefore, can be known only through God; he can be known only when he himself allows himself to be known" (*GJC*, 112–13).

As the prelude to his trinitarian theology, Kasper seeks to rehabilitate natural theology and thereby demonstrate the reasonableness of a faith which provides a "prophetic interpretation of reality" by giving us access to "the ultimate ground and the ultimate meaning and goal of all reality" (*GJC*, 78–79). His first step in this direction is to illustrate the openness of human experience to religious experience by demonstrating the mutually-influential relationship of faith and experience to each other, their "critical correlation." We encounter them as a "hermeneutic circle" (*GJC*, 81): faith is necessarily mediated by our finite historical experience, while our experience itself can be questioned and expanded by its encounter with the transcendental object of faith, the word of God. The major goal in this first step is to demonstrate the openness of finite experience to infinite transcendence so that, in the spirit of Anselm, one might describe human rationality as fundamentally the "pre-apprehension [*Vorgriff*] of irreducible mystery" (*GJC*, 114). "We must take as our point of departure a general understanding of experience and then show how the dimension of religious experience opens up 'in, with and under' everyday human experience" (*GJC*, 81).

This analysis of human experience discloses a number of crucial aspects which, when taken together, give strong testimony to the inherent openness of experience and its fundamental orientation

---

114. See the discussion of the ontological argument above in section 2.1.

beyond any "closure" within the finite.[115] First, experience involves both *objective and subjective elements in a dialectical relationship;* that is, the person as subject is affected by reality and interprets this inter-action in a meaningful way through words, images, and symbols. Experience is also *historical, emerging over time* and involving the past (memory, including those "dangerous memories" of unresolved injus-tices which challenge our complacency) and the future (hope) con-verging in the present. What is non-negotiable is the openness of experience to the future, to what is new; thus experience is never closed or "completed." And experience is *historical* in yet another way: it never occurs "in general" but is always situated and influ-enced by the horizon of understanding which is dominant during any historical epoch.

Experience is also always *hermeneutical,* always *interpreted experi-ence.* "We never experience reality in itself; we always experience it as something that has a specific meaning for us; objective experience and interpretation of experience can never be completely separated" (*GJC,* 81). The meaning of experience is contextualized and arrived at through images, models, concepts, and language. We never sim-ply see or experience something; we always *see it as* or *experience it as* something meaningfully interpreted within a context. Finally, experience always *involves* us with *what is other than us,* the crucial "non-I" element which is not simply an extension of myself or a projection but which *offers resistance* to us and our expectations. "The experiences that are fruitful are not our everyday experiences but rather those contrasting experiences that challenge us to a decision" (*GJC,* 84).

---

115. The following two paragraphs summarize the analysis of experience in *GJC,* 82–87. Kasper's position closely parallels the analyses offered by Hans-Georg Gadamer and Edward Schillebeeckx. Cf. Hans-Georg Gadamer, *Truth and Method,* 2d rev. ed., trans. rev. Joel Weinsheimer and Donald G. Marshall (New York: Continuum, 1989), esp. 346–79; Edward Schillebeeckx, *Christ: The Experience of Jesus as Lord,* trans. John Bowden (New York: Crossroad, 1981), esp. 27–79; Schillebeeckx, *Interim Report on the Books "Jesus" and "Christ,"* trans. John Bowden (New York: Crossroad, 1981), esp. 3–19. See also Max Müller, *Erfahrung und Geschichte: Grundzüge einer Philosophie der Freiheit als transzendentale Erfahrung* (Freiburg/Br.: Herder, 1971) and the additional literature cited in *GJC,* 345 n. 30.

In sum, the convergence of these aspects reveals experience to be both thoroughly contextual and thoroughly open beyond itself because of its inherent incompleteness. A practical example is our use of language to fulfill our desire to communicate. Language has a "depth dimension" that is revealed in the way we use metaphors to communicate more than the words literally mean and analogies that connote more than we can ostensibly point out. The very act of communication expresses a longing for an interpersonally shared understanding which is not yet empirically present and a hope for future agreement which is guided by "a pre-apprehension of an ideal communication community, an anticipation of a life unmarked by alienation" (*GJC*, 92) and grounded in universal consensus.[116] But in the end no experience of any kind is ever enough to give us the fully settled certainty we crave. There is always more to be learned, new aspects of reality to be discovered which can either expand our "fund" of experience or totally shatter our expectations. While we live out of our expectations at every moment—because they enable knowledge to take place at all—at every moment, too, their insufficiencies are exposed because there is always something "new" and "different" to experience which is not already part of our expectations. Kasper notes that while awareness of our finitude brings us suffering (as we chafe against the limits inherent to the human condition), such suffering is a positive sign, for it points to the depth dimension of our experience, our openness to a future and to a newness which can never be completely known. "No one has experienced humanity to the full unless he or she has experienced its finiteness and suffering. But then experience becomes a way leading into an open immensity, into a mystery that is even greater and never to be completely plumbed" (*GJC*, 84).

The very structure of experience, then, opens us to infinite mystery which is nothing less than the condition of the possibility or the transcendental horizon of all human experience. At this point, we have discovered the religious dimension of human experience.

> Religious experience is an indirect, not a direct type of experience; it is an experience which we have "in, with and under" our

---

116. Kasper relies here on the communicative action theories of Karl Otto Apel and Jürgen Habermas. See *GJC*, 347 nn. 55–56.

other experiences. It is therefore not just one experience alongside other experiences, but rather the basic experience present in our other experiences; it is an experience that presides over and gives a pervasive tone to all other experience. (*GJC*, 84)

Religious experiences are thus *always indirect* and have the character of "disclosure situations" that occur within everyday life. They point beyond themselves to the overarching mystery that effectively clarifies our entire experience.[117] This infinite mystery forms the unthematized unifying horizonal "background" to the thematic "foreground" of our everyday experience. This mystery can never be apprehended directly as such but only glimpsed, only known in traces and hints.[118] Since perfect clarity escapes us, religious experiences can be profoundly ambiguous. "Insofar as this experienced mystery is an inaccessible horizon of all our experience, it encounters us as the Wholly Other, a frightening abyss, a wilderness of nothingness. Insofar as it is close to us in everything, it appears to us as a protecting Ground, as grace and fulfillment" (*GJC*, 86).

This first step, then, demonstrates the fundamental openness of historically-situated human experience to transcendent mystery. The second step is the attempt to articulate this mystery's character, as far as we are able within our rational abilities, from the viewpoint of human experience, thus highlighting the natural access-point of faith. For Kasper, contemporary philosophy's critique of classical metaphysics and its close analysis of subjectivity are quite helpful. The crucial clue to the character of the all-encompassing mystery can be found in modern philosophy's insistence that *freedom*, not substance, is the true overarching condition of reality. "Not observable fact but

117. Kasper's "disclosure situations" (*GJC*, 85–86) are similar to the "signals of transcendence" described by Peter Berger in *A Rumor of Angels* and cited by Hans Küng (see above, sec. 2.3). Kasper borrows the term from Ian T. Ramsey, *Religious Language: An Empirical Placing of Religious Phrases* (London, 1969); see *GJC*, 90, 347 n. 51.

118. Again language can serve as an example. Its essential character as "a pre-apprehension of the total meaning of reality" is "a remembering of an unfulfilled hope of the human race and an anticipation of this hope." Thus "even before language becomes explicitly religious language, it always already implies a religious dimension" (*GJC*, 94).

free activity is the reality that alone brings the self-disclosure of the world. Being, therefore, is act, accomplishment, happening, event. Not self-contained being but existence, or freedom that goes out of itself and fulfills itself in action, is now the starting point and horizon of thought" (*GJC*, 153). That the finite human person is intentionally geared to this infinite horizon of freedom is clear, as we have seen, from the taste of everyday experience: it is shot through with incompleteness, with suffering, with the "melancholy of fulfillment" which arises when finite values and persons do not pay off with the infinite returns we seek. These experiences alert us to the unconditioned fulfillment we desire and fully intend but which is unavailable within the realm of human action.[119] "Only in encounter with absolute freedom can the person reach inner peace and inner fulfillment. In every other exercise of freedom there is a hopeful but always unsatisfied pre-apprehension of the complete realization of freedom" (*GJC*, 105). The absolute freedom which would grant us this unconditioned fulfillment is the transcendental condition of the possibility of all individual free acts. But we have no objective grasp of this, only a pre-apprehension (*Vorgriff*) and "fragmentary anticipations" (*GJC*, 105) of its character.

How, then, can we ever be fulfilled? The human person, whose self-identity is constituted by means of experience and is thus dependent to a large degree upon the "non-I" catalyst of experience, can only be fulfilled in a *personal* way, through relationships where the non-I has a personal character. "In the concrete a human person is not even able to live unless accepted and affirmed by other persons and unless he or she receives and at the same time gives love. We attain to fulfillment only by emptying ourselves out in love, so as to realize our own intentional infinity" (*GJC*, 155). But in this, too, we seem to be blocked by the human condition: every one of these specific relationships with our fellow human beings, no matter how intense they may be, shares in the limits imposed by our finite con-

---

119. Cf. also Kasper's *An Introduction to Christian Faith*, trans. V. Green (New York: Paulist, 1980), 28–35, especially the claim (framed in terms of critical theory's analysis of modernity) that the history of suffering generates "the strongest objections to belief in God" (29–30).

dition and can offer only incomplete anticipations of the absolute, conditionless freedom for which we yearn. But despite this roadblock, we still enter into relationships, still hunger for love and acceptance without constraints, still intend the totality of freedom and being which conditions the free acts which constitute our identity. Is this destined to be an intentionality without fulfillment?

Kasper argues that the possibility of the fulfillment of our "dynamic ordering to the totality of being" does indeed exist.

> The human person can reach definitive fulfillment only if it en-counters a person who is infinite not only in its intentional claims on reality but in its real being; that is, only if it encounters an absolute person. Thus a more appropriate concept of person as the always unique "there" of being leads necessarily to the con-cept of an absolute, a divine person. If we understand the person as an always unique realization of being, then the category of person as applied to God does not mean an objectification of God. On the contrary, the concept of person is able to express in a new way the fact that in God being subsists in a unique way, that is, that God is *ipsum esse subsistens* ["subsistent being itself," echoing Thomas Aquinas]. (*GJC*, 154)

Only the recognition of the infinite mystery as the horizon of perfect freedom and only the use of metaphors of personal relationship can give the fullest possible account of the infinite mystery which gives itself to human beings and to the world as horizon and as future fulfillment. True, our ordinary experience (at the point of its ultimate limit, but not only there) can bring us to the point of recognizing our inherent openness to transcendence. And retrospectively we can recognize infinite mystery as the all-pervasive ground which is present "in, with, and under" everyday experience. But Kasper goes further: he believes that rational reflection can detect something of the fundamental character of infinite mystery and the inherent rela-tionship we have with it. Here his argument has something of the flavor of Jean-Luc Marion's argument. Reality manifests a logic that being-language (oriented to objectification and manipulability) misses: a relation to an all-encompassing mystery that grasps us before we grasp it conceptually, which offers the fulfillment that human activity, fueled by hope of personal transformation, intensely intends. The only proper language for the overarching mystery is that of the *personal* which necessarily implies relationality, one's openness to an other. If our use of the term "God" is indeed meant to refer to the all-encompassing infinite mystery and total meaning of reality which forms the horizon of our life and actions, then our human desire for happiness, well-being, and fulfillment—thus, for a completion that is inherently *personal*—gives us a glimpse or hint, a pre-apprehension (*Vorgriff*) of the character of that horizon: a gracious *giver* who takes the initiative to open up to us in a *personal* fashion, the absolute mystery that indeed has us in its grip (so to speak) but that nevertheless graciously grants us the free space that makes our life and actions possible. "Seen in the horizon of the person, the meaning of being is love. . . . To call God a person is to say that God is the subsistent being which is freedom in love" (*GJC*, 155).

Thus Kasper's natural theology brings us much farther than merely an acknowledgment of transcendence in the style of Crossan. In the disclosure situations which occur within our finite experience, we have a *Vorgriff* of the infinite mystery and of its character, for which a personal metaphor is the most adequate description from our side of the relationship (*quoad nos*). We can approach the divine mystery, but we neither fully comprehend it nor control it. We can describe it as infinite freedom and absolute love, but these are only weak analogies formulated in the light of our limited experience. We can glimpse it as the ground of our experience, as the necessary horizon of freedom over against which our free acts become possible. But from within our experience we have *only* an inadequate glimpse, *only* the sketchiest outline. "This 'infinite' is only a pre-apprehension and not a concept; it is a limit-concept which we are unable to turn into a concept" (*GJC*, 116). The infinite mystery itself must reveal to us its inner nature to which we have no access from our side (echoing Thomas' strictures on what is knowable *quoad nos*). Our sketchy *Vorgriff* can only be confirmed and filled out by revelation—in fact, natural theology points to supernatural revelation as its own completion.

The experiential nature of faith (always hermeneutical) and the faith-filled nature of experience (always oriented to universal meaning) are key elements in Kasper's argument. He thus succeeds in depicting how experience, faith, and revelation, while obviously non-identical, are related in a hermeneutical circle: human experience, in its desire for fulfillment, points toward revelation which fills out and provides the true explanation of human experience, which in turn responds to revelation in faith. The natural access-point of faith, then, is within the intentional structure of human experience and is made visible in the operations of that intentionality.

This insight also gives us an expanded understanding of faith in relation to experience. No longer should "faith" be defined in opposition to reason. Rather, the word describes a way of being where one is personally open to absolute mystery, a mode of life which embraces all aspects of human activity, rationality included.

> Faith in this broad sense is not a categorical belief in certain suprarational truths; rather it is the fundamental choice whereby the person opens himself to this dimension of divine mystery and, in terms of it, understands and encounters life, world, man and history. . . . Religious faith exists at the level of a decision regarding life, a decision that embraces the whole person and all his acts. It is a kind of primordial choice, a fundamental option, a decision in behalf of a certain understanding of reality as a whole, together with a decision to adopt a specific practical attitude to this reality. . . . [A person's] decision is an act of primordial trust, understood as an act of self-giving. (*GJC*, 117–18)

Religious experience fills in this outline with reflections based on benevolent experiences with the absolute. The "grammar" of this experience and of a truly contemporary view of God is thus conditioned beforehand by "an understanding of reality in which person and relation have priority" (*GJC*, 310) and by the awareness of a logic of reality which is lost to traditional ontotheology but which can be revealed within a metaphor of personal relationships grounded in experience. "The free turning of God to the world and to us grounds all intra-worldly substantiality. The meaning of being is therefore to be found not in substance that exists in itself, but in self-communicating love" (*GJC*, 156). This redefinition of "being" marks a farewell to any of the usual understandings of "metaphysics" even if Kasper, as we saw earlier, desires to retain the term.[120] For he speaks here of an experience of the all-encompassing mystery that fits into no ontotheological system. The mystery demands, rather, to be experienced through personal relationships which afford finite glimpses of this infinite. This description of experience at the natural access-point of faith allows us to see that supernatural revelation (of the character of God, of God's inner life, and of God's relationship to the world) is not extrinsic to human experience, although it may shatter our expectations. Revelation rather confirms and fills out these glimpses while at the same time exceeding them. Supernatural revelation can thus be seen as the super-abundant fulfillment of the intentional openness of finite human experience and of the natural knowledge of God which flows from that experience.

3. The Consistency and Cogency of Natural Theology

We have examined arguments from across a wide chronological spectrum—from classic medieval formulations all the way to contemporary arguments which at first seem to surpass or even overturn the classic arguments and their principles. I want to summarize our discussion by asking whether there are any "family resemblances" or common threads of concern that we might identify as constitutive of natural theology. Amidst this diversity, is there any consistency? Are the arguments persuasive?

There is indeed consistency, and it guarantees the cogency of the project. Let us focus on three factors.

First, all our examples show clearly that natural theology speaks directly to the issue that we raised at the outset of this chapter, namely its *necessity*—our need to identify some connections between the reality of God and human experience. At that point we noted that

---

120. Cf. also *Theology and Church*, 29–30: "By defining God, the all-determining reality, in personal terms, *being as a whole* is personally defined. This means a revolution in the understanding of being. . . . To put it in more concrete terms: *love is the all-determining reality* and the meaning of being. . . . So wherever there is love, we already find, here and now, the ultimate meaning of all reality" (Kasper's emphases).

the fundamental task of natural theology is to demonstrate that human experience by its very nature is open to transcendence and participates in a dynamic movement toward God which eventually can be more fully articulated through a faith commitment to God and by the action of *intellectus fidei*, faith seeking understanding. Without an experience of God *within* human experience, in terms that can be recognized *by* human experience in so far as that is possible, the person would be stranded and not even know enough to seek God. God would remain extrinsic to experience, and faith in God could not be considered a free and truly human act. Specifying the necessary connection which overcomes this extrinsicism, pointing out precisely how the experience of God is possible *as a human experience*, is crucial to the project of natural theology.

All the arguments we have seen, at their crux, articulate the reality and character of this connection—in differing ways, of course, depending on whether the argument is anthropological, cosmological, or both. Anselm's anthropological argument finds the connection in the actions of rational subjectivity strained to its limits. Thomas Aquinas' cosmological argument discovers it in the metaphysical underpinnings of our experience of the everyday world. Hans Küng, in many ways as traditional as both Anselm and Thomas while responding to the hermeneutes of suspicion, attempts to make both types of arguments at once by highlighting our fundamental trust in both the solidity of our experience of the everyday world and the meaningfulness of our experience of our own lives as pointers to God. Walter Kasper, in his version of the anthropological argument, finds the connection in the depth dimension of everyday experience, especially in those limit-experiences of love and freedom which offer a disclosure and *Vorgriff* of the personal God who is the horizon for those experiences. Even the post-metaphysical "negative" theologies argued by Jean-Luc Marion and John Dominic Crossan, despite their suspicious hermeneutic of human experience (predicting its breakdown when confronted by transcendence), are anthropological arguments which find the connection somewhere in relation to experience, albeit at its very limits where it shades off into the ineffable.

The consistent factor, though, is the explication of some connection between the experience of God and human experience, no matter how tenuously that connection is portrayed. The key issue is the intersection of the *givenness* of God to human experience with the finite human articulation of that givenness. As the critical reflection on the natural access-point of faith, natural theology sits squarely in this intersection. Its role is to establish and clarify the reality of the divine, as far as this is possible from the perspective of our categories of understanding. "As far as this is possible . . ." implies that natural theology is always faced with limits and is forced to concede the inadequacy of its categories in the face of the transcendent character of God. How that inadequacy is evaluated is, as we have seen, remains a point of dispute. Marion and Crossan view it as a burden, a problematic surd, while Anselm, Thomas, Küng and Kasper view it as an opportunity to experience the depth of the mystery which is its necessary precondition. In either case, human experience is still the necessary clearing wherein the experience of God takes place. Natural theology attempts to articulate precisely where within human experience this openness to transcendence occurs.

A second point which is implied in the first is that each of the arguments is an example of a "transcendental move," the ability of human subjectivity to experience the presence of infinite transcendence and something of its character from within our finite perspective. To clarify this experience of "the infinite within the finite," Crossan's metaphor (despite the negative baggage that it carries) is very appropriate here: we acknowledge the transcending expanse which lies beyond the edges of our raft from the viewpoint of those very edges themselves and from the limited domain of experience represented by the raft and its boundaries. We don't *become* the infinite in order to know it—such an experience is impossible, for how could we ever throw off our finitude? But we can understand something of the divine transcendence which is more than our finite situation by approaching it as the never-objectifiable horizon of that situation. The transcendental move is the attempt to think both the finite "foreground" as well as the infinite "background" which is its necessary condition.

The term "transcendental method" and the "horizonal" thinking just described have been closely associated with the twentieth-century theological methods of Karl Rahner, Bernhard Welte, Bernard Lonergan, and other theologians influenced by transcendental Thomism.[121] But we are justified in generalizing beyond this school and applying its insight into the fundamental operation of thought in a more extended fashion. The transcendental move can be defined as the ability "to uncover the universal in the particular" and more specifically as "a critical examination of the concrete human subject [that] can yield genuine insight into elements that go beyond particular experience" and that ultimately grasps "the conditions which make [experience] possible at all."[122] This describes particularly well what all the arguments of this chapter have set out to accomplish: thematizing as clearly as possible the transcendent presence of divinity that is both the condition for and the goal of the human intentional experience of meaning. And if we cast the definition a bit more broadly and say, along with the philosopher Maurice Blondel, that an analysis of human subjectivity demonstrates clearly "that the very notion of immanence [i.e., the meaningfulness of thought and action within the human sphere] is realized in our consciousness only by the effective presence of the notion of the transcendent" and that the transcendent is "indispensable and at the same time inaccessible" for finite human beings,[123] we reach the heart of the natural theology enterprise, an insight into the particular operation of subjectivity as it attempts to think and speak about God. The "transcendental move" names the act where "thinking necessarily transcends itself, inasmuch as it thinks something which it is essentially incapable of thinking out any further, because the infinite cannot be captured in any finite concept."[124] As investigations into the

121. See Francis Schüssler Fiorenza, "The New Theology and Transcendental Thomism," in James C. Livingston, et al., *Modern Christian Thought, Volume II: The Twentieth Century*, 2d ed. (Upper Saddle River, NJ: Prentice-Hall, 2000), 197–232. See also Rahner's own description of "transcendental theology" in Karl Rahner, ed., *Encyclopedia of Theology: The Concise "Sacramentum Mundi"* (New York: Crossroad, 1982), 1748–51.

122. Roger Haight, *Dynamics of Theology*, 2d ed. (Maryknoll, NY: Orbis, 2001), 6.

123. Maurice Blondel, *The Letter on Apologetics*, in *The Letter on Apologetics and History and Dogma*, trans. Alexander Dru and Illtyd Trethowan (Grand Rapids: Eerdmans, 1994), 158, 161.

124. Kasper, *GJC*, 112–13. Kasper applies this to Anselm's argument in particular, but it can be applied to all of the examples in this chapter.

natural access-point of faith, natural theology's various arguments are consistent in wishing to clarify what Blondel termed "the point of insertion,"[125] the locus of the intersection between finite human experience and transcendence where the transcendent becomes available to thought. These arguments, by clarifying the character of this insertion or intersection, articulate the nature of the realities on either side of this "point" or limit-concept, as far as this is possible: the character of finite intentional experience, of course, but also the veiled character of transcendence which is the condition for the possibility of the finite desire for absolute meaning and completes its intentional strivings. We become aware of not only the transcendent mystery of God but also the intentional openness of human subjectivity and the ability of human experience to transcend its empirical limitations.

Finally, there is implicit in the previous two points something which is absolutely crucial for the basic claim of this book. These natural theology arguments clearly respond to and reproduce the dialectical presence-absence structure that is fundamental to our encounter with the reality of God, who is available yet uncontrollable, knowable yet mysterious, immanent yet transcendent. The arguments that we have highlighted, when taken together, can serve as an antidote to the extrinsic view of God which has been assumed to be equivalent to the basic Christian view but which, as we have seen in the previous chapter, is fundamentally a modern fiction and a distortion of biblical revelation.

Previously we saw that the key problem with which all the arguments wrestle is the possibility of establishing and clarifying the givenness of the infinite God from the perspective of our finite experience and categories of understanding. This problem is caused by the paradox which lies at the heart of the reality of God, the dialectic which the Bible comfortably narrates but which rational argumentation struggles to demonstrate.[126] Each argument handles this problem by making a clear statement of what we can know and what we cannot know about God. Natural theology, as we have described it,

---

125. Blondel, *Letter on Apologetics*, 163.
126. We will say more about this paradox and the presence-absence dialectic in the concluding chapter.

is an exercise in affirmation and denial. Every affirmation (presence) includes a denial (absence): God is present *yet* exceeds our categories; our finite perspective gives us some knowledge of God *but* never a comprehensive understanding. At every turn natural theology is confronted with limit (". . . than which nothing greater can be thought"). It is forced to concede the inadequacy of its categories in the face of the uncontrollable, mysterious, transcendent character of God who exceeds those limits.

But this does not cancel the fact that natural theology does indeed make affirmations, although the arguments differ precisely on what is affirmed of God. Crossan stops at the bare fact of God's transcendence. Marion goes a bit further to speak of the quality of transcendence as love and the agapic personality of the Giver. At first glance Anselm seems to offer little more than a vision of God's transcendence; in its barest form the ontological argument seems to reach the conclusion that in the concept of "the being than which nothing greater can be thought" what we comprehend about God is that God is incomprehensible. But a closer examination shows that in this limit-concept one affirms of God all the perfections. Thomas Aquinas and Küng go further still to search out appropriate "names" for God ("unmoved mover," "support," etc.). Kasper goes the furthest: in arguing that the infinite mystery is the horizon of absolute freedom and that the fundamental character of absolute freedom is love, he opens the way to claiming that the infinite mystery is inherently personal: "to call God a person is to say that God is the subsistent being which is freedom in love."[127]

Kasper's argument, I believe, is the most expansive of those we have seen because it is able to take up and account for all the issues raised by the other arguments, whether the evidence is anthropological or cosmological. And it is the one which is the most fully reflective of the presence-absence structure of the biblical revelation of God, which is consistently presented in terms of personal relationships. By means of his particular version of natural theology, we can argue vigorously (always *quoad nos*, from our limited perspective) for an affirmation of the relational character of the divine mystery.

---

127. *GJC*, 155.

We have a way, then, of characterizing the "natural access-point of faith" as a personal appeal for a personal encounter with transcendent divine mystery. Kasper shows us how it is most plausible (always *quoad nos*) to expect that our encounters with God will be personal ones best described in terms of personal relationships. We thus have a solid point of departure to begin to reflect upon the other part of the Christian answer to the problem of God—namely, what Christianity regards as the center of its faith, the trinitarian confession of one God in three persons.

CHAPTER FOUR

The Christian Response, II: Theological Theology

1. The Link between Natural and Theological Theology

The heart of Christian belief and the explicitly Christian way of speaking about God is to confess God as Trinity—one God in three persons, Father, Son, and Holy Spirit. As the Nicene Creed puts it, "We believe in one God, the Father almighty, maker of heaven and earth . . . and in one Lord Jesus Christ, the only-begotten Son of God . . . and in the Holy Spirit, the Lord and Giver of life."[1]

With the creed the Church makes three assertions. First, the heart of Christian life is the revelation of God's saving love for us in the life, death, and continuing presence of the risen Christ, and our ongoing participation in divine life through the power of the Holy Spirit.[2] Second, the creed offers a specific view of reality *as creation*, in terms of its fundamental relation to God, the "maker of heaven and earth." Lastly, something definitive is expressed about the believer, the faithful hearer who understands: not only is "Trinity" *precisely* how God is revealed as the author of salvation, but "Trinity" is also *precisely*

---

1. More precisely the "Nicene-Constantinopolitan" creed, the "symbol" of Nicaea (325) as expanded by the first council of Constantinople (381), trans. in J. Neuner and J. Dupuis, *The Christian Faith in the Doctrinal Documents of the Catholic Church* [hereafter ND], 6th ed. (New York: Alba House, 1996), ND 12 (pp. 9–10) = DH 150. See also Norman P. Tanner, ed., *Decrees of the Ecumenical Councils* [hereafter *DEC*], 2 vols., (London: Sheed and Ward/Washington: Georgetown University Press, 1990), 1:24 (Grk./Lat. orig. and Eng. trans. on facing pages).

2. *Compendium of the Catechism of the Catholic Church* (Washington, DC: United States Conference of Catholic Bishops, 2006), 19 (no. 44): "The central mystery of Christian faith and life is the mystery of the Most Blessed Trinity."

how Christians speak of God when they reflect on how they have encountered God as "God-for-us."[3]

Belief in the Trinity, the central mystery of Christianity, thus pushes believers beyond the constraints of natural theology. Thomas Aquinas' caution that "it is impossible to come to the knowledge of the Trinity of divine persons through natural reason" is worth noting:

> Through natural reason one can know God only from creatures; and they lead to the knowledge of him as effects do to their cause. Therefore by natural reason we can know of God only what characterizes him necessarily as the source of all beings. . . . Whoever tries to prove the trinity of persons by natural powers of reason detracts from faith in two ways. First . . . the object of faith is those invisible realities which are beyond the reach of human reason. . . . Secondly . . . when someone wants to support faith by unconvincing arguments, that person becomes a laughing stock for the unbelievers, who think that we rely on such arguments and believe because of them.[4]

But doesn't this distinction leave us with an intractable problem? As we have seen, Western culture's commonly-held view has been that natural knowledge of God and supernatural divine revelation are distinct and completely separate. Our approach—presenting a natural theology first, then showing its necessary connections with a revelational theology of God as triune—may seem to involve a contradiction or disconnection. Fortunately, there is no real dilemma or forced "either-or" choice here. That would arise only if one were to approach the question of God with the Enlightenment's assump-

---

3. See Catherine Mowry LaCugna, *God For Us: The Trinity and Christian Life* (San Francisco: HarperCollins, 1991), 1; Jürgen Werbick, "Trinitätslehre," in *Handbuch der Dogmatik*, ed. Theodore Schneider, 2 vols. (Düsseldorf: Patmos, 1992), 2:481–576, at 481–82. For our earlier discussion of faith as "a hearing that understands," see chap. 3, sec. 1.

4. Thomas Aquinas, *Summa theologiae* Ia, q. 32, a. 1, resp. (in *Summa theologiae*, vol. 6 [Ia. 27–32]: *The Trinity*, trans. Ceslaus Verlecky [1965; repr., Cambridge: Cambridge University Press, 2006], 102–05; translation modified). Hereafter cited as *ST*, part, question (q.), article (a.), response, reply (ad), followed by volume and page(s) in the Latin-English Blackfriars edition, 60 vols. (1964–76; repr., Cambridge: Cambridge University Press, 2006).

tion of a complete disjunction between so-called "pure nature" and the supernatural. But that assumption (which unfortunately still colors much of the discussion of God in Western culture) stems from a minimalist view of rationality, faith, and natural theology.

In this book, we already have worked out "natural theology" in a much more positive and inclusive way.[5] Faith and reason, while distinct, are mutually related aspects of human experience. Faith is always both "faith seeking understanding" (*fides quaerens intellectum*) and "faith developed in understanding" (*intellectus fidei*). The believer always approaches the truth of God's gratuitous offer of salvation in an active way, interpreting one's life in relation to God and then affirming this relationship as the most meaningful way to actualize the possibilities of human existence. This implicit interaction leads to the more adequate description of natural theology as *the search for the natural access-point of faith.* The "natural" and the "supernatural" are distinct but not dichotomous; they intersect in everyday, historically-shaped lived experience. Within the natural, one recognizes the presence of the mystery of the supernatural, "not as optional like a gift which is proposed but not imposed . . . not as so ineffable as to lack all foothold in our thought and our life, but . . . as indispensable and at the same time inaccessible" to finite human experience.[6] This intersection marks the "clearing" where knowledge of God unfolds, where faith's desire for God becomes visible, where revelation begins to be encountered.

We also emphasized the limits of this search, agreeing with Thomas that the natural knowledge of God permits us only an inadequate glimpse of the character of transcendence, never any full comprehension of its nature.[7] Despite this limitation, natural theology discloses something remarkable: the fundamental *religious* character of the structure of human experience, its intentional openness to infinite mystery that forms its transcendental horizon. True, the *precise* character of this mystery is revealed only by the mystery itself. But

5. See the detailed discussion in chap. 3, sec. 1.

6. Maurice Blondel, *The Letter on Apologetics*, in *The Letter on Apologetics and History and Dogma*, trans. Alexander Dru and Illtyd Trethowan (Grand Rapids: Eerdmans, 1994 [Fr. orig., 1896]), 161.

7. See chap. 3, sec. 2.2. Cf. Thomas Aquinas, *ST* Ia, q. 2, a. 2 (2:8–11).

the natural knowledge of God opens a vista onto the revelation of the true nature of divine mystery, without daring to claim to actually reach it—similar to Moses, on the heights of Mount Nebo, glimpsing the promised land without being allowed to enter it (Deut 34:1–4).

What about this issue when seen within the history of theology? Our approach might appear to echo a fundamental difficulty that has plagued mainstream Christian theology since the thirteenth century, and particularly Catholic theology since the late nineteenth century, namely a perpetuation of the gulf between a theology that emphasizes the nature and unity of God (the theological treatise *de Deo uno*) and one that deals specifically with God as triune (the treatise *de Deo trino*). More recently, this division of labor "made the doctrine of the Trinity appear as an afterthought, as something added on to a prior, independent philosophical concept of God."[8] It led to the situation described in Karl Rahner's famous complaint: "despite their orthodox confession of the Trinity, Christians are, in their practical life, almost mere 'monotheists'. . . . Should the doctrine of the Trinity have to be dropped as false, the major part of religious literature could well remain virtually unchanged."[9]

It is ironic that Thomas Aquinas was the first to develop the study of God in this general manner.[10] He began by taking up the earlier scholastic tradition that had been passed down chiefly through Peter Lombard's *Sentences* (*Sententiarum libri IV*, c. 1155–58), the compendium that dominated the study of theology through the latter half of the medieval period. The *Sentences* had divided the material of theology into four treatises (God and Trinity, creation and sin, the Incarnation and the virtues, the sacraments and the four last things). In writing the *Summa theologiae*, however, Thomas reorganized the material dealing with God, under the influence of late Neoplatonism (espe-

8. Catherine Mowry LaCugna, "The Trinitarian Mystery of God," in *Systematic Theology: Roman Catholic Perspectives*, ed. Francis Schüssler Fiorenza and John Galvin, 2 vols. (Minneapolis: Fortress, 1991), 1:172.

9. Karl Rahner, *The Trinity*, trans. Joseph Donceel (New York: Crossroad, 1997 [Ger. Orig., 1967]), 10–11.

10. Noted also by Rahner (*The Trinity*, 16). For what follows, see LaCugna, *God for Us*, 146–48; W. J. Hankey, *God in Himself: Aquinas' Doctrine of God as Expounded in the Summa Theologiae* (Oxford: Oxford University Press, 1987), 1–35.

cially as conveyed through the writings of Pseudo-Dionysius) and in particular the Neoplatonic *exitus-reditus* schema (i.e., creatures' procession from and return to God).[11] While the *Sentences* had treated the nature of God within the opening section devoted to the Trinity (*de mysterio Trinitatis*), Thomas was more influenced by the structure of Pseudo-Dionysius' *The Divine Names.* He divided the treatise on God into two distinct parts, later called *de Deo uno* and *de Deo trino*.[12] The former (*ST* Ia, qq. 2–26) examines the issues surrounding the nature of the one God and our knowledge of that nature, while the latter examines the distinction of persons in the Trinity and their relations (*ST* Ia, qq. 27–43).

Thomas never designates one part as purely philosophical and the other as purely theological. Rather, both are *theological* because they investigate matters that have been revealed to faith and pursued under the rubric of "sacred teaching" (*sacra doctrina*). He insists at the outset that theology (also termed *sacra doctrina*) is a discipline practiced from the perspective of faith which has its grounding in revelation. It is a science whose principles flow "from founts recognized in the light of a higher science, namely God's very own which he shares with the blessed."[13] One cannot appeal, then, either to the

11. See Paul Rorem, *Pseudo-Dionysius: A Commentary on the Texts and an Introduction to Their Influence* (New York/Oxford: Oxford University Press, 1993), 172–74. As major influences, he cites Boethius, Proclus (whose *Liber de causis* was considered by Thomas to have been authored by Aristotle), and the Pseudo-Dionysian corpus, particularly *The Divine Names*.

12. Cf. Hankey, *God in Himself*, 10–12. The author of *The Divine Names* had divided them into "the unified names [that] apply to the entire Godhead" (such as "transcendently good," "transcendently existing," "beautiful," "life-giving") and those "expressing distinctions, the transcendent name and proper activity of the Father, of the Son, of the Spirit" (*The Divine Names*, chap. 2, sec. 2, in Pseudo-Dionysius, *The Complete Works*, trans. Colm Luibheid and Paul Rorem, The Classics of Western Spirituality [New York/Mahwah: Paulist, 1987], 60). In the prologue to *ST* Ia, q. 2 (2:3), Thomas clearly mentions a *tripartite* outline (the nature of God, "the distinction of persons in God," and "the coming forth from him of creatures"). But only the first two parts deal explicitly with the nature of God.

13. *ST* Ia, q. 1, a. 2, reply (1:11). See also Ia, q. 1, a. 8, ad 2 (1:31–32): "The premises of this teaching [i.e., *sacra doctrina*, Christian theology] are revealed truths, accepted on the word of the teacher who reveals them. . . . All the same *sacra doctrina* also uses human reasoning, not indeed to prove the faith, for that would

structure or the arguments of the *Summa theologiae* to justify the identification of Thomas' *de Deo uno* with the kind of philosophically
extrinsicist natural theology we criticized earlier.[14]

After Thomas' death, his two-fold division of the study of God was
widely imitated in the medieval West and became the model for
subsequent discussions. Only much later, with nineteenth-century
Roman Catholic Neoscholasticism, was the distinction between the
two treatises turned into a rigid disjunction that did away with
Thomas' carefully-crafted plan. The Neoscholastic theological man-
uals identified *de Deo uno* with the philosophical discussion of the
one divine nature and *de Deo trino* with the theological consideration
of mysteries of the Trinity "in the strict sense" (*mysteria stricte dicta*)
whose content lay beyond the grasp of human reason and was made
available only by means of supernatural revelation. This arrangement
clearly reflected the intent of Neoscholastic apologetics to defend
both the legitimacy of Christianity and the objective certainty of
supernatural revelation against the criticisms leveled by modern
natural religion.[15] The tract *de Deo uno* contained the proofs for the

---

take away from the merit of believing, but to make manifest some implications of
its message. Since grace does not do away with nature but brings it to perfection,
so also natural reason should assist faith as the natural loving bent of the will
yields to charity. . . . For our faith rests on the revelation made to the prophets
and apostles who wrote the canonical books, not on a revelation, if such there
be, made to any other teacher" (translation modified).

14. See William J. Hill's comment on Thomas' "five ways": "What Aquinas
seeks out at the very beginning of the work (q. 2) are 'ways' (*viae*, not 'proofs,'
'arguments,', or 'demonstrations') by which the human spirit, in its powers of
transcendence, might ascend to an affirmation of God—and in actual fact, that
God who has already addressed his Word to man" (*The Three-Personed God: The
Trinity as a Mystery of Salvation* [Washington: Catholic University of America
Press, 1982], 63).

15. Neoscholasticism attempted to defend the truth of Catholicism against
what it argued were the heresies of modernity by using what amounted to
modern means of assuring objective certainty. See Francis Schüssler Fiorenza,
"Systematic Theology: Task and Methods," in *Systematic Theology: Roman Catholic
Perspectives*, ed. Francis Schüssler Fiorenza and John P. Galvin, 2 vols. (Minneap-
olis: Fortress, 1991), 1:27–34; Fiorenza, "The New Theology and Transcendental
Thomism," in James C. Livingston, et al., *Modern Christian Thought, Volume II: The
Twentieth Century*, 2d ed. (Upper Saddle River, NJ: Prentice-Hall, 2000), 198–200;

existence of God, the discussion of the nature and attributes of God (e.g., simplicity, immutability, and eternity), and an analysis of the divine operations (knowledge, will, providence, predestination, and omnipotence). *De Deo trino* discussed the distinction, procession, and mission of the divine persons, as well as the intelligibility of the mystery of the Trinity and its philosophical analogues.[16]

Reacting to the perduring influence of this extreme separation, Karl Rahner objected that "the treatise of the Trinity locks itself in even more splendid isolation, with the ensuing danger that the religious mind finds it devoid of interest. It looks as if everything which matters for us in God has already been said in the treatise *On the One God.*"[17] Our own approach, though, has nothing to do with the rigorous divisions of Neoscholasticism. Rather, it has more in common with the method originally suggested by Thomas' *Summa theologiae*, where the study of the nature of the one God and the study of the Trinity are seen as two different yet complementary moments of our encounter with revelation. What I have proposed are two interlocking Christian responses to the problem of God in Western culture and thus a genuine connection between our experience of God and a theological (i.e., revelational) theology of the Trinity.

If our contemporary situation is even roughly as we have described it—a time of the celebration of the consumer image, of the dimming of the religious imagination even amidst heightened religious expression, or even as a "dark night" of varying intensities that provokes from many, even those of strong Christian belief, the anguished questions "where is God?" and "who is God?"—then we must make the strongest arguments for the plausibility of divine transcendence and

---

Anthony J. Godzieba, *Bernhard Welte's Fundamental Theological Approach to Christology*, American University Studies, series VII, vol. 160 (New York/Bern: Peter Lang, 1994), 18–30.

16. E.g., see the once-popular seminary manual by Adolphe Tanquerey, *Synopsis Theologiae Dogmaticae, tomus secundus: de Fide, de Deo uno et Trino, de Deo creante et elevante, de Verbo Incarnato*, 24th ed. (Paris: Desclée, 1933).

17. Rahner, *The Trinity*, 17. Rahner's critique applies more to what Thomas' distinction became in the hands of the Neoscholastic manualists than to Thomas himself.

for the real possibility of personally encountering the living God. In this way we can reignite the religious imagination. For if the very notion of "God" or "divine transcendence" seems implausible to many, what chance does the doctrine of the Trinity have of being appreciated and appropriated in a way that is helpful to faith? To first seek and find the "clearing" or the natural access-point of faith is to promote the human capacity to think and experience otherwise than the unending cycle of commodified images and the seeming claustrophobia of consumer culture. An authentic natural theology heightens our expectations regarding our encounters with God. It widens the parameters by demonstrating that one of the fundamental conditions of human experience is its orientation in the direction of God and transcendence. It also gives us a glimpse—but only a glimpse—of the character of the transcendence for which we long. If natural theology can identify this "clearing" within our experience as the place where God may be encountered, then Christian claims concerning the triune nature and personality of divinity will find a footing in human life and thus be more readily heard and appreciated.

In this clearing, at the threshold of the natural access-point of faith, we encounter not only the transcendent horizon of our life and actions, the all-encompassing infinite mystery which we do not hesitate to call "God."[18] We also discover something of its depth, a hint (*Vorgriff*) of the non-negotiable benevolence of that mystery which *gives* itself to us on its own initiative, a glimpse of the character of absolute freedom which reveals itself to us in a relationship that can best be described as *personal* and ultimately fulfilling. The key elements here are the "givenness" of this experience and the personal relationship that this revelatory "giving" engenders. At the limits of our experience, divine transcendence can best be described in personal, relational terms: as a gracious giver who encounters us in a personal fashion, freely granting us the space that makes our life and actions possible. In turn, we give ourselves over to the infinite mystery, trusting it to reveal itself as the loving fulfillment that we believe it to be.

18. Cf. Karl Rahner, *Foundations of Christian Faith: An Introduction to the Idea of Christianity*, trans. William V. Dych (1978; reprint, New York: Crossroad, 1989), 57–75.

What makes this limited yet meaningful vision possible is a *revelatory moment already present* to human experience. Here is where "natural theology" begins to shade over into "theological theology." The givenness of the infinite mystery makes possible the natural access-point of faith, a moment of grace already present to our experience in the sheer fact of this gift and our recognition of it.[19] We respond to it and interpret it by placing it within the context of our previous experiences. With this deepened natural knowledge of God, our argument against extrinsicism bears fruit. The most appropriate way to describe this experience of givenness is to employ a *personal* metaphor: we perceive the givenness which characterizes infinite mystery as a *personal* appeal which creates a *personal* relationship that begins to fulfill us *as persons*. This experience, though, is only a hint, a series of fragmentary anticipations. At this point, natural theology exhausts itself. The presence-absence structure that governs our encounters with God ensures that our affirmations of transcendence, while true, always fall short. Rational reflection can articulate our fundamental openness to the glimpses we receive of divine presence. But the full nature of the giver and the true quality of the relationship always exceed our categories of experience and reflection. They are revealed only in the depths of supernatural revelation itself. If we are to know who God is, then God must reveal God's own self.

At this point the transition between an authentic natural knowledge of God and trinitarian theology becomes clear. Natural theology's pre-apprehension of the authentic character of God is filled out and intensified by the revelatory encounter we have with God the Father who saves us through Jesus Christ and who incorporates us into that salvation by means of the Holy Spirit. While natural theology always arrives late on the scene, so to speak, it grasps in fragmentary form that which preexists and pervades every moment of our experience of God. It emphasizes the disclosure that unfolds in terms of presence-and-absence, an action that can be adequately approached only by a theological theology that takes up where natural theology

19. Indeed, it is the presupposition for our recognition of revelation as *supernatural*. Cf. Henri Bouillard, *The Knowledge of God*, trans. Samuel D. Femiano (New York: Herder and Herder, 1968), 24–31.

necessarily leaves off. Here, then, is a bridge to a theological theology of the Trinity—not a *proof* of the reality of the triune God, of course, since "reason cannot prove the necessity of the Trinity either from the concept of absolute spirit or from the concept of love. The Trinity is a mystery in the strict sense of the term."[20] Rather, we acknowledge the openness of human experience to an encounter with God and speak, as best we can, about what occurs within that encounter.

"Faith seeking understanding" attempts to express both the revelation of God's own self as a triune communion of persons and the intrinsic relevance of the Trinity for Christian life. One of its fundamental goals, then, is to show that Christian belief in the triune God is not a doctrine imposed from "outside," but rather that God, in revealing, wills our happiness. Human life, having discovered its intrinsic orientation to God, will find its desires and its created potential fulfilled when it continues to acknowledge and celebrate its rootedness in the Trinity (doxology) and confess its intrinsic need for the Trinity's loving and saving action (soteriology). To this theological theology of the Trinity we now turn.

2. The Revelation of the Triune God

The origins of Christian belief in the triune God are found "solely in the history of God's dealings with human beings and in the historical self-revelation of the Father through Jesus Christ in the Holy Spirit."[21] In other words, we become aware of the "inner" or "immanent" reality of God as triune (*theologia* in Greek) not through abstract speculation, but rather on God's revelatory initiative alone—by God's salvific self-disclosure in history (*oikonomia*, the divine plan or

20. Walter Kasper, *The God of Jesus Christ* [hereafter *GJC*], new ed., trans. [Matthew J. O'Connell and] Dinah Livingstone (London/New York: Continuum, 2012), 267.

21. Ibid, 237. For the development of trinitarian theology, see Gisbert Greshake, *Der dreieine Gott: Eine trinitarische Theologie* (Freiburg/Br.: Herder, 1997); Hill, *The Three-Personed God*; Kasper, *GJC*, 233–316; LaCugna, *God for Us*; Wolfhart Pannenberg, *Systematic Theology*, 1:259–336; Rahner, *The Trinity*; Stephen Davis, Daniel Kendall, and Gerald O'Collins, eds., *The Trinity: An Interdisciplinary Symposium on the Trinity* (New York: Oxford University Press, 1999).

"economy" of salvation), in events first narrated within a tradition of belief before they are reflected upon systematically.[22] Scripture, the divinely-inspired interpretive narration of these events, is thus the pivotal resource. While biblical exegetes and theologians agree that there is no explicitly developed doctrine of the Trinity in either the Old or New Testament, nevertheless the classical doctrine is firmly rooted in Scripture's testimony to God's relationship with humanity as it has occurred in history. Additional evidence can be found in the spiritual life and liturgical experiences of the early Church, whose members lived under the intense impact and ongoing effects of Christ's resurrection.

Subsequent theological analysis of these formative elements derives from them "the concepts in which the New Testament revelation of the triune God can be formulated as a profession of faith, presents this revelation in its interconnectedness, and renders its meaning recognizable as the center of Christian belief."[23] This very basic description may make development of the doctrine of the Trinity appear to be a simple process, but in reality it is the fruit of centuries of spiritual experience, liturgical practice, and continuing theological reflection. At every point in this development, the Church's fundamental concern has been soteriological, asking how we are to understand "the saving activity of the God of Israel as this was realised in the person and event of Jesus Christ and in the reception of the gift of the Holy Spirit."[24] The theological task, then, is to explain how our salvation is enacted in the intimate communion among the three persons of the Trinity, while at the same time we profess our firm belief in the one God.

22. Greshake, *Der dreieine Gott*, 48. For the background and various meanings of "economy" (Greek *oikonomia*, Latin *dispensatio, dispositio*) in relation to salvation, see G. L. Prestige, *God in Patristic Thought*, 2d ed. (1952; reprint, London: SPCK, 1981), 57–67; LaCugna, *God For Us*, 24–30.

23. Wolfgang Beinert and Francis Schüssler Fiorenza, eds., *Handbook of Catholic Theology* (New York: Crossroad, 1995), 723, s.v. "Trinity: Doctrine of the" (Wilhelm Breuning).

24. Ralph Del Colle, "The Triune God," in *The Cambridge Companion to Christian Doctrine*, ed. Colin E. Gunton (Cambridge: Cambridge University Press, 1997), 122–23.

The primary scriptural resource for belief in the Trinity is the New Testament, which provides the basis for the doctrine of the Trinity on three interconnected levels: it narrates the historically- and culturally-embedded events whereby the triune structure of God's saving activity is revealed; it records the early Christian attempts to express this trinitarian structure in reminiscence and confession; and it reflects on how these events and expressions, taken together, articulate the definitive self-revelation of the triune God as love (1 John 4:8, 16).[25] But trinitarian theology also relies on the Old Testament for crucial data about the experiences that ground the New Testament's claims. None is more central than the confession of the unity of God: "Hear, O Israel! The LORD is our God, the LORD alone. You shall love the LORD your God with all your heart, and with all your soul, and with all your might" (Deut 6:4-5). These verses were later incorporated into the *Shema*, the prayer recited twice daily by every devout Jew. The confession of God's oneness and uniqueness was the central pillar of Judaism immediately before and during Jesus' time, and became the basis for Christianity as well.[26]

The Old Testament evidence, however, also shows that this fully-formed monotheism was not the starting point of Israel's relationship with Yahweh, but rather its mature arrival-point. Israel's belief in the oneness and uniqueness of God took centuries to develop

---

25. Compare Kasper's assessment of the New Testament evidence, a three-step analysis of "1. the trinitarian structure of the revelational event; 2. the trinitarian explanation of this event in the New Testament; and 3. the connection between this explanation and the essential definition of God that is given in the New Testament." Only in this way can theology keep the confession of the Trinity from being relegated to "a later, purely speculative addition to the original faith in Christ" and instead demonstrate that it "provides the basic structure and ground plan of the New Testament witness, and that with it the belief in the God of Jesus Christ stands or falls" (*GJC*, 244).

26. James D. G. Dunn deems monotheism the first of the four pillars of Second Temple Judaism; see *The Partings of the Ways Between Christianity and Judaism and their Significance for the Character of Christianity* (London: SCM/Philadelphia: Trinity Press International, 1991), 19–21. See also Larry W. Hurtado, *Lord Jesus Christ: Devotion to Jesus in Earliest Christianity* (Grand Rapids/Cambridge: Eerdmans, 2003), 29–31; E. P. Sanders, *The Historical Figure of Jesus* (London/New York: Penguin, 1995 [1993]), 33–39 (on the "common Judaism" of first century AD/CE).

into the form that is considered characteristic of Judaism.[27] A number of texts, for example, reflect the character of early Israelite religion when it tolerated other deities (always few in number) alongside Yahweh (e.g., Gen 35:2-3; Josh 24:16; Judg 5:8). Other texts cast light on the conditions of somewhat later Israelite history, when there existed differences between the nationalistic cult of Yahweh promoted by the monarchy and other, more syncretistic cultic practices of popular religion (e.g., Baal worship) that were originally tolerated, but later were strongly condemned as incompatible with the true worship of Yahweh (1 Kgs 18–19; Amos 5:25-27; Hos 2; Jer 10).[28] The Old Testament clearly depicts an historical development in Israel's relationship with God: from a polytheistic Yahwism or henotheism to a practical monotheism (where one worships Yahweh alone, without deciding on the existence or non-existence of other deities), and finally to an ethical monotheism (where Yahweh is regarded as the only God; all others are nonentities). The centrality of monotheism was affirmed only around the time of the exile in Babylon in the sixth century BC/BCE, and only in this post-exilic period did monotheism and monolatry become the fundamental dogmas of Judaism. For example, the author of Second Isaiah (Isa 40–55), writing just before or during the exile and continuing the Isaian prophetic tradition,[29] boldly and unambiguously affirms that Yahweh is the only deity in the cosmos and the God of all peoples: "I am the LORD, and there is no other. . . . There is no other god besides me; a righteous God and a Savior; there is no one besides me. Turn to me and be saved, all the ends of the earth! For I am God, and there is no other!" (Isa 45:5, 21-22). This insistence on God's unity and uniqueness became the outstanding characteristic of Judaism in the post-exilic period and made Israel unique among its neighbors. It also provoked within

---

27. Mark S. Smith, *The Early History of God: Yahweh and the Other Deities in Ancient Israel*, 2d ed. (Grand Rapids: Eerdmans/Dearborn, MI: Dove, 2002), 182–99; John J. Scullion, "God: God in the OT," in *The Anchor Bible Dictionary*, eds. David Noel Freedman, et al., 6 vols. (New York: Doubleday, 1992), 2:1041–48; Kasper, *GJC*, 238–39.

28. Smith, *Early History of God*, 183–84.

29. Cf. Richard J. Clifford, "Isaiah, Book of: Second Isaiah," in *The Anchor Bible Dictionary*, 3:490–91.

Judaism itself "a fierce antipathy to syncretism and virulent hostility to anything which smacked of idolatry,"[30] as Jewish literature from this later period attests (e.g., Jdt 8:18; Wis 13:1–15:6).

In the religious experience mirrored in the Old Testament, monotheism was never merely a theoretical issue verified by intellectual "proofs." It arose rather out of Israel's encounters with Yahweh, revelatory experiences whose decisive meaning had to be worked out over time in the context and categories of ancient Near Eastern religion and politics. At the same time these categories were stretched up to and even beyond their limits. Biblical monotheism is thus "the fruit of religious experience and an expression of practice based on faith." At its heart is "a radical decision in behalf of the one thing necessary," that is, the unshakable truth that "God alone is God; on him alone can one build unconditionally, in him alone can one trust without reserve." A theological analysis of these experiences of faith and of the practices they engender leads to the conclusion that the *oneness* of God necessarily implies the *uniqueness* of God. "Only one God can be infinite and all-inclusive; two Gods would limit one another even if they somehow interpenetrated. . . . The singleness of God is therefore not just one of the attributes of God; rather his singleness is given directly with his very essence."[31]

This strict commitment to monotheism provided the matrix not only for first-century AD/CE Judaism, but also for the Jewish movement that formed around Jesus and for the early Christianity that developed from it.[32] To abandon exclusivist monotheism was to abandon Judaism.[33] This is true even in light of the fact that late Second Temple Judaism (post-exilic Judaism from the second century BC/BCE onward) could entertain beliefs in a variety of heavenly inter-

30. Dunn, *Partings of the Ways*, 20.

31. Kasper, *GJC*, 239.

32. Hurtado, *Lord Jesus Christ*, 29: "What became 'Christianity' began as a movement within the Jewish religious tradition of the Roman period, and the chief characteristic of Jewish religion in this period was its defiantly monotheistic stance."

33. Ibid., 31: "to engage in the worship of other deities was to abandon Judaism. For devout Jews, the core requirement of Judaism was the exclusive worship of Israel's God."

mediary and redeemer figures and even a healthy angelology.[34] While acknowledging the demonstrable elasticity of monotheism within Second Temple Judaism, however, one must make an important distinction between "entertaining a belief in" and "worshipping," and realize how strictly that distinction was held. There is enough evidence that Jewish monotheism during the Roman period certainly "accommodated beliefs and very honorific rhetoric about various principal-agent figures such as high angels and exalted humans like Moses," but at the same time it "drew a sharp line between any such figure and the one God in the area of cultic practice, reserving cultic worship for the one God."[35]

This context makes all the more surprising the extraordinarily high estimation of Jesus of Nazareth among his followers so soon after Easter, as well as early Christianity's worship of Christ as divine, given the fact that belief in Jesus as the son of God arose among first-century AD/CE Jewish disciples who were steeped in exclusivist monotheism.[36] Their fundamental claim was that the historical manifestation of God and God's view of life had occurred most clearly and definitively in the person of Jesus of Nazareth. This belief was anchored in Jesus' preaching of the Kingdom of God, in the presence of God's salvific power which they perceived in Jesus' own life and actions, and in their experiences of the risen Christ after the catastrophe of his

---

34. See James D. G. Dunn, *Christology in the Making: An Inquiry into the Origins of the Doctrine of the Incarnation*, 2d ed. (London: SCM, 1990), 149–59.

35. Hurtado, *Lord Jesus Christ*, 48. See also Hurtado, "First-Century Jewish Monotheism," *Journal for the Study of the New Testament* 71 (1998): 3–26, where he highlights this combination of elasticity and exclusivism: first-century AD/CE Judaism had at one and the same time "a remarkable ability to combine a genuine concern for God's uniqueness together with an interest in other figures of transcendent attributes described in the most exalted terms" and "an exhibition of monotheistic scruples particularly and most distinctively in public cultic/liturgical behaviour"(3–4).

36. For the relatively rapid development of such exalted beliefs in Jesus, see the classic arguments by Martin Hengel in *The Son of God: The Origin of Christology and the History of Jewish-Hellenistic Religion*, trans. John Bowden (Philadelphia: Fortress, 1976) and "Christology and New Testament Chronology" in *Between Jesus and Paul: Studies in the Earliest History of Christianity*, trans. John Bowden (Philadelphia: Fortress, 1983), 30–47.

crucifixion. Throughout the course of his life, as well as in his death and resurrection, "Jesus reveals God as his own Father in an utterly unique and non-transferable way, while it is only through Jesus that we in turn become the sons and daughters of this Father."[37]

Through his life, words, and practices, Jesus proclaimed the Kingdom of God, God's kingly rule and attitude of care toward human life and the world. For Jesus, God's rule transforms situations of negativity, suffering, and dehumanization into situations of positivity, joy, and surprising human flourishing beyond any human accomplishment. Such astounding reversals can be accomplished only by God, whom Jesus portrayed in his parables and in his miracles as a surprising and capricious lover who surpasses human expectations and standards and goes to any lengths to make the offer of love and reversal open to all without qualification.[38] Jesus claimed that this long-awaited arrival of the Kingdom of God and its ongoing fulfillment was tied in a unique way to his own preaching and prophetic actions. Indeed, the salvific presence of God was present in the very paradox of his person. "Jesus had a direct *theo*-logy (God as object of his preaching), which involved an indirect or implicit *christo*-logy (Jesus as final agent of God). Thus Jesus' identity was absorbed into and defined by his mission."[39] In response to Jesus' aims and the effect his person and ministry had on them, his followers struggled to find appropriate categories and titles to express the extraordinary revelatory character and "otherness" of his presence, while at the same time doing justice to their own commitment to Jewish exclusivist monotheism and to the authentic Jewish character and substance of Jesus' life and preaching. This struggle is rooted in what John Meier terms the "basis paradox Jesus presented" to friends and foes alike: "Though he rarely spoke about his status, he implicitly made himself *the* pivotal figure in the eschatological drama he announced and inaugurated. . . . [Jesus] spoke and acted on the presumption that he would be the criterion used for the final judgment.

37. Kasper, *GJC*, 244.

38. For a detailed discussion, see Anthony J. Godzieba, "Method and Interpretation: The New Testament's Heretical Hermeneutic (Prelude and Fugue)," *The Heythrop Journal* 36 (1995): 286–306.

39. John P. Meier, "Jesus," in *The New Jerome Biblical Commentary*, ed. Raymond E. Brown, Joseph A. Fitzmyer, Roland E. Murphy (Englewood Cliffs: Prentice Hall, 1990) 1316–28, at 1323 (§29; emphases original).

That alone involved a monumental claim to a unique status and role at the climax of Israel's history."[40]

God's action of reversal was revealed not only in Jesus' *announcement* of the Kingdom of God, but equally in Jesus' *performance* of its values, especially his overwhelming concern for and action on behalf of the marginalized within first-century Palestinian Jewish society. This "performance" led to the series of events culminating in his crucifixion and resurrection.[41] That the reversal of negativity and the restoration of human well-being is truly God's salvific will was confirmed for Jesus' followers at Easter—his resurrection is the ultimate reversal, that of death into life. The New Testament clearly shows that the eschatological event of Jesus' resurrection and the disciples' Easter experiences of the Risen Lord became the key elements of their interpretation of Jesus' relationship to his Father (*Abba*): Jesus had been revealed as the human face of God, the full self-expression of God's being. "The eschatological character of this revelation indirectly makes it clear as well that from eternity God is the God and Father of Jesus Christ and therefore that as Son of God Jesus belongs to the eternal being of God."[42]

The fundamental importance of these revelatory experiences cannot be underestimated, given the matrix of Jewish exclusivist monotheism within which they occurred. They provoked the unprecedented development of cultic worship and prayer that included Jesus Christ alongside God the Father, public devotion that is reflected in the New Testament epistolary literature (especially letters by and attributed to Paul) and the book of Revelation.[43] For example, the untranslated Aramaic prayer *marana tha* ("O Lord, come!") preserved in Paul's First Letter to the Corinthians (16:22), which finds a Greek parallel in

40. Ibid. (emphasis original).

41. Regarding the advantage of a performance hermeneutic for understanding both Jesus' view of the Kingdom of God and our contemporary appropriation of the truth of Jesus' message, see Godzieba, "Method and Interpretation"; Godzieba, "'. . . And Followed Him on the Way' (Mark 10:52): Unity, Diversity, Discipleship," in *Beyond Dogmatism and Innocence: Hermeneutics, Critique, and Catholic Theology*, ed. Anthony J. Godzieba and Bradford E. Hinze (Collegeville, MN: Liturgical Press, 2017), 228–54.

42. Kasper, *GJC*, 244.

43. See especially Larry W. Hurtado, *At the Origins of Christian Worship: The Context and Character of Earliest Christian Devotion* (Grand Rapids: Eerdmans, 1999), 63–97; Hurtado, *Lord Jesus Christ*, 134–43; LaCugna, *God For Us*, 112–14.

Revelation 22:20 (*Amēn, erchou kyrie Iēsou;* "Amen. Come Lord Jesus!"),
is an invocation for Jesus to be present, whether at the moment of
worship or eschatologically. This prayer has no parallel in Judaism and
provides evidence for "an incorporation of Jesus into the corporate,
public devotional life of early Christians in a way that is otherwise
reserved for God."[44] Another example is the Christian hymn quoted
by Paul in the Letter to the Philippians (2:6-11); it links the universal
confession that "Jesus Christ is Lord" (2:11) with God's exaltation of
Jesus (2:9), an exaltation that mirrors God the Father's glory as well
(2:11). Colossians 3:17 urges Christians to "do everything in the name
of the Lord Jesus, giving thanks to God the Father through him." A
number of doxologies (e.g., 1 Thess 3:11-13; Rom 1:8, 16:27; 2 Cor 1:19-
20) directly link God the Father and Jesus in prayer, offering praise to
God and invoking Jesus as the mediator between God and humanity.[45]
These are thought to quote directly or echo liturgical formulas already
in common use in Christian worship in the 50s AD/CE. These and
similar New Testament indicators, taken together, reflect the consistent
incorporation of Jesus "into an exclusivistic pattern of devotion in
which there is room for only *one God and one Lord* (e.g., 1 Cor 8:5-6),"
a cultic reverencing of Jesus that early Christians believed they were
impelled to offer in light of their experience of God.[46]

For the early Christian communities whose beliefs and practices are
reflected in these texts, it is clear that Jesus was not considered "another
deity of any independent origin or significance; instead, his divine
significance is characteristically expressed in terms of his relationship
to the one God."[47] The practices of these early communities thus disclose the development of a clearly *binitarian* pattern of belief and devotion. As Larry Hurtado puts it, this was "an unparalleled innovation,
a 'mutation' or new variant form of exclusivist monotheism in which
a second figure (Jesus) was programmatically included with God in

---

44. Hurtado, *Lord Jesus Christ*, 141–42.

45. LaCugna, "Trinitarian Mystery," 16; *God For Us*, 112–13.

46. Hurtado, *Origins*, 97 (emphasis original). The hymn quoted by Paul in 1
Cor. 8:5-6 confesses that there is "one God, the Father, from whom are all things
and for whom we exist, and one Lord, Jesus Christ, through whom are all things
and through whom we exist."

47. Hurtado, *Lord Jesus Christ*, 52.

the devotional pattern of Christian groups."[48] This devotion paralleled and fostered the development of what have been called "New Testament symbols implying a second in God,"[49] a range of titles for Jesus that attempted to express his unique relationship to God without compromising the exclusivist monotheist context from which they arose.

One of these titles is "son of God," originally denoting Yahweh's elect (either corporately or individually), but without overtones of divinity.[50] Early Christian practice, spurred on by the sense of intimate sonship with God that Jesus expressed in his sayings and actions (e.g., Matt 11:27/Luke 10:22), applied the term to Jesus and eventually narrowed down its focus to signify the distinctive relationship between Jesus and the Father (e.g., Mark 1:1; Rom 1:3, 8:3, 14-15; Gal 4:6-7; John 1:14; 1 John 4:9). Another is "Lord" (*kyrios*), whose meaning in a Jewish setting was far less ambiguous.[51] In first-century AD/CE diaspora synagogues where Jews spoke Greek rather than Hebrew, whenever the Scriptures were read aloud in translation, the substitution for the never-to-be-uttered *YHWH* would not have been the Hebrew *Adonai* but rather the Greek *kyrios*. The same translation appears in Christian manuscripts of the Greek translation of the Old Testament, the Septuagint. The word thus had clear connotations of divinity when early Christian communities deliberately chose it as one of their key interpretations of Jesus' relationship to God. In doing so, they expressed their belief that now "Jesus could be hailed as Lord and receive the honour due to God alone, because God had so appointed Christ to this status and these roles," while at the same time maintaining a distinction between God the Father and Jesus.[52]

48. Ibid., 64.

49. Hill, *The Three-Personed God*, 6–17.

50. For examples of earlier Jewish usage and of Jesus' own expressions of his sonship, see Dunn, *Partings of the Ways*, 170–71; Dunn, *Christianity in the Making, Volume I: Jesus Remembered* (Grand Rapids/Cambridge: Eerdmans, 2003), 708–24 (especially his conclusions).

51. For what follows, see Dunn, *Partings of the Ways*, 188–91; see also Hill, *Three-Personed God*, 14–15.

52. Dunn, *Partings of the Ways*, 191: "*To call Jesus 'Lord', therefore, was evidently not understood in earliest Christianity as identifying him with God.* What Paul and the first Christians seem to have done was to claim that *the one God had shared his lordship with the exalted Christ.*"

For example, Peter, in his speech at Pentecost, claims that in the Jesus' resurrection and exaltation "God has made him both Lord (*kyrios*) and Messiah (*christos*)" (Acts 2:36). He cites as proof Psalm 110:1, a popular proof-text in early Christianity: "The LORD says to my lord, 'Sit at my right hand until I make your enemies your footstool.'"[53] In Paul's letters, *kyrios* plays a central role. He even claims that preaching "Jesus Christ as Lord" sums up his entire teaching (2 Cor 4:5), and that this name, precisely because it is "the name that is above every name," deserves to be reverenced by all: "every tongue should confess that Jesus Christ is Lord, to the glory of God the Father" (Phil 2:9-11).[54] In 1 Corinthians 8, he uses the title in the absolute sense: despite others' claims of "many gods and many lords," for believers there is "one God, the Father . . . and one Lord, Jesus Christ" (1 Cor 8:5-6). These texts do not spell out the ontological details of the relationship between Jesus and God; such intricate theological discussions developed only later in Christian tradition.

Alongside this binitarian pattern, the New Testament clearly indicates the early development of the *trinitarian* pattern as well, again without compromising the monotheism which governed early Christian experience. Here, too, detailed theological elaboration is bypassed in favor of testimony. The catalyst for this pattern was the immediacy of the presence of God that the earliest Christians continued to experience through the risen Jesus, an intensity of religious experience that led to them to recognize their unity with one another and drew them together into the earliest Christian communities.[55] After Easter, believers claimed that the action of the Spirit (*pneuma*) was the source for their continuing participation in God's power (*dynamis*) that Jesus had promised to those who have faith (Mark 9:24; 10:27). The Spirit's action was also the reason for their inclusion within Jesus' relation-

53. Ibid., 188, 316 n.16.

54. Dunn notes (ibid., 188) how this passage echoes Is 45:22-23: "For I am God and there is no other. By myself I have sworn. . . . 'To me every knee shall bow, every tongue shall swear.'"

55. See James D. G. Dunn, *Unity and Diversity in the New Testament: An Inquiry into the Character of Earliest Christianity*, 3rd ed. (London: SCM Press, 2006), 189–217, esp. 215–16.

ship to his *Abba* and the resulting community fellowship (*koinōnia*).[56] Once again, Jewish tradition provided the model. Various Old Testament texts recount the outpouring of God's "spirit" (in Hebrew *ruah*, "wind," "breath") as a sign of God's activity in the world, whether as vivifying power (e.g. Job 33:4), creative agency (e.g. Gen 1:2), or prophetic presence in human beings (e.g. Isa 61:1), especially in messianic times (e.g. Joel 3:1-5). "Spirit" is understood in these texts more or less impersonally and functionally, as a principle of action.[57] This meaning also governs the use of the term in many New Testament texts. Based on their continuing experience of the risen Christ, however, members of the early Church later began to interpret both the process and the implications of God's revelation in Jesus in a way that emphasized how God's "inspiration" of Jesus' disciples is indeed God's *personal* relationship with them, one best expressed in a *personal* way. They thus expanded the meaning of "spirit" beyond its Old Testament roots in order to acknowledge this distinctive personal divine presence.

This expansion of meaning, however, did not occur all at once. The accounts of the baptism of Jesus in the synoptic gospels (Mark 1:9-11; Matt 3:13-17; Luke 3:21-22), for example, appears to follow the earlier Old Testament model. The "voice from heaven" reveals Jesus as the "beloved Son" of the Father; he is portrayed as receiving the "Spirit" (the "Spirit of God" in Matthew, the "Holy Spirit" in Luke) at the inauguration of his ministry. In Paul's letters, too, *pneuma* often reflects this functional Old Testament understanding.[58] Moreover, in several well-known texts Paul does not clearly differentiate Christ from the Spirit, leaving the relationship ambiguous. In Galatians, for instance, he depicts the role of the Spirit as enabling a believer to replicate in his or her life the intimate relationship with God that Jesus experienced: "And because you are children, God has sent the

56. Kasper, *GJC*, 244–45.

57. Joseph A. Fitzmyer, *The Gospel According to Luke (I–IX)*, Anchor Bible, vol. 28 (Garden City: Doubleday, 1981), 484; John L. McKenzie, "Aspects of Old Testament Thought," *The New Jerome Biblical Commentary*, 1290–91.

58. For this and what follows, see the discussion in Joseph A. Fitzmyer, "Pauline Theology," *The New Jerome Biblical Commentary*, 1396, §§61–65.

Spirit of his Son into our hearts, crying, 'Abba! Father!' " (Gal 4:5).[59] In Romans 8:9-11, Paul uses "Spirit of God," "Spirit of Christ," and "the Spirit of him who raised Jesus from the dead" interchangeably to depict the believer's participation in God's life. And in 2 Corinthians 3:17-18 he goes so far as to claim that "the Lord is the Spirit." However, there are also striking passages where Paul speaks of the Spirit as distinct from the Father (e.g., Rom 8:14-17), having distinguishing characteristics (e.g., 1 Cor 12:3-11) and even comprehensive knowledge of God: "For the Spirit searches everything, even the depths of God. . . . No one comprehends what is truly God's except the Spirit of God" (1 Cor 2:10-11). At times Paul emphatically differentiates God, Jesus, and the Spirit, putting them on an equal footing and thereby providing a basis for the language of "distinct persons" found in later dogmatic statements on the Trinity. Second Corinthians, for instance, concludes with "the grace of the Lord Jesus Christ, the love of God, and the communion of the Holy Spirit be with all of you" (13:13), a triadic formula that seems to echo liturgical practice.

Two other key New Testament instances significantly expand the meaning of "Spirit." One is Matthew 28:19, Jesus' command to "make disciples of all nations, baptizing them in the name of the Father and of the Son and of the Holy Spirit." This parallelism of Father, Son, and Spirit as implicit equals is unprecedented in the gospel; so too is the connection of baptism with Jesus (rather than with John the Baptist). Commentators generally agree that the formula as Matthew presents it most probably originated with the early Church rather than with historical Jesus, and reflects the Church's baptismal practice.[60] But even though the formula may not directly quote Jesus himself, it is warranted by his relationship to his Father and "presents a summary of the early church's development and practice which had been guided by the Spirit of Jesus Christ and to that extent were

59. Cf. Dunn, *Unity and Diversity*, 209.

60. E.g., Daniel J. Harrington, *The Gospel of Matthew*, Sacra Pagina, vol. 1 (Collegeville: Liturgical Press, 1991), 415–17; W. D. Davies and Dale C. Allison, Jr., *A Critical and Exegetical Commentary on The Gospel According to St. Matthew*, 3 vols., International Critical Commentary (Edinburgh: T. & T. Clark, 1997), 3:676–91, esp. 677–78, 684–87. See also LaCugna, *God for Us*, 113–14 and "Trinitarian Mystery," 163–64 (and literature cited there).

authorized by Jesus himself."[61] That is, the Trinitarian baptismal formula expresses what became the core of early Christianity's developing understanding of its identity, namely, that the life of the Church is grounded in God's salvation which has been incarnated in the person and message of Jesus, and that this life now continues to flourish after Christ's resurrection because of the Father's continuing personal presence to the Church through the Spirit. Whoever wishes to join this community of disciples and participate in this offer of personal relationship and salvation must enter through baptism, the origin and ground of Christian life. At baptism, one commits oneself to this trinitarian view of God's saving action. Along with Christ's exalted divine significance, then, early on Christians were called to acknowledge the triune divine life as the necessary precondition for the life of the individual Christian and of the Church.

The other key instance is the reference to the Paraclete in John's gospel, specifically in Jesus' farewell discourse at the Last Supper (John 14–17).[62] There, in intimate conversation with "his own" whom he loved (John 13:1), Jesus promises that, on his return to the Father, he will ask the Father to send "another *paraklētos* to be with you forever. This is the Spirit of truth, whom the world cannot receive" (14:16-17). This Paraclete is "the Holy Spirit, whom the Father will send in my name, [who] will teach you everything, and remind you of all that I have said to you" (14:26). He "comes from (*ekporeuetai*, proceeds from) the Father" and will testify on Jesus' behalf, as the disciples must do as well (15:26-27). He will come only if Jesus departs, and when he comes he will convict the world of its false judgments (16:7b-11). As the "Spirit of truth," he will guide the disciples along the way to truth and glorify Jesus, and will take what belongs to Jesus ("all that the Father has is mine") and declare it to the disciples (16:13-15).

---

61. Kasper, *GJC*, 245.

62. See Raymond E. Brown, *The Gospel According to John XIII–XXI*, The Anchor Bible, vol. 29A (Garden City, NY: Doubleday, 1970), 1135–44; Rudolf Schnackenburg, *The Gospel According to St. John*, 3 vols., trans. David Smith and G. A. Kon, Herder's Theological Commentary on the New Testament (New York: Crossroad, 1968–82), 3:138–54; John Ashton, "Paraclete," *Anchor Bible Dictionary*, 5:152–54. The discourse contains five sayings regarding the Paraclete: John 14:16-17, 14:26, 15:26-27, 16:7b-11, and 16:13-15. The only other use of *paraklētos* in the New Testament is 1 John 2:1, where it is applied to Christ.

No single translation of *paraklētos* (e.g., "Advocate" or "Comforter") can capture the rich complexity of meaning that the Johannine author intends to express throughout these passages. The term has a range of technical (legal) and non-technical meanings in Greek: "one called alongside" (*parakalein*) to help—i.e., an advocate, intercessor, or defense counsel; a mediator or spokesperson; a comforter or consoler; and one who encourages and exhorts. Its use in the gospel has obvious Old Testament antecedents (especially with regard to the prophets as mediators of God's spirit, and personified Wisdom coming to dwell with God's people) as well as precedents in Second Temple Jewish angelology. The Johannine author has creatively combined these traditional meanings and employed them in a unique way to explain how the personal presence of Jesus to the community—its lifeblood as it were—is sustained after Jesus' return to the Father. Indeed, the *paraklētos*, the "Spirit of truth," is "another Paraclete" (14:16), implying that Jesus has already been the first. After Jesus' departure, the Paraclete sent by the Father is portrayed as Jesus' representative, continuing his living presence in the community and personally performing a series of actions: teaching, reminding the disciples of Jesus' words, testifying on Jesus' behalf, defending those disciples suffering persecution and exposing the guilt of the hostile and unbelieving world, guiding the disciples to the truth about the present and the future.[63] The Paraclete's *personal* actions are instrumental in carrying out his multi-faceted relationship to Jesus and to the disciples: "the Paraclete is a *witness* in defense of Jesus and a *spokesman* for him in the context of his trial by his enemies; the Paraclete is a *consoler* and guide of the disciples and thus their *helper.*"[64]

The Johannine author has sculpted these diverse meanings into a remarkable theological portrayal of "the Paraclete as the Holy Spirit in a special role, namely, as the personal presence of Jesus in the

63. Schnackenburg notes (3:142–43) that the Paraclete's "forensic" role as advocate and mediator for disciples who witness to Jesus before hostile persecutors picks up a thread of the early tradition that was known to the synoptics as well (cf. Mk 13:11, Mt 10:20, Lk 12:11).

64. Brown, *John*, 1137. See also ibid., 1135, where all the Paraclete's characteristics noted in John 14–16 are tabulated.

Christian while Jesus is with the Father."[65] This role is so special and distinctive that the author was compelled to bestow a special title and offer a distinctive interpretation of the Holy Spirit, whose presence the community had already accepted.[66] As Raymond Brown notes, this portrait of the Paraclete is the gospel's solution to the "tragedy" of the "death of the apostolic eyewitnesses who were the living chain between the Church and Jesus of Nazareth," and especially the death of the Beloved Disciple, this community's "eyewitness *par excellence.*" How would the community survive without a living connection to Jesus? The Johannine answer is that the connection has been provided by the Spirit, whose presence is due to Jesus and his resurrection (7:39) and who, after the resurrection, enlightened the first disciples so that they would grasp the true meaning of Jesus' earlier words and actions (cf. 2:22, 12:16). In fact, the gospel insists that the Spirit as Paraclete is the Father's gift to the entire community, guiding not only the Beloved Disciple and other eyewitnesses but every other member as well, now and in the future. "The later Christian is no further removed from the ministry of Jesus than was the earlier Christian, for the Paraclete dwells within him as he dwelt within the eyewitnesses. And by recalling and giving new meaning to what Jesus said, the Paraclete guides every generation in facing new situations; he declares the things to come."[67]

The gospel is not a dogmatic theological treatise. The Johannine author is more interested in the similarities between Jesus and the Spirit than in the distinctions accentuated in later trinitarian theology.[68] But the importance of this gospel for later Christian reflection on the Trinity is unmistakable, especially for the debates establishing the personal nature of the Holy Spirit.[69] The crucial active and personal role played by the Paraclete in Jesus' farewell discourse clearly implies that the Johannine community had at least an incipient awareness of the trinitarian pattern of God's salvific actions. The unity in love between the Jesus and the Father, expressed in the

65. Ibid., 1139.
66. Ibid., 1140; cf. Schnackenburg, 3:140, 149–50.
67. Brown, *John*, 1142.
68. Ibid., 1141.
69. Cf. Schnackenburg, 152–53.

"priestly prayer" that concludes Jesus' farewell to his disciples (chapter 17), is now made accessible to all believers through the unity of Jesus with his disciples guaranteed by the Spirit as Paraclete.[70] This participation in divine life is the *true* meaning of life—eternal life. "And this is eternal life, that they should know you, the only true God, and the one whom you sent, Jesus Christ" (17:3).[71] To know the Father means to acknowledge the Father's lordship and to glorify him, thereby discovering that the true meaning of life is communion with God.[72] Jesus makes this communion possible: true life for the disciples means knowing Jesus, the Son who has been sent, and the glory and the love that he has from the Father (17:5, 7, 22-23)—indeed, knowing that "all that the Father has is mine" (16:15; cf. 17:10). The knowledge of God made available through faith in Jesus "brings communion with him and through him with God. . . . The glorification of the Father by the Son thus has for its goal the participation of the disciples in this glorification and in eternal life."[73] To preserve this communion of the disciples with the Father through Jesus is the role of the Paraclete, the Spirit of truth sent by Jesus (14:16-17), who will reveal not only the union of the Father and the Son, but also how the disciples' own unity among themselves participates in the saving love and unity that is the divine life (17:21, 26). This communion is not for the disciples alone; it must be extended to the world as a sign of God's saving love for the world (17:21, 23). In the light of all these relationships that enfold and give life to the community, the Johannine author thus emphasizes the inherent connection between belief in the trinity and God's offer of salvation, a connection that is at the heart of Christian belief. The gospel reveals, in Walter Kasper's words, that "the trinitarian dox-

70. For what follows, see Kasper, *GJC*, 247–48.

71. A more literal translation that preserves the impact of the original word order.

72. Schnackenburg comments: "'Knowing God' has the previously established, O[ld] T[estament] meaning of 'having communion with God'. . [Johannine theology] is content to present community with God as the fulfillment of man's longing for salvation, achieved in believing and loving union with Jesus Christ" (3:172–73).

73. Kasper, *GJC*, 247.

ology is the soteriology of the world."[74] Salvation consists of our union with God through Christ and consequently with each other; the participative love which is the basis of this union must be revealed and made effective in the world. The Father has given over everything to the Son, the Son gives everything over to the disciples, and the Spirit reveals, preserves, and extends the bond of love that is the catalyst for these acts of giving.

Implicit in the gospel is the Johannine community's belief that we are offered a glimpse of the triune divine nature through the revelatory events of Christ's own life, lived in intimate relation with his Father, and with the sending of the Spirit—a glimpse that a later writer from the Johannine school will sum up in the simplest terms: God is love. "Whoever acknowledges that Jesus is the Son of God, God remains in him and he in God. . . . God is love, and whoever remains in love remains in God and God in him" (1 John 4:15-16).[75] Kasper argues that this passage—and the development of trinitarian awareness—is the fundamental summary of the entire message of the New Testament.

> In the revelational event which is Jesus Christ God has shown himself to be love. But this revelational event consists precisely in making known the eternal communion of love, life and reciprocal glorification between Father, Son and Spirit, in order that through this revelation the disciples and, with their help, mankind may be drawn into this same communion of love and life. The revelational statement "God is love" is therefore at the same time a statement about the being of God and, as such, a statement about salvation. Only because God is love can he reveal and communicate himself to us as love. The unity of church and world, the peace and reconciliation of mankind have their ultimate ground and ultimate possibility, as seen by Christians, in the acknowledgement of the glory of God in the love of Father, Son and Spirit.[76]

74. Ibid., 248.

75. The New American Bible, Revised Edition (NABRE) translation, which is more literal and retains the original word order. Regarding the authorship of 1 John, see Raymond E. Brown, *An Introduction to the New Testament*, The Anchor Bible Reference Library (New York: Doubleday, 1997), 389–92.

76. *GJC*, 248.

The love of the triune God and the metaphor of personal relationship are, in Kasper's view, the interpretive keys to the Scriptures and
to reality as a whole. This interpretation gives us a vantage point
from which to summarize and evaluate all the scriptural evidence
we have seen. We can discern a pattern, none other than the dialectic
of "presence and absence" that earlier we argued is the fundamental
logic of God's revelation: the simultaneous knowability-mysterious-
ness, availability-uncontrollability, immanence-transcendence of God.
In the texts we have examined, the traditional categories of divinity
have been stretched up to and even beyond their limits to accommodate revelatory experiences of God who always exceeds human categories—or better put, to respond to God's offer of an always-deeper
relationship to humankind. These experiences demand interpretation;
their surprising new elements provoke believers to reevaluate their
usual expectations and definitions of divinity, a process that takes
place under the "pressure" of revelation (the Old Testament theophanies are examples of this). To call this process "development" is too
weak a description; any connotations of smooth systematic progress
barely hint at the volatility of the call to a deepening personal relationship that occurs when an individual or a community encounters
the incomprehensible mystery of God and finds the normal definitions of God shaken or even shattered.

The various categories used by Israel, by Jesus' first disciples, and
by early Christianity to understand God and God's activity were
constantly expanded and at times surpassed when they were seen
as inadequate to the task. As a response to both the devastation of
exile and Israel's subsequent miraculous return to its homeland,
post-exilic Judaism's rigorous exclusivist monotheism went far
beyond earlier polytheistic and henotheistic categories by making
the radical claim that Yahweh's salvific presence was absolute and
allowed no rivals or subordinates. This revision and expansion continued in the New Testament. Exclusivist monotheism, the essential
religious matrix for Jesus, his earliest disciples, and early Christianity,
was not an obstacle to the eventual recognition of the triune nature
of God, but rather surprisingly acted as a catalyst for new possibilities of understanding and expanding the hard-won faith claim that
God is one. The early growth of the binitarian pattern was one

approach. It was an innovative Christological expansion of the Jewish understanding of God that developed as a way to do justice to the disciples' original experience of Jesus as the human face of God and God as the *Abba* of Jesus, especially in the light of Jesus' resurrection from the dead. The early communities of believers used this pattern to confess their belief that "from eternity God is the God and Father of Jesus Christ and therefore that as Son of God Jesus belongs to the eternal being of God."[77] The trinitarian pattern, clearly reflected in the later texts of the New Testament, surpassed binitarianism and in effect critiqued it as ultimately inadequate to deal with the fullness of the early Christian experience of God. Early Christianity's trinitarianism reveals the deeper and (from hindsight) inevitable realization that the manifestation of the relationship of the Father with the Son to us (*oikonomia*, the externalizing "economy" of salvation) and our sharing in that relationship can take place only on God's personal initiative. The confession of the Spirit is the early Church's way of recognizing and expressing this initiative by God to enter into a continuing personal relationship with us that saves us. The Christian's experience of revelation and salvation is thus fundamentally trinitarian. This recognition of a "third" in God is not a separate, parallel development, but rather a complementary and even more expansive response to the Christological concerns that binitarianism raises.[78] From a historical point of view, the earlier confession of Jesus as Christ and Lord and the questions that are provoked (who is Jesus? why is he significant? how does his presence live on for us after his departure?) set the stage for the dawning New Testament belief that only by means of the Spirit does the community have a continuing personal share in the reality of Jesus. But once this point was reached, it became clear that the believer's ability to recognize Christ as Lord and confess him as such always depended on the already-present power of the Holy Spirit (cf. 1 Cor. 12:3).[79] Thus, Christology and

77. Kasper, *GJC*, 244.

78. Cf. Hill, *Three-Personed God*, 17–28, especially 26: "an implicit trinitarianism is gradually coming to light in the New Testament itself in function of some of its developing Christologies."

79. See ibid., 26–27 and Kasper, *GJC*, 248–49. Hill and Kasper differ on the directionality of the influence. Hill argues that Christology comes first, and that

Trinitarian theology are inseparably linked in a mutually supportive way. At the same time, though, one must say that Christology finds the completion of its intentional drive or its inherent "logic" in the confession of the Trinity, and that the fundamental structure of revelation and of the New Testament message of salvation is trinitarian.

> People believe in Jesus because the Father has raised him from the dead and established him as Lord. Moreover, the saving act of Jesus Christ includes the sending of the Holy Spirit. Only in the Holy Spirit is it possible to confess Jesus as Lord (I Cor. 12.5f.), and only in the Spirit do we have a share in the reality of Jesus. Consequently, a christological confession is possible only in the form of a trinitarian confession.[80]

3. The Trinitarian Rule of Faith and its Interpretation

3.1 From the New Testament to Nicaea (325 AD/CE)

The simpler confessions and doxologies of the first century AD/CE gave way during the following centuries to both shorter and longer creedal formulas and progressively more detailed theological statements of belief in the Trinity. This is not, as the popular stereotype has it, a story of more and greater abstractions being spun out by theologians in the privacy of their own scholarly disputes and divorced from the Church's everyday life. Rather, these developments stemmed directly from the concrete situations of the early Church's prayer and liturgical life, its public worship of the triune God (especially the celebrations of baptism and the Eucharist), and the various prayers and formulas that developed in conjunction with these ritual celebrations. Prayers to God the Father through Christ the mediator, the invocation of the Spirit over the gifts of bread and wine so that they may become the body and blood of the Lord, the three-fold confession of Father, Son, and Spirit at baptism—these

---

"even today it is Christology that provides the way to a confession of the Trinity, and not the other way around" (*Three-Personed God*, 26–27). Kasper, on the other hand, argues that "faith in Christ and existence as a Christian depend on the confession of the Trinity" (*GJC*, 249).

80. Kasper, *GJC*, 249.

liturgical actions raised important questions in the minds of believers regarding the relations among the Father, Son, and Spirit, and the relation of the trinitarian confession to Christian monotheism. These became the fundamental questions that would occupy the greatest theological minds in the early Church over the next few centuries. The development of the trinitarian dogma provides the earliest documentation of the workings of the ancient principle *lex orandi, lex credendi* ("the rule of prayer is the rule of belief"). One of theology's primary tasks is to interpret with as much clarity as possible the truth of faith that believers already express through personal and liturgical prayer, in order to make that truth more accessible and understandable, and guard it against misinterpretations, distortions, and outright denials.[81]

The *lex orandi*, then, was a vital catalyst to trinitarian reflection. The New Testament itself, as we have seen, contains numerous witnesses to both binitarian and trinitarian patterns of prayer and doxology—a clear sign that Christian communities were already pondering the relations among Father, the risen Christ, and Spirit, with the trinitarian pattern ultimately being judged the most appropriate to the Christian experience of God.[82] The trinitarian confession at baptism was crucial because it summarized and structured the entire world of belief that the newly-baptized Christian was entering. Along with the tri-partite baptismal command in Matthew 29:19, other early witnesses to the trinitarian baptismal confession include the *Didache* (late 1st cent. AD/CE), Justin Martyr (first half of 2nd cent. AD/CE), and Irenaeus of Lyons (c. 130–c. 200).[83] These early formulas are the

81. Cf. Jaroslav Pelikan, *Credo: Historical and Theological Guide to Creeds and Confessions of Faith in the Christian Tradition* (New Haven: Yale University Press, 2003), 166–67; Kasper, *GJC*, 251. The original form of the principle can be traced back to the Prosper of Aquitaine, writing in the 5th cent. AD/CE (Pelikan, 166).

82. See LaCugna, *God For Us*, 111–42 for an overview of New Testament and post-New Testament doxologies, eucharistic prayers, and creeds.

83. *Didache* 7:1-3 (*The Apostolic Fathers: Greek Texts and English Translations*, rev. ed., trans. J. B. Lightfoot and J. R. Harmer, ed. and rev. Michael W. Holmes [Grand Rapids: Baker, 1999], 258–59); Justin Martyr, *Apology I*, 61 (*Writings of Saint Justin Martyr*, trans. Thomas B. Falls, The Fathers of the Church, vol. 6 [New York: Christian Heritage, Inc., 1948], 99); Irenaeus of Lyons, *Demonstration of the Apos-*

roots from which the later creeds develop, a process which begins quite early.[84] For example, Irenaeus structures his discussion of the three main "articles" of faith (God the Father and creator of all, Christ as Word and Son, and the Holy Spirit who renews humanity for God) along the lines of the tri-partite baptismal confession.[85] The *Apostolic Tradition* (early 3rd cent. AD/CE), attributed to Hippolytus of Rome, records a rite of baptism wherein the trinitarian profession has been formulated as a series of three questions (similar to the articles contained in later creeds) posed by the bishop to the one about to be baptized.[86] The prayers which accompanied the celebration of the Eucharist also developed a trinitarian structure. In the liturgy as described by Justin, the presider takes "bread and a chalice containing wine mixed with water" and "offers praise and glory to the Father of all, through the name of the Son and of the Holy Spirit."[87] The eucharistic prayer in the *Apostolic Tradition* gives praise and thanks to God through the mediatorship of Christ, pronounces an epiclesis which calls on God to "send your Holy Spirit on the presbytery of the holy church," and prays to God in a concluding doxology "that we may praise and glorify you through your child Jesus Christ, through whom be glory and honor to you, with the Holy Spirit in your holy church both now and to the ages of the ages."[88] These examples give a sense of the prevailing understanding in the early Church whereby the trinitarian pattern of prayer became the orthodox norm.[89]

---

tolic Preaching 3, 7 (*Proof of the Apostolic Preaching*, trans. Joseph P. Smith, Ancient Christian Writers, no. 16 [New York/Ramsey, NJ: Newman Press, n.d.], 49, 51).

84. Cf. Pelikan, *Credo*, 377–83.

85. *Demonstration*, 6 (51).

86. *Apostolic Tradition*, 21 (Hippolytus, *On the Apostolic Tradition*, trans. Alistair Stewart-Sykes [Crestwood, NY: St. Vladimir's Seminary Press, 2001], 110–14).

87. *Apology I*, 65 (*Writings*, 105); see also chap. 67: "For all the favors we enjoy we bless the Creator of all, through his son Jesus Christ and through the Holy Spirit" (ibid., 106).

88. *Apostolic Tradition*, 4:4, 12-13 (64–65).

89. Pelikan, *Credo*, 380: "The trinitarian force of the baptismal formula—and, apparently on that basis, of the Gloria Patri ['Glory be to the Father . . .']— prevailed over any binitarian formulas even though these could claim biblical provenance."

What is also evident is that the *lex orandi* contained ambiguities that provoked questions, both liturgical (how to worship God) and theological (how to think about God). These eventually fueled disputes as to precisely what roles Christ and the Spirit played in relation to the Father and to the divine plan of salvation. The prime example is the *mediatory* pattern that both binitarian and trinitarian prayers consistently took: one prays to the Father *through* or *in the name of* the Son, the Father grants us grace and life *through* Christ and the Spirit.[90] To some who were influenced by the "hierarchies" of being or divinity in Hellenistic thinking, these prayers suggested that the Son was subordinate to the Father because of his mediatory role. For others it raised the question of the subordination of the Holy Spirit, or whether the Spirit was the servant of the Son, the *Logos.* Such contested issues demanded the precision that comes from a more detailed reflection upon the truth of faith. The theological clarifications that occurred between the end of the first century AD/CE and the Council of Nicaea (325 AD/CE) spoke to this need, contributing to the eventual development of the trinitarian dogma and to the official ecclesial statements promulgated at the earliest ecumenical councils.[91]

The Apologists of the second century AD/CE, including such writers as Justin Martyr and Theophilus of Antioch, were committed to the trinitarian pattern and to demonstrating "how the Son and Spirit, who were revealed in the 'Economy' as other than the Father, were yet inseparably one with him in his eternal being."[92] They said much less about the Holy Spirit, however, due to their focus on Christology. They adapted the Hellenistic philosophical concept of *logos* in order

90. Cf. LaCugna, *God For Us*, 22. She notes that "virtually all extant liturgical texts of the pre-Nicene church are marked by a mediatory pattern of prayer, particularly in the anaphoras and doxologies" (ibid., 114).

91. For what follows, see Kasper, *GJC*, 251–63; LaCugna, "Trinitarian Mystery," 162–74; LaCugna, *God For Us*, 24–30; Pannenberg, *Systematic Theology*, 1:264–80; *The Trinitarian Controversy*, trans. and ed. William G. Rusch, Sources of Early Christian Thought (Philadelphia: Fortress, 1980), 1–27; Edmund J. Fortman, *The Triune God: A Historical Study of the Doctrine of the Trinity* (Philadelphia: Westminster, 1972), 35–170; Wilhelm Breuning, "Gotteslehre," in *Glaubenszugänge: Lehrbuch der katholischen Dogmatik*, ed. Wolfgang Beinert (Paderborn: Schöningh, 1995), 1:274–97.

92. Fortman, *The Triune God*, 108.

to assert Christ's divinity, to explain both his distinction from and his eternal relationship with the Father, and preserve Christianity's commitment to monotheism. *Logos* (meaning both "word" and "reason") had been used in the first century AD/CE by the Stoics and by the Jewish philosopher Philo of Alexandria to name the foundational rational principle that unifies and governs reality, the necessary condition for reality's inherent intelligibility and meaningfulness that ultimately is revealed in the rational human mind (also defined as *logos*).[93] Philo further taught that the divine Logos spoke through Israel's prophets and was the means by which the transcendent God of Israel (the "One" or "Monad") was related to the finite materiality of creation.[94] The Apologists, building on these arguments and on the biblical use of *logos* in John 1:1 ("In the beginning was the Word [*Logos*], and the Word was with God, and the Word was God"), developed a two-stage "Logos Christology." The Logos is divine and eternally begotten of the one God, preexisting in the mind of the Father as the "immanent Word" (*logos endiathetos*); in the historical coming of Christ, the Logos became incarnate as the Son and the Father's "expressed Word" (*logos prophorikos*). In this way, the Apologists attempted to recognize the unity in being as well as the evident plurality in the eternal Godhead (termed "Father," the author of all that exists), and to articulate the distinction between God the Father and Christ in a way that would avoid any overtones of natural, temporal generation.[95] However, the early development of this Christology with its terminological limitations did not succeed in avoiding a

93. Cf. Christopher Stead, *Philosophy in Christian Antiquity* (Cambridge: Cambridge University Press, 1994), 46–48, 58–60, 150–58; Henry Chadwick, "Philo and the Beginnings of Christian Thought," in *The Cambridge History of Later Greek and Early Medieval Philosophy*, ed. A. H. Armstrong (1967; reprint, Cambridge: Cambridge University Press, 1980), 137–92, at 137–57; Friedo Ricken, *Philosophy of the Ancients*, trans. Eric Watkins (Notre Dame: University of Notre Dame Press, 1991), 190, 194–98, 229; Kasper, *GJC*, 185–86. The roots of the *logos* concept go back as far as Heraclitus (c. 6th cent. BC/BCE).

94. Chadwick, "Philo," 144: "The Logos is God immanent, the vital power holding together the hierarchy of being, who as God's viceroy mediates revelation to the created order so that he stands midway on the frontier between creator and creature."

95. See, e.g., Justin, *Apology I*, 21 (*Writings*, 56–57).

hierarchical subordination of the Logos (seen at times as a second or secondary God) to the Father. This is due to the lack of an adequate correlation between the Hellenistic philosophical conception of the impersonal *logos* (the universal "substance" of reality) and the irreducibly particular, personal, historical reality of Christ, the biblical "Word" who "became flesh" (John 1:14).[96]

Irenaeus of Lyons took a somewhat different approach due to his struggle against the Gnostics. He was opposed to their view of an utterly inconceivable and ineffable God, their theory of the emanation of the world from the divine (in ever more diluted stages of being), and their dualistic separation of the world from God. Against their overly "Hellenized" view of the Godhead, Irenaeus insisted on the Church's rule of faith, "received from the apostles and their disciples . . . in one God the Father Almighty, the Creator of heaven and earth and the seas and all things that are in them; and in the one Jesus Christ, the Son of God, who was enfleshed for our salvation; and in the Holy Spirit, who through the prophets preached the Economies. . . ."[97] His incipient reflections on the Trinity and on the roles of Christ and the Spirit in the history of salvation are bound up with his strong theology of creation. They assert the inherent goodness and dignity of all things, based on their direct creation from nothing by the one God, "the only Lord, Creator, and Father, who alone contains all things and gives them being."[98] On this basis, Irenaeus emphasized most strongly the fundamental unity of creation and redemption in the one economy of salvation: the one and

96. Cf. Kasper, *GJC*, 185–86, 252.

97. *Adversus haereses* I, 10 (*Against the Heresies, Volume I, Book I*, trans. and ed. Dominic J. Unger and John J. Dillon, Ancient Christian Writers, no. 55 [New York/Mahwah, NJ: Paulist, 1992], 49). "Economies" here means God's plan of salvation as revealed in the Old and New Testaments (ibid., 185 n.6).

98. *Adv. haer.* II, 1, 1 (*Contre les hérésies, livre II*, ed. and trans. Adelin Rousseau and Louis Doutreleau, Sources chrétiennes [hereafter SC] 294 [Paris: Les Éditions du Cerf, 1982], 26–27 [my translation]). He thereby denies any idea of intermediary stages after an initial creation, and thus rejects the Gnostics' claim of a presently-existing "evil" world which differs from the initial intent of the creating demiurge. Cf. G. W. H. Lampe, "Christian Theology in the Patristic Period," in *A History of Christian Doctrine*, ed. Hubert Cunliffe-Jones and Benjamin Drewery (Philadelphia: Fortress, 1980), 21–180, at 43–44.

the same God and Father freely creates and saves, and does so by means of his two "hands," Word (Christ the Son) and Wisdom (the Spirit), who are always with God.[99] Irenaeus' position is a type of "economic trinitarianism," arguing that while God's ineffable being is a unity, the Godhead contains within himself from eternity the distinctions of his Word (the *Logos* or *Verbum*) and his Wisdom that are made known to us only when revealed in the economy. Thus, the Son is divine and *always* the Son; he does not become so simply at the incarnation. In discussing the Logos, Irenaeus purposely avoids the Apologists' language of "begetting." The Son is *logos ensarkos*, "the enfleshed Word," at once both *logos endiathetos* and *logos prophorikos* (the "immanent Word" and "expressed Word" of the Apologists). In the incarnation, Christ as Son and divine Logos-made-flesh fully reveals the Father,[100] and fully participates in and recapitulates (sums up) all of humanity, thus saving humanity by divinizing it and restoring all creation's communion with God.[101] "God has become man. The purpose of the divine exchange is that man might become what God is. . . . The end of all things is the participation of God in man and of man in God."[102] The role of the Spirit is to reveal the effects of this wondrous exchange as God's plan. The operations of the entire Trinity, then, are the necessary conditions for salvation.

> For those who are bearers of the Spirit of God [i.e., the baptized] are led to the Word, that is to the Son; but the Son takes them and presents them to the Father; and the Father confers incorruptibility. So without the Spirit there is no seeing the Word of God, and without the Son there is no approaching the Father;

---

99. *Adv. haer.* IV, pref., 4; 20, 1 (*Contre les hérésies, livre IV*, ed. and trans. Adelin Rousseau, SC 100/2 [Paris: Les Éditions du Cerf, 1965], 390–91, 626–27).

100. *Adv. haer.* III, 6, 2 (*Contre les hérésies, livre III*, ed. and trans. Adelin Rousseau and Louis Doutreleau, SC 211 [Paris: Les Éditions du Cerf, 2002], 68–71): "Thus, through the Son, who is in the Father and who has the Father in himself, the God 'who is' manifests himself—the Father giving witness to the Son, and the Son announcing the Father."

101. *Adv. haer.* III, 16, 6; 19, 1 (SC 211, 312–15, 374–75).

102. Eric Osborne, *Irenaeus of Lyons* (Cambridge: Cambridge University Press, 2001), 22.

for the Son is knowledge of the Father, and knowledge of the
Son is through the Holy Spirit.[103]

Irenaeus has no fully developed theory of the distinction of persons
in the Trinity, and his thought is not without elements which subordinate both Logos and Spirit to the Father. He develops, rather, a
theology of the economy of salvation that articulates the relationship
between God and the world and combats the Gnostics' dualism and
their inadmissible separation of God the Creator (Old Testament)
from God the Father of Jesus (New Testament). Within this theology,
he succeeds in crafting a way of explaining the distinctions within
the Godhead while insisting on the unity of God, and rooting this
distinction-in-unity firmly in the biblical evidence. By showing how
this divine unity is the basis for the unity of creation and salvation,
and by emphasizing that in the economy the distinctive divinizing
roles played by the Son's incarnation and the Spirit's revelation could
be effective only if they were truly the "two hands" of the Father from
eternity, he shows "how the Son and the Spirit disclosed in the economy as other than the Father were also one with him in his intrinsic
being."[104] Incarnation and soteriology are thus inextricably linked in
God's plan: "the unity of God thus grounds the unity of the order of
salvation, while the order of salvation in turn presupposes the con-
substantiality of the Son with the Father. In this brilliant vision of
Irenaeus the economic Trinity and the immanent Trinity are one."[105]
His insights will prove to be influential in later trinitarian debates.

Both Tertullian (c. 160–c. 225) and Origen (c. 185–c. 254) furthered
the development of the doctrine by contributing pivotal clarifications
and important terminological distinctions. Tertullian attempted to
steer a middle course between the extremes of subordinationism and
the "modalism" of the Monarchians. Third-century AD/CE Monarchianism had grown out of a backlash against Apologists' Logos-
christology, for fear that it undermined the unity of God and led to
ditheism. The Monarchians, in order to safeguard monotheism,
argued that the Godhead is an absolute monad—one sole power or

103. *Demonstration*, 7 (51–52).
104. Rusch, *The Trinitarian Controversy*, 7.
105. Kasper, *GJC*, 253.

substance, a "monarchy" (in Greek *monarchia*, from *monē archē*, "sole origin") devoid of all distinctions. Modalistic Monarchianism, the more philosophically sophisticated of the two versions of modalism extant in the early Church, argued that the distinctions that Christians confess—Father, Son, and Spirit—are not real distinctions at all, but merely the different operations, projections, or modalities (*modi*) by which the one absolute Godhead manifests himself in the economy of salvation at different times. This version was argued by such early third-century AD/CE figures as Sabellius (whose teachings came to be seen as modalism's examplar ["Sabellianism"] and gained an important foothold in Rome), Noetus of Smyrna, and the shadowy Praxeas (which may or may not be a nickname).[106]

Tertullian strove to refute this type of modalism. Its fundamental error, he argued, lay in claiming "that the Father himself came down into the virgin, himself born of her, himself suffered, in short himself is Jesus Christ . . . he [Praxeas] put to flight the Paraclete and crucified the Father."[107] Against this unitarian "patripassianism" (God the Father suffered and died as the Son), he cites the apostolic rule of faith and its trinitarian confession as the authoritative foundation of his whole position, namely, that the Father is the one from whom the Son proceeds, the Son is born "both man (*hominem*) and God" of the virgin and is named Jesus Christ, who suffered, died, and was raised. The Father and the Son send the Holy Spirit, the Paraclete, who sanctifies those who believe.[108] The ancient rule of faith thus emphasizes that "the threefoldness of God's intrinsic being is disclosed in creation

---

106. Another version, called "dynamic monarchianism" or "adoptionism," held that the man Jesus was never more than human, but was adopted by the Godhead and endowed with divine power (*dynamis*) or inhabited by the Logos, one of the Father's attributes, thus becoming "Son of God." Proponents of this version included Paul of Samosata (bishop of Antioch) and Theodotus of Rome.

107. *Adversus Praxean* 1 (*Adversus Praxean liber/Treatise Against Praxeas*, ed. and trans. Ernest Evans [London: SPCK, 1948], 89–90 [Latin]; 130–31[English]). Hereafter, page numbers for the Latin original [L] and the English translation [ET] are separated by a slash [/]).

108. Ibid., 2 (90–91 [L]/131–32 [ET]). The rule of faith is the authoritative touchstone because it "has come down from the beginning of the Gospel" and existed before heresy, and because "whatever is earliest is true and whatever is later is counterfeit" (ibid., 90 [L]/132 [ET]).

and redemption."[109] Tertullian's interpretation of this confession was the first to introduce the terms "trinity" (*trinitas*) and "person" (*persona*) into the discussion—a theological breakthrough.

> They [Father, Son, and Holy Spirit] are of the one, namely by unity of substance (*per substantiae scilicet unitatem*) while none the less is guarded the mystery of that economy which disposes the unity into trinity (*quae unitatem in trinitatem disponit*), setting forth Father and Son and Spirit as three, three however not in quality but in sequence (*gradu*), not in substance (*substantia*) but in aspect (*forma*), not in power but in [its] manifestation (*specie*), yet of one substance and one quality and one power, seeing it is one God from whom those degrees and aspects and manifestations are reckoned out in the name of the Father and the Son and the Holy Spirit.[110]

In interpreting these relationships, he retained the concept of *monarchia* but understood it in a more active sense than did his Monarchian opponents. He combined with it his revision of the theory of emanation and with the Apologists' Logos-christology, along with a deep concern for the economy of salvation, similar to that of Irenaeus. What resulted was a theology of the immanent Trinity that preserves both unity and distinction in God. A key element is that the *monarchia* of the Father, from which everything proceeds, is not divided by the emanation of the Son and the Spirit. Tertullian argues, against the Gnostics, that emanation does not necessarily imply separation.

> Everything that proceeds from something must of necessity be another beside that from which it proceeds, but it is not for that reason separated [from it]. . . . In this way the Trinity, proceeding by intermingled and connected degrees from the Father, in no respect challenges the monarchy, while it conserves the quality of the economy [i.e., the distinctions as they have been revealed in history].[111]

109. Rusch, *Trinitarian Controversy*, 10.

110. *Adv. Prax.* 2 (90–91[L]/132 [ET]).

111. Ibid., 8 (97 [L]/139–40 [ET]). Earlier in the same chapter, he employs natural analogies to make his point: "the Son was brought forth from the Father, but not made separate. For God brought forth the Word . . . as a root brings

And contrary to the modalists' explanation, in God there is a distinction of persons, not substances.[112] Tertullian uses *substantia* to refer to the unity of the essential being of Father, Son, and Spirit. Each of the three persons is God, without the Godhead being partitioned: the Father is "the whole substance" (*tota substantia*), the Son second in the sequence (*gradus*) of procession from the whole, and the Spirit third. The Son proceeds from the substance of the Father "not . . . by diversity, but by distribution, not by division but by distinction," and the Holy Spirit proceeds from the Father through the Son.[113] On the basis of these understandings of *monarchia* and emanation/procession, Tertullian proposes a formula "unrivalled in its accuracy"[114] that exerted tremendous influence in later trinitarian discussions:

> So the close series of the Father in the Son and the Son in the Paraclete makes three who cohere, the one attached to the other. *And these three are one substance, not one person* (*qui tres unum sunt, non unus*) in the sense in which it was said "I and the Father are one" [John 10:30], in respect of unity of substance, not of singularity of number.[115]

The other key element to his thought, already hinted at with the terms "distribution" and "distinction," is that *relationality* is an essential characteristic of what it is to be God. "The rules God has made, he himself observes. A father must have a son so as to be a father, and a son must have a father so as to be a son."[116] The terms "Father," "Son," and "Spirit" (Tertullian often uses the Johannine "Paraclete")

---

forth the ground shoot, and a spring the river, and the sun its beam: for these manifestations also are 'projections' [Tertullian uses the Greek *probolai*, the usual term for "emanations"] of those substances from which they proceed" (ibid., 97 [L]/139 [ET]).

112. Ibid., 7 (96 [L]/138 [ET]): "Whatever therefore the substance of the Word was, that I call a Person, and for it I claim the name of Son: and while I acknowledge him as Son I maintain he is another beside the Father."

113. Ibid., 7 (94–96 [L]/137–38 [ET], describing the processions); 9 (97–98 [L]/140 [ET], "whole substance" and "distribution . . . distinction"); 13 (103 [L]/147 [ET], each is God [*pater deus et filius deus et spiritus sanctus deus*]).

114. Kasper, *GJC*, 254.

115. *Adv. Prax.* 25 (121 [L]/169 [ET], emphasis added, translation modified).

116. Ibid., 10 (/141 [ET]).

designate those relations without which the specific actions of each divine person in the economy could not be understood. The relation of the distinct persons—and therefore plurality—lies at the very center of both the one inner being of God and the revelation of God in the economy of salvation, a "unity in trinity" which is the essential attribute of the immanent as well as the economic Trinity. This insight underlies Tertullian's insistence that Father, Son, and Spirit be called "persons," individual centers of action which have specific roles in the history of salvation.[117]

Despite Tertullian's brilliance in perceiving the issues at stake and fending off modalism, his thought does not completely avoid subordinationist tendencies. His portrayal of the Father as "the whole substance" and the Son as "an outflow and portion of the whole (*derivatio totius et portio*),"[118] his depiction of the "perfect birth of the Word (*sermonis*), when it proceeds from God" at creation,[119] and other such metaphors of emanation/procession/utterance/extrapolation, are signs that his thought remains under the shadow of the Apologists' *logos endiathetos/logos porphorikos* distinction, and that he understands the divine generation of the Son or Logos from the Father to have occurred in a gradual fashion.[120] Nevertheless, the precision and clarity of his formulations, as well as his terminological innovations, played a major role in the discussions of the Trinity up to the council of Nicaea.

Origen's contribution flows from his grand enterprise of constructing a comprehensive Christian view of reality that rests on two pillars: the revelation of the incomprehensible God as found in Scripture (properly interpreted to discover its deeper spiritual meaning) and celebrated in the liturgy, and his interpretation of this revelation within

---

117. See, e.g., *Adv. Prax.* 12 (101 [L]/145 [ET]), where Tertullian explains that at the creation, God says "Let us make man after our image and likeness" (Gen. 1:26) because "there already was attached to him the Son, a second Person, his Word, and a third Person, the Spirit in the Word. . . . He was speaking with the Son who was to assume manhood, and the Spirit who was to sanctify man, as with ministers and mediators in consequence of the unity of the Trinity."

118. Ibid., 9 (97 [L]/140 [ET], translation modified).

119. Ibid., 7 (94 [L]/136 [ET], translation modified).

120. Johannes Quasten, *Patrology, Volume II: The Ante-Nicene Literature after Irenaeus* (1950; reprint, Westminster, MD: Christian Classics, 1984), 326.

a philosophical framework influenced mainly by the Middle Platonism he had learned from its premier exponent, Ammonius Saccas (c. 175–242 AD/CE).[121] Origen's starting point is the belief handed on by the "apostolic teaching." God is one, the creator who created all things from nothing, and who sent the Lord Jesus Christ to call both Jews and Gentiles to salvation. "This just and good God, the Father of our Lord Jesus Christ, himself gave the law, the prophets and the gospels, and he is God both of the apostles and also of the Old and New Testaments." He emphasizes God's unity and goodness in order to show how the rule of faith decisively refutes the various Gnostic arguments. Christ was "begotten of the Father before every created thing" and was the means by which the Father created the universe. Christ became fully human at the incarnation, truly died, was raised, and ascended into heaven. The Holy Spirit "is united in dignity with the Father and the Son" and inspired the prophets and saints, but the Spirit's origins ("whether he is to be thought of as begotten or unbegotten") are unclear and remain an open question in the Church.[122]

In clarifying the meaning of this rule of faith for his contemporaries, Origen employed a Platonic philosophical framework, albeit one tempered by revelation.[123] God as Father is absolutely transcendent, incomprehensible, ungenerated, incorporeal, indivisibly one. He is purely spiritual, "a simple intellectual existence [that] is Unity (*Monas*) [or] Oneness (*Henas*) throughout, and the mind and fount from which originates all intellectual existence or mind."[124] The Father, in free-

---

121. Ammonius Saccas would also later teach Plotinus. Cf. Chadwick, "Philo and the Beginnings of Christian Thought," 182–83; John Anthony McGuckin, "The Life of Origen," in *The Westminster Handbook to Origen*, ed. John Anthony McGuckin (Louisville: Westminster John Knox, 2004), 1–23, at 5. McGuckin notes also the influence of Aristotle and Pythagoras, and calls the "heart" of Origen's work "the weaving together of the philosophic and mystical imperatives."

122. Origen, *Peri Archon (De principiis)*, pref. 4 (*On First Principles*, trans. G. W. Butterworth [1936; repr., Gloucester, MA: Peter Smith, 1973], 2–4).

123. For what follows, in addition to the sources noted in nn. 91 and 93, see *The Westminster Handbook to Origen*, q.v. "Christology" (C. Kannengieser), 73–78; "God" (R. E. Heine), 108-13; "Trinitarianism" (C. Markschies), 207–09.

124. *Peri Archon* I.1.6 (10). The ancient Latin translation by Rufinus (*De principiis*, the only complete version of *Peri Archon* extant) retains the original Greek terms.

dom, has created all reality through his only-begotten Son, who is Wisdom and Logos, the "image of the invisible God" (Heb. 1:3) who reflects the Father's being to rational creatures and is their way of return to the Father. The relationship of Father and Son is eternal, their union one of love and action.[125] Natural analogies utterly fail to explain "how the unbegotten God becomes Father of the only-begotten Son. This is an eternal and everlasting begetting. . . . For he does not become son in an external way through the adoption of the Spirit, but is Son by nature."[126] The better comparison for this ceaseless incorporeal generation, according to Origen, is the operation of the intellect, specifically how "an act of will proceeds from the mind without either cutting off any part of the mind or being separated or divided from it, [thus] in similar fashion has the Father begotten the Son."[127] This description of the generation of the Son as a continuous act of the Father's will, an "immanent intellectual procession" that excludes all materiality, is one of the earliest uses of this intellectual metaphor that will eventually come to dominate Western trinitarian thinking.[128] In comparison, Origen has less to say about the Holy Spirit. The Spirit is divine, "united in honor and dignity with the Father and the Son," proceeds from the Father, and "is ever with the Father and the Son; like the Father and the Son he always is, and was, and will be."[129] However, as noted above, he was undecided about the Spirit's origins and unsure about the Spirit's precise relation to the Son.

While asserting the union of the Father, Son, and Spirit, Origen emphasizes their distinction as well. He refers to the Father and the Son as "two distinct existences (*hypostases*), but one in mental unity, in agreement, and in identity of will."[130] Of the Trinity, he is "persuaded

---

125. Ibid., I.2.2–6 (16–20); II.9.2 (130); IV.4.1 (313–16).

126. Ibid., I.2.4 (18). Origen thus rejects the Apologists' two-stage Logos-christology.

127. Ibid., I.2.6 (19).

128. Fortmann, *The Triune God*, 56.

129. *Peri Archon* pref. 4 (3); I.2.13 (28); *Commentary on Romans* 6.7, quoted in Fortman, *The Triune God*, 57.

130. *Contra Celsum* VIII.12 (*Contra Celsum*, trans. Henry Chadwick [Cambridge: Cambridge University Press, 1965], 460–61).

that there are three *hypostases*, the Father, the Son, and the Holy Spirit."[131] Origen here uses *hypostasis* in its more generic Middle Platonic sense of "substance," "real existence," or "essence," thus nearly equivalent to *ousia* (the usual word for "substance"), rather than the more precise meaning of "individuality" which developed later, after the Council of Nicaea.[132] He criticized those who would reduce the Father and the Son to one hypostasis, and rejected the use of the term *homoousios* ("of the same substance," "consubstantial") to describe their relationship.[133] However, the three hypostases could be considered "consubstantial" in the sense that, "because their respective and specific nature is that of substantial goodness, they can be said to be "cosubstantive" . . . and to this extent, as cosubstantively good, they are devoid of internal subordinate distinctions."[134] At the same time, however, Origen's position admits a subordinationist interpretation. Only the Father is God in the absolute sense (*autotheos ho theos*, "God in himself, the God"). Since the Son/Logos participates in the Father's divinity, "it would be more just not to call him 'the God' (*ho theos*) but rather 'God' (*theos* [without the article])."[135] The Son/Logos is eternally generated from the Father; nonetheless the Father "caused it to exist."[136] He goes so far as to call the Son "a creature" (*ktisma*)[137]

131. *Commentary on John* II.10.75 (*Commentaire sur Saint Jean, tome I [Livres I–V]*, ed. and trans. Cécile Blanc, SC 120 [Paris: Les Éditions du Cerf, 1966], 254–55 [my translation]).

132. Markschies, "Trinitarianism," *Handbook*, 208. Cf. Rusch, *Trinitarian Controversy*, 14; Stead, *Philosophy in Christian Antiquity*, 174–80.

133. Markschies, "Trinitarianism," *Handbook*, 208, citing the *Commentary on Matthew* 17.14. This rejection may be based on the fear that, during this period, *homoousios* implied the "improper idea of a generic being shared by members of a class" (209).

134. Ibid., 209. Markschies cites *Peri Archon* I.6.2, I.8.3, and the *Homilies on Numbers* 12.1.

135. *Commentary on John* II.2.17 (SC 120, 216–19).

136. *Peri Archon* I.2.9 (23). Earlier in this section, he says that the Son "comes into existence . . . subsisting in its own proper nature, a kind of breath . . . of the first and unbegotten power of God."

137. Ibid., IV.4.1 (314). Rufinus, in his Latin translation of *Peri Archon*, omits the mention of the Son as creature (cf. p. 314 nn. 3 and 6), probably in order to distance Origen from accusations of heresy.

and even "a second God" (*ton deuteron theon*).[138] In emphasizing an immanent hierarchy and the Son's eternal dependence on the Father, Origen is most probably arguing against Gnostic theories of naturalistic emanation. The Spirit is "united in dignity with the Father and the Son" and proceeds from "the original goodness" of God the Father.[139] However, in other texts clearly implying a hierarchy, he claims that the Spirit "needs the mediation [of the Son] in order to be subsistent (*tē hypostasei*)," and places it at the lowest rank, while insisting that it "has more dignity than all the rest and a rank superior to all which has come from the Father through Christ."[140] The three hypostases have different specific actions: the Father has the widest sphere of activity, the Son smaller, and the Spirit smaller still.

> The God and Father, who holds the universe together, is superior to every being that exists, for he imparts to each one from his own existence that which each one is; the Son, being less than the Father, is superior to rational creatures alone (for he is second to the Father); the Holy Spirit is still less, and dwells within the saints alone. So that in this way the power of the Father is greater than that of the Son and of the Holy Spirit, and that of the Son is more than that of the Holy Spirit, and in turn the power of the Holy Spirit exceeds that of every other holy being.[141]

However, despite such traces of subordinationism throughout his overall schema, Origen's understanding of salvation is fully Trinitarian; that is, salvation is unobtainable apart from the whole Trinity. As the revealed image of God, Christ who is savior, Son, and Logos is the only means by which human beings, created "in the image and likeness of God" (Gen. 1:26), can gain knowledge of the Father and of "the truth of the noble qualities that are within us."[142] Our understanding of the Son's revelation, in turn, is made possible only by the

138. *Contra Celsum* V.39 (296; *Contre Celse, tome III [Livres V et VI]*, ed. and trans. Marcel Borret, SC 147 [Paris: Les Éditions du Cerf, 1969], 118–19).

139. *Peri Archon*, pref. 4; I.2.13 (28).

140. *Commentary on John* II.10.76 (mediation), II.10.75 (rank) (SC 120, 254–57).

141. *Peri Archon* I.3.5 (33–34). Rufinus omits this potentially troublesome passage from his translation.

142. Ibid., I.2.6 (20).

Holy Spirit,[143] the source of that grace whereby we become holy and thus "capable of receiving Christ afresh in his character of the righteousness of God."[144] Origen's vision of reality follows the circular Neoplatonic schema of *exitus-reditus* (outflow and return), while always guided by the apostolic rule of faith: the Father, the absolutely transcendent and incorporeal *autotheos*, freely created the universe through the mediation of the Son and the Spirit who are with him eternally, and then calls all back to himself through the grace of the Holy Spirit which allows us to recognize the revelation of his image in the Son. Without the entire Trinity, we would have no access to the "gifts of God" and thus would be unable to receive salvation.[145] Rather than the determinism that grounds the Gnostic view of reality, Origen finds at the heart of reality the freedom, love, and providence of God.[146]

Because of its desire to "think everything," Origen's theology is full of complexities that at times shade over into obscurities and contradictions. Indeed, Christoph Markschies calls attention to its "unfinished and experimental character" which set off "a struggle at [an] international level over the authoritative interpretation of Origen's Trinitarian schema."[147] His many-faceted synthesis can confound us as well, making his theology of the Trinity difficult to unravel.[148] For example, alongside clearly subordinationist passages

143. Ibid., I.3.4 (32–33). Origen bases his interpretation on one of the Paraclete passages in John's gospel: "When the Spirit of truth comes he will guide you into all the truth" (John 16:13).

144. Ibid., I.3.8 (38).

145. *Commentary on John* II.10.77 (SC 120, 256–57.)

146. Kasper, *GCJ*, 256: "Origen's entire system has a voluntaristic or, as we would say today, historical character which is profoundly opposed to the naturalism inherent in the gnostic idea of emanation."

147. "Trinitarianism," *Handbook*, 207.

148. Markschies notes how Origen's approach admits both subordinationist and "consubstantial" interpretations, depending on one's emphasis. See his "Theologische Diskussionen zur Zeit Konstatins: Arius, der 'arianische Streit' und die Konzil von Nicaea, die nachnizänischen Auseinandersetzungen bis 337" and "'. . . et tamen non tres Dii, sed unus Deus . . .': Zum Stand der Erforschung der altkirchlichen Trinitätstheologie," in, *Alta Trinità Beata: Gesammelte Studien zur altkirchlichen Trinitätstheologie* (Tübingen: Mohr Siebeck, 2000), 99–195, at 108–10; 286–309, at 298–99.

such as *Peri Archon* I.3.5 (quoted above), Origen can also say that "nothing in the Trinity can be called greater or less, for there is but one fount of deity, who upholds the universe by his word and reason, and sanctifies 'by the spirit of his mouth' all that is worthy of sanctification."[149] In the midst of a difficult discussion of the eternal relationship of the Spirit with the Father, Origen diagnoses the problem he faces as one having to do with the limits of language:

> Of course, these terms that we use, such as "always" or "has been," or any similar ones that bear a temporal significance, must be interpreted with reservations and not pressed; for they relate to time, but the matters of which we are now speaking, though described in temporal language for the purposes of discussion, in their essential nature transcend all idea of time.[150]

Despite the difficulties, we too need to wrestle with his theology because of its immense influence on the discussions that led to great doctrinal definitions of Nicaea, Constantinople (381 AD/CE), and Chalcedon (451 AD/CE).[151] Origen's detailed argumentation and his introduction of the terms *hypostasis* and *ousia*, played out against a background of mystical spirituality, had a clarifying effect on the Trinitarian discussion. He forced it to move to a deeper ontological level in order to handle the still-lingering questions about the relations among Father, Son, and Spirit and the effects on the economy of salvation, questions that became more complex as Christianity grew and had to face rival Hellenistic accounts of reality and divinity. In this way, Origen extended the insights of Irenaeus and Tertullian, and along with them helped the Church "develop a trinitarian doctrine of its own in which the economic Trinity and the immanent Trinity are inseparably conjoined."[152] Even more specifically, in view

149. *Peri Archon* I.3.7 (37). Some commentators hold that Rufinus altered this passage in his translation.

150. *Peri Archon* I.3.4 (33).

151. As Markschies puts it, "the so-called 'Neo-Nicene' formula (*mia ousia, treis hypostaseis;* 'one substance, three persons') . . . dogmatized through the creed of the Council of Constantinople 381 . . . is a structure of thinking about the Trinity which is fundamentally based on Origen's thinking ("Trinitarianism," *Handbook*, 207).

152. Kasper, *GJC*, 257.

of developments in the period immediately following Origen, his approach determined the fundamental "architecture" of orthodox Trinitarian doctrine, and remains definitive today.

> The development of Trinitarian theology in all parts of the church over the two centuries following him did little other than develop the schema he himself had first sketched out, by clarifying the loose ends of his concept. After the fourth century the whole body of Trinitarian doctrine was left alone, and to this day its architecture (as witnessed in the Neo-Nicene statements) shows the marks of the compromise (that sought-after balance of disparate emphases) we first find in Origen: a well-balanced mixture of Nicene Antisubordinationism (as in the coequality of the Persons) with legitimate subordinationism (e.g., the taxonomy observed in the Trinitarian aspects of prayer and liturgy and soteriological function).[153]

At the close of the third century AD/CE, then, many of the basic elements of a Trinitarian "solution" were in place. The next phase of development dealt not only with the clarification of these elements, but also with the noticeably increasing dissonance between biblical revelation and the Hellenistic philosophical framing of the God-issue which had governed much of the discussion so far. Middle Platonism, the revival and extension of Plato's thought in late antiquity, had provided most of this framework.[154] Its adherents understood God to be the changeless divine monad or sole principle (*archē*) that absolutely transcends time, history, and matter, and created the physical world through a secondary divine figure or demiurge (a concept borrowed from Plato's *Timaeus*; from the Greek *dēmiourgos*, "craftsman"). This doctrine, taught by philosophers such as Numenius (fl. c. mid-2nd century AD/CE), appeared under different guises and with many variations in various Christian treatises. However, it clashed with the person- and event-centered understanding of God and God's economy of salvation that had been narrated in the Old

153. Markschies, "Trinitarianism," *Handbook*, 209.
154. Cf. Stead, *Philosophy in Christian Antiquity*, 54–75; John M. Dillon, *The Middle Platonists, 80 B.C. to A.D. 220*, rev. ed. (Ithaca, NY: Cornell University Press, 1996).

and New Testaments. Signs of this growing dissonance surfaced especially during the late third and early fourth centuries, not only in the disputes over the reception of Origen's theology, but in the growing resistance to the subordinationism which, as we have seen, had been a consistent aspect of Christian reflection on God from the Apologists all to way up to Origen.

The controversy sparked by Arius and Arianism put the problem at center stage.[155] Rather than affirm the ambiguous subordinationism that pervaded Origenist descriptions of trinitarian relations, Arius (d. 336 AD/CE) rejected it by absolutizing and radicalizing it. His strict adherence to the Middle Platonic doctrine of God's absolute transcendence determined his interpretation of Scripture, his theology of creation, and his Christology. Arius excluded all plurality in the divine monad, any gradations within divinity, and any inherent connection between God and the material world.[156] In response to complaints raised against his preaching, he defended his position in a letter to his bishop, Alexander of Alexandria:

> We know one God—alone unbegotten (*agennēton*), alone eternal, alone without beginning, alone true, alone possessing immortality, alone wise, alone good, alone master, judge of all, manager, director, immutable and unchangeable . . . who begot an only-begotten Son before eternal times, through whom he made the ages and everything. . . . Thus there are three *hypostases.* God being the cause of all is without beginning, most alone; but

---

155. See the summary by Aloys Grillmeier, *Christ in Christian Tradition, Volume 1: From the Apostolic Age to Chalcedon (451)*, 2d ed., trans. John Bowden (Atlanta: John Knox Press, 1975), 219–48, and the literature cited there, especially G. C. Stead, "The Platonism of Arius," *Journal of Theological Studies* n.s. 15 (1964): 16–31 and Friedo Ricken, "Das Homousios von Nikaia als Krisis des altchristlichen Platonismus," in *Zur Frühgeschichte der Christologie. Ihre biblischen Anfänge und die Lehrformal von Nikaia*, ed. Bernhard Welte, Quaestiones Disputatae 51 (Freiburg/ Br.: Herder, 1970), 74–99. See also J. N. D. Kelly, *Early Christian Doctrines*, 5th ed. (1977; reprint, London/New York: Continuum, 2000), 223–51.

156. Cf. Ricken, "Das Homousios von Nikaia," 99: "Im Arianismus verabsolutiert sich ein mittleplatonisches Denkschema. . . . Der Arianismus stellt insofern eine erste Krisis des mittleplatonischen Denkens dar, der er herausstellt, daß es für den christlichen Glauben keine Stufung des Göttlichen und damit kein Drittes zwischen Transcendenz und geschaffener Welt gibt."

the Son, begotten by the Father, created and founded before the ages, was not before he was begotten. Rather, the Son begotten timelessly before everything, alone was caused to subsist by the Father. For he is not eternal or as eternal or as uncreated as the Father. Nor does he have identical being with the Father. . . . But God is thus before all things, as Monad (*monas*) and Beginning of all (*archē*). Therefore he is also before the Son, as we have learned from you when you preached throughout the midst of the church.[157]

All the basics of Arius' position are here. God the Father is uncreated, eternal, utterly transcendent; he is the unique Monad, the *hypostasis* from whom all duality is excluded. Due to the Godhead's absolute transcendence, there can be no direct relationship between divinity and the finite material world. The essence of Godhead is indivisible; it cannot be shared, participated in, or communicated, since this would imply divisibility (and thus change) or even, in the case of participation, a duality of gods. The Son of God, on the other hand, is a true creature, inferior to the Father yet superior to all other creatures, created by the Father before time and yet not eternal— according to the oft-repeated Arian slogan, "there was when he was not."[158] Thus, the Son is not co-eternal with the Father, as Origen held, but had a beginning: he was created before the time of the material world began, and was the mediating instrument (demiurge) by which the utterly transcendent Father created. Since the Son is of a different order of existence than the Father, he has no direct knowledge of the Father, no communication with him. Whatever divine titles he has ("Word," "Wisdom," "Son of God," etc.) are by courtesy alone: "Even

157. *Letter to Alexander of Alexandria*, 2, 4 (in Rusch, *The Trinitarian Controversy*, 31–32 [translation modified, following Stead, "The Platonism of Arius," 18, and Grillmeier, 226]).

158. Quoted at Nicaea (in the anathema accompanying the creed; see below) and by Athanasius, *Contra Arianos*, oratio I, 5 (*Patrologiae Cursus Completus, Series Graeca* [= PG], ed. J.-P. Migne [Paris: 1857-1866], 26:21A–B). In his *Letter to Eusebius of Nicomedia*, 5, Arius says that "before [the Son] was begotten or created or defined or established, he was not. For he was not unbegotten. But we are persecuted because we say, 'The Son has a beginning, but God is without beginning'" (in Rusch, *The Trinitarian Controversy*, 30).

if he is called God, he is not God truly, but by participation in grace. . . . He too is called God in name only."[159] The Arians' main concern, then, was to portray God the Father as the monad who by his very nature cannot enter time and history but relates to the world only by means of intermediaries, and to portray as occupying this intermediate sphere the Son, "produced by decree of the will of the Father and not by the communication of his nature or essence," who is on the side of creatures rather than divinity, yet who is the supreme creature and demiurge through whom the transcendent Father creates.[160]

Early in 325, a local council in Antioch condemned the Arian position. Only with the emperor Constantine's explicit intervention was a general council called later that year in Nicaea, with the goal of definitively settling the conflict and thereby securing ecclesial unity. The solution—less definitive than anticipated—was contained in the creed or "symbol" agreed to by the bishops at Nicaea, namely, the definition that the Son was "consubstantial [one in being] with the Father" (*homoousios tō patri*).

> We believe in one God the Father all powerful, maker of all things both seen and unseen. And in one Lord Jesus Christ, the son of God, the only-begotten (*monogenē*) begotten from the Father (*gennēthenta ek tou patros*), that is from the substance (*ousia*) of

159. In Athanasius, *Contra Arianos*, oratio I, 6 (PG 26:24A; translation from Kelly, 229).

160. I. Ortiz de Urbina, *Nicée et Constantinople*, Histoire des conciles œcuméniques I (Paris: Éditions de l'Orante, 1963), 76. See also LaCugna, "Trinitarian Mystery," 167; Grillmeier, 231–32. As LaCugna notes (*God For Us*, 32), the Arians could cite scriptural support for their position (e.g., Prov. 8:22, John 14:28) as well as for the widespread subordinationist interpretation of the Church's common intercessory prayers to the Father through the Son. For a somewhat different approach, see Frances M. Young, *From Nicaea to Chalcedon: A Guide to the Literature and its Background* (Philadelphia: Fortress, 1983), 58–64, who views Arius' teaching as driven more by intra-ecclesial exegetical debates than by philosophical argumentation. She describes his major concern as "not so much of demoting the Son as exalting the Father" in order "to avoid attributing physical processes like emanation or generation to God," and Arius himself as being "a reactionary, a rather literal-minded conservative who appealed to scripture and tradition as the basis of his faith" (63–64).

the Father, God from God, light from light, true God from true God, begotten not made, consubstantial (*homoousion*) with the Father, through whom all things came to be, both in heaven and those in earth; for us humans and for our salvation he came down and became incarnate, became human, suffered and rose up on the third day, went up into the heavens, is coming to judge the living and the dead. And in the holy Spirit.

[*Anathema:*] And those who say, "there once was when he was not," and "before he was begotten he was not," and that he came to be from things that were not, of from another hypostasis or substance, affirming that the son of God is subject to change or alteration—these the catholic and apostolic church anathematizes.[161]

The bishops at Nicaea most probably took up a previously-familiar baptismal creed and inserted various elements and anathemas that specifically ruled out Arianism as a legitimate Christian interpretation of God and God's salvation. In this way, they intended to avoid any divergence between the Church's liturgical and pastoral practice and its theological reflection.[162] The creed presents "the saving economy of the Trinity which shows that the Father communicates himself to us in the true Son (and in the Holy Spirit), while at the same time showing the truly divine status of the Son and also his soteriological relevance. . . . Jesus Christ is the one true Son of the Father, not a creature."[163] Since the immediate theological discussion focused on Christology, specifically the nature and role of the Son, the baptismal model's brief mention of the Holy Spirit was left undeveloped.

The concept of *homoousios* ("of the same being/substance," "consubstantial") was the most crucial of the additional elements, and the most contested. The term's presence in the creed was initially objectionable to many in the fourth-century Church, both at Nicaea and afterwards, because of its non-biblical character, its various shades of meaning,[164]

161. *DEC* 1:5 [see n. 1].
162. Grillmeier, 266.
163. Ibid., 267.
164. "Are we to understand 'of the same nature' in the 'generic' sense in which Origen was alleged to have employed *homoousios*, or are we to take it as having the meaning accepted by later Catholic theology, viz. numerical identity

its origins in Valentinian Gnosticism (where it meant a "similarity of being" between different beings), and the fact that the Arian party had been the first to employ it at this stage of the discussion (in order to ridicule and reject it).[165] Nevertheless, the council employed it, at the behest of Constantine and his theological advisor Ossius of Cordoba, in order to refute the Arian doctrine and to craft a statement to which no Arian could subscribe. In doing so, "the Fathers of Nicaea had the courage to maintain the tradition of the 'Son of God' to be found in Bible and church in all its strictness, in part with unbiblical words."[166] In a terse, kerygmatic fashion, the concept of *homoousios* summarizes how Sonship relates to the one being of God. It expresses the Church's belief that the Son is eternally begotten (*gennēthenta*), not created (*poiē-thenta*), thereby uncoupling the concept of "begetting" from any naturalistic concept of "being created in time."[167] Thus, the Son is fully God ("true God from true God"): he belongs on the side of God rather than that of creatures, and possesses the unique and indivisible divine nature that is proper to the Father, without being the Father. Despite its inherent ambiguities, then, *homoousios* can be interpreted in the context of the creed as a whole to mean "unity of being," rather than "same being" (which could connote tritheism) or "identity of being" (which could lead to Sabellian modalism).[168]

The context of the creed as a whole has a very specific character: it is trinitarian from the start and follows the pattern of the economy of salvation, rather than beginning with any sort of philosophical notion of the one being of God. In other words, it does not confess

---

of substance? The root word *ousia* could signify the kind of substance or stuff common to several individuals of a class, or it could connote an individual thing as such" (Kelly, 234).

165. For the Gnostic pre-history of *homoousios*, see Ricken, "Das Homousios von Nikaia," 92–95. For Arius' first use, see Grillmeier, 269–70 and Lampe, 98.

166. Grillmeier, 270.

167. The discussion at Nicaea thus begins the resolution of the persistent ambiguities that had plagued early church discussions of the relationship of the Father with the Son that centered around the linguistic pairs "begotten-unbegotten" (*gennētos-agennētos*) and "created-uncreated" (*genētos-agenētos*)— note the slight but important variation in spelling. See LaCugna, *God For Us*, 32–34; Grillmeier, 267; Kelly, 227–28.

168. Kasper, *GJC*, 257–58; Kelly, 235–36.

belief in a formal and abstract notion of "divinity" or Godhead. "The creed starts rather with the Father and understands him as the 'summit of unity' in which the Son and the Spirit are comprehended. We thus have a genetic conception of the divinity, in which the divinity originates in the Father and streams forth in the Son and the Holy Spirit."[169] We also have a clear denial of the Arian argument that the essence of divinity is "self-enclosed" being, and a clear affirmation that it includes relationality and relationship.[170] It turns out, then, that the general trinitarian "architecture" that had been sketched earlier by Origen (and by Tertullian with his reformulation of *monarchia*) remains valid: a dynamic understanding of divine being which balances the coequality of the divine persons (the antisubordinationist affirmation, against the Arians) with a legitimate recognition of the Son's difference from and dependence on the Father (clearly affirmed in the gospels and numerous other biblical texts),[171] while ruling out any naturalistic understanding of "begetting" or any separation of being between Father and Son. What the symbol of Nicaea articulated, then, was the great Church's deepest intuition that Christ was not simply "a bridge between the atemporal God and human history; rather, Christ was the coming of *very God* into the world, and our means of transformation and union with God."[172]

This was as far as Nicaea's affirmations could go. Despite the emperor's intentions, the problem of reconciling unity and trinity in God remained, and became even sharper. The council's basic purpose, after all, had been negative: to rule out Arianism as a legitimate Christian interpretation. It gave no further guidance on how *homoousios* should be more precisely and positively defined, since it lacked "the

169. Kasper, *GJC*, 258, citing Ortiz de Urbina, *Nicée et Constantinople*, 75–76. Ortiz de Urbina emphasizes that, according to Nicaea, the unity of the persons is "directly revealed and affirmed in its source, who is the Father. It is not deduced by reflection which compares the three persons among themselves" (76; my translation).

170. Cf. Greshake, *Der dreieine Gott*, 91–92.

171. See Bernhard Welte, "Zur Christologie von Chalkedon" [1954/1965], *Auf der Spur des Ewigen: Philosophische Abhandlungen über verschiedene Gegenstände der Religion und der Theologie* (Freiburg: Herder, 1965), 429–58, at 452–58; also in *Gesammelte Schriften*, vol. IV/2: *Wege in die Geheimnisse des Glaubens*, ed. Peter Hünermann (Freiburg: Herder, 2007), 131–62, at 156–62.

172. LaCugna, "Trinitarian Mystery," 167.

conceptual tools for expressing in an adequate way the unity of being and distinction of persons. . . . The clear distinctions which Tertullian had already made could win adherence only after a long and difficult process of clarification."[173]

3.2 From Nicaea to Constantinople I (381 AD/CE)

This process began immediately after Nicaea, with the meaning of *homoousios* as a focus.[174] Some, like Eusebius of Caesarea (c. 260–c. 340), objected to its materialistic connotations. Others, like the important group of mid-fourth-century theologians known as Homoiousians (misleadingly labeled "Semi-Arians" by one of their contemporaries), tried to develop an orthodox position between the Nicene symbol and the interpretations of the still-active Arian parties. These theologians held just as high a Christology as Nicaea and rejected Arian doctrines, but objected to the un-biblical *homoousios* as well as to the political tactics used by the various parties at the council. They especially feared that confessing the Son as "one in being" with the Father would lead to the Sabellian identification of Father and Son without distinction—i.e., the fear that *homoousios* ("consubstantial") truly meant *tautoousios* ("identical in substance"). They preferred the term *homoiousios* ("like in substance"), and the declaration of the council of Ancyra (358) codified their view that "the Son, who is an *ousia* (here denoting 'individual entity' or 'person') and not an impersonal divine activity . . . is like the Father in respect of substance."[175] Later statements reflected the Homoiousians' revulsion at the growing radicality of the Arians' claims, as well as the narrowing gap between their own thinking and that of the Nicene party.

Their initial "moderate" compromise solution, unfortunately, could not do justice to the soteriological insight that Nicaea attempted to safeguard with the *homoousios*. Nor did they sort out in any clear fashion the confusing meanings of *ousia* and *hypostasis* that continued to plague the ongoing discussion. (Did *ousia* mean "individual" or

173. Kasper, *GJC*, 258. In fact, Constantine considered this lack of precision advantageous; it allowed the various feuding parties to agree to Nicaea's symbol, according to the different shadings of meaning that they accepted.

174. See Kelly, 237–51; Lampe, 99–111.

175. Lampe, 110; see also Kelly, 250.

something more generic? To what precisely did *hypostasis* refer? Did *ousia* and *hypostasis* mean roughly the same thing?) Some progress began to be made with Athanasius of Alexandria's interventions, both in his post-Nicaea writings and during his leadership of the synod of Alexandria (362).

Athanasius (c. 296–373) staunchly defended the Nicene doctrine because he grasped the soteriological issue that lay at its core: only if the Son is truly divine and eternal can he bestow eternal life and save humankind. And the Son can be this and do this only if he is the eternal Son of the eternal Father. "For he [i.e., the *Logos*, the Word of God] himself was made human, so that we might become God; he rendered himself visible by his body, so that we might have an idea of the invisible Father; he took on the insults of men, so that we might have a share in immortality."[176] On seeing how closely the ongoing Homoiousian discussion approximated the Nicene dogma, and despite the inconsistent and even contradictory trinitarian formulas used by the various parties ("three *hypostaseis*" by some, "one *hypostasis*" by others), Athanasius was able to win over the Homoiousians and other moderates. He demonstrated that their concern to avoid the dreaded Sabellianism by maintaining the distinction of persons in the divine Triad, without ever denying the unity of divine being, was yet another legitimate way of expressing Nicaea's concern to affirm the unity of being of Father and Son (i.e., one *ousia*) without denying the distinctions. The Church could tolerate both positions and both *hypostasis* formulas; what had separated the parties was fundamentally a difference in emphasis.[177] Athanasius is also responsible for focusing attention again on the nature and role of the Holy

---

176. Athanasius, *De incarnatione* 54, 3 (*Sur l'incarnation du Verbe*, ed. and trans. Charles Kannengiesser, SC 199, 2d rev. ed. [Paris: Les Éditions du Cerf, 2000], 458–59). Kannengiesser notes that "these three propositions are rightly considered as summarizing the essentials of the treatise's teaching" (459 n.1). They echo a theme seen earlier in Irenaeus of Lyons.

177. See Athanasius, *Tomos ad Antiochenos* 5–6 (PG 26:800–04). See also Kelly, 252–55; Lampe, 110–11; Joseph T. Lienhard, "*Ousia* and *Hypostasis:* The Cappadocian Settlement and the Theology of 'One *Hypostasis*'," in *The Trinity: An Interdisciplinary Symposium* [see n.21], 99–121, at 104–05.

Spirit.[178] Against those who interpreted Scripture as teaching that the Spirit was a creature, his most compelling argument was again soteriological. Citing Paul's challenge "Do you not know that you are the temple of God, and that the Spirit of God dwells in you?" (1 Cor 3:16), he argued that "if the Holy Spirit were a creature, we should have no participation in God through him; we would be united to a creature and alien from the divine nature. . . . If he makes men divine, his nature must undoubtedly be that of God."[179] The Spirit is consubstantial (*homoousios*) with the Father and the Son, and hence, due to this indivisible essence, their activity (*energeia*) is one and the same. Whatever the Father accomplishes is effected through the Son in the Holy Spirit.[180]

Athanasius' theology is part of the complex history of Nicaea and its immediate aftermath. The series of animated and at times volatile fourth-century theological discussions helped resolve some (but never all) of the dissonance between the biblically-grounded person- and event-centered understanding of the triune God and the Middle Platonic philosophical framework employed to interpret it. Revelation's "excessive" character makes this a necessary dissonance. The biblical view of the loving God who encounters Israel in the Old Testament and all creation through Jesus Christ and the Spirit in the New Testament—in other words, the revelation that God is both immanently and economically *relational*—clashes with, indeed exceeds, Greek ontological categories. The partial resolution in this case was clear: the encounter with the God of the biblical narratives and the incarnational impulse of revelation were given priority over Middle Platonic concepts of absolute transcendence and non-relational divinity. The categories of being, substance, and divinity had to be rethought and reshaped under the "pressure" of revelation in order to communicate more adequately the realities of the *oikonomia*, the salvific relationship of the triune God with creation that is initiated by the Father and brought to fulfillment in the incarnation of the Son and the persistent power of the Spirit.

178. See Kelly, 255–58.
179. *Ad Serapionem* 1, 24 (PG 26:585–88; translation from Kelly, 258).
180. Ibid., 1, 27–28 (PG 26:593–96).

If the conflict with Arianism indeed provoked, in Friedo Ricken's phrase, "the crisis of the ancient church's Platonism," then the discussions both at and after Nicaea demonstrate that a parallel crisis of scriptural interpretation had to be faced as well. In an ironic turn of events, the reformulated understandings of the un-biblical notions of *ousia* and *hypostasis* helped to guard the biblical Christian experience of the triune God from being swamped by philosophical rigorism. The confession that the loving Father is the source of all things, the recognition of Jesus' intimate sonship with his "Abba" (an intimacy he offers to share with us), the acknowledgment of the Spirit's necessary role in the recognition of Jesus as Lord and as the human face of God—these biblical affirmations are rooted in experiences with God that had provided the basis for early Christianity's fundamental trinitarian structure and its biblical expression. During the early fourth century, however, the meaning of these biblical affirmations came into question. Arius' radically subordinationist interpretation of the Son's relation to the Father had seemed as compelling as the interpretations of those who had emphasized the co-equality of the Father and the Son. To solve this dilemma, the soteriological heart of Christianity, the belief that Christ saves us by the power of the Father and gives us a share in the eternal life of God, was brought most strongly to the fore, despite the long tradition of subtly subordinationist liturgical prayer and biblical exegesis.[181] The result of the Nicene and post-Nicene discussions was the differentiation of two types of subordinationism—one permitted, one banned—similar to what we had seen earlier in the evaluation of Origen's trinitarian "architecture." When speaking of the nature of God and the relations among the divine hypostases, a *logical* subordination of God the Son to God the Father, without any hint of inferiority or superiority of being, is legitimate and permitted, since fathers are logically prior to sons; as the Nicene symbol puts it, "the son of God [is] the only-begotten begotten from the Father." But any *ontological* subordination, implying the superiority of one type of being over another or implying temporal priority, is ruled out.[182] Thus, the soteriological insight that "the Logos himself

181. Cf. LaCugna, *God For Us*, 22, 32, 114; "Trinitarian Mystery," 164, 166.
182. See Markschies, "Trinitarianism," *Handbook*, 209; LaCugna, "Trinitarian Mystery," 166 n.32.

was made human so that we might become God"—a belief grounded in Christian experience, conveyed by the living tradition of the Church, and summed up in the time-honored phrase echoed by Athanasius— became the ultimate standard by which the Church interpreted those places in Scripture and in liturgical prayer where the mediatorship of Christ could possibly be misrepresented as an "inequality" between the Father and the Son. And what aided theologians in articulating this insight, as well as marking the first steps toward understanding the role of the Holy Spirit, were the un-biblical concepts of *ousia* and *hypostasis*, along with reformulated notions of divinity and being. These categories clarified the soteriology in Scripture in a way that biblical exegesis alone could not. The Nicene symbol itself is a mixture of these two types of language, one a more scriptural presentation of the economy of salvation, the other more abstract, conceptual, argumentative. The life, death, and resurrection of Jesus are narrated in biblical terms, whereas the preceding section on the identity of Christ argues with the technical, abstract terms of Greek philosophy. "The answer to the question about what Christ did and suffered required not only a focus on the one who acted and suffered, but also a language that could interpret and determine this narrative as clearly as possible. Thus, problems raised with regard to the history of salvation, the *oikonomia*, required a reflection on the level of God-self, the *theologia*."[183]

A final point in connection with this "crisis" is that both the final form of the creed and the subsequent debates over *homoousios* demonstrate the necessity of theological reflection. Rowan Williams is correct in emphasizing the significance of Nicaea's theological hermeneutics (the process of interpretation which clarifies the meanings of Scripture and the lived Christian tradition) for the early Church as well as for today.

> There is a sense in which Nicaea and its aftermath represent a recognition by the Church at large that *theology* is not only legitimate but necessary. The loyal and uncritical repetition of

183. Herwi Rikhof, "Trinity," in *The Theology of Thomas Aquinas*, ed. Rik Van Nieuwenhove and Joseph Wawrykow (Notre Dame: University of Notre Dame Press, 2005), 36–57, at 38.

formulae is seen to be inadequate as a means of securing continuity at anything more than a formal level; Scripture and tradition require to be read in a way that brings out their strangeness,
their non-obvious and non-contemporary qualities, in order that
they may be read both freshly and truthfully from one generation
to another. They need to be made more *difficult* before we can
accurately grasp their simplicities. Otherwise, we read with eyes
not our own and think them through with minds not our own;
the "deposit of faith" does not really come into contact with
ourselves. And this "making difficult," this confession that what
the gospel says in Scripture and tradition does not instantly and
effortlessly make sense, is perhaps one of the most fundamental
tasks for theology.[184]

The conflict of Christological interpretations in the early fourth century AD/CE had exposed the problem of relying on Scripture itself
to provide the means necessary for clarifying its meaning. This
method failed because of the plurality of plausible interpretations.
The danger within Arianism was not only its claim that God was
disconnected from the world, but that Scripture could be interpreted
to support this claim. It led to the fear that salvation mediated by the
ontologically subordinate, non-divine Son might not really be salvific
at all. The reality of salvation and the means by which God accomplishes it would thereby be obscured, the Old Testament creation
narrative and image-of-God theology would be contradicted, and
the role of the Son would be diminished. Without the reflections on
being and divinity that used non-biblical, more philosophical categories (that is, from "outside" the biblical narrative but always in
light of biblical revelation), the meaning of Scripture would have
remained ambiguous and contested, and its life-giving force in the
Church undermined. The use of reason to clarify faith claims had
been part of Christian tradition from its earliest days. But the official
approbation that Nicaea gave to theological reflection, to the point
of including its results in the confession of faith that previously had
been purely liturgical and doxological, was a momentous step. It
provided a model for all subsequent creedal statements. The Church

---

184. Rowan Williams, *Arius: Heresy and Tradition*, rev. ed. (Grand Rapids:
Eerdmans, 2001), 236.

insisted that Scripture demands interpretation; the mere recitation of scriptural proof-texts is no guarantee that one has successfully grasped the truth of revelation.

The balanced application of both faith and reason was especially necessary during the polemics of the late fourth century. Despite the agreements reached in 362 at the synod of Alexandria, as well as Athanasius' later interventions, it still remained unclear how the distinctions among the divine persons were to be characterized and how *ousia* and *hypostasis* could be used to articulate them. Their overlapping meanings contributed to the confusion; for many writers of the fourth century, *ousia* and *hypostasis* functioned as synonyms meaning "something that subsists."[185] Some, like Marcellus of Ancyra (d. c. 374), argued that Christian monotheism could be defended only by a miahypostatic (one *hypostasis*) theology. In this tradition, "there is one God, who subsists; He is one *hypostasis*, one *ousia*. . . . This one God utters a Word, or begets a Son, and sends forth his Holy Spirit. . . ." However, as Joseph Lienhard notes, this tradition "hesitates to assign any plurality to the Godhead. In general in speaking of God, saying 'one' is always safe, whereas saying 'two' is always dangerous."[186] Many later fourth-century theologians tenaciously held this, arguing that any notion of three *hypostaseis* was tantamount to tritheism.

Through the concerted efforts of the Cappadocian theologians Basil of Caesarea, his friend Gregory of Nazianzus, and Basil's brother Gregory of Nyssa, a way was found to express both the unity and distinction in God as authentically as possible, one that led eventually to the classic orthodox trinitarian formula of "one *ousia*, three *hypostaseis*." The solution stemmed from their attempts to work out the explicit distinction between the two terms and then explain how they were related.[187] Basil (c. 330–79) developed a two-fold argument that addressed both the *ousia-hypostasis* question as well as the begotten-created distinction. He followed Stoic philosophy in claiming that

185. Lienhard, "*Ousia* and *Hypostasis*," 103–04.

186. Ibid., 109.

187. For what follows, see esp. Basil Studer, *Trinity and Incarnation: The Faith of the Early Church*, trans. Matthias Westendorff, ed. Andrew Louth (Collegeville, MN: Liturgical Press, 1993), 139–153; Lienhard, 105–07.

ousia and *hypostasis* have different meanings: *ousia* refers to what is common and shared (*ta koinon*); *hypostasis* to what is proper (*to idion*), the particular way in which *ousia* is received. Each *hypostasis* of the Trinity is thus distinguished from the others by its proper characteristic: paternity (Father), sonship (Son), sanctification (Holy Spirit).[188] Against Arians such as Eunomius of Cyzicus who identified unbegottenness (*agennēsia*) with God's essence (*ousia*) and thus concluded that the Son, as begotten, had to be of a different essence and could not be God, Basil contended that unbegottenness is not part of the *ousia* of God, but rather is a proper characteristic of the *hypostasis* of the Father, just as begottenness is a proper characteristic of the Son.[189] "Peculiar to the Father is the fact that he owes his being to no other cause; peculiar to the Son is his generation from the Father; peculiar to the Holy Spirit is that he is known after and with the Son and that he has his substance from the Father."[190]

Gregory of Nazianzus (329/30–389/90) brought clarity of expression as well as further theological depth to this discussion. He coined various concise formulas to describe the Trinity and was perhaps the first to employ the phrase "one nature and three hypostases."[191] For example, in his Fifth Theological Oration (preached at Constantinople in 380), after presenting a series of arguments against those who

188. Ep. [Letter] 214, 4 in *Saint Basile: Lettres*, ed. and trans. Yves Courtonne, 3 vols. (Paris: Les Belles Lettres, 1957–66), 2:205–06; *Saint Basil: The Letters*, ed. and trans. Roy J. Deferrari, 4 vols., Loeb Classical Library 190, 215, 240, 270 (Cambridge, MA: Harvard University Press, 1962–86), 2:234–35. See also Ep. 236, 6 (3:53–54 [Courtonne]; 3:400–03 [Deferrari]).

189. Lienhard, 105, citing Basil, *Contra Eunomium* 2, 26 (PG 29:637). For Eunomius' teaching, including his claim that God's essence can be completely comprehended by human reason, see LaCugna, *God For Us*, 55–56. As Lampe notes (114), Basil's typology of peculiar properties remains unsatisfactory, since "paternity" and "sonship" are modes of subsistence, while "sanctification" is an activity that logically cannot be restricted to the Spirit.

190. Kasper, *GJC*, 259.

191. Cf. Anthony Meredith, *The Cappadocians* (Crestwood, NY: St. Vladimir's Seminary Press, 1995), 44. See, e.g., the passage from the Fifth Theological Oration, below. In Oration 26, 19, Gregory uses *mia physis, treis idiotētes* ("one nature, three personalities") (*Discours 24–26*, ed. and trans. Justin Mossay and Guy Lafontaine, SC 284 [Paris: Les Éditions du Cerf, 1978], 270–71).

denied the divinity of the Holy Spirit (known as the Pneumatomachians or "Spirit-fighters"), he summarized the formal doctrine of the Trinity with great precision.

> The very fact of not being begotten, of being begotten and of proceeding give[s] them whatever names are applied to them— Father, Son, and Holy Spirit respectively. The aim is to safeguard the distinctness of the three hypostases within the single nature (*mia physis*) and quality (*axia*) of the Godhead. The Son is not Father; there is *one* Father, yet he is whatever the Father is. The Spirit is not Son because he is from God; there is *one* Only-begotten. Yet whatever the Son is, he is. *The three are one in their Godhead and the one is three in personalities* (*idiotēsin*).[192]

To refer to the unity in God, Gregory used *ousia* sparingly, preferring *physis* ("nature") or *theotēs* ("deity," "Godhead"). To indicate what is three in God, he used *idiotētes* ("peculiar qualities," "properties") and *prosōpa* ("persons") along with *hypostaseis*, and applied the Nicene *homoousios* to all three.[193] He defined what is proper to each hypostases as unbegottenness (Father), generation (Son), and procession (Spirit).[194]

Gregory of Nyssa (c. 330–c. 395) clarified these distinctions even further. He equated *ousia* with the generic, as did Basil. But his analysis of *hypostasis* is more detailed: it refers to "that which is said proper to the individual (*to idiōs*)" and "the conception which, by means of specific notes that it indicates, restricts and circumscribes in a particular thing what is general and uncircumscribed. . . ."[195]

---

192. Oration 31 (= Fifth Theological Oration), 9 in *Discours 27–31 (Discours théologiques)*, ed. and trans. Paul Gallay and Maurice Jourjon, SC 250 (Paris: Les Éditions du Cerf, 1978), 292–93; *On God and Christ: The Five Theological Orations and Two Letters to Cledonius*, trans. Frederick Williams and Lionel Wickham, Popular Patristics Series (Crestwood, NY: St. Vladimir's Seminary Press, 2002), 123 (my emphasis; translation modified).

193. E.g., Oration 31, 10 (SC 250, 292–93; *On God and Christ*, 123): "What then? Is the Spirit God? Certainly. Is he consubstantial (*homoousios*)? Yes, if he is God."

194. E.g., Oration 25, 16 (SC 284, 198–99): *agennēsia* (Father), *gennēsis* (Son), *ekpempsis* (Spirit).

195. *On the Distinction between "Ousia" and "Hypostasis"* (once attributed to Basil as his Ep. 38), 2–3 (*Basile: Letteres*, 1:82–83 [Courtonne]; *Basil: Letters*, 1:200–01 [Deferrari]).

However, the analogy he used to illustrate how *ousia-hypostasis* is equated with generic-particular (namely, "man" as the genus, "Peter," "James," and "John" as particular instances of that genus), along with the pronounced individuation it seemed to advocate, led some to accuse him of tritheism (three Gods who share a common divine being). He defended himself by arguing that language and analogies are only approximations that never succeed in completely comprehending the mysteries of the divine nature and that, unlike the three men in the analogy who are distinguished by the differences in their activities, in the Trinity there is but a single operation or activity (*energeia*) that reveals a unity of being:

> Therefore, then, the holy Trinity works every activity (*energeia*) according to the manner stated, not divided according to the number of the *hypostases*, but one certain motion and disposition of goodwill occurs, proceeding from the Father through the Son to the Spirit.

> For . . . the principle of the power of oversight and beholding in Father, Son, and Holy Spirit is one. It starts off from the Father as from a spring; it is effected by the Son, and by the power of the Spirit it completes its grace. No activity (*energeia*) is divided to the *hypostases*, completed individually by each and set apart without being viewed together.[196]

This demonstrates one of the consistent aspects of the Cappadocians' trinitarian thought: it not only affirms the oneness of nature shared by Father, Son, and Spirit, but emphasizes the distinction of persons within "a dynamic understanding of God [that] retains the biblical emphasis on the economy of salvation" and views God the Father as the font of divinity, "the unoriginate origin, source, and principle of Godhead"[197]—a dynamic and monarchical understanding of divinity, but without subordinationist or Sabellian overtones.[198] By uniting the

196. *To Ablabius: That There Are Not Three Gods* (PG 45: 125D–127A, 127C–D; *Gregorii Nysseni Opera*, eds. Werner Jaeger et al., vol. 3/1 [Leiden: Brill, 1958], 48–49; 50; translation in Rusch, 155, 156.) Cf. Hill, *Three-Personed God*, 48.

197. LaCugna, "Trinitarian Mystery," 168.

198. In light of this belief, Gregory of Nyssa feels comfortable describing the distinctions in terms of causality: "While confessing the unchangeableness of

Origenist teaching of three hypostases with the Athanasian concern for the unity-in-equality of the Godhead, the Cappadocians' "one nature, three hypostases" formula represents an advance over both positions. By reinterpreting the more abstract Nicene *homoousios* in terms of the saving action of the Trinity confessed at baptism, they bring together the theological concern for the divine unity with the liturgical affirmation of the Trinity's operation in the *oikonomia*.[199]

These crucial terminological clarifications serve as a prelude to the Cappadocians' major contribution, the development of the concept of *relationality* in support of their arguments. This was a key move in solving much of the unity-distinction dilemma as well as resolving (as far as possible) the dissonance between the biblical narrative of the economy and Greek philosophical categories.

Gregory of Nazianzus states the point succinctly: " 'Father' designates neither substance (*ousia*) nor activity (*energeia*), but is the name of a relation (*scheseōs*) which holds good between the Father and the Son."[200] Basil had first proposed such an understanding of the hypostases in order to defeat Eunomius' claim that by identifying God's *ousia* with unbegottenness and seeing "Father" and "God" as equivalent, one might grasp the essence of God and render God rationally comprehensible. According to Basil, neither "unbegotten" nor "Father" is equivalent to the divine *ousia*. Neither term allows unmediated access to "what" God is—God remains incomprehensible. Rather, they are terms of relation expressing the specific manner of God-being-Father. "Unbegottenness" signifies one proper characteristic, namely, that divine Fatherhood is absolutely independent of any origin. The term "Father" functions similarly as a term of relation, being defined "by relation to the Son, and not just by the

---

the nature, we do not deny the difference in cause and causality, by which alone we seize the distinction of the one from the other. It is by the belief that one is the cause [i.e., the Father] and the other is from the cause [i.e., the Son]. We also consider another difference of the one who is from the cause. There is the one which depends on the first, and there is that one [i.e., the Spirit] which is through that which depends on the first" (*That There Are Not Three Gods* [PG45:133B; *Opera*, 3/1: 55–56; Rusch, 160]).

199. Cf. Studer, 144–45.

200. Oration 29 (= Third Theological Oration), 16 (SC 250, 210–11; *On God and Christ*, 84 [translation modified]).

absence of all relation to an antecedent term [of origin]. The notion of Father necessarily includes the notion of Son."[201] The terms thus signify *how* God is rather than *what* God is. The mystery of the divine essence is thereby preserved. Gregory of Nyssa extended this understanding by arguing that the Son and the Spirit are everything the Father is (thus there is one nature), except that the Son is neither Father nor Spirit, and the Spirit is neither Father nor Son (thus there are three *hypostaseis*). In agreement with Basil, he held that the Father, Son, and Spirit are distinguished from each other not by essence (*ousia*) or nature (*physis*), but only in terms of the eternal relation (*schesis*) they bear toward one another. The Father is eternally the Father, and thus the Son must be eternally Son and with the Father as well; no interval separates them. One cannot think of the Father without the Son, nor the Son without the Father.[202] Indeed, Gregory pushes this line of thinking even further to speak of how Father and Son inhere in each other:

> Everything that the Father is is seen in the Son, and everything that the Son is belongs to the Father. The Son in his entirety abides in the Father, and in return possesses the Father in entirety in himself. Thus the hypostasis of the Son is, so to speak, the form and presentation by which the Father is known, and the Father's hypostasis is recognized in the form of the Son.[203]

This marks the beginning of the development of the doctrine later known as *perichōrēsis* (Greek) or *circumincessio* (Latin), the mutual permeation or inherence of the persons without any loss of difference in relation.

Finally, the Cappadocians were instrumental in advancing the understanding of the Holy Spirit. All three affirmed the Spirit's divinity, while not quite certain how to differentiate between the Spirit's relation to the Father and the Son's unbegottenness. Basil argued that the Spirit is not

---

201. LaCugna, *God For Us*, 61, citing Basil's *Contra Eunomium*.

202. *On the Distinction* (= Basil's Ep. 38), 7 (1:90–91 [Courtonne]; 1:220–21 [Deferrari]); cf. Studer, 147.

203. *On the Distinction*, 8 (1:92 [Courtonne]; 1:226–27 [Deferrari]; translation from Kelly, 264).

to be ranked with creatures but is inseparable from the Father and Son and "completes the all-praised and blessed Trinity." The Spirit shares in "the common [divine] nature (*kata tēn physin koinōnias*) and "is described to be *of God* . . . because he proceeds from the mouth of the Father, and is not begotten like the Son."[204] Basil never explicitly calls the Spirit "God" or refers to the Spirit as consubstantial, partly out of deference to the terms used of God in Scripture. However, he indirectly affirms the *homoousios* of the Spirit by affirming that the Spirit partakes of the same ineffable nature as the Father and the Son and thus deserves the same honor and adoration that they receive.[205] In light of this, he began to use the liturgical doxology "Glory to the Father *with* the Son, *together with* the Holy Spirit" alongside the more traditional form which gave glory to the Father *through* the Son *in* the Spirit.[206] For Basil, the ultimate convincing argument was the liturgy, since it reflected the long tradition of belief in the Spirit that "was unassailably inherent in the souls of the faithful." The touchstone is especially the long-revered trinitarian baptismal formula, which imposes certain obligations: "the proof of orthodox opinion is not to separate him from the Father and the Son (for we must be baptized as we have received the words of baptism, and we must believe as we are baptized, and we must give glory as we have believed to the Father, the Son, and the Holy Spirit)."[207]

204. *Peri tou hagiou pneumatos* 18, 45–46 (*Sur le Saint-Esprit*, ed. and trans. Benoît Pruche, 2d ed., rev., SC 17bis [Paris: Les Éditions du Cerf, 2002], 408–90; *On the Holy Spirit*, trans. David Anderson [Crestwood, NY: St. Vladimir's Seminary Press, 1980], 72–73 [translation modified]). This treatise was directed against increased opposition from the Pneutomachians. See also Ep. 125, 3 (2:33–34 [Courtonne]; 2:266–69 [Deferrari]). Basil was originally reluctant to mention the Spirit's divinity in his public homilies, not wishing to create dissension among the members of his congregation.

205. Ibid., 19; 22 (SC 17bis, 416–25, 440–43; *On the Holy Spirit*, 75–79, 83–85). Cf. Kelly, 260–61; Yves Congar, *I Believe in the Holy Spirit*, trans. David Smith, 3 vols. in 1, Milestones in Catholic Theology (New York: Crossroad, 1997), 1:74.

206. *Peri tou hagiou pneumatos* 1, 3 (SC 17bis, 256–59; *On the Holy Spirit*, 17). Basil reports that some in his congregation felt this to be contradictory. Kasper describes Basil's formulation as "a doxology based on the one nature or substance of God [that] takes its place alongside the doxology that reflects the history of salvation" (*GJC*, 261).

207. Ep. 125, 3 (2:33 [Courtonne]; 2:266–69 [Deferrari]).

Gregory of Nazianzus, as we have seen, had no reservations in declaring the Spirit both divine and consubstantial with the Father and the Son in the face of the varied contemporary opinions that denied the Spirit's full divinity, including those who identified "consubstantial" with "begotten" and thus argued that the Spirit could not be another Son. Against the Pneumatomachians, Gregory asserted that the Spirit is truly divine, and differentiated the only-begotten Son's relation to the Father (generation or "filiation") from that of the Spirit, which Gregory called "procession"—without, however, being able to explain it further.[208] Gregory of Nyssa also applied *homoousios* to the Spirit. Taking the other Gregory's insights a step further, he proposed an understanding of the Son as the mediator of the Spirit's procession from the Father, thus assuming a two-fold procession of the Spirit (from the Father through the Son).[209]

The treatises and letters of the Cappadocians represent the concluding moves in series of contentious debates that lasted for more than a half-century after Nicaea. What were the results? The Cappadocians' insights and success at clarifying the language and concepts used in discussing the Trinity were confirmed at the First Council of Constantinople (381) and in the report of the council sent by the synod of Constantinople (382) to Pope Damasus and the other bishops in Rome.[210] In the wake of the recent controversies with Arians, Sabellians, Pneumatomachians, and others, those at the council took up a

208. Oration 39, 12, in *Discours 38–41*, ed. Claudio Moreschini, trans. Paul Gallay, SC 358 (Paris: Les Éditions du Cerf, 1990), 174–75: "The Holy Spirit is truly the Spirit coming forth (*proïon*) from the Father, not by filiation (for it is not by generation) but by procession (*ekporeutōs*), if I may coin a phrase for the sake of clarity" (my translation).

209. See, e.g., the passage mentioned earlier (n. 196) from *That There Are Not Three Gods* (PG45:133B; *Opera*, 3/1: 55–56; Rusch, 160]): the Spirit's relation to the Father is "through that which depends on the first [i.e., through the Son]." Studer (146 n.50, 152 n.101) also cites *Contra Eunomium* 1, 280, 378 (PG 45:336D, 369A) and *Adversus Macedonianos* 6 (PG 45:1308B; *Opera* 3/1: 92–93). Cf. also Kelly, 262–63.

210. The council's acts have not survived; the only contemporary record is found in the synod's letter summarizing the council's decisions. The council's creed appears in the acts of the Council of Chalcedon (451), where it is quoted alongside the Nicene Creed. Chalcedon declared both creeds to be authoritative

version of the earlier Nicene creed, made its teaching on the Son's divinity more precise in light of recent theological developments (e.g., omitting the phrase "from the substance [*ousia*] of the Father," adding references to the history of salvation), and greatly expanded the teaching on the Holy Spirit.

> We believe in one God the Father all-powerful, maker of heaven and of earth, and of all things both seen and unseen. And in one Lord Jesus Christ, the only-begotten Son of God, begotten from the Father before all ages, light from light, true God from true God, begotten not made, consubstantial (*homoousios*) with the Father, through whom all things came to be; for us humans and for our salvation he came down from the heavens and became incarnate from the holy Spirit and the virgin Mary, became human and was crucified on our behalf under Pontius Pilate; he suffered and was buried and rose up on the third day in accordance with the scriptures; and he went up into the heavens and is seated at the Father's right hand; he is coming again with glory to judge the living and the dead; his kingdom will have no end. And in the Spirit, the holy, the lordly and life-giving one, proceeding forth from the Father, co-worshipped and co-glorified with Father and Son, the one who spoke through the prophets; in one, holy, catholic and apostolic church. We confess one baptism for the forgiving of sins. We look forward to a resurrection of the dead and life in the age to come. Amen.[211]

The synodal report of 382 makes it clear that the creed's confession of faith in the Trinity is to be understood along the general conceptual lines introduced by the Cappadocians, namely, "that the Father, the Son and the holy Spirit have a single Godhead (*theotētos*) and power (*dynameōs*) and substance (*ousias*), a dignity deserving the same honour and a co-eternal sovereignty, in three most perfect hypostases, or three perfect persons (*prosōpois*)."[212]

---

doctrinal teaching. See *DEC* 1:21–23 (introduction); 24 (Constantinople I's creed); 25–30 (synodal letter); 84–85 (affirmation by Chalcedon).

211. Ibid., 1:24 (= ND 12, DH 150).

212. Ibid., 1:28. The creed, however, avoids mention of *homoousios* in connection with the Spirit.

244 A Theology of the Presence and Absence of God

The creed and the synodal letter together signal the resolution of the major Trinitarian controversies and comprise the Church's definitive statement of what we earlier referred to as the fundamental "architecture" of the Trinity. They also reflect the terminological consensus that had been reached within Eastern (Greek) Christianity by the end of the fourth century AD/CE. The Western (Latin, Roman) Church, diverging from this consensus to some degree, tended to translate *hypostasis* with the Latin *substantia*. Western Christians thus had trouble with the Eastern confession of three *hypostases;* it seemed like a belief in three divine substances, i.e., three Gods. Official Roman statements, such as the "Tome" of Pope Damasus (382) which confirmed Constantinople's decree, spoke instead of one *substantia* and three *personae*, following on Tertullian's insights.[213] Eastern Christians, for their part, had trouble with the Western use of *persona*, since the Greek equivalent *prosōpon* did not connote substantial individuality but rather a mask or mere appearance. The West's use of *personae* sounded like modalism to Eastern ears.

Contemporary commentators have often posited a more profound theological difference behind these terminological distinctions, arguing that the East's trinitarian reflections tended to begin with the distinction of the divine persons and their actions in the economy of salvation, and that the West took a more abstract approach, starting from the unity of the divine nature.[214] For example, Walter Kasper claims that "while the creeds of Nicaea and Constantinople start with the Father and then confess the Son and the Spirit to be one in being or substance with the Father, the West replaces this dynamic conception with a more static approach that starts with the one substance

---

213. DH 168 (*de divina substantia*), 173 (*tres personas . . . veras*), 177 (*veram solam unam divinitatem et potentiam, maiestatem et substantiam*) (= ND 306/16, 21, 24).

214. The roots of this typology go back to Théodore de Régnon, *Études de théologie positive sur la Sainte Trinité*, 3 vols. (Paris: Retaux, 1892–98). Regarding the inadequacies of de Régnon's schema, despite its pervasive influence, see LaCugna, *God For Us*, 11–12; Michel René Barnes, "Augustine in Contemporary Trinitarian Theology," *Theological Studies* 56 (1995): 237–51; idem, "Rereading Augustine's Theology of the Trinity," in *The Trinity: An Interdisciplinary Symposium* [see n.21], 145–76.

and then says that it subsists in three persons."[215] In light of recent research it is clear that a strict application of any "East=dynamic-vs.-West=static" schema is an oversimplification; an "Eastern" approach would be just as concerned with the unity of God as a "Western" one. But that schema, more broadly conceived, at least points up the differing conceptual starting points behind the obvious terminological distinctions, without turning them into mutually exclusive positions. Eastern trinitarian reflection did seem to be more comfortable with understanding the relations among the divine hypostases in terms of the monarchial metaphor, where God the Father is "the unoriginate origin, source and principle" of the eternal being of God and where "every act of God in creation originates with the Father, proceeds through the Son, and is perfected by the Holy Spirit."[216] On the other hand, the West, in order to rule out all traces of Arianism and subordinationism, seemed more comfortable starting its reflections with the notion of the one divine *substantia* before moving on to treat the distinction of persons.

These differences did not divide the Church, however, but rather revealed "the possible plurality and wealth of theologies that are based on a single common faith."[217] These legitimate approaches were brought together at the Second Council of Constantinople (553). Its Trinitarian formula is a synthesis of speculative, technical language and more biblical language that reflects the history of salvation:

> If anyone will not confess that the Father, Son and holy Spirit have one nature (*mian physin, unam naturam*) or substance (*ousian, substantiam*), that they have one power and authority, that there is a consubstantial Trinity (*triada homoousion, trinitatem consubstantialem*), one Deity to be adored in three subsistences (*hypostasesin, subsistentiis*) or persons (*prosōpois, personis*): let him be anathema. There is only one God and Father, from whom all things come, and one Lord, Jesus Christ, through whom all things are, and one holy spirit, in whom all things are.[218]

215. Kasper, *GJC*, 259–60.
216. LaCugna, "Trinitarian Mystery," 168–69.
217. Kasper, *GJC*, 260.
218. *DEC* 1:114 (First Anathema against the "Three Chapters" [in both Lat. and Grk.] = DH 421 [Grk. version only]).

This statement brings the major segment of the historical development of the doctrine of the Trinity to a close. Constantinople II confirms as the Church's pivotal belief what we have been calling the fundamental architecture of the doctrine of the Trinity—the expression of the divine trinitarian reality in the language of "nature," "substance," and "person." All subsequent theological reflection on the Trinity in the history of Christian theology is commentary on this doctrinal claim—not "mere" commentary or trivial additions to a basic core, but rather developments that are as legitimate and necessary as what occurred at Nicaea. This is precisely because Christianity has a mandate to proclaim the good news of salvation in every situation, in every epoch. There is the continual need to discern and draw out the doctrine's implications and possibilities and then apply them in contexts far beyond the imaginations of any thinkers in the early Church.

4. The Doctrine of the Trinity in a Contemporary Context

From the moment of baptism ("in the name of the Father, the Son, and the Holy Spirit"), the Trinity is at the core of Christian life. By expressing "the eschatologically definitive and universal truth about God from which all other talk about God can derive its full truthfulness"—namely, that "God has given of himself through Jesus Christ through the working of the Holy Spirit"—the trinitarian confession "holds the entire edifice together like the keystone of a Gothic arch."[219]

The crucial issue we face in rendering the trinitarian doctrine accessible today is explaining what Kasper calls the doctrine's "practical relevance to Christian life."[220] "Relevance" here does not mean cutting down the mystery of the Trinity to fit ever-shifting cultural standards. Rather, we need to underscore the central truth that the Trinity has been revealed "for us and for our salvation"—for us as we are in the twenty-first century. The connection with the ordinary lives of Christians must be disclosed if the doctrine is to be teachable, preachable, and existentially meaningful for those for whose salvation it has been

219. Kasper, *GJC*, 233.
220. Ibid.

revealed.[221] Once we say this, though, we begin to recognize the temporal and conceptual distance that exists between the confession of the Trinity as developed in ancient Christianity and our attempts to understand it and live it in the aestheticized postmodern (or even post-postmodern) consumer world of the West. After all, the doctrine's "architecture" and the comprehensive view of reality that it engenders have long been expressed in the metaphysical language of "nature" and "substance" and with a quite different view of "person"—ways of thought foreign to a postmodern Western culture seemingly allergic to metaphysics. How do we bridge this hermeneutical gap and disclose how central the belief in the Trinity is for our times, for a context that in countless ways outruns the imagination of the ancient Church?

The keys to bridging the gap are an adequate theological method and an insightful metaphor. First, the method itself must be hermeneutical, based on the recognition that temporal distance and tradition are not disabling factors but rather *enabling* ones. They allow both the historical rootedness and the necessary newness of our contemporary Christian beliefs and practices to appear in bold relief. Temporal distance and tradition do not prevent understanding; rather, they make a fuller understanding of the trinitarian confession possible through the application of its truth to our present context and its possibilities. That context always exhibits the dual truth of difference *and* continuity: it necessarily differs and stands *apart from* the originating context of the tradition, and yet because of the historically-rooted beliefs, practices, and questions that have formed it, it is nonetheless always *a part of* the tradition. This is the blunt reality of Christian thought and practice.

Graham Ward's comments regarding Christology as a "cultural operation" are pertinent here. Starting with Thomas Aquinas' view that "God is not known to us in his own nature, but through his works

---

221. Because of this particular kind of "practical relevance," Kasper argues strongly that a theology of the Trinity necessarily recover the "soteriological motives" that led to the development of the doctrine to begin with and "to develop a comprehensive and specifically Christian vision of reality on the basis of the trinitarian confession" (ibid., 263).

(*ex operationibus*) or effects (*effectibus*),"[222] Ward says that the fundamental Christological question is thus not "who" or "what" is Christ, but "where is the Christ?" "The Christological enquiry therefore does not begin with the identity of the Christ, what in dogmatics is the nature as distinct from the work of Christ; it begins with an analysis of the operations whereby Christ is made known to us. And in being made known we participate in him."[223] This echoes the burning contemporary question "Where is God?" that we raised at the beginning. "Participation in Christ" is another (very Johannine) way of saying "salvation," and *our* participation, most obviously, begins and develops in the epoch and culture in which we dwell. The Christ-event, while eschatologically oriented, is always culturally situated and inflected as well: "Not that the past is irrelevant, for the horizons of today's questions are always configured by what has been handed down to us—including the historical Jesus himself recorded in the Scriptures. But because Jesus Christ is a confession of faith, and faith is a present operation with respect to salvation, then God is made known to us today in ways that differ from [the past]."[224]

The same holds true of the trinitarian confession. The continuous, centuries-long reception of the doctrine—through the practices of liturgy, devotion, and the theological reflections of such thinkers as Augustine and Thomas Aquinas—creates a stream of interpretive and interpreting effects that flow into our own epoch, shape our current framework of beliefs, and connect the ancient confessional statements with our own confession. The trinitarian confession is present to us and for us precisely because of the culturally-inflected Christian traditions which stream toward us and touch us with their force. It is clear, then, that "bridging the gap" means that one takes seriously the whole of the economy of salvation as a "revelatory event" and asks the basic question: how is the Trinity revealed to us, in our own situation? Any answer must take into account the context-inflected ways in which belief in the Trinity has been interpre-

---

222. *ST* Ia, q. 13, a.8, reply (3:78–79; translation modified).
223. Graham Ward, *Christ and Culture*, Challenges in Contemporary Theology (Malden, MA: Blackwell, 2005), 1.
224. Ibid., 6.

tively handed down to us throughout the Christian tradition and articulated "for us and for our salvation." A productive method, then, must look both ways: a "backward glance" at the tradition, and a "forward glance" at our context and our future.

The second key to "bridging the gap" is the employment of an insightful metaphor that fuses this historical rootedness with our own context and speaks to our contemporary life of faith. And a successful metaphor opens the way to realizing new possibilities of belief and understanding. The aspect of the ancient confessions of the Trinity that most prominently threads its way into our own faith is the Cappadocian insight into relationality and the use of the metaphor of "person" to explicate the insight and its way of conceiving distinctions in the Trinity. Relationality, the heart of the trinitarian confession of divine unity-and-plurality, is what the theological traditions have labored to articulate—with greater or lesser success—in the centuries after the ancient doctrinal settlements, and our reception of these reflections form the foundation of our own endeavors of *fides quaerens intellectum.*

The Catholic understanding of the trinitarian confession has been shaped—and to some extent determined—by Augustine and Thomas Aquinas and the ways each chose to format the issue. Augustine (354–430) reflected on the Trinity throughout his career as a Christian theologian, and most especially in the major work *De trinitate*, which "stands alone as a meditation on the trinitarian mystery as a mystery at once of theology and anthropology."[225] His early studies of Neo-Platonism strongly influenced him and led him to see not only the structure of the world as manifesting the being of God (in accordance with Paul in Romans 1:20: "his eternal power and divine nature, invisible though they are, have been understood and seen through the things he has made"),[226] but most especially the soul as a reflection of its Creator and thus containing a vestige or image of the Trinity. The way inward through introspection and contemplation thus becomes an ascent toward God. *De trinitate* clearly reveals Augustine's

225. *Augustine Through the Ages: An Encyclopedia*, ed. Allan D. Fitzgerald, et al. (Grand Rapids, MI: Eerdmans, 1999), s.v. "*De Trinitate*" (by Rowan Williams), 850.

226. Augustine, *De trinitate* 5.1.1; ET: *The Trinity*, trans. Edmund Hill, ed. John E. Rotelle, The Works of Saint Augustine, pt. I, vol. 5 (Brooklyn, NY: New City Press, 1991), 395. Hereafter cited as *De trin.* in the text.

overriding concern for the oneness of God, in order to rule out any trace of Arian subordinationism: "Let us believe that the Father and Son and Holy Spirit are one God, maker and ruler of all creation; and that the Father is not the Son, and the Holy Spirit is neither the Father nor the Son, but that they are a trinity of persons related to each other, and a unity of equal being" (*De trin.* 9.1.1. [271]).

Starting from this emphasis on unity, his argument is driven by the desire to think how oneness and threeness belong together in God, who is made manifest to us in the love of Christ.[227] In books 5–7 of *De trinitate* he confronts the Arians on the issue of the one divine substance and makes the important point that distinctions in the Trinity do not belong to the substance of divinity but rather to the mutual relations of the inner-trinitarian life.[228] "Father" and "Son" describe the relation between the first and second persons, while the Holy Spirit is "supreme charity conjoining Father and Son to each other and subjoining us to them . . ." (*De trin.* 7.3.6 [224]). However, the central question remains, for if "the Father is God and the Son is God and the Holy Spirit is God," how are believers to understand "that this threesome is not three gods but one God" (*De trin.* 1.5.8 [70])? Augustine developed various approaches in response to this question,[229] but the most famous and the one with the most impact on the subsequent tradition was the psychological analogy that compared the operations of a person's inner life with the relations within the Trinity. As the human mind is one substance that exists with the distinct powers or operations of memory, understanding, and will, without that substance being divided (the knower remains the same person while

227. Cf. Wilhelm Breuning, "Gotteslehre," in *Glaubenszugänge: Lehrbuch der katholischen Dogmatik*, ed. Wolfgang Beinert, 3 vols. (Paderborn: Ferdinand Schöningh, 1995), 1:289–93, at 290.

228. See *De trin.* 5.8.9 (195): "Whatever that supreme and divine majesty is called with reference to itself is said substance-wise (*substantialiter*); whatever it is called with reference to another is said not substance- but relationship-wise (*non substantialiter, sed relative*)."

229. Cf. Olivier du Roy, *L'Intelligence de la foi en la Trinité selon saint Augustin* (Paris: Études Augustiniennes, 1966).

exercising these powers),[230] so the one God exists as Trinity, without division or confusion, in the Father's generation of the Word and the procession of the Holy Spirit. All the divine actions are attributable to the entire Trinity: "the trinity works inseparably in everything that God works" (*De trin.* 1.5.8 [70]).[231] Any attempt to give a more precise description, however, is defeated by the transcendent mystery of the Godhead. Whatever term is used to answer Augustine's famous question "Three what?"—whether "substance" (*hypostasis*, the preference of "the Greeks") or "person" (Augustine's reluctant choice)—will be merely an inadequate semantic placeholder.[232] This is because "the total transcendence of the godhead (*divinitatis*) quite surpasses the capacity of ordinary speech. God can be thought about more truly than he can be talked about, and he is more truly than he can be thought about" (*De trin.* 7.4.7 [224–25]). In the final book (book 15), Augustine admits his frustration at not being able to find adequate ways of expressing the distinctions in the Trinity. Yet this does not block our experience of God. There is still the possibility of mystical ascent through prayer to a contemplative union with the Trinity when one experiences love as a pure gift from God and becomes aware of the presence of God who is love, as 1 John 4:16 proclaims (*De trin.* 8.7.10–8.12 [251–54]). "Augustine means to say in effect that the Christian experiences love as the pure gift of God—as grace, thus as a sharing in that love which is proper to God. But to this he now adds his own expanded understanding (not explicit in any Father before Augustine) that such love in God is the Holy Spirit."[233] Subsequent Latin tradition, though, emphasized Augustine's psychological analogy rather than this anagogical method. The medieval

230. See *De trin.* 10.11.18 (298): "These three then, memory, understanding, and will, are not three lives but one life, nor three minds but one mind. So it follows of course that they are not three substances but one substance."

231. See also ibid., 5.14.15 (199): "With reference to creation Father, and Son, and Holy Spirit are one origin, just as they are one creator and one lord."

232. Ibid., 5.9.10 (196): "Yet when you ask 'Three what?' human speech labors under a great dearth of words. So we say three persons, not in order to say that precisely, but in order not to be reduced to silence."

233. Hill, *Three-Personed God*, 58.

scholastic tradition also adopted Augustine's focus on the unity of the Godhead and his principle that the divine persons, sharing the same essence, act as one in the economy of salvation (thus the axiom *opera trinitatis ad extra indivisa sunt*). As Catherine LaCugna notes, Augustine's principle "tends to blur any real distinctions among the divine persons and thereby formalizes in Latin theology the breach between *oikonomia* and *theologia*. . . . Once it is assumed that the Trinity is present in every instance where Scripture refers to God, and once the axiom *opera ad extra* is in place, no longer, it seems, is there any need to single out any one person in relation to a particular activity."[234] This determined the subsequent shape of Western trinitarian theology.

Thomas Aquinas (c. 1225–1274), inheriting this tradition, took up Augustine's psychological analogy and ontologized it.[235] That is, he moved "beyond the psychological processes of the soul to its very beingness. The resultant relationality is an ontological one, grounded in being itself as a dynamism and not merely a self-referencing achieved by way of the soul's activity."[236] For Thomas, the persons of the Trinity are defined more specifically as "subsistent relations" (*ST* Ia, q. 40, a. 2 [7:144–49]) that in turn are grounded in the inner-divine processions.

Thomas' starting point is the revelation of the Trinity in Scripture, a revelation grasped by faith. Scripture speaks of the distinction of persons within the one God—a distinction characterized by relations—and it is this truth of faith that Thomas attempts to render intelligible. In the *Summa theologiae* he begins by examining the "immanent processions" or "notional acts," the inner-divine actions that bring about these real relations. In God there are two types of immanent action, intelligence and will. The first, the procession based

---

234. LaCugna, *God For Us*, 99.

235. For summaries of Thomas' trinitarian theology, see Hill, *Three-Personed God*, 62–78; Gilles Emery, "The Doctrine of the Trinity in St. Thomas Aquinas," in *Aquinas on Doctrine: A Critical Introduction*, ed. Thomas G. Weinandy, Daniel A. Keating, and John P. Yocum (London: T&T Clark, 2004), 45–65. This section is based largely on Emery's essay. References to the *Summa theologiae* are given in the text, following the system in n. 4.

236. Hill, *Three-Personed God*, 70.

on intellect (*per modum intellectus*) is the speaking of the Word, the generation of the Son (which also establishes the fatherhood of the Father); the other, the procession based on love (*per modum amoris*), is the procession of the Spirit. These processions cause real relations, not imposed from without ("accidental") but rather generated from within ("substantial"). They are real distinctions in God, standing "in relative opposition to each other. Therefore since in God there is a real relation . . . relative opposition must also be there [and] such opposition implies distinction" (*ST* Ia, q. 28, a. 3, resp. [6:34–35]). The real relations allow us to distinguish the persons in the Trinity while asserting the unity of the divine essence. "While relation in created things exists as an accident in a subject, in God a really existing relation has the existence of the divine nature and is completely identical with it. . . . Therefore it is clear that in God relation and nature are existentially not two things but one and the same" (*ST* Ia., q. 28, a. 2, resp. [6:30–31]). There are four real relations: active generation or paternity (the relation of the Father to the Son), passive generation or sonship (the Son's relation to the Father), "active spiration" (the relation of the Father and Son to the Spirit), and "passive spiration" or "procession" (the relation of the Spirit to the Father and the Son) (*ST* Ia. q. 28, a. 4 [6:34–39]). Gilles Emery offers this clarification:

> Of these relations, three constitute the persons themselves: fatherhood, sonship and procession. For this reason the three relations of origin are known as "personal properties," since they constitute the persons in the unity of the divine essence which is communicated. The relation of "active spiration" . . . is not a personal property, since it is common to the Father and the Son: the Father and the Son are not constituted by the spiration of the Spirit, but by their fatherhood and sonship.[237]

The relations are the focal point of Thomas' argument against both Arianism (diminishing the divinity of any of the persons) or Sabellianism (modalist diminishing of the distinction of persons). "Everything converges in relation, because the divine relation contains both the element of personal distinction (*ratio*), and the element of the

---

237. Emery, "The Doctrine of the Trinity," 53.

hypostatic divine subsistence (*esse*). These two aspects together con-stitute the theological notion of a divine person."[238] Borrowing Boe-thius' definition of "person" ("an individual substance of a rational nature," (*ST* Ia, q. 29, a. 1 [6:40–47]) with its implications of distinction, existence, and free action (intellect and will), Thomas finds it to be a fitting term for the subsistent relations in God, since "person" refers to that which "is most perfect in the whole of nature, namely what subsists in rational nature" (*ST* Ia, q. 29, a. 3, resp. [6:52–53]). Thus, he defines the divine persons more specifically as "subsistent relations" and thus avoids both Arian subordinationism and Sabellian modalism. "The divine persons are their own subsisting relations. . . . The divine persons are not distinct in the being wherein they subsist nor in any-thing else absolute, but exclusively in their being related to one another. Relation, then, is enough to set them apart from each other" (*ST* Ia, q. 40, a. 2, ad 1–2 [7:146–49]). With this definition of "person" Thomas can safeguard a strict trinitarian monotheism.

Between these great medieval syntheses and our own time, the field has shifted and the presuppositions behind the notion of "per-son" have changed. In modernity and especially the Enlightenment, "person" came to be defined psychologically (characterized by self-consciousness) and in terms of autonomy, thereby rendering the earlier use of "person" as defined ontologically (e.g., the Boethian "individual substance") unintelligible in this new context. In reaction to this legacy, Karl Barth (1886–1968) and Karl Rahner (1904–84) both argued that the use of "person" with regard to the Trinity is prob-lematic and suggested alternative formulations. Barth claimed that it was preferable "to say not 'Person' but 'mode of being,' with the intention of expressing by this concept the same thing as should be expressed by 'Person,' not absolutely but relatively better, more sim-ply and more clearly" because it was judged closer to the ancient church's use of the term *hypostasis*.[239] Thus God is one in three distinct and absolutely essential modes of being. Rahner, beginning with God's free self-communication in history and his analysis of human

238. Ibid., 54.
239. Karl Barth, *Church Dogmatics*, vol. 1, pt. 1: *The Doctrine of the Word of God*, trans. G. T. Thomson (1936; reprint, Edinburgh: T&T Clark, 1963), 412–13.

subjectivity in its openness to the transcending horizon of absolute mystery, preferred to say that "the one God subsists in three distinct manners of subsisting."[240] As Walter Kasper notes, while their approaches differ, neither Barth nor Rahner starts with the traditional formula "one substance, three persons"; rather, "they think of God not as substance but as subject, whether as subject of a self-revelation (K. Barth) or as subject of a self-communication (K. Rahner)."[241]

Their alternative formulations flow from their presuppositions. For Barth the starting point of our reflection on the Trinity is the reality of God's revelation that occurs as an act of divine sovereignty and that "is a ground which has no sort of higher or deeper ground above or behind it, but is simply a ground in itself. . . ."[242] Revelation is summed up in the statement "God reveals Himself as the Lord." This is "the root of the doctrine of the Trinity," which states that "God who has revealed Himself according to the witness of Scripture, is the same in unimpaired unity, yet also the same in unimpaired variety thrice in a different way." The doctrine is not revelation itself but rather the Church's work of understanding it,[243] since revelation means "the self-unveiling, imparted to men, of the God who according to His nature cannot be unveiled to man."[244] Rejecting the quest for vestiges of the Trinity in the world, Barth insists that only Scripture discloses God's freedom to distinguish himself from himself, and that God does so as Revealer, Revelation, and Revealedness, a formula that corresponds both to the unfolding of biblical revelation as well as the Church's doctrine of the Trinity. Thus God is understood as the sovereign subject of his own revelation as well as the self-unveiling that makes the human acceptance of revelation possible.[245] While the Church traditionally used "person" to explicate this, "the Church doctrine of the Trinity has nothing directly to do with

240. Rahner, *The Trinity*, 109. He judges this to be "better, simpler, and more in harmony with the traditional language of theology and the Church" than Barth's phrase (ibid., 110).

241. Kasper, *GJC*, 300.

242. *Church Dogmatics* 1/1, 350.

243. Ibid., 351–52.

244. Ibid., 373.

245. Ibid., 361.

'personality,' " which would lead to tritheism. Rather, in the doctrine, "we are speaking not of three divine 'I's,' but thrice of the one divine I. The concept of the equality of essence (*homoousia, consubstantialitas*) in Father, Son, and Spirit is thus at every point preeminently to be regarded in the sense of identity of essence. From the identity follows the equality of essence in the 'Persons.' "[246]

Rahner, for his part, understands the Trinity in terms of the mystery of salvation as revealed in history. Faith in this holy mystery is the source of his famous axiom: "The basic thesis which . . . presents the Trinity *as* a mystery of salvation (in its reality and not merely as a doctrine) might be formulated as follows: *The 'economic' Trinity is the 'immanent' Trinity and the 'immanent' Trinity is the 'economic' Trinity.*"[247] Any theological reflection on the Trinity, then, must start with salvation as historically revealed: the free self-communication of God in the world in Christ and in the Spirit, understood upon reflection "as moments, innerly related to each other, yet distinct from one another, of the *one* self-communication of God. . . ."[248] This can only be the authentic self-communication of God if the economic Trinity is indeed the immanent Trinity. Any reflection on this must avoid the idea that in God there are three distinct subjectivities and centers of activity—this is the *cul-de-sac* to which the modern concept of "person" leads. By always using the history of salvation as the benchmark, Rahner believes that a more adequate formulation can be found. That formulation is "distinct manners of subsisting."

> The one self-communication of the one God occurs in three different manners of given-ness, in which the one God is given concretely for us in himself, and not vicariously by other realities through their transcendental relation to God. God is the concrete God in each one of these manners of given-ness—which, of course, refer to each other relatively, without modalistically coinciding. If we translate this in terms of "immanent" Trinity, we may say: the one God subsists in three distinct manners of subsisting.[249]

246. Ibid., 403.
247. Rahner, *The Trinity*, 21–22 (his emphasis).
248. Ibid., 84–85.
249. Ibid., 109–10.

There are in the Trinity three really distinct subsistences, each identical with the simple essence of God. Historical revelation testifies to the oneness of God and also to the distinction between the Father and the Son, which reflects an eternal differentiation in the immanent Trinity, and between these two and the Holy Spirit, the expression the mutual love of Father and Son. The true meaning of this doctrine is ultimately not to be found in an abstract formulation about the immanent Trinity, but in how adequately it describes God's salvific activity.

> God himself as the abiding and holy mystery, as the incomprehensible ground of man's transcendent existence is not only the God of infinite distance, but also wants to be the God of absolute closeness in a true self-communication, and he is present in this way in the spiritual depths of our existence as well as in the concreteness of our corporeal history.[250]

These influential contemporary attempts to rethink the doctrine of the Trinity respond to the real problem of detraditionalization that affects the classical formulation of the doctrine: what happens to the meanings of "nature," "substance," and "person" when the original experiential context fades and presuppositions change?[251] With regard to Barth and Rahner, Walter Kasper makes the judicious comment that, even though they are valiant attempts to address current understandings of faith, both leave us with problems:

> It is not enough that the trinitarian confession should be marked by logical clarity; this confession is also to be fit for doxological use. But no one can invoke, adore and glorify a distinct manner of subsisting. . . . If, then, we are not to conjure up new misunderstandings and if we are not to turn the trinitarian confession completely into a book with seven seals for the "ordinary"

250. Karl Rahner, *Foundations of Christian Faith: An Introduction to the Idea of Christianity*, trans. William V. Dych (1978; reprint, New York: Crossroad, 1989), 137.

251. On the problem of detraditionalization, see Lieven Boeve, *Interrupting Tradition: An Essay on Christian Faith in a Postmodern Context*, Louvain Theological and Pastoral Monographs 30 (Leuven/Dudley, MA: Peeters, 2003).

> Christian, we have no choice but to retain the traditional language of the church and interpret it to the faithful.[252]

Rather than rejecting the recent concept of "person" as unusable in the doctrine of the Trinity, Kasper suggests that it can be retrieved and joined to the key Cappadocian insight of relationality that led to the official teaching of "one substance, three persons." Here we join in that constructive retrieval.

While "person" will always be an inadequate term for the divine plurality, it is the most fitting word we have, since God relates to us in love and we relate to God in gratitude for creation and salvation. The genius of the post-Nicene theological tradition, signaled by the language of procession and *perichōrēsis*, was to recognize that belief in the Trinity always has at its core a recognition of relationality, even during those periods when there was an emphasis on substance as the starting point of trinitarian reflection.

> [T]he two processions in God ground three really distinct relative oppositions. The latter are prototypes and primal ground of the dialogical and relational interaction and co-presence of Father, Son and Spirit in the history of salvation. . . . In God substance and relation are really identical; God is relation and exists only in the intra-divine relations; he is wholly love that surrenders and bestows itself. This relational reality of God, which is identical with his being or substance, presupposes real, mutually distinct relational realities. . . . Thus the distinctions based on the relations once again bring out the ecstatic character of God's love.[253]

The term "person" is best situated to bring out this ecstatic, dynamic character because it is a fundamentally relational category. This is a point that the Orthodox theologian John Zizioulas has emphasized by combining the Cappadocian insight with a contemporary understanding of personal existence in order to understand "person" once again in an ontological framework. To say "I am," to assert one's particular being in the face of possible non-being (and thus also acknowledge the threat of death) "is the recognition of the

252. Kasper, *GJC*, 288.
253. Ibid., 280.

limitations or limits of being. It is a *kataphasis* implying an *apophasis*, the possibility or rather the actuality of a *beyond*, a movement of *transcendence*."[254] To be a person, then, is to be ecstatic intentionality with a claim to uniqueness that in turn implies relationship. "Both in the case of God and of man the identity of a person is recognized and posited clearly and unequivocally, but this is so only in and through a *relationship*, and not though an objective ontology. . . . Personal identity is totally lost if isolated, for its ontological condition is relationship."[255] He employs this analysis in order to retrieve the Cappadocian fine-tuning of the principle of *monarchia* without subordinationist or modalist overtones:

> The fact that God exists because of the Father shows that His existence, His being is the consequence of a free person; which means, in the last analysis, that not only communion but also *freedom*, the free person, constitutes true being. True being comes only from the free person, from the person who loves freely—that is, who freely affirms his being, his identity, by means of an event of communion with other persons.[256]

Kasper, starting from the modern philosophy of freedom, takes a similar tack. Freedom is more originary than self-contained being or substance: "freedom that goes out of itself and fulfills itself in action, is now the starting point and horizon of thought."[257] Viewed in terms of freedom, the human person is revealed as a unique intentional being marked by two characteristics. First, the person "finds its fulfillment only in the communion of love" and thus exists "only in mutual giving and receiving."[258] Second, the person is marked by a

254. John D. Zizioulas, "On Being a Person: Towards an Ontology of Personhood," *Communion and Otherness: Further Studies in Personhood and the Church*, ed. Paul McPartlan (New York: T&T Clark, 2006), 99–112, at 100.

255. Ibid., 112.

256. John D. Zizioulas, *Being as Communion: Studies in Personhood and the Church* (Crestwood, NY: St. Vladimir's Seminary Press, 1985), 18. Cf. also p. 42: "God 'exists' on account of a person, the Father, and not on account of a substance."

257. Kasper, *GJC*, 153.

258. Ibid., 306.

tension between an "irreplaceable individuality" and "an unlimited openness to the whole of reality," a restlessness that cannot be stilled by anything finite but demands definitive fulfillment. This *personal* desire can only be fulfilled in a *personal* way, that is, "only if it encounters a person who is infinite not only in its intentional claims on reality but in its real being; that is, only if it encounters an absolute person" characterized by perfect freedom. Since "person" implies relationality, perfect relationality means the complete emptying of oneself in love. "Seen in the horizon of person, the meaning of being is love. . . . To call God a person is to say that God is the subsistent being which is freedom in love. Thus the definition of God's essence brings us back to the biblical statement: 'God is love' (I John 4.8, 16)."[259]

A trinitarian theology can be built upon this insight into the category of "person" as most fundamentally free, intentional, and relational. One can express the divine unity not as some rigid and monolithic unity, but as selfless giving and bestowing that characterizes biblical monotheism:

> If God is to remain God and not become dependent on the world or man, then he must be co-existent within himself. Within the unity and simplicity of his being he must be a communion in love, and this love cannot be a love marked by need but only a love that gives out of the overflowing fullness of his being. . . . Because God in his perfection and simplicity is everything and does not possess anything, he can give only himself. . . . God's oneness must be thought of as love that exists only in the giving of itself.[260]

One can express the distinction of persons with similar "ec-static" language:

> The Father as pure self-giving cannot exist without the Son who receives. But since the Son does not receive something but everything, he exists only in and through the giving and receiving. . . . On the other hand, he would not have truly received the self-

259. Ibid., 155.
260. Ibid., 306.

giving of the Father were he to keep it for himself and not give it
back. . . . But this reciprocal love also presses beyond itself; it is
pure giving only if it empties itself of, and gives away, even this
two-in-oneness and, in pure gratuitousness, incorporates a third
in whom love exists as pure receiving, a third who therefore exists
only insofar as he receives his being from the mutual love between
Father and Son. The three persons of the Trinity are thus pure
relationality; they are relations in which the one nature of God
exists in three distinct and non-interchangeable ways. They are
subsistent relations.[261]

One advantage of this language is that it follows the biblical prec-
edent: human relationships with God are spoken of in terms of the
metaphor of personal relationship, and the New Testament claim that
"God is love" (1 John 4:8, 16) can take its rightful place at the core of
Christian life. Another is that the connection between the Trinity and
creation is made clear: if creation is grounded in God, and God's
being is to be a loving communion-in-unity, then "the trinitarian
communion-unity shows itself to be the model for a Christian understanding of reality . . . in which person and relation have priority"
and in which "the meaning of being is the selflessness of love."[262] A
final advantage is that we can claim the doctrine of the Trinity to be
"the summation of the entire Christian mystery of salvation and, at
the same time, its grammar,"[263] that is, the structuring principle that
acts as the backbone of every Christian claim to truth and the *telos* of
all of those claims together.

5. Ongoing Points of Discussion

The current "state of the question" in trinitarian theology includes
a number of significant issues.[264] Here at the end of this chapter we

261. Ibid., 309.
262. Ibid., 310.
263. Ibid., 310–11.
264. For an overview of the current discussion, see Gerald O'Collins, "The
Holy Trinity: The State of the Questions," in *The Trinity: An Interdisciplinary Symposium* [n. 21], 1–25. He sorts the issues into general categories: the recovery of
the centrality of trinitarian belief; trinitarian issues in Scripture and early Chris-

focus on three: the issue of "social trinitarianism"; trinitarian theology in ecumenical discussion; and the links between belief in the Trinity, liturgy, and the lived experience of Christian life.

5.1. Relationality and Social Trinitarianism

"Social trinitarianism" is the theory that the perichoretic relationship of the Trinity should provide the model for relationships in human society. According to this argument, the Trinity can be shown in this way to have direct implications for everyday life. The impetus for this strongly influential view comes from the contemporary retrieval of the Cappadocians' "relationality" as a prime element in trinitarian thinking, coupled with a theological anthropology that emphasizes the human person as *imago Dei*. A "social doctrine of the Trinity" is most closely associated with the Protestant theologian Jürgen Moltmann and his work *The Trinity and the Kingdom of God*. He argues that if one follows Rahner's axiom that "the economic Trinity is the immanent Trinity, and vice versa," and if "God is a community of Father, Son and Spirit, whose unity is constituted by mutual indwelling and reciprocal interpenetration," then "we find the earthly reflection of this divine sociality, not in the autocracy of a single ruler but in the democratic community of free people, not in the lordship of the man over the woman but in their equal mutuality, not in an ecclesiastical hierarchy but in a fellowship church."[265] He proposes the social doctrine as the authentic Christian antidote to a "monotheism" viewed as having long been used to justify domination and repression through monarchical, hierarchical, and patriarchal systems in government, church, and human

---

tian history; the Trinity, Christian life, and interreligious dialogue; and current theological issues, including the relation of the immanent and economic Trinity, the use of personal language, and theological method. See also the diverse topics (historical, ecclesiological, aesthetic, etc.) discussed in Marmion and Thiessen, eds., *Trinity and Salvation* [n. 4].

265. Jürgen Moltmann, *The Trinity and the Kingdom: The Doctrine of God*, trans. Margaret Kohl (1981; reprint, Minneapolis: Fortress, 1993), 160 (Rahner's axiom), viii ("mutual indwelling," reflection of divine sociality). Citations are from the reprint edition, with a new preface.

relations.[266] Moltmann's student Miroslav Volf has refined this argument further by characterizing it as a "social vision" rather than a "social program." He grounds this vision in the identity of the Trinity as "mutual indwelling" (*perichōrēsis*) and as self-donation that is "enacted in the cross by the power of the Spirit" and that translates into a "divine welcome in Christ" that the New Testament (especially Paul) encourages all believers to emulate.[267] In Catholic theology, a major representative has been Leonardo Boff, who expands on Moltmann's basic position in his book *Trinity and Society*: "From the perichoresis-communion of the three divine Persons derive impulses to liberation: of each and every human person, of society, of the church and of the poor, in the double—critical and constructive—sense." Humanity is thus called to forsake egoism and live the vocation of communion, society is called to create structures that are "humane, open, just and egalitarian," the church is called to reduce inequalities and practice "unity as co-existence in diversity," and the poor are called to see the Trinity as "the model for a human society based on mutual collaboration—all on an equal footing—and individual differences."[268]

However, others criticize social trinitarianism as being guilty of overreaching, and perhaps even of hubris. Since "the concepts of personhood and community are concepts we import into the process of analysis, synthesis, and construction," social trinitarianism, by

266. See, e.g., Jürgen Moltmann, *History and the Triune God: Contributions to Trinitarian Theology*, trans. John Bowden (New York: Crossroad, 1992), xii: "The unity of the triune God is no longer seen in the homogeneous divine subject nor in the identical divine subject, but in the eternal *perichoresis* of Father, Son and Spirit. . . . The monarchical, hierarchical and patriarchal ideas used to legitimate the concept of God are thus becoming obsolete. 'Communion,' 'fellowship,' is the nature and the purpose of the triune God."

267. Miroslav Volf, " 'The Trinity is Our Social Program': The Doctrine of the Trinity and the Shape of Social Engagement," *Modern Theology* 14 (1998): 403–23, at 415–16. See also his summary claim: "[The] primacy of grace in the establishment of its own proper truth and justice is . . . inscribed in the inner logic of divine justification, which is the inner logic of the cross, which is the inner logic of Trinitarian love translated into the world of sin" (417).

268. Leonardo Boff, *Trinity and Society*, trans. Paul Burns (Maryknoll, NY: Orbis, 1988), 236–37.

using such concepts to claim an insight into the immanent Trinity, is accused of ignoring the obvious disjunction between these concepts and the reality of God who infinitely exceeds them: "God alone is God [and] we as creatures cannot copy God in all respects."[269] An even more trenchant criticism accuses social trinitarianism of projecting modern or post-Enlightenment notions of "person" and "egalitarianism" onto the term *perichōrēsis*, then claiming to discover in the immanent Trinity these very notions and to present this discovery "as an exciting resource Christian theology has to offer the wider world in its reflections upon relationships and relatedness."[270] Rather than viewing this or any doctrine of the Trinity as a "first order discourse" that provides "a deep understanding of the way God really is" and demonstrates God's relevance, Karen Kilby suggests that it should be seen rather as "grammatical" or as a second order "structuring principle" that "specifies how various aspects of the Christian faith hang together."[271] Finally, social trinitarianism has been criticized for misunderstanding the notion of "person" that emanates from the Cappadocian discussion (especially the work of Gregory of Nyssa) and for trying to assimilate it too closely to contemporary philosophical views of the self.[272]

Each side of this contested issue makes an important point. On the one hand, as we emphasized at the outset, the Trinity is and remains an infinite mystery, and so "we cannot deduce the immanent Trinity by a kind of extrapolation from the economic Trinity."[273] Without a doubt there is "a strongly apophatic sensibility [that] attends any talk of the 'essence' of God"[274] that should make theologians think twice about making stronger-than-necessary claims about the immanent

269. Ted Peters, *God as Trinity: Relationality and Temporality in Divine Life* (Louisville, KY: Westminster/John Knox, 1993), 185–86.

270. Karen Kilby, "Perichoresis and Projection: Problems with Social Doctrines of the Trinity," *New Blackfriars* 81/957 (Nov. 2000): 432–45, at 442.

271. Ibid., 443–44.

272. Sarah Coakley, " 'Persons' in the 'Social' Doctrine of the Trinity: A Critique of Current Analytic Discussion," *The Trinity: An Interdisciplinary Symposium*, 123–44.

273. Kasper, *GJC*, 276.

274. Coakley, " 'Persons' in the 'Social' Doctrine," 135.

Trinity. On the other hand, the creed's assertion that the revelation of God in history happens "for us and for our salvation" gives theology a mandate to discern, as far as it is able, how the salvific presence of the triune God occurs "for us." "Relevance" here (*pace* Kilby and other critics) is not code for any attempt to reduce God to fit our limited categories, but rather signals the Christian conviction that there is a connection between the Trinity and history and that it is possible to express in a meaningful way how God's presence interlaces with everyday lived experience, even if the means of expression is ultimately flawed. This conviction stems not only from the belief that the Incarnation changes everything, but also from the recognition that the historical revelation of God in Christ ("Rather, he emptied himself . . . coming in human likeness; and found human in appearance" [Phil 2:7 NABRE]) and in the work of the Spirit discloses at the very least a "rhythm of self-giving" that forms "the inner justification, indeed the necessity, of a new trinitarian ontology" that grounds reality and gives us a glimpse (but, again, only a glimpse) of the character of divine life.[275] Theological reflection on the Trinity does not end with the accomplishments of the fourth century AD/CE; the creed demands that the mystery and its implications for human life continue to be explored. Indeed, contemporary philosophical reflection on intersubjectivity, relationality, and "the gift" can help theology illuminate the centrality of the Trinity for human life in ways that supplement the Cappadocians' reflections in unexpectedly productive ways.

One way to do justice to both sides—arguing on behalf of the "social" metaphor while preserving the infinite mystery of the Trinity—would be to follow Yves Congar and Walter Kasper in revising Rahner's fundamental axiom. Congar emphasizes that "there is a distance between the economic, revealed Trinity and the eternal Trinity. The Trinity is the same in each case and God is really communicated, but this takes place in a mode that is not connatural with the being of the divine Persons."[276] Kasper's rephrasing of the axiom runs

---

275. Klaus Hemmerle, *Thesen zu einer trinitarischen Ontologie*, Kriterien 40 (Einsiedeln: Johannes Verlag, 1976), 55 (my translation).

276. Congar, *I Believe in the Holy Spirit*, 3:15.

thus: "in the economic self-communication the intra-trinitarian self-communication is present in a new way, namely, under the veil of historical words, signs and actions, and ultimately in the figure of the man Jesus of Nazareth." A trinitarian theology must therefore respect both "the kenotic character of the economic Trinity" and "the apophatic character of the immanent Trinity," while recalling that "the immanent Trinity is and remains a *mysterium stricte dictum* in (not: behind!) the economic Trinity."[277]

5.2. The Trinity in Ecumenical Discussion

Enormous strides have been made in the ecumenical dialogues held in the decades after Vatican II. Regarding belief in the Trinity, official Roman Catholic discussions with Lutheran, Reformed, Methodist, and Anglican churches have led to a remarkable consensus.[278] For all those involved in these dialogues, the Trinity is the foundation and ultimate goal of Christian faith, and belief in it is possible because of the life, death and resurrection of Christ and the sending of the Spirit. While the mystery of divine life exceeds human language and concepts, nonetheless it can be affirmed that the triune God is "a unity of self-communicating and interdependent relationships" (Anglican-Catholic dialogue [ARCIC]) and "an invisible *koinonia*" (Methodist-Catholic dialogue) who calls the Church into being for the redemption of humankind. The Father is the source of the processions of the other persons and the source of salvation history. Christ is the Son and Incarnate Word sent by the Father, truly divine and truly human, the unique Lord and mediator who reconciles God and humanity. The Holy Spirit is the bond of unity between Father and Son and bond of communion who unites all Christians. The Spirit is active throughout the history of salvation, bringing transformation and participation in God.

One area that remains controversial is the dispute over the *Filioque* ("and from the Son") that continues to separate Roman Catholicism

---

277. Kasper, *GJC*, 276.

278. See Walter Kasper, *Harvesting the Fruits: Basic Aspects of Christian Faith in Ecumenical Dialogue* (London/New York: Continuum, 2009), 16–30, which forms the basis of what follows.

(the Latin West) and the Eastern Orthodox churches.[279] Eastern Christianity holds that the Holy Spirit proceeds from the Father, while according to the West (since the early medieval period) the Holy Spirit proceeds from the Father and from the Son. The West's position (*qui ex Patre Filioque procedit*, "who proceeds from the Father and the Son") was first interpolated into the Nicene-Constantinopolitan creed of 381 in Spain in 589. Despite criticisms and attempts to suppress the formula (e.g., by Pope Leo III [d. 816]), it spread through western Europe as a safeguard against resurgent Christological heresies and was eventually adopted in Rome by 1014. The *Filioque* was resisted by the East from the beginning, was condemned by Patriarch Photius of Constantinople in 867, and figured prominently in the mutual exchange of anathemas in 1054 that accelerated the break between Eastern and Western Churches. The Latin-led Council of Florence in 1439 declared the reunion of the Churches and approved the addition of the *Filioque*, but this decree was never officially accepted in the East and was formally rejected in 1484. Despite increasing dialogue and liturgical sharing over the past half-century, this separation remains.

The controversy over the *Filioque* is really two-fold, involving theological and ecclesiological issues. The theological issue is "rooted in subtle but significant differences in the way key terms have been used to refer to the Spirit's divine origin." The Greek terms *ekporeuesthai* ("proceed, issue forth") and *ekporeusis* ("procession") connote "a 'passage outwards' from within some point of origin. . . . Greek theology almost always restricts the theological use of this term to the coming-forth of the Spirit from the Father," thus preserving the monarchical role of the Father among the divine persons (i.e., the

---

279. For a history of the controversy and recent developments, see A. Edward Siecienski, *The Filioque: History of a Doctrinal Controversy*, Oxford Studies in Historical Theology (Oxford/New York: Oxford University Press, 2010). See also the Pontifical Council for Promoting Christian Unity, "The Greek and Latin Traditions Regarding the Procession of the Holy Spirit," *L'Osservatore Romano*, English edition, 20 September 1995 (also at http://www.ewtn.com/library/curia/pccufilq.htm), as well as the statement of the North American Orthodox-Catholic Theological Consultation, "The *Filioque*: A Church-Dividing Issue?" (25 October 2003), http://www.usccb.org/seia/filioque.shtml.

"one origin" or "principle without principle").[280] *Proienai* ("movement forwards"), on the other hand, is used more to describe the Spirit's mission in history. Early Latin translations, however, used *procedere* ("movement outwards") and *processio* to translate both meanings. The West thereby attempted to signify "the communication of the consubstantial divinity from the Father to the Son and from the Father, through and with the Son, to the Holy Spirit."[281] However, the East understood the Western use of *procedere/processio* as compromising the role of the Father as the sole *archē* of divine life. The recent North American Orthodox-Catholic discussion, attempting to avoid the theological polemics of the past, has acknowledged a number of consensus points in trinitarian belief, including agreement that "the Holy Spirit is a distinct hypostasis or person within the divine Mystery, equal in status to the Father and the Son," that "the Father is the primordial source (*archē*) and ultimate cause (*aitia*) of the divine being, and thus of all God's operations," and that "both traditions affirm that the three hypostases or persons in God are constituted in their hypostatic existence and distinguished from one another solely by their relationships of origin, and not by any other characteristics or activities."[282] Such a consensus, building on earlier dialogue agreements and formulas (e.g., "The Spirit proceeds from the Father of the Son," "The Spirit proceeds from the Father through the Son") has led to calls in Catholic circles for a return to the creed of 381 without the *Filioque* interpolation.[283]

The ecclesiological issue involves the teaching authority in the Church, specifically regarding the authority of the bishop of Rome to confirm and even alter conciliar decisions. "So while Orthodox theology has regarded the ultimate approval by the Popes, in the eleventh century, of the use of *Filioque* in the Latin Creed as a usurpation of the dogmatic authority proper to ecumenical Councils

280. "The *Filioque*,," III.1, par. 1. The Eastern understanding is rooted in its interpretation of John 15:26: "When the Advocate comes whom I will send you from the Father, the Spirit of truth that proceeds from the Father (*para tou patros ekporeuetai*), he will testify to me."
281. "The Greek and Latin Traditions," [par. 14].
282. "The *Filioque*," III, par. 3.
283. E.g., by Congar, *I Believe in the Holy Spirit*, 3:214.

alone, Catholic theology has seen it as a legitimate exercise of his primatial authority to proclaim and clarify the Church's faith."[284] This is a serious issue that, at present, seems less amenable to consensus; indeed, it "remains the root issue behind all the questions of theology and practice that continue to divide our communions."[285]

5.3. Trinity, Liturgy, and the Christian Life

We would be remiss if we did not recall an important point, namely a more fundamental version of the "relevance" issue: the ongoing task of advocating the centrality of belief in the Trinity for Christian life. The long-assumed "irrelevance" of Trinity that was mentioned at the outset, the portrayal of trinitarian doctrine as too esoteric for ordinary believers, and an impoverished theology of the Holy Spirit (pneumatology) are problems that much contemporary trinitarian theology has worked hard to overcome. But the results have hardly filtered into the everyday life of Catholics, and more must be done "to bring together the mystery of God and the mystery of salvation."[286]

We can mention two issues that need further discussion. The fundamental importance of these issues is undeniable, especially when one acknowledges the truth of Timothy Radcliffe's succinct identification of "the point of Christianity": "If Christianity is true, then it does not have a point other than to point to God who is the point of everything."[287] How does one acknowledge this ultimate divine point (an exercise in doxology) and live so as to make one's life conform to this point (the experience of salvation, studied by soteriology)?

First, there is a need to underscore an important insight noted both in the early Christian tradition and throughout the history of Christian spirituality: that salvation is indeed "deification" (*theōsis*), "participating in the very life of God, being made like Christ . . . for through Christ we are made sharers in the divine nature (2 Peter 1:4)," and that "the doctrine of the Trinity is the specifically Christian

284. "The *Filioque*," III.2.b, par. 1.
285. Ibid., III.2.b., par. 2.
286. LaCugna, "Trinitarian Mystery," 186.
287. Timothy Radcliffe, *What is the Point of Being a Christian?* (London/New York: Burns and Oates, 2005), 1.

way to explicate the meaning of participation in the life of the triune God."[288] If humanity is created in the image of God, then there is already a path toward that "point," but because of creaturely finitude and the effects of sin this transformative participation cannot be achieved without God's grace. The key to the reaching that "point" is summed up by Paul: "The grace of the Lord Jesus Christ, the love of God, and the communion of the Holy Spirit be with all of you" (2 Cor. 13:13). We have access to the love of God through the grace of Christ offered to us in discipleship (living a Jesus-like life in light of the Paschal Mystery) and perduring in us and in the midst of our world through the power of the Spirit who offers us fellowship, a participation in that divine love. Alongside and in consort with the developed Christology that already exists in the Church, a more developed understanding of the Holy Spirit (whom some have called "the forgotten person of the Trinity") is needed, along with the development of a trinitarian spirituality that shows how both together ground a life lived according to the values of the Kingdom of God.

> Union with God (deification) is therefore union with the life of God in the economy. It is at once mystical and active. In a trinitarian spirituality neither a pneumatological or a christological focus may overtake the other. Christ and the Spirit are the two foci of Christian life. The economy of the Spirit (deification) and the economy of the Son (incarnation) comprise the one divine economy.[289]

Second, there is the importance of the liturgy for a living trinitarian faith, and the retrieval of liturgical theology as a locus for trinitarian theology. For where else is the doctrine of the Trinity as the "summation of the entire Christian mystery of salvation" (Kasper) most often recalled and threaded through our lives than liturgical prayer, especially the celebration of the Eucharist? Right here is a link to the genius of the Cappadocians: recall that Basil of Caesarea considered the ultimate convincing argument for the divinity of the Spirit to be

---

288. LaCugna, "Trinitarian Mystery," 189 (definition of deification), 190 (doctrine as explication).
289. Ibid., 189.

liturgical prayer, especially the trinitarian baptismal formula, since it was a reflection of the long tradition of belief "in the souls of the faithful." The same confidence in the liturgy and the "sense of the faithful" is reflected in Catherine LaCugna's summary of the liturgy as the celebration of the triune God who is revealed "for us and for our salvation": "Doxology is the praise of God, the appreciation of God as God apart from the benefits of God. In praising God we make no distinction between who God is as God, and who God is for us."[290] Here the awareness of our salvation—our incorporation into God's life on God's initiative—is expressed in prayer that unites us "to God's triune mystery and to all believers throughout time, as we place ourselves into the whole history of redemption, particularly its eschatological movement of return to God."[291] Theology should constantly recall, then, how remarkable it is that the simplest prayer to the Trinity can express, as Kasper puts it,[292] how soteriology passes over into doxology: "Glory be to the Father, and to the Son, and to the Holy Spirit."

290. Ibid., 186.
291. Ibid., 187.
292. Kasper, *GJC*, 315.

CHAPTER FIVE

The Presence and Absence of God

No one has ever seen God. It is God the only Son [*monogenēs theos*], who is close to the Father's heart, who has made him known.

—John 1:18

Whoever is seeking God by ways is finding ways and losing God, who in ways is hidden.

—Meister Eckhart, Sermon 5b
("In hoc apparuit charitas dei in nobis")

Here at the end, let's recall Walter Kasper's provocative claim that we quoted at the outset:

The mystery which God is for the religious man or woman generally, is interpreted by the Christian faith as the mystery of an unfathomable and incomprehensible love, and hence as a personal mystery. *This mystery of God's love is the answer to the mystery of the world and human beings,* the answer to the deepest human longing for acceptance and love.[1]

Are we any closer to confirming this restatement and amplification of "God is love" (1 John 4:16)? It is audacious and paradoxical, at once particular and universal. In other words, the fundamental Christian attitude is belief in the triune God and in the mystery of divine love that exceeds all categories and descriptions: a truly *personal* love that reaches inward and touches each of us at the most personal and

1. Walter Kasper, "Revelation and Mystery: The Christian Understanding of God," in *Theology and Church*, trans. Margaret Kohl (New York: Crossroad, 1989), 30.

unique core of one's being, and yet a love that has a *universal* range as well—the ultimate response to all questions and all desires, a love that binds all together.

And what about the simple questions that we had posed originally, namely "Who is God?" and "Where is God?" (We rejected "What is God?" as an extrinsicist distortion.) They are startling, too, even in their "chastened" form. They distill Kasper's claim to its basics by suggesting an intimacy that would not be even possible unless the desires that motivate those questions were met by an experience of God that we do not coerce but rather is given to us: both familiar and unfamiliar, comforting yet discomforting, unmistakably *present* by fulfilling our innermost desires for love and meaning yet disturbingly *absent* by shattering our expectations and escaping our limited categories of description and understanding. We meet the unfathomable mystery, to the point that we feel disoriented, even adrift in "unknowing."

Throughout this book, the metaphor "presence and absence" has played subtly in the background, shaping our theological reflections. Here at the conclusion we need to deal with this paradox of belief and come clean about the use of this metaphor. I want to show how it helps us deal not only with Kasper's audacious claim and our chastened questions, but also with the *key question* that grounds all these issues, the basic conundrum that remains in the face of the divine mystery: *how is the ineffable God available to us within our embodied, time-bound life?* How is that intimacy given? How is God even accessible? We need as much clarity about this as we can achieve, because we need to be able to perform with our lives what we believe about the triune God "who in ways is hidden." Whatever clarity we can gain will help us connect doxology and soteriology—to uncover the crucial link between confession-and-contemplation (the faith commitment "to point to God who is the point of everything"[2]) and the actions by which one makes everyday living conform to this point (the actual experience of salvation). Discovering this link is crucial because the previous chapters' claims about God and Trinity are not disconnected abstract speculations, but rather intensely practical

2. Timothy Radcliffe, *What is the Point of Being a Christian?* (London/New York: Burns and Oates, 2005), 1.

considerations that apply to contemporary Christian life—they map out ways by which we can live lives of discipleship in the real world. *Performance* is the key to "faith seeking understanding."

1. Paradox

The conundrum is easy to express, hard to unpack. The Gospel of John presents it with delicious irony. "No one has ever seen God," the evangelist says, yet at the same time believers have indeed seen God because "the only Son . . . has made him known" (John 1:18). Later in the gospel, it is made clear (to the hearer or reader) that this revelation in fact has not brought clarity for the inner circle of disciples; indeed, they demand a further certainty bordering on fulfillment. "Lord," Philip asks, "show us the Father, and we will be satisfied" (John 14:8). Irony reappears in Jesus' reply: "Whoever has seen me has seen the Father. . . . Do you not believe that I am in the Father and the Father is in me?" (John 14:9, 10).

We are swamped, then, with impossibility and contradiction: God is not seen and yet revealed; we have no direct access, yet access is given through Jesus, the Son. How can this paradox even be approached, let alone grasped with any kind of understanding? How is God accessible in limited human experience? More precisely, does the ineffable God have any *phenomenality* that allows us to encounter God in our temporally-situated lives? "Phenomenality" is taken here in its root Greek meaning: what appears or comes into view (*phainomenon*), what shines or is lit up (*phainō*) for seeing and experiencing. How does God, whom no one has ever seen, appear "for us and for our salvation" (Nicene Creed)?

We encountered this paradox already in the first chapter when we spoke of God's "discretion." As we followed Anselm's seeker withdrawing into contemplation, along with the seeker we found that the question "where is God?" leads not only to the stark awareness that God dwells in "light inaccessible," but that nonetheless we acknowledge an intense desire for God. With the seeker, we experienced the transfiguration of this desire on realizing that it does not spring up from nowhere but has a catalyst, a dim awareness of God that we already possess. Absence becomes a signal of presence; faith is rooted in an already gratuitous divine action of giving. "I will never find you," the seeker exclaims, "unless you show yourself to me." Desire is transfigured when we acknowledge that it can point to the presence of God, "a little of your truth which my heart *already* believes and loves."[3]

Desire kicks off the search for God in the first place, but doesn't erase the need for the search. The reason is God's discretion. As Christian Duquoc puts it, "God does not give himself in experience; he announces himself in witnesses . . . . Nothing defines his identity or his essence *except the action he takes* within a framework which he has fixed, the covenant, and a promise which opens up the present to the future in a positive way."[4] God evades our direct perceptual experience because God is not an "object of knowledge" the way other objects are; our epistemological expectations are confounded. God does not impose or overwhelm but holds back so that reality, having its foundation in God, might have space to be. If considered as a static essence or a collection of attributes, God's identity is ungraspable. Rather, it is revealed only in divine action immersed in the running course of time and history. This insight is already present in the theophany of the burning bush: "Moses' vision represents a break: God gives his Name as a guarantee of his liberating action (Ex. 3.14)."[5] The basic structure of revelation is that divine discretion is not stasis or non-action, but rather an act of giving, a granting of time to exist in order to actualize the possibilities of one's identity in relation to others and to God.

Edward Schillebeeckx relates a poignant instance of this. A woman religious, a missionary, had written to him about struggles in her prayer life, how it had become more difficult, even empty. "I feel utterly alone," she says, "as if I belonged to no one. I live in cold faith. Our dear Lord wants us to love him, to please him, yes, but never to

3. *Proslogion*, in *The Prayers and Meditations of Saint Anselm*, trans. Benedicta Ward (Harmondsworth/New York: Penguin, 1973), 240, 243, 244 (my emphasis). "Light inaccessible" echoes 1 Timothy 6:16: "It is he alone who . . . dwells in unapproachable light, whom no one has ever seen or can see. . . ."

4. Christian Duquoc, " 'Who is God?' becomes 'Where is God?': The Shift in a Question," trans. John Bowden, in *Where is God? A Cry of Human Distress*, ed. Christian Duquoc and Casiano Floristán, Concilium 1992/4 (London: SCM Press, 1992), 2–3 (my emphasis).

5. Ibid., 3.

see anything, never once to be in his shortlived presence." Her situation, for Schillebeeckx, represents "a basic law of the spiritual life. God never shows himself."[6] He warns us that whoever seeks God should never mistake God's gifts for God's own self; one must practice "an obstinate refusal to confuse God with any creature whatever. . . . If you are really in search of God, you must reconcile yourself to living in religious darkness."[7] Schillebeeckx's interpretation of this spiritual state, though, might strike us as counter-intuitive. That darkness and unsettling silence of God, which Jesus also experienced on the cross, is not a sign of God's non-existence, Schillebeeckx insists, but rather witnesses to God's nearness and "utmost interest" in us and our unfolding life story. "Silence is an element of any conversation or any dialogue. . . . Therefore God can answer only when our fleeting life on earth is ended. We must let God be God, give God time to listen to our story. . . . Because God is greater than our human heart, God never comes as a human voice into the depths of our being but as a divine silence, a silence which only becomes a voice and a visible face after our death."[8]

But what signals of this nearness and interest do we have in this life? We are thrown back into our conundrum: God as ineffable, yet available; not seen, yet seen; absent, yet present. In the midst of the silence of God's discretion, what signals do we have that God is love, and that this love is directed to us?

2. Phenomenality

All the problems that human understanding has in grasping the mystery of the triune God come together and confront us at this point.

---

6. Edward Schillebeeckx, "The Believer's Complaint: 'You are a hidden God' (*Isaiah 45.15*)," *For the Sake of the Gospel*, trans. John Bowden (New York: Crossroad, 1990), 85–87, at 85.

7. Ibid., 86. Elsewhere, Schillebeeckx puts it this way: "When confronted with any manifestation of the divine, God's essential reserve is always experienced; God can never be reduced to one of the forms in which he is manifested. Reality continues to surprise us" (Schillebeeckx, *Christ: The Experience of Jesus as Lord*, trans John Bowden [New York: Crossroad, 1981], 55).

8. "The Believer's Complaint," 86–87.

God dwelling in "light inaccessible" means that God does not appear within our field of experience in the fashion that all creation appears, that God is not a "phenomenon" or an object of thought the way all other objects can be.

Notice, however, the language that we have used thus far—and that is normally used—to describe experiences or non-experiences with God: "to see God," "light inaccessible," "appear," "religious darkness," "show us the Father," "unless you show yourself to me." The *visual metaphor* governs all these expressions; in other words, experiencing, believing, and knowing are like seeing. There is nothing new about this comparison. The metaphor is present in the Bible (as, for example, in the Johannine passages cited earlier), and in a more "objective" way it pervades those areas of Western culture that have been most influenced by philosophy's claim that what counts as "true" is whatever is clearly seen (e.g., earlier with the Platonic Forms, later with Descartes' "clear and distinct ideas"). Even our use of "phenomenality" in connection with God's presence brings vision into play: the "phenomenal," after all, is what appears.

The more objective use of the metaphor also assumes a peculiar way of framing experience and knowledge. The danger is that, in the wake of the development of the modern rational, autonomous, ascetic self after 1500, the taken-for-granted metaphor can easily seduce us into positing the seeing/knowing "I" as the fixed central vantage point, with everything else that is "real" positioned outside and around this point. To "see" something "clearly" from this central point and to express it with this metaphor is to engage reality, but always at a distance, with a gap that must be bridged.

What if we shift the metaphor? That does not eliminate the paradox (how could it?) but it does make it more approachable. The philosopher and theologian Kevin Hart, using the language of phenomenology, puts it this way:

> When we pray to the Trinity, we do not constitute the triune God as phenomenon; we dispose ourselves so that we receive him as mystery. We do not bring God into presence; we enter into his presence, which may be quite different from human modes of presence. The triune God is not an object or a being, nor strictly

being itself but rather *ipsum esse subsistens omnibus modis indeter-minatum*, to use Aquinas's fine expression, that is, wholly unde-termined subsistent "to be" itself. God is an absolutely singular *event*, and doubtless His triune nature is an index of that singularity.[9]

Let's focus on the characterization of God as "an absolutely singu-lar *event*." The language of "event" is more in line with a biblical understanding, where God is encountered in terms of action within the framework of creation. It would be incorrect to say that God's action "enters history," as if history somehow preexisted God's crea-tive impulse as a kind of already-established arena. This is because the triune God "cannot be conceived as an object embedded on an intentional horizon. God overflows all horizons."[10] Rather, God's subsistent and dynamic "to be" brings time and history into being, and is woven throughout their flow within the framework of the covenant God makes with humanity. Although literally inconceivable and unobjectifiable, it is the character of this "to be" that we need to clarify . . . and there's the visual metaphor again. It seems unavoid-able. But while admitting its necessity and usefulness, we must attempt to surpass it and thus come closer not only to the disclosure of God in the theophanies we examined in chapter two, but also to the revelation of the triune God as a communion of persons in love.

How do we encounter God's subsistent and dynamic "to be" within our necessarily limited frame of experience? Expanding our notion of experience helps to provide an answer. Our embodied conscious awareness is always "consciousness of . . ." something. Conscious-ness has a directedness, an "aboutness." It is an active field including both the knower's "streaming" awareness (called "intentionality") and the known, the target of meaning toward which the streaming

---

9. Kevin Hart, "Notes toward a Supreme Phenomenology," *Kingdoms of God* (Bloomington: Indiana University Press, 2014), 159–78, at 168. He cites Thomas, *Summa theologiae* Ia, q. 11, a. 4, resp.: "[God] exists supremely, because he has not acquired an existence which his nature has then determined, but is subsistent existence itself (*ipsum esse subsistens*), in no way determined" (*Summa theologiae*, vol. 2 [1a. 2–11]: *Existence and Nature of God*, trans. Timothy McDermott [1964; repr., Cambridge: Cambridge University Press, 2006], 166–69).

10. Hart, "Notes," 170.

intentionality is directed.[11] This bypasses the usual static subject-object description of knowledge (e.g., the mind is a camera, concepts are the pictures) and does justice to the dynamic flow of our embodied awareness and the real referents of our ideas. Using the terms of phenomenology, we can call the poles of this intentional flow *noesis* (the knowing subject's acts of conscious awareness, responsible for constituting the meaning that it grasps) and *noema* (the perception *"through which* the object is grasped").[12] We can also widen the description of intentionality beyond mental acts to include diverse aspects of lived experience immersed in the world.[13] The key insight is that conscious awareness, no matter how narrowly or widely construed, is a fluid field that includes both *noetic acts* and the *noematic correlates* of those acts. Our awareness streams outward from the self toward what is beyond the self, in order for us to know this "non-I" through our perceptual relation to it.

At first glance, this explanation seems counter-productive for our purposes. What is the phenomenality that "lights up" the triunity of God for it to be the focus of our intentionality? There isn't any. There is no perceptual experience that would give us the specific noematic correlate "trinity."[14] How, then, do we have any inkling whatsoever

11. See Martin Heidegger, *History of the Concept of Time: Prolegomena*, trans. Theodore Kisiel (Bloomington: Indiana University Press, 1985), 29: "*Intentio* literally means *directing-itself-toward.* Every lived experience, every psychic comportment, directs itself toward something. Representing is a representing of something, recalling is a recalling of something, judging is judging about something, presuming, expecting, hoping, loving, hating—of something."

12. Edmund Husserl, *Ideas Pertaining to Pure Phenomenology and to a Phenomenological Philosophy, First Book: General Introduction to a Pure Phenomenology*, trans. F. Kersten (The Hague: Nijhoff, 1983), 198–200, 211; Dermot Moran, *Introduction to Phenomenology* (London/New York: Routledge, 2000), 156, 157.

13. As was done by Husserl's later followers, including Heidegger ("Being-in-the-world") and Maurice Merleau-Ponty (the "lived body" with its body-consciousness). See Martin Heidegger, *Being and Time*, trans. John Macquarrie and Edward Robinson (New York: Harper and Row, 1962 [Ger. orig. 1927]); Maurice Merleau-Ponty, *Phenomenology of Perception*, trans. Donald A. Landes (London/New York: Routledge, 2012 [Fr. orig. 1945]).

14. See Hart, "Notes," 168: "If I engage in *epochē* and reduction in an attempt to figure the Trinity as phenomenon, I may find a noesis but I cannot find a

of God as triune? The ultimate answer, of course, is faith. But faith needs a starting point within our experience, a catalyst, a phenomenality to launch a progressively deepening encounter. It goes without saying that faith's object is God and is evoked by God's self-revelation, but at the same time it is also a human act that includes the process of embodied and temporally-saturated understanding.[15] A "double apriori" is in operation here, a simultaneous two-fold presupposed dependency: God's self-giving occurs in the midst of and through the conditions of human experience, while at the same time the very possibility of human experience is always already grounded in God who gives it space to be.[16] In this mutual dependency, God constrains divinity to "fit" humanity—another surprising act of discretion.

The natural theology that we pursued in chapter three, where we discerned the natural access-point of faith, helps us articulate the "clearing" within our experience where clues of divine transcendence make their appearance. Kasper's analysis, based on "freedom" as the overarching reality rather than "being," extended that discernment to the point of being able to suggest that the absolute transcendence we meet at the limits of our experience can be characterized as the Absolute Person.[17] The Christian tradition does not stop there, though, but presses on to speak of the Triune God as a communion of persons in love (as Kasper eventually demonstrates). "Trinity," then, is more than concepts of "divine transcendence" and "absoluteness." Where do we find the clues for that?

---

noema, what my intentional act aims at, since the Trinity exceeds human thought, as much in the transcendental attitude as in the natural attitude."

15. Walter Kasper, *The God of Jesus Christ* [*GJC*], new ed., trans. [Matthew O'Connell and] Dinah Livingstone (London/New York: Continuun, 2012), 71–72; Bernhard Welte, *Heilsverständnis: Philosophische Untersuchungen einiger Voraussetzungen zum Verständnis des Christentums*, in *Gesammelte Schriften*, vol. IV/1: *Hermeneutik des Christlichen*, ed. Bernhard Casper (Freiburg: Herder, 2006), 32–60, esp. 33–35.

16. Klaus Hemmerle, *Thesen zu einer trinitarischen Ontologie*, 2nd ed., Kriterien 40 (Einsiedeln: Johannes Verlag, 1992), 18–19.

17. Kasper, *GJC*, 154–55. See Anthony J. Godzieba, "The Promise and the Burden of Natural Theology," in *The Theology of Cardinal Walter Kasper: Speaking Truth in Love*, eds. Kristin M. Colberg and Robert A. Krieg (Collegeville, MN: Liturgical Press, 2014), 42–58.

Those clues are best found in the gospels—in the life, preaching, practices, death, and resurrection of Jesus the Christ. We have already shown how Jesus' active presence is *theophanic:* he claimed that the long-awaited arrival of the God's Kingdom (*basileia tou theou*) and its ongoing fulfillment were tied in a unique way to his own person, preaching, and prophetic actions: he comforts the suffering, heals the sick, feeds the hungry, raises the dead, forgives sinners, creates an inclusive community that overcomes gender, class, and ethnic hierarchies, and preaches parables that describe the active reign of God and challenge his audiences to experience the world in the throes of this outpouring of divine love. "We can study the phenomena of his practices of eating and preaching, how he brings forth sin and forgiveness as phenomena, his phenomenology of proper relations with the Father (by way of the *basileia*), the phenomenon of his death and the saturated phenomenon of his bodily resurrection."[18] And we can examine more closely Jesus' command to us to put aside the ordinary taken-for-granted arrangements of the world that obscure the fundamental structures and conditions of our lives. In phenomenology, this "bracketing" of preconceptions and business-as-usual approaches to experiences is called "the suspension of the natural attitude" or *epochē*. Its goal is to eliminate distortions and help us focus on and examine the essential aspects of our experiences which are thereby made more easily open to display.[19] As Hart notes, Jesus practices his own version of the *epochē*. In the gospels, Jesus is "perpetually confronted with a version of the natural attitude, 'the world,' in its various forms" and with its various human arrangements of power. He responds "by leading his audience (and us) back to something that has a prior claim on us, the *basileia* or Kingdom" and using his preaching and practices to challenge his hearers to experience differently and imagine "a better arrangement and harmony in which the Father is regarded as absolute, not his creation or anything in it. The power of the *imperium mundi* must be bracketed for us to see what is radically prior to it, the loving rule of the Father."[20]

18. Hart, "Notes," 171.

19. For a thumbnail sketch of Husserl's notions of *epochē* and the phenomenological reduction, see Moran, *Introduction to Phenomenology*, 11–12.

20. Hart, "Notes," 171–72.

It is this ensemble of Jesus' practices—his proclamation of the values of the Kingdom, and his actions and relationships which incarnate those values—that reveal the all-embracing love of the Father for all creation. He is the catalyst of a series of interpersonal actions that embody the revelation of God's love *in performance.* Jesus not only describes in parables the divine act of reversal that the Kingdom of God represents (a reversal from a negative situation to a positive one beyond our own abilities), but also actualizes it. "Go and tell John what you have seen and heard: the blind receive their sight, the lame walk, the lepers are cleansed, the deaf hear, the dead are raised, the poor have good news brought to them" (Luke 7:22). That performance is *theophanic.* Graham Ward, in a nice turn of phrase, calls this "the Christological operation; the divine as it works in, through, with and as the body of this Jewish man who is the Christ. For, after all, the Messiah in Jewish and then Christian thinking is not just a person but an eschatological operation. The person is identified only in the mission."[21] As we emphasized in the previous chapter, personal identity is only constituted in relationality and in actions over time that incarnate that relationality.[22] Our identification of Jesus the Christ as the revelation of the Father's faithful love is based on our perception of his actions in the gospel accounts: he challenges and sets aside humanly-constructed, self-serving construals of reality so that we might experience the most fundamental basis of reality in the unfolding love of God—a love that surpasses death to reveal eternal life. The mystery of the ineffable "singular event" that is the triune God is revealed in the events instigated by Jesus of Nazareth, the accessible phenomenality of that event. These noematic clues continue to be available in the ongoing effects and affects in the communities that flow from Jesus' death and resurrection and that continue to be vivified by the Holy Spirit.

As Hart puts it, we enter into God's presence, not the other way around. In other words, the very being of the triune God is always

---

21. Graham Ward, "The Schizoid Christ," *Christ and Culture* (Oxford/Malden, MA: Blackwell, 2005), 60–91, at 63.

22. Kasper, *GJC,* 155; John D. Zizioulas, "On Being a Person: Towards an Ontology of Personhood," *Communion and Otherness: Further Studies in Personhood and the Church,* ed. Paul McPartlan (New York: T&T Clark, 2006), 99–112, at 112.

already active ahead of our encounter with and knowledge of God; it is the necessary precondition for the very possibility of that encounter. We do not control or force that presence; rather, we respond to a prior and active givenness, one that "overflows" any restriction to a particular object. This is different from all our other encounters. The clue to the character of this givenness is the revelatory and yet discreet phenomenality of Christ in action in the gospels. He gives us a glimpse of the primordial source of this transfiguring power: the all-encompassing love of God for all that God has created. "We love because he first loved us" (1 John 4:19). The fundamental character of this love is so absolute that the theologian Klaus Hemmerle does not hesitate to argue that it forces us to re-read reality itself according to a new understanding of being, a "trinitarian ontology."[23] The very being of God as a communion of persons in love enters into all aspects of reality and transforms them by "the rhythm of self-giving" and by the invitation to participate fully in divine life.[24] The mystery of the Trinity as communion-in-love as the divine grounding and sustaining of everything (*ipse esse subsistens* taken truly dynamically) compels us to experience the fundamental nature of reality itself as open-ended and relational rather than static. The self-giving at the heart of the trinitarian mystery of God, rendered "phenomenal" not only in the preaching and actions of Christ but also in the ongoing life of the Spirit wherever Christ is followed and the values of the Kingdom are performed, ensures that God could never be construed definitively as a divine object grasped by human categories of thought or governed by traditional metaphysical principles. God, to use Hart's phrase, is an absolutely singular *event*. This fundamentally relational understanding of being, which cannot be deduced but only revealed,

---

23. Hemmerle, *Thesen*, 38–60, esp. 54: "This perspective becomes apparent in the structure of all being, all thinking, and all events; it leads to a re-reading in faith of what the phenomenon reveals in direct reference to this perspective. Thinking itself learns anew from this phenomenology; it becomes transformed insofar as, in accompanying the path of self-giving, it becomes a path of love" (my thanks to Francis Schüssler Fiorenza for the translation). See also Anthony J. Godzieba, "Prolegomena to a Catholic Theology of God between Heidegger and Postmodernity," *Heythrop Journal* 40 (1999): 319–39, esp. 331–33.

24. Hemmerle, *Thesen*, 38.

breaks the constraints of metaphysics. Thus, God's love has both ontological and eschatological consequences: the experience of God as love can be both immediately active and anticipated, since it is of the character of love to increase in the act of loving.[25]

3. Performance

The gospels make this obvious: in order to participate in this love that God is and has for us, our own actions must mirror it. Divine love is given and is transfiguring, but its possibilities must be received, applied, and activated as well. This activation, this mirroring, is *discipleship*, living a Jesus-like life in the midst of our particular historical and cultural situations. But beyond the obvious, something deeper is also at stake, and that is the other aspect we need to explore. To do this effectively, we need to perform our own *epochē* on the phenomenality of Christ made available in the gospels.

Let's focus on the "Christological operations," the series of Jesus' personal actions that embody the revelation of God's love *in performance*. If we bracket the particular content of these actions (a healing, a teaching, a dramatic parable, and so on), the commonality that they share becomes more apparent: these are all *effective performances* (that is, they reverse a negative situation into a positive one) that occur *in time* and *in relationships.* The disclosure of the mystery of the triune God, the revelation of the love of God in Christ, occurs for us in a time-bound, not timeless, way. The absolutely singular event of God inhabits time and its duration. Here, then, is an additional paradox: the "absolute" is available to us only in time and history. Time is not the enemy of divine mystery; rather, *it is the precondition of its revelation.*

But how can this be? Don't the divine, the absolute, the infinite all belong to the realm of the timeless? Like the so-called classical transcendentals (the good, the true, the beautiful, and being itself), doesn't the perfection of divine love dwell beyond the temporally-drawn limits of our experience? But in Christian practice and belief, the essential phenomenality plays out otherwise: Christ indeed makes

25. Ibid., 44–46, 54, 59–60.

this love accessible in what he *does*, both in the gospels and in those who continue his mission by performing the values of the Kingdom of God today in their particular ways and places. The performance that makes God's self-giving love available precedes any speculative explanation. The particular, the material, the temporal are the focal points of our attention. The gospels insist that the mystery that transcends the particular is only revealed by the particular.

This further paradox—the revelation of the Trinity in time, or the absolute in history—has shadowed Christianity since its origins, and has generated a long history of reflection that we cannot rehearse here. We approach it from a different angle, an *aesthetic* one, since the arts have always employed various material means of arousing particular sentiments in order to bring the viewer or listener to an experience that transcends the limits of the senses. As the painter Mark Rothko put it, art "must provide the implications of infinity to any situation."[26] And so first we will examine our *contemporary experience of time*, which forms the background for our current encounter with the mystery of the love of the triune God. Then we will turn to *three different aesthetic ways* of exploring time and meaning—painting, architecture, and music—to expand our notion of experience and to help us navigate the conundrum with, we hope, a bit of success.

3.1. The Experience of Time: Social Acceleration

Whether we are aware of it or not, the contemporary experience of time has a major effect on our awareness of the meaning of discipleship and how we experience the values of the Kingdom of God. Time is shrinking, and is even in danger of being blotted out. That is not an alarmist statement but rather a sober description. Recent

---

26. Mark Rothko, *The Artist's Reality: Philosophies of Art*, ed. Christopher Rothko (New Haven: Yale University Press, 2004), 95, as cited in Susie Paulik Babka, *Through the Dark Field: The Incarnation through an Aesthetics of Vulnerability* (Collegeville, MN: Liturgical Press, 2017), 7 n 13. Babka's introduction and opening chapter offer an insightful and often moving introduction to the intertwinings of art and religious experience. She suggests that, like art, theology's task should be that of "exposing the infinitely Other reality which is past-all-grasp" (11).

cultural studies have shown that the accelerated pace of contemporary life leads paradoxically to its "de-temporalization," the experience of the loss of time or the loss of any forward movement through time.[27] We complain about "having no time" to get things done, "running out of time," being "squeezed for time"—all this despite the promise of various strategies and digital technologies to help us control the constant onslaught of obligations and fragmentary waves of information. But this hope to get things under control is a false one. As one commentator has put it, "not only have our devices outpaced us, they don't even reflect a here and now that may constitute any legitimate sort of present tense. They are reports from the periphery, of things that happened moments ago."[28] We always come late to the present.

Contemporary culture is thus experiencing the erasure of time. In the words of media theorist Douglas Rushkoff, we suffer from "narrative collapse" due to the loss of optimism about the future, an attitude brought on by overwhelming events like terrorism, the implosion of the economy, and climate change. That collapse is mirrored in the presentist popular culture that shapes much of how we understand the world, including Christian beliefs and practices. For example, goal-directed narrative arcs once used by television dramas have been replaced by shows "characterized by frozenness in time, as well as by the utter lack of traditional narrative goals."[29] Today, the popular search for meaning looks instead to drama generated by disconnected spectacles of immediate attention-grabbing behavior, such as reality TV's stock-in-trade of humiliation and personal

---

27. This section borrows material from my essays "'. . . And Followed Him on the Way' (Mark 10:52): Unity, Diversity, Discipleship," in *Beyond Dogmatism and Innocence: Hermeneutics, Critique, and Catholic Theology*, ed. Anthony J. Godzieba and Bradford E. Hinze (Collegeville, MN: Liturgical Press, 2017), 228–54, and "Who is the 'Polis' Addressed by Political Theology? Notes on a Conundrum" (International Edward Schillebeeckx Seminar, Katholieke Universiteit Leuven [Belgium], November 2016; forthcoming in print). See these essays for more details on "social acceleration."

28. Douglas Rushkoff, *Present Shock: When Everything Happens Now* (New York: Current/Penguin, 2013), 74.

29. Ibid., 31.

tragedy, or raucous disputes among the panelists that are stoked by the hosts of cable TV and radio talk shows. As Rushkoff puts it, "Without the traditional narrative arc at their disposal, producers of reality TV must generate pathos directly, in the moment. . . . What images and ideas can stop the channel surfer in his tracks?"[30] The loss of narrative is also disappointingly mirrored in contemporary politics, which is mostly crisis management trying to appear authoritative, but is lost in chaotic, hair-on-fire decision-making and the inability to construct or even envision long-term goals.[31]

The social theorist Hartmut Rosa has a name for the proximate cause of such "now-ism": *social acceleration.* This, he argues, is now the structure of contemporary society. It has three elements: *technical acceleration* ("the intentional . . . acceleration of goal-directed processes"), the *acceleration of social change* (where past experiences no longer meet present expectations, causing the present as a time-span of social stability to "contract"), and *acceleration of the pace of life* (where we experience the contraction of the present as "the scarcity of time resources" and the anxious compulsion to "keep up").[32]

The combination of all three elements leads to radically altered circumstances. The acceleration of the pace of life has two components, the "shortening or condensation of episodes of action" and a decrease in off-times or resting times between actions (the *objective* component),[33] and our growing sense "that one lacks time or is pressed for time and in a stressful compulsion to accelerate as well as in anxiety about 'not keeping up'," accompanied by "the *feeling* that time itself is going by faster" (the *subjective* component).[34] This

---

30. Ibid., 37

31. Ibid., 47: "What used to be called statecraft devolves into a constant struggle with crisis management. Leaders cannot get on top of issues, much less ahead of them, as they instead seek merely to respond to the emerging chaos in a way that makes them look authoritative."

32. Hartmut Rosa, *Social Acceleration: A New Theory of Modernity*, trans. Jonathan Trejo-Mathys (New York: Columbia University Press, 2013), 71–80, at 71 (goal-directed), 76 (contraction of the present), 79 (scarcity); Rosa, "Social Acceleration: Ethical and Political Consequences of a Desynchronized High-Speed Society," *Constellations* 10/1 (2003): 3–33, at 6–10.

33. Rosa, *Social Acceleration*, 78–79, 152.

34. Ibid., 79 (here and elsewhere, emphasis in the original).

acceleration of the pace of life is encouraged (and at times even caused) by technical acceleration, the "introduction of new techniques" that help us do things faster. This technical solution to the scarcity of time in turn leads to the realization that "the *more scarce time resources become, the greater is the need for techniques and technologies of acceleration and hence the faster the pace of life becomes too.*"[35] The middle component, the acceleration of social change, is also affected: if "our relationships to space, time, things, and other actors" changes as a result of technical acceleration, then "practices of socialization and subjectivation, and hence patterns of identity and personality structures" change as well. Finally, if the accelerating tempo of individual life demands more technical acceleration, and the latter causes social acceleration, then the cycle is completed when one sees how social acceleration affects the tempo of one's individual life: *"the heightening of the pace of life in view of newly scarce time resources is thus a direct (and in the end unavoidable) consequence of the acceleration of social change."*[36] When past experiences no longer provide secure and trustworthy solutions because they no longer meet accelerated expectations, individual actors and organizations alike are already down the slippery slope of constantly revising their actions *and* expectations to meet the rapidly changing circumstances. What occurs is "an erosion of all conceivable resting places: *standing still* inevitably becomes a form of *falling behind* not only in the economy but in all dimensions of social life."[37]

What also occurs as a result of all this frantic effort seems counterintuitive: the *collapse of time*, the "de-temporalization" of both the individual and the social. "Life is no longer planned along a line that stretches from the past into the future," but rather is governed by short-term decisions in response to constant waves of "unforeseeable contingencies" and the overwhelming needs and desires of the moment. Only the isolated moment matters; any flow of time from

35. Ibid., 152.

36. Ibid., 156.

37. Ibid., 155. See also Rosa's discussion of the "circle of acceleration" (156–59). This circle "turns out to be largely immune to *individual* attempts to interrupt it," he argues, since the person who attempts it falls behind, "loses opportunities," and "must drop out of some contexts of interaction" (157).

the past through the present into the future disappears. The result, Rosa argues, is an "incapacity to engage in long-term commitments," leading in turn to "a paradoxical backlash in which the experience of frantic change and 'temporalized time' give way to the perception of 'frozen time' without (a meaningful) past and future and consequently of depressing inertia."[38] This "de-temporalization of time" affects not only individual identities; social identities and political decisions are also pervaded by directionless inertia masquerading as frantic change, resulting in the "disappearance of politics."[39] We are left with an apparently unsolvable dilemma: social acceleration reveals a range of human possibilities that is wider than ever, but our abilities to survey these possibilities and decide among them remain as truncated as before. We are overwhelmed and can't keep up. The result is ominous: the pace of everything around us ("increasingly contingent and revisable") accelerates, while our own "loss of direction, priorities, and narratable 'progress'" causes us to decelerate into inertia.[40]

This squeezed, truncated contemporary situation is where Christian life and our encounter with the triune God occur, at the very least where globalization and consumer capitalism and its technologies prevail. Discipleship runs counter to this de-temporalization because it implies *duration*, time to unfold and develop. The incarnation of the values of the Kingdom of God needs to be lived over time for the power of grace to be revealed and effective. But contemporary inertia recognizes these actions only as momentary, disconnected blips. And so the encounter with the dynamic phenomenality of God seems to be short-circuited by contemporary culture.

One reaction to the current dominance of frantic, de-temporalized change has been contemporary Catholic dogmatism of various types, which are ultimately attempts to reduce Catholicism to a single timeless identity-marker or a "brand." However, these are capitulations to de-temporalized inertia, even while they claim to resist the culture that provokes it. They are anxiety-prone reactions to the accelerated

---

38. Rosa, "Social Acceleration," 19–20; see also 25: "The inability to control social change has brought an overwhelming sense of directionless change in an 'iron cage' that itself has become fundamentally inert."

39. Ibid., 20–22.

40. Ibid., 27. See also *Social Acceleration*, 80–93.

speed of social change and overwhelming difference. While dogma-
tist construals of religious identity make a show of resisting a so-called
"culture of relativism," they are implicated in postmodern inertia
when they equate a particular time-bound synthesis with the
"essence" of the Christian tradition, and then go on to claim that
synthesis as perennial (a temporal claim) and/or absolute (a metaphysical claim). This minimizes the gospel call to ongoing discipleship—*living* a Jesus-like life—as a key moment of divine revelation,
and ignores how these practices reveal the truth of the gospel and
the activity of the triune God throughout time and shifting situations.

3.2. Aesthetic Clues for Breaking the Spell

In this accelerated, presentist context, how do we make God's discretion understandable? And how do we communicate the claim that
the divine mystery that transcends the particular (Rothko: "the implications of infinity") is necessarily revealed only by the particular? To
explore those aspects of our embodied experience that resonate with
our claim—aspects that tend to be obscured by our persistent "now-
ism"—we should turn to the arts. They are adept at disclosing glossed-
over aspects of our experience and navigating the porous boundaries
of the visible and the invisible, time and transcendence, materiality
and "timeless" beauty—placing us inside the paradox.

Take, for example, the confluence of the visible and the invisible
that occurs in *painting.* Michelangelo Merisi da Caravaggio's earlier
version of *Supper at Emmaus* (1600–01), one of the most famous depictions of the post-resurrection appearance of Christ in the Gospel of
Luke (24:13-35), is an excellent example.

Caravaggio has chosen to portray the extraordinary within the
ordinary, the supernatural within the everyday, by means of heightened concentration upon the ordinariness of the scene and its elements, with almost the precise observational skills of a natural
scientist. The work is as luminous as it is virtuosic. The richness of
the scene almost defies description; its visual immediacy involves the
viewer directly in the experience. Drama is achieved through the
contrast of deep dark colors and brilliant highlights, by the sensuous
fullness of the figures, and by a dazzling use of perspective. The table
is set close to the viewer, but with enough room so that the disciple

1. Michelangelo Merisi da Caravaggio, *Supper at Emmaus* (1600–01)
(National Gallery, London)

on the left can be seated before it. He grasps the arms of his chair as if he is about to leap out of it in utter astonishment at the dramatic revelation of Christ and push it through the picture plane—a move typical of Baroque art, which dissolves the boundary between the viewer and the work. The basket of fruit perched precariously on the edge of the table looks as if it will drop into our laps at any moment. The disciple on the right, wearing the pilgrim's shell, throws out his arms in a gesture of amazement (perhaps symbolizing the crucifixion). His left arm, extended toward the viewer and also seeming to break the picture plane, unites the disciples with us, who are also amazed.

All attention is focused on Christ, whose beardless face is perhaps Caravaggio's solution to the problem of why the disciples "were kept from recognizing him" (Luke 24:16) on the road. Christ's face is illuminated by light falling from the left; its radiance is highlighted even further by the shadow cast by the uncomprehending innkeeper on the wall behind, almost as a kind of dark halo. The light falling from the upper left bespeaks its divine origin and signals God's transfiguration of this ordinary scene and the revelation of the identity of the risen Christ at the moment the meal is blessed and shared.

And how that scene is transformed: a delicate light passes through the water pitcher and casts both water-reflected light and shadow on

2. Michelangelo Merisi da Caravaggio, *Supper at Emmaus* (detail)

the tablecover in a scene of incredibly eloquent brilliance (fig. 2). The same light is reflected from the tablecover onto the face of the disciple on the left, allowing us to see and know his reaction even though we catch only the barest glimpse of his face.

The fundamental interpretation of the Emmaus episode, by Luke and by Caravaggio's contemporaries as well, is Eucharistic. The work as a whole "preaches" the Eucharistic meaning of the Emmaus episode: not only the presence of Christ in the breaking of bread, but also a manifestation of the sacramental imagination and care for ordinary materiality which Caravaggio shared with the popular spiritual reform movements of his time. Indeed, to borrow the title of a classic commentary on art, we witness "the transfiguration of the commonplace."[41] Caravaggio's complex composition choreographs our performances as viewers and believers—and it *is* a performance; even *looking* takes time. As our eyes move around the image, the ordinary, without giving up one bit of its materiality, is slowly revealed to be extraordinary; by means of the natural, the supernatural is revealed, to us as well as to the two disciples. They finally recognize Jesus in

41. Arthur C. Danto, *The Transfiguration of the Commonplace: A Philosophy of Art* (Cambridge, MA: Harvard University Press, 1981).

the blessing and breaking of the bread—in a shared relationship that is, by the incarnational initiative of God, the precondition for the revelation of Christ's identity and the meaning of salvation.

Caravaggio's brilliant technique, especially his employment of dramatic light-dark contrasts known as *chiaroscuro*, gives a two-dimensional image the depth and richness of three dimensions. It reflects a sacramental vision that conveys how the finite mediates the infinite, how material particularity (including the very materials of the image) can disclose transcendent beauty that presupposes the goodness of God's creation (Gen 1). In short, we experience more than we can see. The beauty of the particular acts as a vehicle for divine grace which transcends the particular: the rootedness of creation in God's love, intensified by the incarnation of God in Christ, is confirmed by the resurrection of Christ as our destiny as well. Again, though, discretion rules the scene: in the Emmaus episode, what transcends the particular can only be revealed by the particular, and God's salvific self-giving is experienced in what turn out to be the very mundane actions: in the midst of a relationship initiated by a conversation, confirmed by an invitation ("Stay with us, because it is almost evening" [Luke 24:29]), and embodied in a shared meal.

The light which falls from the left-hand side of the image is part of this performance of discretion, perhaps even its most fundamental element. The light *per se* and its source are not seen, but make everything else visible, beautiful, shimmering with life, intimate. In noting the connection between painting and architecture, the architect Juhani Pallasmaa remarks that "light tends to be experientially and emotionally absent—we see objects rather than light. Light must be contained by space, or concretized by the surface or matter that it illuminates to be recognized."[42] And that illumination is neither random nor aimless, but provides order and meaning:

> Illumination directs our movements and attention creating hierarchies and points of foci and importance. The paintings of Rembrandt, Caravaggio, and Georges de la Tour demonstrate

42. Juhani Pallasmaa, "Light, Silence, and Spirituality in Architecture and Art," in *Transcending Architecture*, ed. Julio Bermudez (Washington, DC: Catholic University of America Press, 2015), 19–32, at 24.

the power of illumination in defining hierarchy and dominance. In these paintings, human figures and objects are wrapped in a soothing embrace of soft light and merciful shadows. Focused light provides the human figures with a radiant halo, creating an air of significance and holiness. A mere candle suffices to create a drama.[43]

When speaking of focused light, shadow, and holiness, perhaps Pallasmaa has in mind de la Tour's spectacular *Christ and St. Joseph in the Carpenter's Shop* (c. 1642), which intensifies Caravaggio's *chiaroscuro* in order to create a scene of quiet, intimate communion tinged with melancholy (fig. 3).

Here is a moving and perhaps even more obvious depiction of the presence-absence metaphor. The candlelight that creates the circle of illumination of the two figures (doing so from between them, holding them in relationship) as well as the deep shadows that envelop them

3. Georges de la Tour, *Christ and St. Joseph in the Carpenter's Shop* (c. 1642) (Musée de Louvre, Paris)

43. Ibid.

has its source in the flame hidden behind the hand of the child Jesus. We perceive the source's effects, yet the source itself is inaccessible to our direct vision. The necessary precondition for the composition of the scene is hidden within the scene itself—a quintessential illustration of discretion and of the interlacing of absence and presence.

A consideration of *architectural beauty* augments the element of temporality in discretion. We have a subtle awareness that the stolidity—the solid permanence—of great buildings is actually something of an illusion: what looks to be a massive static presence is subtly affected by the rhythms of time. Juhani Pallasmaa, for example, who has highlighted the multi-sensory role of the human body in creating and dwelling within architecture, strongly suggests that "architecture articulates our experiences of time as much as of space" and that "every moving encounter with art—ancient, modern or contemporary—slows down and suspends the understanding of time and opens up a view to a calm and tranquil duration."[44]

Pallasmaa here reacts to two issues. The first is a variant of our earlier discussion of the collapse of time and the dominance of "now-ism." After the heyday of modernism, he argues, "our own celebrated buildings often appear to be rushing as if time were just about to disappear altogether. This architectural hurry is expressed in two opposing ways: in the overwhelming number of motives, materials and details on the one hand, and the forced simplicity of buildings intended to impress us through a single simultaneous image on the other" (ibid.). The other issue is Karsten Harries' famous thesis that architecture, as a "domestication" of space, is both an attempt to fend off the "terror" of homelessness (which overtakes humanity after the biblical Fall from paradise) and, more essentially, a defense against the flow of time that leads all humans to death: "Thus, if we can speak of architecture as a defense against the terror of space, we must also recognize that from the very beginning it has provided defenses against the terror of time."[45] Much of the history of

---

44. Juhani Pallasmaa, "Inhabiting Time," *Architectural Design* 86, no. 1 (Jan.–Feb. 2016): 50–69, at 54.

45. Karsten Harries, "Building and the Terror of Time," *Perspecta: The Yale Architecture Journal* 19 (1982): 59–69, at 59.

architecture, having been influenced by Plato's aesthetic of "timeless beauty" and pure forms, has put beauty in opposition to time. Beauty's timeless state becomes the antidote to time's morbid terror. Harries summarizes Plato's view this way: "Desiring, yet lacking being, we are haunted by dreams of a plentitude, a satisfaction that our present temporal situation must deny us; by dreams of an escape from time. Beauty promises an answer to such dreams. . . . Given this Platonic aesthetic, the language of beauty is the language of a timeless reality in which the spirit feels at home because it is of the spirit. . . . That the embodied self cannot take comfort in such beauty is evident."[46]

Pallasmaa, though, argues that time and beauty can co-inhere. "Profound buildings are not self-centered monologues. Buildings mediate deep narratives of culture, place and time, and architecture is in essence always an epic art form."[47] In the midst of our encounter with such buildings, they evoke from us both intense feeling and a rich extension of our intentionality. "A sense of melancholy lies beneath all moving experiences of art; this is the sorrow of beauty's immaterial temporality. Art projects an unattainable ideal, the ideal of beauty that momentarily touches the eternal."[48] Some structures of epic beauty give us a sense of "slow or dense time" (e.g., a medieval cathedral), while others seem to suspend time altogether (e.g., the Temple of Karnak in Luxor, Egypt). But this experience of being "liberated from the flow of time" or of "a duration or permanence" is not an experience of being taken *out of time* altogether but rather of being *immersed in* a dense accumulation of memories in a deeper temporal continuum that only seems to us to be timeless because of its monumentality. "Great works always enter into a dialogue with the past," Pallasmaa says, "making us sense time as an authoritative and calming presence and continuum, not

46. Ibid., 63 (his summary of Plato's argument in the *Symposium*).

47. Juhani Pallasmaa, "Newness, Tradition and Identity: Existential Content and Meaning in Architecture," *Architectural Design* 82, no. 6 (Nov. 2012): 14–21, at 20.

48. Juhani Pallasmaa, *The Eyes of the Skin: Architecture and the Senses*, 3rd ed. (Chichester, West Sussex: Wiley, 2012), 58.

a momentary or disappearing instant."[49] Indeed, this applies to more than epic structures; even the most ordinary architectural settings and objects can immerse us "in the continuum of lives through centuries": for example, "an ancient paved street, polished to a clean shine by centuries of walking; stone steps carved by millions of feet; or a patinated bronze door pull, polished by thousands of hands, turning it into a warm gesture of welcome."[50] And every building, epic or not, is bathed in and pierced by the shifting light of the rhythms of the day and the seasons, and thus presents different looks at different times on different days, while at the same time offering a manifestation of time in the aging of the building's materials.[51] Architecture thus registers its own kind of presence and absence: "Geometry and form speak of permanence, whereas materials—through the very laws of nature—trace the passing of time."[52] What looks massive and static is thus caught up in a wave of time that connects the present with the past and the future—a reflection of the deep, invisible temporal continuum that transcends and underpins the particularity of the visible.

As a final clue, *music* offers a model for navigating the paradox of time and transcendence that brings together the clues disclosed by

49. "Inhabiting Time," 55. As an example, he cites Marcel Proust's description in *À la recherche du temps perdu* of the church in Combray, France, "an edifice occupying, so to speak, a four-dimensional space—the name of the fourth being Time—extending through the centuries its ancient nave, which, bay after bay, chapel after chapel, seems to stretch across and conquer not merely a few yards of soil—but each successive epoch from which it emerged" (ibid., citing Marcel Proust, *In Search of Lost Time, Vol. 1: Swann's Way*, trans. C. K. Scott Moncrief and Terence Kilmartin [London: Random House/Vintage, 1996], 71).

50. "Inhabiting Time," 57.

51. An example is provided, surprisingly, by Harries himself in a small pavilion he designed for the Puerto Rican island of Vieques that creates the "presencing of time": "An oculus allows the space to be a 'sun-, moon-, and star-dial, mediating life-time and world-time,' giving views in the night of constellations and the changing light of the moon on the floor and walls. Generous doors to the east bring in intense morning sun. . . ." (Karen A. Franck, "Visiting Karsten Harries and Revisiting his 'Building and the Terror of Time'," *Architectural Design* 86, no. 1 [Jan.–Feb. 2016]: 128–35, at 131).

52. Pallasmaa, "Inhabiting Time," 57.

painting and architecture. This is because a musical work is temporal to its core—it necessarily moves through time while offering an aural and affective experience that transcends the physical generation of sounds and the written score that guides their realization.[53]

A musical work, from the shortest melodic fragment to the longest opera, is the intended goal of a set of actions stretched out over time, often (but not always) guided by notation. The performance of music occurs *in* and *through time.* Performances are the foundation for the various interpretations and critiques of the work which itself perdures over time, although its identity cannot be reduced to any unique performance, nor to the fixed system of notational signs which provide directions for its temporal realization. In addition, there is a prior "layer" of interpretative activities that are also part of the work, carried out by the performers in order to fulfill the intentionality of the score and bring it to aural realization. These activities are guided by the score, but are by no means determined by it, since the score is a schematic representation of the musical ideas and of the realization of the musical sounds. The elements of the performance, crucial to the real-time realization of the musical work, could never be completely scripted. In coming to terms with a host of interpretive layers—a composer's marks, the historical setting and genre of the piece, the "appropriate" affect and style of delivery, the construction of the instrument(s), the timbre of voices and instruments, the variable blends of sounds, the reverberation time of the room, the reception of the listeners, etc.—the performer comes to terms with an ensemble of elements that are not fully textual and which only come together in the reality of the moment of performance.[54]

---

53. For a more detailed discussion of the following points, see Anthony J. Godzieba, "Method and Interpretation: The New Testament's Heretical Hermeneutic (Prelude and Fugue)," *The Heythrop Journal* 36 (1995): 286–306; Godzieba, "*Ut Musica Christianitas:* Christian Tradition as a History of Performances," in *The Shaping of Tradition: Context and Normativity*, ed. Colby Dickinson, Lieven Boeve, and Terrence Merrigan (Leuven: Peeters, 2013), 91–99; Godzieba, " '. . . And Followed Him on the Way' (Mark 10:52): Unity, Diversity, Discipleship" [see n. 27]. The following paragraphs draw on some of this material.

54. Bruce Ellis Benson notes that "even the interpreter who is fully committed to the goal of respecting the text and the author's intentions is never simply

It is true that textual strategies have often been used to analyze musical works and their performances.[55] But music outruns its notation. The diversity in performance styles, ornamentation possibilities, and rhythmic variability cannot be adequately codified and analyzed with discourse strategies derived from theories of literature or linguistics. Nor can encoding capture the wider intentionality of the musical work, because it exceeds the specific "local" intentions of the composer.[56] The meaning of musical works can be determined only in the performance and its "incarnated" effects. The musical text's inherent schematic nature, no matter how thickly encrusted with performance directives, insures that no performance will ever duplicate another of the same work. Each constitution of the possibilities inherent in the score will occur at different times, in different material contexts, encountering different moods.[57]

The process of realizing the possibilities inherent in the musical score and thus constituting the real work has the strange result of bringing to the listeners a work which is *always* the same (as an object always intending *this* particular configuration of tones and rhythm and *this* particular order of events) yet *never* the same in its spatio-temporal realization, in its effects upon the audience's varied perceptual experiences, and in its constituted meaning. The phenomenality of the musical performance subverts any attempt to reduce it to its "text." Rather, musical performance practice maintains an

---

'repeating' the text (or score). If texts and scores are 'underdetermined,' then the reading that results from an interpretation is *always* improvisatory" (Benson, "The Improvisation of Hermeneutics: Jazz Lessons for Interpreters," in *Hermeneutics at the Crossroads*, ed. Kevin J. Vanhoozer, James A. K. Smith, and Bruce Ellis Benson [Bloomington, IN: Indiana University Press, 2006], 193–210, at 205).

55. Eighteenth-century commentators, for example, explained the affects produced by a performance through the use of the terms and concepts of classical Roman rhetoric.

56. See John Butt, *Playing with History: The Historical Approach to Musical Performance* (Cambridge: Cambridge University Press, 2002), 74–95, esp. 94–95.

57. David Fuller, "The Performer as Composer," in *Performance Practice: Music After 1600*, ed. Howard Mayer Brown and Stanley Sadie (London: Macmillan, 1989), 119: "No musician . . . can harbour any illusions about a 'code of performance', or indeed any combination of notation and written description that would enable him to reproduce a performance he has not heard."

exquisite balanced relationship between the freedom of the composer's, the performer's, and the listener's subjectivities on the one hand
and the constraints of a codified structure on the other, both sides of
which inhabit and interact within every interpretational endeavor.[58]
From this interactive encounter between freedom and structure arises
what the philosopher Manfred Frank has termed "style," the "unfore-
seeability of interpretation." Style, as a uniquely new and unprecedented reality, results from the realization of interpretation as *this
particular interpretation.* It is determined neither by the structure alone
nor by subjectivity alone; never could it be codified in a system of
rules or discourse, or be coerced.[59]

A fulfilled understanding of the work and the experience of its
affective force occurs in performance, the unique temporal realization
of the provocations which create the work and that also engender
real meaning for audience and critics alike. Something is "going on"
in the work, beyond its script, that is generated in real time, even
when listeners are not directly aware of something going on: say, a
feeling of sublime beauty and power (Bach's *Mass in B minor*, Bee-
thoven's Ninth Symphony), or joy ("Happy Birthday"), or warmth
(a song that one's parent used to hum or sing), or the comfort of a
beloved tradition (a Christmas carol or a national anthem), or sim-
mering protest (Billie Holiday singing "Strange Fruit"), or unbridled
freedom (Bruce Springsteen's "Born to Run").

3.3. Trinitarian Ontology: Performing Light Inaccessible

What our ways of performance—painting, architecture, music—
bring to the fore is the kinetic, multi-dimensional character of phenomenality. In other words, "what appears" is never a flattened

58. For the elements of "structuring" and "individual lived experiences" and
their interaction within interpretation, see Manfred Frank, "Toward a Philosophy
of Style," trans. Richard E. Palmer, *Common Knowledge* 1 (1992): 54-77, and Frank,
What is Neostructuralism?, trans. Sabine Wilke and Richard Gray (Minneapolis:
University of Minnesota Press, 1989). In his view, this freedom of the individual
exists *prior* to the structured system of signs, for signs are artificial and have had
their meaning assigned through the free exercise of human subjectivity ("Toward
a Philosophy of Style," 55–56, 65–66; *What is Neostructuralism?*, 93–95).
59. Frank, "Toward a Philosophy of Style," 54–55, 76.

singularity but rather a rich event of multiple elements of affect and meaning. What, then, is the connection to the triune God? How do our three ways of performance help point us in the direction of the Trinity as "the answer to the mystery of the world and of human beings" (Kasper)? How do they help us respond to our basic conundrum: how is the ineffable God available to us within our embodied, time-bound life?

They certainly do not offer any sort of direct divine revelation, nor could they ever directly produce faith in the Trinity. Rather, they highlight a particular dynamic aspect of human experience, wherein the limits of experience shade over into what transcends those limits—or, more theologically speaking, where natural intentionality bleeds into the supernatural. Now, any phenomenology of experience-over-time has its limits. Here we heed Maurice Blondel's warning that human constructions of meaning that start with everyday experience, move outward and upward, and sketch out the places where experience opens out to transcendence (the "method of immanence") can take us no further than that clearing. They should not "reach the reality of the supernatural order," only recognize it.[60] But our ways of performance do recognize it by generating a distinct and discreet "revelation" of their own, disclosing what we have called the "porous boundaries" of the visible and the invisible, time and transcendence, materiality and "timeless" beauty. They open our experience to these porous boundaries and immerse us in paradox, breaking the spell of detemporalized inertia and evoking the deeply-rooted human capacity to surpass the constraints of an anxiety-ridden "now." In the process, they subtly shift our emphasis from a merely "intellectualist" account of natural theology to a more robustly embodied understanding of experiences of God. The search for the natural access-point of faith expands to include the mystery of the whole person.

Even though much contemporary Western culture is mesmerized by forms of presentism, the arts reveal an aspect of embodied human

---

60. Maurice Blondel, *The Letter on Apologetics*, in *The Letter on Apologetics and History and Dogma*, trans. Alexander Dru and Illtyd Trethowan (Grand Rapids, MI: Eerdmans, 1994 [Fr. orig., 1896]), 160. The main discussion of the "method of immanence" is in the *Letter*, 156–61.

experience that is forgotten or glossed over in more theoretical or rationalist discussions of God: *affect*, and most especially *desire*. They disclose our already-active intentions to experience what is beyond the "now" and the limits of the material-empirical: the invisible suggested by the visible. Their ensemble of practices evoke, by means of time, our encounter with those values usually thought to transcend time: *beauty, sublimity, happiness, affective fulfillment*. But aren't these really euphemisms for our temporal fulfillment *as persons*? We are addressed personally, we "intend" personally, and we are touched, each to one's personal core, in the midst of events shared with others. In other words, the arts perform in time the presence-absence metaphor by bringing to the fore the real affects and effects that fulfill our insatiable desire for a fuller and deeper experience but are not immediately perceptible, realities that are necessary for our well-being and break through the cultural bubble of detemporalized immediacy. By activating the powers of the imagination, especially in its religious form intending ultimacy, the arts move us to "think and act otherwise" than the status quo, to desire and effect more than business-as-usual experiences which ultimately get exposed as insufficient, unfulfilling, repetitive.[61]

In focusing on desire's intimate link with experiences of God, rather than taking up any of the prominent recent (and especially postmodern) discussions of it, I want to steer us back to our unexpected medieval resource, Anselm's *Proslogion*. He not only makes us aware of the perennial paradox of searching for God who exceeds our perceptual limits, he also gives us the clue for beginning to unravel the conundrum we face. From our earlier discussion,[62] we recall the seeker's three-stage prayer that makes up the *Proslogion's* first chapter. In the first, the seeker is invited to withdraw into contemplative solitude and set off on a journey of discovery, beseeching God for help in finding God. But in the second stage, the journey appears utterly impossible: God dwells "in light inaccessible," beyond the reach of

61. See Anthony J. Godzieba, "The Catholic Sacramental Imagination and the Access/Excess of Grace," *New Theology Review* 21/3 (August 2008): 14–26; Godzieba, "Imagination, the Body, and the Transfiguration of Limits," in *At the Limits of the Secular: Reflections on Faith and Public Life*, ed. William A. Barbieri, Jr. (Grand Rapids, MI: Eerdmans, 2014), 199–225.

62. Chap. 1, sec. 2.

the understanding of the "wretched" seeker who is burdened by sorrow, desire, ignorance, and sin: "I was my own impediment."[63] Imploring God for guidance, the seeker prays that the desire for God, which at first seemed a burden, an unfulfillable hunger, be transformed into something positive that directs one toward an understanding of God. The key moment of the transfiguration of this desire, the third stage, occurs when the seeker realizes that this desire does not spring from nowhere but is sparked by a dim understanding of God that he already possesses.

> I cannot seek you unless you show me how,
>   and I will never find you unless you show yourself to me.
> Let me seek you by desiring you,
>   and desire you by seeking you;
>   let me find you by loving you,
>   and love you in finding you.
>   I confess, Lord, with thanksgiving,
>   that you have made me in your image,
> so that I can remember you, think of you, and love you.[64]

Feelings of emptiness and exile from God begin to dissipate in the knowledge that there is "a little of your truth which my heart already believes and loves."[65]

What Anselm offers us is a transcendental argument of the type we examined previously when dealing with natural theology. But here I want to approach it from another angle and emphasize its somewhat different flavor: it sketches a desire for love and ultimacy in a phenomenological mode, a desire whose partial fulfillment is the result of a contemplative journey stretched out over time. Desire and its transfiguration form the centerpiece for both the possibility of Anselm's later ontological argument (which relies on a strong *imago Dei* theology, hearkening back to Genesis 1:26–27) and for the whole enterprise of *fides quaerens intellectum* (faith seeking understanding) that he announced at the outset.

63. *Proslogion* [n. 3], 240 (light inaccessible), 243 (impediment).
64. Ibid., 243.
65. Ibid., 244.

There are two important points to make. First, *temporality* is embedded in desire. A nagging consciousness of lack, the ache of frustration, suffuses every experience, even in a radically presentist culture: the present is neither the past nor the future, and it is never enough. Desire is acute: we want what we don't have *now*, we suffer a lack *now*. And to fill that lack we seek both to retrieve lost affective memories of the past (recall Proust wandering through a church resonant with centuries of tradition) and to anticipate future personal fulfillment. In fact, the taste of fleeting love, satisfaction, or enjoyment from the past whets our appetites for future fulfillment without limits. This temporal ache pervades every desire, even the desire for ultimacy. That gap between one's present lack of satisfaction and the anticipated fulfillment in the future can be addressed only within a succession of moments of action.

An insight from Maurice Merleau-Ponty helps clarify this point. He argues that time, as "the order of co-existences as well as that of successions, is a setting to which one can gain access and which one can understand only by occupying a situation in it. . . ."[66] When discussing how the body and its operations are saturated with time, he highlights a crucial aspect of our perception of the world: we treat those perceptions and our knowledge of the world as completed syntheses and therefore true, and yet there is no way such a completion should be possible: "How can any thing ever really and truly *present itself* to us, since its synthesis is never a completed process, and since I can always expect to see it break down and fall to the status of a mere illusion? Yet there *is* something and not nothing." The contradiction disappears when we acknowledge "the ultimate conditions of our experience," namely, that "we operate in time [and] understand time as a measure of being. The synthesis of horizons is essentially a temporal process . . . it merges with the very movement whereby time passes."[67] And so while a relentless presentism can blot out immediate awareness of the temporal flow of desire and its fulfillment, that flow persists as desire's driving intentionality—indeed, as a fundamental structure of incarnate human subjectivity. *The particular is the new uni-*

66. Maurice Merleau-Ponty, *Phenomenology of Perception*, trans. Colin Smith (London: Routledge and Kegan Paul, 1962), 332.
    67. Ibid., 330 (emphasis original).

versal: the most particular experience of a desire fulfilled within a temporal flow also reveals the universal temporal structure of all desires.

Secondly, there is the seeker's specific desire for ultimacy that Anselm demonstrates is the desire for God. Despite the eventual "intellectualist" resolution of the seeker's journey in "that than which nothing greater can be thought" (in chapters 2 and 3 of the *Proslogion*), the prayer makes it clear that the catalyst for the search is an *affective* state with its roots in a theology of the *imago Dei.* The transfiguration of desire into fulfillment, surpassing what the seeker calls his "wretched" despair, is not due in the first place to the seeker's own strivings (important as they are), but rather to the dimly-perceived image of God "which my heart already believes and loves," which will be filled out in the hermeneutic circle of faith and understanding: "I do not seek to understand so that I may believe, but I believe so that I may understand; and what is more, I believe that unless I do believe I shall not understand."[68] The seeker already has a relation to God, even before the search begins ("you have made me in your image"). This, in fact, gets the search started in the first place: it is a response to the initiative and presence of God in creation, an intentionality stretched out over time until it finds fulfillment.

Note that the *imago Dei*, already present and operative, sets off the search for ultimacy, without being recognized as such. This divine discretion can be expressed in metaphysical terms, as in the "transcendental" anthropology and Christology popular in Catholic theology in the latter half of the twentieth century. But it can also be transposed (more dynamically and productively, I believe) into a more praxical and phenomenological key. A "natural theology of desire," the real root of a theological aesthetics, can confirm this insight of Edward Schillebeeckx's: "God and his initiative of salvation are a reality independent of human consciousness, and independent of our expression of God in experience. But our expression of God and his saving initiative is dependent both on that divine initiative and on the historical context in which human beings express him."[69]

68. Anselm, *Proslogion*, 244.
69. Edward Schillebeeckx, *Church: The Human Story of God*, trans. John Bowden (New York: Crossroad, 1990), 13.

This brings us back to the dogged question of phenomenality and the Trinity. If this divine initiative is always already active ahead of our recognition of it, how does it become a phenomenon for us? Where do we see it play out? The first clue, from Anselm, stares us in the face: "you have made me in your image, so that I can remember you, think of you, and love you." In other words, *we are already participants in the divine revelation that we desire and pursue, by the sheer fact of creation and our existence within it.* This remains true despite the brute reality of our sinfulness—the fact that, as Anselm puts it, we are our "own impediment." But how do we clarify the quality of that participation? (That, after all, is the task that Anselm assigns to theology.) God's self-giving in the act of creative divine discretion gives us space to be and act freely and fruitfully; the divine initiative is already active at the roots of our being. But how is that activity in us expressed?—literally, how do we "press it out" (*ex-primere*) in the open in real time? What guide do we have as to what direction that participative expression should take?

This leads to the second and crucial clue: the phenomenality of Christ's *performance* in the gospels and our commitment to model that performance in our time-saturated lives and contexts. Here we are thrown back on the theophanic Christological operations in the New Testament and our perception of Jesus' actions that lead us to identify him as the revelation of God's love. By comforting the suffering, healing the sick, feeding the hungry, raising the dead, forgiving sinners, and including all in the relationship of the Father's loving care, Jesus performs in time and space what he preaches: the outburst of absolute divine love that signals the active reign of God and challenges the usual human arrangements of power. His salvific actions that reverse negative situations and create situations of grace and care, under the rubric of the values of the Kingdom of God, are temporal realizations of his loving relation to the Father and the Father's continuing love for all creation. We are called to model these actions of reversal in our own particular situations by our contemporary performances over time as disciples led by the power of the Spirit.[70] Thereby we encounter

---

70. For more on the quality and applicative nature of this call, see Godzieba, "'. . . And Followed Him on the Way'," 232–37.

the reality of the triune God, the communion-of-persons-in-love, through the grace of the Father in Christ, offered to us in disciple-ship—living a Jesus-like life in light of the Paschal Mystery. That grace perdures in us and in the world through the ongoing work of the Spirit who offers us fellowship—an intensified participation in divine love and a relationship with all those who live as disciples, and indeed with all creation.

Participation and *relationship* imply *embodied action.* We live our everyday lives performing and thereby *incarnating* our participation in the grace and love of God. Discipleship-as-applicative-perfor-mance—that is, living a Jesus-like life and activating the values of the Kingdom of God in the specific context of our historical and cultural situation—is therefore a necessity, as Jesus insisted: "Go and do likewise" (Luke 10:37). The truth of God who is love (1 John 4:16) is revealed in the applicative moment, and that truth expands and deepens in the ensemble of applicative actions over a lifetime. The situation of the disciple is akin to the movement of time in architec-ture and in music: just as in epic buildings the movement of light incarnates the deep continuum of time and slowly discloses a build-ing's mysteries, and in music the unfolding sequence of melodies and harmonies stretched out over time incarnates the rich identity of the work, so the movement of time incarnates the activated pos-sibilities of following Jesus and thus the truth of revelation for each person and for reality as a whole.

This intersection of unity and diversity is possible because of the overlapping three-fold sequence of events that are at the core of all Christian faith and practice: the rootedness of creation in God's self-giving love, the intensification of this love in the incarnation of God in Christ, and the confirmation of this love in the death and resurrection of Christ, which confirms the availability of God's love and eternal life for us as well. The Incarnation makes visible "what has been hidden from the foundation of the world" (Matthew 13:35), the discreet universal self-giving of God in creation. Christ's embod-ied performance should be understood as the historically particular application and focused intensification of that divine intentionality which has been active from creation onwards. The continual pres-encing of that love is guaranteed by the Easter events as the "initial ignition" of the communities of believers and the immense outpour-ing of the Spirit that follows.[71]

Christ's phenomenality, the revelatory access to the divine triunity that he makes possible, and the wave of ongoing effects that it sets off throughout history all incarnate the underlying trinitarian ontol-ogy of reality, the fundamental structure constituted by the love and freedom of God's self-giving. Here, in fact, is the goal of the perfor-mative sequence that this book has followed. We have moved from a search for "the natural access-point of faith" (our working definition of natural theology), to an awareness of the deeply personal out-ward-striving intentionality made visible at that point and the infinite mystery we meet there.[72] If our use of the term "God" refers to this all-encompassing infinite mystery and total meaning of reality which forms the horizon of our life and actions, then our desire for a fulfill-ment that is inherently *personal* gives us a pre-apprehension of the character of that horizon: that of a gracious *giver* who takes the ini-tiative to open up to us in a *personal* fashion—the absolute mystery that graciously grants us the free space which makes our life and our actions possible. "Seen in the horizon of the person," as Walter Kasper emphasizes, "the meaning of being is love. . . . To call God a person is to say that God is the subsistent being which is freedom in love."[73] This pre-apprehension, discovered at the natural access-point of faith, gets filled out by revelation of the personal quality of this infinite love in and over time, specifically by the life, praxis, death, and res-urrection of Jesus Christ, by the sacramentality of our actions, and by the ongoing presence of the Spirit who reveals and supports per-formances of this love and grace in time and history.

We saw earlier that Kasper does not hesitate to call the Trinity "the mystery of perfect love that communicates and empties itself," and truly "the grammar and summary of the entire Christian mystery of salvation."[74] If so, then we are encouraged to understand the quality of reality in a more authentic and relational way: a trinitarian ontol-

---

71. Walter Kasper, *Jesus the Christ*, new ed., [trans. V. Green] (London/New York: T&T Clark, 2011), 112.

72. See chapter 3, esp. sec. 2.5.

73. Kasper, *GJC*, 155.

74. Kasper, *GJC*, 314.

ogy moves us "into an understanding of reality in which person and relation have priority. Here the ultimate reality is here not the independent substance but the person, who is fully conceivable only in the relationality of giving and receiving. We might even say: the meaning of being is the selflessness of love."[75]

To this characterization one must add, as we have done, an emphasis on the necessity of performance in the thickness of time.[76] That is, this fundamental divine relationality becomes truly salvific for us only when we experience the effects of Christ's phenomenality—the ensemble of his life and actions which incarnate the values of the Kingdom of God—and their perdurance through the power of the Spirit in the particular actions of our temporally-saturated lives. Our discipleship, our applicative performances occurring over time, follows the gospel mandate that we immerse ourselves in paradox: we experience the mystery of God's infinite love when we personally incarnate its particular effects in our time-bound everyday lives. Here precisely is the presence-absence metaphor in performance: that God's absolute, infinite, unfailing love is never graspable as such, but only in particular, fallible performances. We can recall Merleau-Ponty's insight into the movement of time and apply it to our experience of divine love. "How can any thing ever really and truly *present itself* to us, since its synthesis is never a completed process. . . . Yet there *is* something and not nothing. . . . The synthesis of horizons is essentially a temporal process . . . it merges with the very movement whereby time passes."[77] Despite the time-bound fallibility of our particular performances and our inability to grasp the Trinity as such, we still participate in the mystery of divine love and grace. In the way that the arts mediate a never-isolatable "timeless" beauty in an always time-bound and timely way, so discipleship mediates the "timeless" goodness of God in the only way we could

75. Ibid., 310. The concept of trinitarian ontology derives originally from Klaus Hemmerle (see n. 16).

76. Cf. Hemmerle, *Thesen*, 60: "Such a Trinitarian present . . . admittedly stands under the law of time. As present, it is a self-giving into a future whose gift is still suspended. . . . Trinitarian ontology is as such eschatologically open" (my translation).

77. Merleau-Ponty, *Phenomenology of Perception*, 330 (emphasis original).

310 A Theology of the Presence and Absence of God

possibly experience it: in time and action. We should pay heed, then, to the "two men in white robes" who admonish the apostles at the site of Christ's ascension: "Why do you stand looking up toward heaven?" Jesus, they say, "will come in the same way as you saw him go into heaven" (Acts 1:10–11), namely, through his active disclosure in the world of the Father's love for the world. Performance is everything: "Go and do likewise."

4. The Presence and Absence of God

What about the conundrum we outlined at the start of this chapter? We began with the claim that the mystery of God is "the mystery of an unfathomable and incomprehensible love," and hence a personal mystery (Kasper). We then asked the key question: how is this ineffable mystery of God available to us within our embodied, time-bound life? How is this intimate love given? How is God accessible? We must admit that neither the conundrum nor the question has been "solved"—that is, if we stick closely to the word's root meaning (from the Latin *solvere*: to unravel, unbind, untie). In fact, the conundrum seems more tightly bound up than ever.

What if, after all, this is precisely the point? There is no unraveling the "double apriori" that is operative in reality: God's self-revelation occurs in the conditions of human experience, and the very possibility of human experience is grounded in God whose discretion gives it freedom to be. It is a mutual dependency, occasioned by divine discretion. Revelation, from biblical times until now, ties presence and absence closely together. God is *present* by fulfilling our innermost desires for love and meaning, and yet disturbingly *absent* by shattering our expectations and escaping our attempts at a complete synthesis or a definitive understanding, exceeding our limited categories of description and understanding. Our awareness of the infinite triune reality of God (the "immanent Trinity") cannot occur without an encounter with the love of God in partial and fallible performances of grace in real time (the "economic Trinity"). Our experience and confession that "God is love" must have some real-time catalyst, some footing in reality, and some continuity in history. Since these encounters keep on occurring, no definitive synthesis of knowledge is ever possible, only the fragile certainty of faith.

One reason for this fragility is that, for the most part, these encounters with God, "the subsistent being which is freedom in love" (Kasper), do not verge on the spectacular. They occur as part of the ordinariness of everyday life that participates in divine presence by the sheer fact of its existence: the person who finds love against the odds; unexpected help from a kind stranger on the street; the hopeless one who is given a reason to go on; the destruction of a community's life overcome by that community's trust in one another and in grace; forgiveness offered when there is no reason to expect it; an overwhelming liturgical experience after a string of blandly rote attendances; one's spirit deeply moved by a piece of music one has heard a million times; a nation's trust in justice and peace over violent confrontation. The shattering of expectations that occurs in these events is not because they are other-than-normal, but rather that the normal includes experiences on the porous boundary between the visible and invisible, that from within immanent time we can access the mystery of God's love, the transcendental horizon that is always present but never isolatable on its own.

The upshot of such experiences is not merely that we can reply to the big yet very abstract question "why is there something rather than nothing?" Stopping there would leave us in the realm of natural theology. Instead, in the light of Christ's phenomenality such events move us further to wonder "what is the source of this change in my life?," or better, "*who* is the source of such change, such fulfillment, such beauty, such happiness that addresses me personally?" Or more simply, "why this constant love for us, despite our limitations and sins, our own failures to love?" This reconfigures in a personal key the issue raised by Ludwig Wittgenstein's famous proposition, "not *how* the world is, is the mystical, but *that* it is."[78] At the same time, our reply made in the light of Christ's phenomenality and our discipleship contests Wittgenstein's earlier insistence that "God does

---

78. Ludwig Wittgenstein, *Tractatus Logico-Philosophicus*, trans. C. K. Ogden (1922; reprint, Mineola, NY: Dover, 1999), 107 (proposition 6.44, emphasis original).

not reveal himself *in* the world."[79] For where else and how else would the triune God be revealed? In the light of the range and depth of Christ's phenomenality, we believe that revelation occurs *in performative relationships, in personal actions in time.*

Thus we can confirm Kasper's contemporary restatement and amplification of "God is love" that draws out its audacious paradox. The mystery of the triune God is indeed "the mystery of an unfathomable and incomprehensible love" and "a personal mystery"—an unfathomable love with universal scope and intimate particular application, disclosed in time. This is the authentic core of the revelation of the triune God that the gospel's phenomenality provides, the absolute personal divine love that binds all together.

Finally, what about the presence-absence metaphor? "Presence" we have used as shorthand for what we are able to experience, say, and think about the mystery of God, and "absence" for the ineffability of the divine mystery that exceeds what we can say or think. Once the metaphor is put in the context of revelation-as-personal and revelation-as-event, it is almost self-explanatory. For the most part we are following the very traditional Christian path of categorizing approaches to God as kataphatic (the *via affirmativa* or affirmative way) and apophatic (the *via negativa* or negative way). These categories are ancient, coming into early Christian reflection on the spiritual life primarily by way of Neoplatonism and the influential mystical synthesis of Greek and Jewish ideas in the work of the first-century CE Jewish philosopher Philo of Alexandria. This approach was crystallized by the late fifth- or early sixth-century writer who called himself (Pseudo-)Dionysius the Areopagite, and later taken into the medieval theological syntheses and later reflections on spiritual practices.[80]

The kataphatic or affirmative way maintains that we can achieve some limited knowledge of God "by attributing all the perfection of the created order to him as its source," while the apophatic or nega-

79. Ibid. (proposition 6.432, emphasis original).

80. See Dierdre Carabine, *The Unknown God: Negative Theology in the Platonic Tradition: Plato to Eriugena*, Louvain Theological and Pastoral Monographs 19 (Leuven: Peeters/Grand Rapids, MI: Eerdmans, 1995), 1–5.

tive way insists on the absolute transcendence and ineffability of God, emphasizing that "one cannot transfer creaturely attributes to the divine nature without diminishing the unrestricted aspect of God's transcendence."[81] Many contemporary thinkers, reacting to overblown medieval and modern claims to either delineate sharply or dismiss the existence and attributes of divinity, have taken a cue from Martin Heidegger's critique of ontotheology and his call for a "god-less thinking" (*gott-lose Denken*) which, in his words, "is more open to Him than onto-theo-logic would like to admit."[82] This argument has had an influence on this book's approach as well. I have argued earlier, however, the critique of metaphysics and of ontotheology carried out by Heidegger and his followers only clears the decks of various metaphysical "sins" of the past; it offers little constructive help in where to go next. This is why an approach such as Walter Kasper's, who takes the critique of ontotheology seriously while moving past critique in the direction of "freedom," "person," and "relation" (categories that are at once more biblical and more contemporary) is the approach this book has largely followed. It is more productive and respects the personal givenness which, *quoad nos*, is the fundamental character of the mystery of God who reaches out to all creatures in love and invites all reality to participation in divine love.

What we have added to this "theological theology" is the crucial and inescapable element of performance-in-time. This emphasis helps us avoid a serious drawback with the presence-absence metaphor, the danger that it could be understood as too static or as a simplistic binomial opposition, where "presence" is seen as divine substance with definitive metaphysical attributes to be played off against "absence" as a lack, or emptiness, or irrationality. What we have stressed, over and over, is the interlacing of presence and absence, the kataphatic and the apophatic, experienced most intensely in the performance of the actions of love and care in Christological

81. Ibid., 2.

82. Martin Heidegger, *Identity and Difference*, trans. Joan Stambaugh (New York: Harper and Row, 1969), 72 (Eng.), 141 (Ger. orig.). See our earlier discussion in chap. 3, sec. 2.4.

operations, the grace of God in the incarnation of Christ as perpetuated and intensified by the Spirit. An appropriate image that conveys this is one we have seen earlier: Juhani Pallasmaa's description of the role of light. On the one hand, "light tends to be experientially and emotionally absent—we see objects rather than light. Light must be contained by space, or concretized by the surface or matter that it illuminates to be recognized."[83] On the other hand, the movement of "experientially absent" daylight through a building, disclosing its varied looks, also reveals the movement and effects of equally "absent" time. This is a fair analogy for trinitarian ontology: we experience particular performances of transformative love that express (as far as they are able) the ineffable trinitarian communion of love that, like light, permeates these particular performances of discipleship by making them possible and rendering their effects visible in a revelatory way.

It is yet a further irony, then, that the Trinity continually offers us an intimate relationship that is realized in time and history, and yet much of Western modernity, on encountering God, has responded by preferring the "timeless," or a philosophical essentialism, or dogmatic certainty turned into an infinitely repeatable brand or trademark. However, the persistent paradox that both the Johannine author and Meister Eckhart sketched out at the head of this chapter (no one has seen God, only the Son makes God known; God "in ways is hidden") defeats these attempts at definition. Instead, it opens us up to participation, to experience the rhythm of divine self-giving that makes possible particular performances of discipleship and the reversals that they provoke.

A practical way to make this point is to use Pope Francis' pithy comment "time is greater than space." Here is how he explains the connection between time and action:

> Giving priority to time means being concerned about initiating processes rather than possessing spaces. Time governs spaces, illumines them and makes them links in a constantly expanding chain, with no possibility of return. What we need, then, is to give priority to actions which generate new processes in society

83. Pallasmaa, "Light, Silence, and Spirituality," 24.

and engage other persons and groups who can develop them to the point where they bear fruit in significant historical events.[84]

The pope reinforces our emphasis on performance with his oft-repeated message that Christian life is a journey, which implies time, duration, choice, action. Christian discipleship, for Francis, includes "accompaniment"—believers joining and journeying with those who suffer or need healing, or are alone and alienated from society, church, or God. His biblical model, most fittingly, is Luke's Emmaus story. The disillusioned disciples travel back to what is probably their home village after the stunning collapse of the narrative they had embraced about Jesus of Nazareth. They appear, according to the pope, "utterly vanquished, humiliated, even after the third day," and they now "set off on the road alone, with their disappointment."[85] But the Emmaus pilgrims' return to the supposed certainty of a known past takes an unexpected turn: when accompanied by the risen Jesus, it becomes a journey into a surprising salvific future commencing with a deeply meaningful interpretation of Scripture and the shared breaking of bread, a practice of hospitality (Luke 24:27, 30-31). The journey with Jesus is transformative; the reversal of their bereft situation occurs in their participative performance with Jesus—walking, questioning, listening, sharing in eucharistic hospitality. The pope urges all believers to learn this "art of accompaniment."[86] In order to warm disillusioned hearts just as "Jesus warmed the hearts of the disciples of Emmaus," those who have experienced the mystery of divine love and grace must be "a Church . . . which accompanies them on their journey; a Church able to make sense of the 'night' contained in the flight of so many of our brothers and sisters from Jerusalem. . . ."[87]

---

84. Pope Francis, Apostolic Exhortation *Evangelii Gaudium* (24 November 2013), §223, https://w2.vatican.va/content/francesco/en/apost_exhortations/documents/papa-francesco_esortazione-ap_20131124_evangelii-gaudium.html.

85. The quotations come from the pope's address to the Brazilian bishops on World Youth Day, §3, http://w2.vatican.va/content/francesco/en/speeches/2013/july/documents/papa-francesco_20130727_gmg-episcopato-brasile.html.

86. *Evangelii Gaudium*, §204.

87. Pope Francis, address to the Brazilian bishops, §3.

From the diverse types of transformative accompaniment that are possible, Pope Francis specifies one way that this performance can occur in real time by highlighting the dislocation and alienation in contemporary society that are ripe for reversal. "The rapid pace of change," he remarks, makes us ignore all those whom society judges to have "no right to be part of the city." Despite this attitude, "Jesus still walks our streets" and "God is living in our cities," and so we continue to have "a hope which liberates us from the forces pushing us to isolation and lack of concern for the lives of others. . . ."[88] In these and other examples, the pope challenges the indifference and isolation brought on by a presentist culture by emphasizing rhythm of divine self-giving that courses through life. The mystery of God's love for human beings and the world, governed by God's discretion, continues to unfold, even when default cultural categories refuse to recognize it. The pope urges us to imagine reality more authentically, in a way that reawakens the desire for life lived under the sign of grace and transforms the social world through the unfolding possibilities of mercy that is performed. This is the phenomenality of the infinite mystery of divine love—"absent" only because excessive—that is made present through the particular, namely, performances of discipleship, our participation in the rhythm of divine self-giving in real time and real places.

***

At the end, then, is our beginning: "So we have known and believe the love that God has for us. God is love, and those who abide in love abide in God, and God abides in them" (1 John 4:16). Our discussion of trinitarian ontology has been a way of offering an expanded explication of the most essential act of Christianity: "to point to God who is the point of everything."[89] And God to whom Christians point is the absolutely singular and subsisting event of divine self-giving,

88. Pope Francis, Homily at Mass at Madison Square Garden, New York City (25 September 2015), http://w2.vatican.va/content/francesco/en/homilies/2015/documents/papa-francesco_20150925_usa-omelia-nyc.html.
    89. Radcliffe, *What is the Point of Being a Christian?* [n. 2], 1.

"the mystery of an unfathomable and incomprehensible love . . . a personal mystery . . . the answer to the mystery of the world and human beings."[90] To believe in the triune God is to confess that "God is love," a truly personal self-giving that is at once particular and universal: a love that touches each person to the most unique core of their being and yet also grounds all reality. This is the nexus where divinity and reality are joined, on God's creative initiative—primordial and more fundamental than any other category or attribute, where God's discretion is active in the perduring gift of grace and the constant invitation to participate in divine life.

Here, then, is why we have insisted, along with Walter Kasper, that belief in the Trinity is not sequestered off into a timeless contemplative bubble. Rather, the revelation of God as a communion of persons in love, the "glory" of the mystery that evokes our contemplation and praise (doxology), provokes the time-bound performative participation in divine grace that transforms and saves the world (soteriology). The glory of God is mediated by acts of justice and mercy. "The unity, peace and life of the world thus come about through the revelation of the glory of the Father, Son and Holy Spirit. The trinitarian doxology is the soteriology of the world."[91] Paradox, phenomenality, and performance all join together where praise and contemplation (doxology) and action (soteriology) intersect.

In fact, in our embodied experience of faith we work "upwards" toward the mystery. Our particular performances of the myriad possibilities of incarnated grace, made available through the work of the Spirit, mirror and expand the phenomenality of the operations incarnated by Christ, who "show[s] us the Father" (John 14:8). Paradox remains; God still dwells, as Anselm insisted, in light inaccessible. But that "light," experientially absent and invisible in itself (to use Pallasmaa's image), is made present through the embodied performances it illuminates, the prayer that it evokes, and the liturgy it engenders. The Christian tradition that holds fast to this belief in this paradox, the available ineffability of God "who in ways is hidden," finds its

90. Kasper, "Revelation and Mystery" [n. 1], 50.
91. Kasper, *GJC*, 248.

summary in the astonishing insight delivered with jaw-dropping simplicity by the author of the First Letter of John:

> In this is love, not that we loved God but that he loved us and sent his Son to be the atoning sacrifice for our sins. Beloved, since God loved us so much, we also ought to love one another. No one has ever seen God; if we love one another, God lives in us, and his love is perfected in us. (1 John 4:10-12)

Selected Bibliography

Anselm of Canterbury. *Proslogion.* In *The Prayers and Meditations of Saint Anselm.* Translated by Benedicta Ward. Harmondsworth/New York: Penguin, 1973.

Augustine of Hippo. *The Trinity.* Translated by Edmund Hill. Edited by John E. Rotelle. The Works of Saint Augustine, pt. I, vol. 5. Brooklyn, NY: New City Press, 1991.

Blondel, Maurice. *The Letter on Apologetics* (1896). In *The Letter on Apologetics and History and Dogma.* Translated by Alexander Dru and Illtyd Trethowan. Grand Rapids, MI: Eerdmans, 1994.

Buckley, Michael J. *At the Origins of Modern Atheism.* New Haven: Yale University Press, 1987.

Burrell, David. *Knowing the Unknowable God: Ibn-Sina, Maimonides, Aquinas.* Notre Dame, IN: University of Notre Dame Press, 1986.

Congar, Yves. *I Believe in the Holy Spirit.* Translated by David Smith. 3 vols. in 1. New York: Crossroad, 1997.

Crossan, John Dominic. *The Dark Interval: Towards a Theology of Story.* Rev. ed. Sonoma, CA: Polebridge Press, 1988.

Davis, Stephen, Daniel Kendall, and Gerald O'Collins, eds. *The Trinity.* Oxford/New York: Oxford University Press, 1999.

Dunn, James D. G. *The Partings of the Ways Between Christianity and Judaism and their Significance for the Character of Christianity.* London: SCM/ Philadelphia: Trinity Press International, 1991.

Duquoc, Christian. " 'Who is God?' becomes 'Where is God?': The Shift in a Question." Translated by John Bowden. In *Where is God? A Cry of Human Distress*, edited by Christian Duquoc and Casiano Floristán, 1–10. Concilium 1992/4. London: SCM Press, 1992.

Greshake, Gisbert. *Der dreieine Gott. Eine trinitarische Theologie.* 2nd ed. Freiburg: Herder, 1997.

Hart, Kevin. "Notes toward a Supreme Phenomenology," 159–78. In *Kingdoms of God.* Bloomington: Indiana University Press, 2014.

Heidegger, Martin. "The Onto-Theo-Logical Constitution of Metaphysics," 42–74. In *Identity and Difference.* Translated by Joan Stambaugh. New York: Harper and Row, 1969.

Hemmerle, Klaus. *Thesen zu einer trinitarischen Ontologie.* 2nd ed. Kriterien 40. Einsiedeln: Johannes Verlag, 1992.

Hill, William J. *The Three-Personed God: The Trinity as a Mystery of Salvation.* Washington, DC: Catholic University of America Press, 1982.

Hurtado, Larry W. *Lord Jesus Christ: Devotion to Jesus in Earliest Christianity.* Grand Rapids/Cambridge: Eerdmans, 2003.

Johnson, Elizabeth A. *She Who Is: The Mystery of God in Feminist Theological Discourse.* 1992. Reprint, New York: Crossroad, 2002.

Kasper, Walter. *The God of Jesus Christ.* New ed. Translated by Matthew J. O'Connell and Dinah Livingstone. London/New York: Continuum, 2012.

———. "Revelation and Mystery: The Christian Understanding of God." In *Theology and Church*, 19–31. Translated by Margaret Kohl. New York: Crossroad, 1989.

Kelly, J. N. D. *Early Christian Doctrines.* 5th ed. 1977. Reprint, New York: Continuum, 2003.

Kolakowski, Leszek. "The Revenge of the Sacred in Secular Culture." Translated by Agnieszka Kolakowska and Leszek Kolakowski. In *Modernity on Endless Trial*, 63–74. Chicago: University of Chicago Press, 1990.

Küng, Hans. *Does God Exist? An Answer for Today.* Translated by Edward Quinn. 1980. Reprint, Eugene, OR: Wipf and Stock, 2006.

LaCugna, Catherine Mowry. *God For Us: The Trinity and Christian Life.* San Francisco: HarperCollins, 1991.

Macquarrie, John. *In Search of Deity: An Essay in Dialectical Theism.* The Gifford Lectures 1983–4. London: SCM, 1984.

Marion, Jean-Luc. *God Without Being: Hors-Texte.* Translated by Thomas A. Carlson. Chicago: University of Chicago Press, 1991.

Murray, John Courtney. *The Problem of God.* New Haven: Yale University Press, 1964.

Pannenberg, Wolfhart. "Anthropology and the Question of God." In *The Idea of God and Human Freedom*, 80–98. Translated by R. A. Wilson. Philadelphia: Westminster, 1973.

Prestige, G. L. *God in Patristic Thought.* 2nd ed. 1952. Reprint, London: SPCK, 1981.

Rahner, Karl. *The Trinity.* Translated by Joseph Donceel. 1970. Reprint, New York: Crossroad, 1997.

Ricœur, Paul. "The Critique of Religion" and "The Language of Faith." Translated by R. Bradley DeFord. In *The Philosophy of Paul Ricœur*, edited by Charles E. Reagan and David Stewart, 213–38. Boston: Beacon Press, 1978.

Rosa, Hartmut. *Social Acceleration: A New Theory of Modernity.* Translated by Jonathan Trejo-Mathys. New York: Columbia University Press, 2013.

Rusch, William, ed. *The Trinitarian Controversy.* Sources of Early Christian Thought. Philadelphia: Fortress, 1980.

Smith, Mark S. *The Early History of God: Yahweh and the Other Deities in Ancient Israel.* 2nd ed. Grand Rapids: Eerdmans/Dearborn, MI: Dove, 2002.

Studer, Basil. *Trinity and Incarnation: The Faith of the Early Church.* Translated by Matthias Westerhoff. Edited by Andrew Louth. Collegeville, MN: Liturgical Press, 1993.

Tanner, Norman P., ed. *Decrees of the Ecumenical Councils.* 2 vols. London: Sheed and Ward/Washington: Georgetown University Press, 1990.

Thomas Aquinas. *Summa theologiae*, vol. 2 [1a. 2–11]: *Existence and Nature of God.* Translated by Timothy McDermott. 1964. Reprint, Cambridge: Cambridge University Press, 2006.

———. *Summa theologiae*, vol. 6 [Ia. 27–32]: *The Trinity.* Translated by Ceslaus Verlecky. 1965. Reprint, Cambridge: Cambridge University Press, 2006.

Turner, Bryan. *Religion and Social Theory.* 2nd ed. Theory, Culture and Society. London/Newbury Park, CA: Sage, 1991.

Index